"Lucid, compelling, and conversational, David Farina Turnbloom's *Speaking with Aquinas* connects the sacramental theology of the *Summa Theologica* with Thomas Aquinas's soteriology and ethics. By examining the relationship between grace and the virtues, Turnbloom uncovers the presuppositions of Thomas Aquinas's treatises on the sacraments and on the Eucharist. Aquinas's 'multiple grammars' allow him to treat the paradoxical agency of both Christ and the Christian in the sacraments. As a result, in this nuanced but accessible treatment, the Holy Spirit and the Christian life of faith emerge as the center of Aquinas's sacramental theology. *Speaking with Aquinas* reveals the links between Christology, sacrament, the Eucharist, and ethics, showing how Aquinas's sacramental soteriology can still speak to readers today."

— Kimberly Belcher, PhD
University of Notre Dame

"David Turnbloom invites us into an entirely new conversation about how the Eucharist nourishes our moral lives. Into the circle of contemporary theologians like Chauvet, Morrill, and Baldovin, Turnbloom invites Thomas Aquinas and gives him room to speak about his grammar of grace and virtue. As Turnbloom channels Thomas, we hear the thirteenth-century theologian with a whole new voice speaking to us about the spiritual life of friendship with God as a pilgrim community. Refreshingly satisfying discourse for hungry Christians on the move!"

— James F. Keenan, SJ
Boston College

Speaking with Aquinas

A Conversation about Grace, Virtue, and the Eucharist

David Farina Turnbloom

Foreword by
Bruce T. Morrill, SJ

A Michael Glazier Book

LITURGICAL PRESS
Collegeville, Minnesota

www.litpress.org

A Michael Glazier Book published by Liturgical Press

Cover design by Monica Bokinskie.

1	2	3	4	5	6	7	8	9

Library of Congress Cataloging-in-Publication Data

Names: Turnbloom, David Farina, author.
Title: Speaking with Aquinas : a conversation about grace, virtue, and the
    Eucharist / David Farina Turnbloom.
Description: Collegeville, Minnesota : Liturgical Press, 2017. | "A Michael
    Glazier book." | Includes bibliographical references.
Identifiers: LCCN 2016045750 (print) | LCCN 2017003422 (ebook) |
    ISBN 9780814687802 | ISBN 9780814687819 (ebook)
Subjects: LCSH: Thomas, Aquinas, Saint, 1225?–1274. | Grace (Theology) |
    Virtues. | Lord's Supper.
Classification: LCC B765.T54 T865 2017 (print) | LCC B765.T54 (ebook) |
    DDC 230/.2092—dc23
LC record available at https://lccn.loc.gov/2016045750

This book is dedicated to all my teachers at:

St. John's Elementary School,
Woodland Middle School,
Hibbing High School,
The University of St. Thomas,
Weston Jesuit School of Theology,
and
Boston College.

I am still learning to recognize how much you gave me.

Contents

FOREWORD
Bruce T. Morrill, SJ   xi

PREFACE
Conversion through Conversation   xv

INTRODUCTION
Finding a Lost Voice   xvii

    I. Grammars   xvii

    II. Scholastic Grammars   xx

    III. Modern Grammars   xxiv

    IV. The Problem: Lacking Context   xxvii

    V. The Solution: Finding a Lost Voice   xxx

CHAPTER ONE
Why the *Secunda Pars*?   1

    I. Lamenting the Loss of a Loss   2

        1. The Deadly Dichotomy   2

        2. Consequences of the Deadly Dichotomy   5

    II. The Purpose of the *Summa Theologiae*   9

III. Signification and Causality   11

IV. Baptism and Penance: Infusing Charity   16

V. The Eucharist: Increasing Charity   20

VI. Unanswered Questions   25

CHAPTER TWO
Grace as the Embodied Spiritual Life   27

I. The Teleological Nature of the Spiritual Life   28
  1. The Structure of the *Summa Theologiae*   29
  2. The Place of the *Prima Secundae* in the *Summa*   32

II. Grace and the Spiritual Life   33
  1. Grace Actualizing the Image of God   35
  2. The Spiritual Life Conforming to Grace   39

III. Belief and Signs   40

IV. Conclusion: Cooperative Participation   47

CHAPTER THREE
The Theological Virtues Founding the Embodied Spiritual Life   49

I. The Theological Virtues: Orders and Degrees   50
  1. Faith, Hope, and Charity   51
  2. Orders of Generation and Perfection   52
  3. Three Degrees of Charity   56

II. Falling in Love with God   57
  1. Justification   58
  2. Infusion   61

III. Growing in Love for God   64
  1. Sanctification   64
  2. Increase   66

IV. Being Saved by Love   70

CHAPTER FOUR

The Moral Virtues Manifesting the Embodied Spiritual Life 73

I. Moral Virtues 74
1. The Codependence of Moral Virtues 75
2. Acquiring and Increasing Moral Virtue 84

II. Embodying Friendship with God 87
1. Operating *Ex Caritate* 87
2. Dispositive Acts of Charity 92
3. Communal Embodiment of Friendship with God 97

III. Grammars of Grace and Virtue 100

CHAPTER FIVE

The Eucharist Nourishing the Embodied Spiritual Life 103

I. Jesus Establishes the Way 104
1. Paschal Mystery as Sacrificial Sign of God's Love 104
2. Provocation as Possibility of *Theosis* 108

II. Sacraments Show the Way 111
1. Writing the Signs through Religion 112
2. Reading the Signs through Faith 115
3. Graced Cooperation 118

III. Eucharist as Nourishment for the Way 120
1. Writing Christ through the Eucharist 121
2. Spiritually Eating through Faith 123
3. The Unity of the Church:
The Fellowship of Sinful Saints 129

CHAPTER SIX

A Liturgical Theology of Right Religion 133

I. A Self-Defeating Tendency 133

II. Goodness and Rightness 138

III. Religious Signification   140

IV. Right Religion   142
    1. Religious Prudence   143
    2. Striving for Right Religion   144

    V. Writing a Diverse Christ for a Plural World   148
    1. Prudently Writing Christ   148
    2. How Do We Write Christ?   150

CONCLUSION
Speaking with a Lost Voice   155

Bibliography   157

Index   163

FOREWORD

Good, powerful academic theology always draws from significant pastoral experience, from some well-founded practical motivation. This is no less true for sacramental-liturgical theology than for any other theological subdiscipline. Indeed, all too often the challenges posed to the sacramental-liturgical scholar from both without and within this particular field of theology arise from modern propensities for excessively dividing theory from practice. In the post-Enlightened modern academy, Catholic and Protestant, theological faculties tended for a combination of reasons to relegate the study of sacraments and liturgy, whether on the grounds of method or content or both, either to historical-material treatment or to the pastoral realm. In the latter case, there could arise the implication of a certain intellectual inferiority inherent to the subject matter. An air of defensiveness on both "sides," i.e., systematic versus liturgical theologians, could prove palpable in such situations, which, thankfully, now seem to be on the wane. The disciplinary quest and sporadic polemics over the nature and mission of practical theology have, for all their difficulties, at least helped systematic theologians explicitly acknowledge that practical concern (practice of the faith), however implicit, underlies their scholarship. Now, with vigor and enthusiasm, young theologians are following the example of their deceased predecessors in the *ressourcement* begun more than a half century ago, reaching back beyond rationalism and idealism for critical engagement in the liturgical practice–based thought of Christian theologians of the ancient through medieval eras.

Meanwhile liturgical theology has had its own internal problems, among which a significant one has comprised often misguided, pragmatic pursuits of palpable, practical results in the pastoral field. The Constitution on the Sacred Liturgy's mandate that "full and active participation in liturgical celebrations by all the people [be] the aim to be considered before all else" has, to follow the formulations of my doctoral mentor Don Saliers, suffered distortion by liturgists playing to surface-level feelings rather than to depth of emotion. Isolating parts or even the entirety of liturgy, not a few liturgical theologians (across denominations and continents) have worked at creating diagnostics for determining whether full, conscious, and active participation is actually taking place. This can amount to asking of the liturgy, and thereby of the people engaged in it, what it in itself, in its ritual components—and, thus, they in their ritual performances alone—cannot yield. The liturgy in itself is not the value. The liturgy (to invoke the other celebrated line in *Sacrosanctum Concilium*) as the source and summit of the life of the faithful is. Surely, the content and form of the liturgy—reformed and renewed—matter. But this type of "liturgiology" alone is incapable of informing the deeper connection between liturgy and life essential to gospel faith. Scholarly service to the character of lives the church hopes to foster through sacramental rites requires capacious reflection on the dynamics of grace as conveyed through scripture and tradition.

Study of the monumental achievement of Thomas Aquinas in the *Summa Theologiae* is invaluable for gaining not only insight into the anthropological and ecclesial characteristics of the sacraments within the entire economy of grace but also methodological strategies for pursuing such insights. Every contributor to the development of sacramental theology over the past century has reckoned in one way or another with Aquinas. That David Turnbloom has been able to achieve such a fresh, insightful reading of the *Summa* is due not only to his carefully developed, keen theological intellect but also to the generous and compassionate pastoral and personal life of faith he brings to his scholarly work. His is a clear and compelling voice among a new generation of theologians practicing their vocations with an admirable desire to eschew ideological divides in the late-modern church while nonetheless asserting solid theological propositions and religious pedagogical strategies true to the demands of living the faith in our time. I am privileged to invite readers to enter with Turnbloom into this particular exploration of grace, virtue, and sacrament so as to better recognize what a living body of Christ is and can be like.

Bruce T. Morrill, SJ
Edward A. Malloy Professor of Catholic Studies
Vanderbilt University

Conversion through Conversation

I want to begin by making a distinction between what this book is *about* and what this book is *for*. In order to describe what this book is about, I would speak about the relationship between liturgical rituals and the moral identity of individuals and communities. As you will see, the content of these pages is primarily an analysis of the theology of St. Thomas Aquinas and the way he understands the relationships between grace, the virtues, and the Eucharist. However, behind the examinations that fill the following pages lies my preoccupation with the method of theological discourse. Put differently, this book is *for* theological conversation.

Through conversation we exchange ourselves with one another. We give of ourselves and simultaneously receive who we are. This book is, most fundamentally, aimed at facilitating the self-exchange that occurs in conversation. Etymologically speaking, conversation implies choosing to share life with another person. We receive ourselves in conversation because language gives us the possibility of experience. Sharing a common grammar (i.e., a common way of speaking) is the possibility of approximating a common experience. As such, conversation is also about living toward a common reality with someone. *Theological* conversation, then, is one way a community lives toward God. The purpose of this book is to provide a way of speaking that aids theological conversation.

In the end, I am most concerned with the effect the following pages might have on existing conversations about Christian worship and its relationship to the lives of Christians. Specifically, my hope is that this book will help others see the good in the positions they fear. Seeing the good in a position we dislike allows us to overcome the biases that would keep us from conversion through conversation. This book is an attempt to mitigate the biases that plague contemporary liturgical theology, thereby helping to overcome that which blocks our conversion to greater communion.

INTRODUCTION

Finding a Lost Voice

The theological importance of St. Thomas Aquinas need not be defended. However, his continued relevance as a positive resource for sacramental theology at the beginning of the twenty-first century is not as self-evident. Since the Second Vatican Council, a plurality of grammars has developed within sacramental theology. Certain Thomists have scrupulously retained a scholastic grammar, while other theologians, influenced by *Nouvelle Theologie*, have opted for grammars more heavily rooted in patristic theology. Still others have adopted grammars that take much influence from more modern sources such as phenomenology, anthropology, linguistics, and sociology. In this introduction, I simply want to point out the obvious: this plurality exists and causes a problem in need of a solution.

Broadly speaking, this book seeks to offer a grammar that helps bridge the disconnection between other grammars. In this brief introduction, I will justify such a project by pointing out that there is a problem, namely, a disconnection between certain grammars of sacramental theology. I will then argue that this problem is, if not overcome, at least mitigated by the use of a common grammar.

I. Grammars

I would like to begin by being clear about how I will use the word "grammar." Simply put, a grammar dictates the ability of its lexicon to mediate meaning. Brian D. Robinette defines a grammar as "a deep structural tendency in expression or thought; a characteristic and coherent pattern of understanding; an identifiable and habitual mode of articulation which results in relatively consistent thematization." [1] Or, put more simply, a theological grammar is "a characteristic pattern of Christian speech." [2] I will not use the term "grammar" as strictly as some linguists might demand (e.g., I will not spend time distinguishing between syntax, morphology, phonology, etc.). *Rather, I use the term to emphasize the importance of recognizing patterns in the relationship between words.* Fidelity to an author's thought demands far more than adoption of a vocabulary; it demands scrutiny of the vocabulary's application. While individual words are used to mediate meaning, it is the grammar within which a word is used that determines the possibility and parameters of that mediation. Grammars are more than just word choice; grammars include words, the relationship between those words, and the rules that govern those relationships. To alter the relationships between words is to alter the grammar, and to alter a grammar is to alter (whether positively or negatively) its ability to mediate meaning.

Here, I will briefly highlight three points about the use of grammars. First, grammars dictate the possibility and content of thought. As George Lindbeck puts it, "There are numberless thoughts we cannot think, sentiments we cannot have, and realities we cannot perceive unless we learn to use the appropriate symbol systems." [3] In this passage, Lindbeck is speaking more broadly about cultural and linguistic forms, but his claim is easily applied to grammars as well. Adopting a vocabulary and a particular understanding of how those words relate opens the mind to the possibility of understanding. To paraphrase one of Lindbeck's illustrations, imagine that a man who is completely unfamiliar with sports is shown a video clip of a game in which a player uses a stick to hit a ball into a giant crowd of people. If the man is then asked to explain the phrase "ground rule double," he will fail because he does not have the appropriate grammar needed to understand his experience of the game. If the man is then given a

---

[1] Brian D. Robinette, *Grammars of Resurrection* (St. Louis, MO: Crossroad, 2009), 184.

[2] Ibid., 181.

[3] George A. Lindbeck, *The Nature of Doctrine: Religion and Theology in a Postliberal Age* (Louisville, KY: Westminster John Knox Press, 1984), 34.

rule book for golf and asked to use that rule book to explain the phrase "ground rule double," he will fail again. This time, however, not only will he fail to explain "ground rule double," but it is quite likely that he will incorrectly describe the game in terms of the rule book that he has been given. So, while grammars make understanding and communication possible, grammars taken out of context invariably lead to misunderstanding and miscommunication.

The second point that I wish to highlight is the risk involved when using multiple grammars. Returning to Lindbeck, we have seen that "it is necessary to have the means for expressing an experience in order to have it, and the richer our expressive or linguistic system, the more subtle, varied, and differentiated can be our experience."[4] Put in terms of grammar, the presence and utilization of a plurality of grammars can afford the mind deeper and more nuanced understanding. For example, a human being can be described through many different grammars. Taxonomically speaking, a human is a *Homo sapien*. Chemically speaking, a human is a mass of molecules that are largely based on carbon. Theologically speaking, a human is made in the *imago Dei*. Anthropologically speaking, a human is a storytelling animal. When we adopt differing grammars, we open up the possibility for greater depth of understanding and greater breadth of communication.

The use of a particular grammar provides an epistemological framework that constitutes a subject's perspective. The use of multiple grammars can provide multiple perspectives. While there is obvious benefit in having multiple grammars, there is also risk. The more distinct two grammars are, the more difficult communication between them becomes. For example, a physicist will be able to discuss color more readily with an ophthalmologist than with a painter. The common use of a scientific grammar that understands color primarily in terms of wavelength will facilitate communication. While multiple grammars may afford deeper understanding, that does not necessarily imply a greater ability to communicate that understanding. Simply put, certain grammars are more compatible than others.

---

[4] Ibid., 37.

The third point is the danger implicit in absolutizing a particular grammar. To absolutize a grammar is to afford it a place of such privilege that it leads to the exclusion of other grammars, whether intentionally or accidentally. While I will return to this danger later in this introduction, for now I would like to simply point out that excluding other grammars limits the possibility of thought. Admittedly, there are times when such limitations are advisable. It is not controversial to claim that one of the main functions of doctrine is to limit the use of speech.[5] However, it should be self-evident that when treating a Mystery, the absolutizing of any grammar is detrimental. In article 2, question 1 of the *Tertia Pars*, Aquinas points out ten different perspectives from which the incarnation can be explained as being "necessary." He then ends the article by pointing out that these ten perspectives are in no way exhaustive; nor does he privilege one perspective to the detriment of any other. Aquinas understands that in dealing with Mystery, the use of language is an exercise in approximation in which careful verbosity brings advantage. What I am *not* doing in this book is retrieving a grammar to be absolutized. On the contrary, the grammar I will retrieve is always to be used in cooperation with others.

II. Scholastic Grammars

I want to be clear about what I am *not* doing when I talk about "scholastic" grammars of the sacraments. I am not trying to define a type. *Rather, I am highlighting the tendency in which a dogmatized scholastic vocabulary is given such privilege that its use is seen as prerequisite to authenticity.* Put another way, failure to explicitly use this scholastic vocabulary is to automatically invite a hermeneutic of suspicion. In order to provide a simple example of this tendency, I turn to Pope Paul VI's 1965 papal encyclical, *Mysterium Fidei*.

In this text, Paul VI focuses on the importance of language when talking about the Eucharist. Of particular note is section 24:

---

[5] The potential danger in this view of doctrine is the tendency to mistake lexicon for grammar. For example, saying that Jesus sinned is instantly problematic. Nevertheless, before such a statement can be deemed heretical (i.e., be excluded), the word "sinned" must be defined in terms of its relations in the grammar being used compared to the use of ἁμαρτίας in the grammar used in Heb 4:15.

And so the rule of language which the Church has established through the long labor of centuries, with the help of the Holy Spirit, and which she has confirmed with the authority of the Councils, and which has more than once been the watchword and banner of orthodox faith, is to be religiously preserved, and no one may presume to change it at his own pleasure or under the pretext of new knowledge. Who would ever tolerate that the dogmatic formulas used by the ecumenical councils for the mysteries of the Holy Trinity and the Incarnation be judged as no longer appropriate for men of our times, and let others be rashly substituted for them? In the same way, it cannot be tolerated that any individual should on his own authority take something away from the formulas which were used by the Council of Trent to propose the Eucharistic Mystery for our belief. These formulas—like the others that the Church used to propose the dogmas of faith—express concepts that are not tied to a certain specific form of human culture, or to a certain level of scientific progress, or to one or another theological school. Instead they set forth what the human mind grasps of reality through necessary and universal experience and what it expresses in apt and exact words, whether it be in ordinary or more refined language. For this reason, these formulas are adapted to all men of all times and all places.[6]

Throughout the entire encyclical, there is an emphasis on a pseudo-grammar of "sacrifice" and "substance."[7] The text asserts that the Mystery of the Eucharist is most properly understood and expressed

---

[6] *Mysterium Fidei* 24.

[7] I use the term "pseudo-grammar" because specific terms are defended through an appeal to (what is portrayed as) their univocal use throughout Christian tradition. In other words, emphasis is placed on words and not their historically and culturally conditioned relationships to one another. This problematic tendency finds it roots in the encyclical's fundamental misunderstanding of the nature of language. The notion that formulaic language can "set forth what the human mind grasps of reality through necessary and universal experience and what it expresses in apt and exact words, whether it be in ordinary or more refined language" misunderstands language, seeing it as a tool and not mediation. For more on this misunderstanding, see Louis-Marie Chauvet, *Symbol and Sacrament: A Sacramental Reinterpretation of Christian Existence*, trans. Patrick Madigan and Madeleine Beaumont (Collegeville, MN: Liturgical Press, 1995), chap. 3.

by utilizing these grammars.[8] Any future development that might add clarity must be a development of these dogmatic *formulae*. Simply put, Paul VI moves beyond lauding a traditional grammar and its beauty to absolutizing that grammar.

Adopting this tendency, other theologians have made similar claims about the foundational role of scholastic grammars. For example, in his essay "Transubstantiation Revisited," Reinhard Hütter states:

> The *intellectus fidei*, however, relies on *received* reality—that is another way of saying *objective* reality—and this reliance is accounted for in our case, Eucharistic transubstantiation, by a most central *metaphysical* principle, a principle that antecedes and transcends culture as much as history, human subjectivity as much as the philosophy *du jour*, in short, the metaphysical principle of *substance*.[9]

For Hütter, the metaphysical concepts of substance, accident, and quantity are indispensible. This metaphysical grammar is not merely one grammar among equals, all of which can be utilized in eucharistic theology. What we see here is a radical claim about the primacy and indispensability of scholastic vocabulary. The vocabulary of scholastic metaphysical inquiry, in Hütter's view, is not so much a grammar as it is an innate aspect of the human intellect. He maintains that "metaphysical contemplation . . . remains indispensable in properly understanding the inner constitution of the reality on which the human intellect qua intellect . . . relies in its very act of understanding."[10] For Paul VI and Hütter, grammars that fail to utilize metaphysical language when discussing the Eucharist are disabled. As such, scholastic grammars are absolutized, and this absolutizatition has consequences. As Lindbeck points out, the grammars we use dictate what experiences we can have. The same is true of these scholastic grammars. When we examine the Eucharist solely through scholastic

---

[8] Cf. section 39 in which "real" presence is described as "presence par excellence, *because it is substantial*" (my emphasis).

[9] Reinhard Hütter, "Transubstantiation Revisited," *Ressourcement Thomism: Sacred Doctrine, the Sacraments, and the Moral Life*, ed. Matthew Levering and Reinhard Hütter (Washington, DC: The Catholic University of America Press, 2010), 27.

[10] Ibid.

grammars of substance, the manner in which we experience and understand the eucharistic presence of Jesus Christ will suffer the influence of these grammars.

A simple example: in his 2003 encyclical, *Ecclesia de Eucharistia,* Pope John Paul II says that "from [the Eucharist] the Church draws her life. From this 'Living bread' she draws her nourishment."[11] Here, John Paul follows the tendency in eucharistic theology that is a consequence of absolutizing scholastic grammars of substance. In this sentence, the Eucharist, a ritual, is confused with the consecrated species. The rite is replaced by one of its parts.

In contrast, the Second Vatican Council's Constitution on the Sacred Liturgy famously asserted a fourfold presence of Christ in the liturgy.[12] According to this document, Jesus Christ is present in the assembly, in the proclaimation of the Scriptures, in the presiding minister, and in the consecrated bread and wine. Absolutizing the scholastic grammar of substance leads eucharistic theology to myopically focus on the substantial presence of Christ that subsists in the consecrated bread and wine. Affording such privilege to grammars of substantial presence does damage to what sacramental theologian John Baldovin has called a "many faceted jewel." The fourfold presence of Christ is replaced by a singular, circumscribable presence. When these scholastic grammars are absolutized, perspectives are marginalized and lost. In turn, there is a tendency to reduce an elaborate and historically rich sacrament to a substantial presence or a moment of consecration.

This use of scholastic grammars finds its generation in what I call a preferential option for the language of tradition. Dogmatized language should indeed be given privilege. However, if privilege is to remain a preferential option, it must always avoid absolutization. While these scholastic grammars arise from a preferential option, the option is quickly turned into an exclusive obligation. Sacramental theology then finds itself carrying an absolutized grammar rather than walking with a living tradition. I want to be clear: I am not setting scholastic grammars up as a straw man to be dismissed. On the contrary, later in this project I will forward Thomistic grammars as particularly helpful to modern sacramental theology. Rather, I am

---

[11] *Ecclesia de Eucharistia* 7.
[12] *Sacrosanctum Concilium* 7.

highlighting scholastic grammars that tend to be absolutized and criticizing them *as absolutized*. When these scholastic grammars are absolutized, any contemporary sacramental theology which fails to incorporate these grammars becomes suspect.

III. Modern Grammars

If scholastic grammars cease to be options and are absolutized into obligations, then any eucharistic theology that fails to incorporate scholastic grammars falls short in its ability to express the sacrament *par excellence*. Such disabled grammars, then, open themselves up to suspicion. Anyone familiar with the theological context from which *Mysterium Fidei* emerged is aware of the eucharistic theologies to which it was responding. When Paul VI rhetorically asks "who would ever tolerate that the dogmatic formulas used by the ecumenical councils for the mysteries of the Holy Trinity and the Incarnation be judged as no longer appropriate for men of our times, and let others be rashly substituted for them," he has specific people in mind. In this section, I will examine three theologians and their eucharistic theologies. As with the previous section, I am not concerned with the intricacies of the eucharistic theologies mentioned. Rather, they are being mentioned to demonstrate the existent plurality in eucharistic theology that has arisen in the last century of Roman Catholic sacramental theology.

Earlier I mentioned that some modern theologians have developed grammars for eucharistic theology that are heavily rooted in patristic sources. The first of our three examples of modern grammars of the Eucharist comes from one such theologian. In 1944, the French Jesuit Henri de Lubac published a book titled *Corpus Mysticum: The Eucharist and the Church in the Middle Ages*.[13] In this text, de Lubac bemoans the loss of an intimate connection between the sacramental body of Christ and the ecclesial body of Christ. This loss is manifested in history by the shift in use of the words *corpus mysticum* ("mystical body") and *corpus verum* ("true body"). Once used to signify Christ's presence in the Christian community, *corpus verum* gradually came to signify the presence of Christ in the consecrated bread and wine.

---

[13] Henri de Lubac, *Corpus Mysticum: The Eucharist and the Church in the Middle Ages; Historical Survey*, trans. Gemma Simmonds (London: SCM Press, 2006).

Likewise, the words *corpus mysticum* began to be used in reference to the Christian community rather than the consecrated species. Simply put, in the early Church the "true body" of Christ was the Christian community and the "mystical body" of Christ was consecrated bread and wine. By the Middle Ages, the designations had been switched.

This *ressourcement* project laid the ground for later theologians like J. M. R. Tillard who would begin studying the relationship between the Church and the Eucharist as it was treated in patristic writing.[14] These historical projects have become the foundation for the retrieval of grammars that seek to understand the Eucharist and Christ's presence within it. For our current purposes, it is most important to note that these projects offer us grammars that are not scholastic yet claim to speak about the Eucharist and Christ's presence with validity that is at least equal to the metaphysical language of scholasticism.

Twenty-three years after de Lubac published *Corpus Mysticum* and six years after the opening of the Second Vatican Council, the Dutch theologian Edward Schillebeeckx published the book *Christus' Tengenwoordigheid in de Eucharistie* (later published in English as *The Eucharist*). In this work, Schillebeeckx forwards what he boldly calls "a new approach to the formulation of faith."[15] He sets out to offer a formulation of the doctrine of Christ's real presence that "will not be from the philosophy of nature, but from anthropology."[16] Like de Lubac, Schillebeeckx focuses on making the relationship between the Church and the Eucharist primary. By beginning with anthropology, Schillebeeckx moves toward an understanding of eucharistic conversion that is constructed in terms of phenomenology, meaning, and signification. While Schillebeeckx defends the need for a theory of transubstantiation,[17] his construction of a theory of transignification is carried out employing a grammar that is not scholastic yet claims to formulate the Church's faith with equal depth and precision. This turn to the anthropological is an instance of modern eucharistic theology's willingness to engage its context as a positive source. As one

---

[14] Cf. J. M. R.Tillard, *Flesh of the Church, Flesh of Christ* (Collegeville, MN: Liturgical Press, 2001).

[15] Edward Schillebeeckx, *The Eucharist* (New York: Continuum Books, 1968), 87.

[16] Ibid., 93.

[17] Ibid., 150.

might expect, this willingness is a catalyst for the development of multiple grammars.

Finally, the French liturgical theologian Louis-Marie Chauvet has adopted the theory of symbolic exchange to examine eucharistic rituals.[18] Unlike Schillebeeckx, Chauvet is less conservative when it comes to retaining the need for a theory of transubstantiation. Putting Chauvet's critiques of scholasticism aside for the moment, I want to highlight the fact that Chauvet's grammars are, like those of Schillebeeckx, rooted in an honest willingness to engage the reality of eucharistic theology's modern context. Specifically, Chauvet treats the sacrament as the ritual that it is. Heavily relying on the anthropological "turn to the subject," Chauvet explores the Eucharist as a historically and culturally conditioned ritual performed by a communal subject. By first establishing a method in which the sacraments are seen as rituals that mediate the relationship between God and Christian community, Chauvet develops a grammar of symbolic exchange and Christian identity. The sacraments are examined in terms of their role in this economy of religious identity. In short, Chauvet concerns himself primarily with what the sacraments are as celebrations of the Church, as opposed to doctrines discussed by theologians.

This brief description of Chauvet's project should make it evident that there are fundamental differences between the grammars employed by Chauvet and the scholastic grammars we previously mentioned. However, it is clear that Chauvet is not simply trying to add clarity to traditional doctrinal formulae; his project is far more constructive. Likewise, his sacramental theology is not weakened by its departure from metaphysical language.

These three modern grammars of the Eucharist do not view themselves as disabled. They are forwarded as viable options for engaging the Eucharist theologically and communicating that faith. Their distance from the scholastic primacy of metaphysical inquiry is not seen as inhibitive. On the contrary, such distance is almost always a reaction to a need left unfulfilled by such metaphysical inquiry. Whether that unmet need be ecclesiological, as with de Lubac; cognitive, as with Schillebeeckx; or pastoral/ethical, as with Chauvet, modern grammars arise to effectively communicate a faith in a way that

---

[18] Chauvet, *Symbol and Sacrament*.

addresses that need. And so, there arises a plurality of grammars. Catholic sacramental theology finds itself in a state of extensive plurality—a state in which not everyone is comfortable.

IV. The Problem: Lacking Context

This plurality has led to the problem of a twofold disconnection. First, there is a contextual disconnection being ignored in the transplantation of certain scholastic grammars. Second, there is a disconnection between the grammars being used in Roman Catholic sacramental theology today. The latter disconnection issues from the former.

Transplanting a grammar is what happens when a grammar is retrieved from one context and inserted into another with little or no attention paid to its relationship to that new context. For example, if a theologian began using terms like "spectroscopic lines," "electron configurations," and "angular momentum quantum numbers" to talk about the consecrated bread and wine without any previous discussion of what those terms mean or how they are being applied within a theological conversation, that would be an instance of transplanting a chemistry grammar of orbitals into a theological context. The disconnection that results from transplanting a grammar is a consequence of failing to translate that grammar *for its new context*. What *Mysterium Fidei* attempts to do is transplant scholastic grammars. Denying the historically conditioned nature of metaphysical language, the encyclical tries to rehabilitate these scholastic grammars through historical theology and explanation. As Edward Schillebeeckx has said, "It is difficult to see how simply repeating the dogma word for word in our present age could do anything but impose an unnecessary and unjustified burden on our Christian faith."[19] Schillebeeckx points out that scholastic theology's use of Aristotelian metaphysics was a new way of understanding the presence of Christ in the Eucharist. He does this because he goes on to offer his own new approach to eucharistic presence which takes anthropology as its point of departure.[20] The point that we must stress, however, is

---

[19] Schillebeeckx, *The Eucharist*, 90.
[20] Ibid., 92.

how Schillebeeckx understood the newness of these formulations of the faith. It will be beneficial to quote him at length on this issue.

> Only a generation of believers living at a later period in the development of human consciousness and therefore further removed from the Aristotelian metaphysical philosophy of nature in its medieval form—and capable at least of seeing this philosophy more clearly if they have not rejected it altogether—can be aware that this medieval mode of thought was historically conditioned and hence, in the concrete sense, a form of "wording" for what the Council of Trent was really trying to express. But, in this case, this later generation will not be able to grasp the genuine *content of faith* of the Council of Trent if they methodically set aside their own (and later) way of thinking. If we, living in the twentieth century, are to discover the genuine content of the Tridentine faith in connection with Christ's presence in the Eucharist, we must also enter intimately into this content of faith, reassessing it and making it actual and present, because we can never really grasp at it in its "pure state."[21]

Newness, for Schillebeeckx, is not radical (i.e., a complete break with tradition), but it is honest. Modern eucharistic theology cannot transplant the grammars of the past into the present and expect that they will function in the same way as they once did; we must give assent to the loss that comes with time. To make something new is to make the past "actual and present" within and for the history of the present.

When grammars are transplanted, they are radically decontextualized. Denying their need for context (i.e., claiming their universality and absolutizing that grammar) does not undo that damage. Language is of a particular historical moment. To responsibly move a grammar from one context to another can be done only through translation. Or, as Schillebeeckx has put it: "The contemporary context of our life leads us to reinterpret the world of ideas with which the dogma of transubstantiation has come down to us, precisely in order to be able to preserve in a pure form the basic meaning of the dogma and to make it capable of being freshly experienced by modern man."[22] Translation and reinterpretation are done from and for a

---

[21] Ibid., 62.
[22] Ibid., 90.

particular context. *Ressourcement* theologians like de Lubac do not want to transplant patristic grammars into our modern discourse. They recognize the impossibility of such a project. The defining characteristic of true *ressourcement* is maintaining the object of study as a source to be translated, as a source from which to progressively develop a meaningful theology. When a grammar is transplanted, its contextuality is denied. To deny contextuality is to claim universality. Any grammar that is universalized is absolutized. As I pointed out above, the plurality of grammars in modern eucharistic theology includes such transplanted and absolutized scholastic grammars. The decontextualized state of those grammars brings about a disconnection in communication between these scholastic grammars and other modern grammars.

Alasdair MacIntyre, in his book *After Virtue*, points out that ethical issues are often unresolved within intellectual communities when proponents of opposing sides refuse to recognize and acknowledge the simple fact that each side is employing a grammar that is incompatible with the other's grammar.[23] In short, for conversation to be meaningful and productive, a common grammar is needed. As I pointed out above, it is possible to use multiple grammars when treating a subject. It is also possible, however, to have two grammars that are mostly incompatible. Difficulties arise when dialogue partners are using grammars that do not translate easily or are incompatible. This incompatibility between scholastic grammars and other modern grammars is rooted in the lack of a shared context. Any time a grammar is absolutized, the shared context that is a precondition for communication is denied. The criticism, then, that modern grammars want to level at scholasticism cannot find (acknowledged) footing from which to begin. Likewise, there is nothing any nonscholastic grammar could say that would mitigate the suspicion earned by being a contextualized grammar.

What I want to do in this book is show that modern grammars are not disabled. They offer us a way to understand the Eucharist that is at least as robust as the language of the *Terita Pars*. Likewise, by retrieving the context of the scholastic grammars found in the *Tertia Pars*, I want to defend them from some of the modern critiques. If,

---

[23] Alasdair MacIntyre, *After Virtue: A Study in Moral Theory*, 3rd ed. (Notre Dame, IN: University of Notre Dame Press, 2007), 8.

by retrieving a Thomistic grammar of grace and virtue, we can show the similarities between these disconnected grammars, then we have moved toward leveling the playing field between the two grammars. By retrieving a grammar of grace and virtue as the context for the grammars in the *Tertia Pars*, I attempt to show that those grammars are indeed contextualized grammars. If they are contextualized grammars, such recognition is a recognition of their possible translation.

V. The Solution: Finding a Lost Voice

In an article titled "Whether the Eucharist Is Necessary for Salvation?" Aquinas sums up in six words what is, for him, at the heart of the Eucharist: "Spiritual food changes man into itself."[24] For Aquinas, the sacrament of the Eucharist has as its end the human person's union with the Godhead manifested by the unity of the mystical body that is Christ's Church. While reflecting on this point may seem to be simply belaboring the obvious, it is a common tendency in eucharistic theology to allow the *means* to this end (i.e., "Real Presence") to obfuscate the true purpose of the Eucharist—unity.

The retrieval of a Thomistic grammar of grace and virtue is not an abandonment of the scholastic language dogmatized by Trent. On the contrary, this retrieval is an attempt to honestly translate the sacramental theology of Thomas without irresponsible transplantation. More and more, however, such references to Thomas are presented as an apology in which the sacramental grammar of scholasticism (e.g., accident, substance, form, matter, etc.) is reworked, not to communicate what Thomas meant, but to make that grammar meaningful to those who hear it with a modern ear.[25] Once dogmatized by Trent, this scholastic grammar of the Eucharist laid a claim on Roman Catholic theology that has primarily manifested itself in preoccupation with terms rather than with meaning. In other words, adherence to a particular grammar is given privilege above and beyond the

---

[24] S.T. III.73.3.ad2. Quotations from the *Summa Theologiae* are from *The Summa Theologiae of Saint Thomas Aquinas, Latin-English Edition* (Scotts Valley, CA: NovAntiqua, 2008).

[25] An excellent example of this mentality would be the twentieth-century debate between Carlo Colombo and Filipo Selvaggi. For an insightful examination of this debate and its continued significance, see P. J. Fitzpatrick, *In Breaking of Bread: The Eucharist and Ritual* (Cambridge: Cambridge University Press, 1993), chap. 1.

success of communicating the ideas that particular grammar was created to mediate.

Are grammars important? Certainly. Can we simply disregard grammars that are so deeply traditional as to have been dogmatized? Certainly not. Nevertheless, we must always guard against any tendency to mistake the grammar for the message, the medium for the mediated. Such a tendency confuses repetition with being traditional. The only way to truly honor a grammar is to communicate, as faithfully as possible, the message it mediates; this is called translation. Translation is not only necessary; it is unavoidable. We must be honest about the fact that we can no longer hear the Latin or Greek words of doctrine in the same way they were heard by the people who wrote them. Any notion that adopting a universal language might free us from the need for translation ignores the necessary relationship between culture and language. We must recognize and affirm that, in translation, change occurs. Not only can we say that the Church does change; we must say that it can do nothing but change. Failure to change is a failure to live.[26] So, when we seek to be traditional, our first instinct should not be to look to the *Enchiridion Symbolorum* for the word bank we have been handed by our Tradition. Rather, we should look to Tradition for the truths it passes on to us through the mediation of an inculturated and contingent grammar.

Interpretation must precede translation if translation is to be accomplished honestly, because, in the end, our only choices are good translation or bad translation. All this has been to say that *the absence of a particular grammar does not mean it is has been dismissed*. On the contrary; it is very possible that an absent grammar is exerting a great amount of influence in any given work of theology. Likewise, the explicit employment of a grammar does not necessarily imply fidelity to that grammar *qua* grammar. If we insist on utilizing a grammar to the detriment of proper translation, we run the great risk of abusing and obfuscating that doctrine.

At the beginning of this introduction, I said that, broadly speaking, this book seeks to offer a grammar that helps bridge the disconnection between grammars. Speaking more specifically, this book seeks

---

[26] For a brief discussion of the importance of change, see Micahel Himes, *The Mystery of Faith: An Introduction to Catholicism* (Cincinnati, OH: St. Anthony Messanger Press, 2004).

to retrieve a Thomistic grammar of grace and virtue that will help bridge the disconnection between scholastic grammars of eucharistic presence and modern grammars. The retrieved grammar will function to help translate the disconnected grammars in a way that allows for meaningful dialogue. I say that this retrieval is tantamount to finding a lost voice, not because the Thomistic grammars of grace and virtue have gone unnoticed and undiscussed (far from it!), but because these grammars have gone largely unnoticed and undiscussed in connection with Aquinas's treatment of the sacraments.

By constructively using the grammars of grace and virtue, I will show that Aquinas's way of addressing grace and the virtues still has much to offer contemporary sacramental theology. In short, this book provides a retrieval of a more robust Thomistic sacramental theology. By refusing to be confined to what is explicitly sacramental in the *Summa Theologiae*, I will have opened up the traditional scholastic grammar in a way that encourages other approaches to sacramental theology. This grammar both protects against narrow readings of Aquinas's sacramental theology and broadens the spectrum of issues that can and ought to be included in sacramental theology. Replacing the scholastic obsession with transubstantiation with Aquinas's obsession (i.e., charity) not only removes a stumbling block for Roman Catholic theological conversations but also can serve to mitigate a point of ecumenical division by offering a theology better equipped to engage the plurality of grammars being employed in the discussion.

CHAPTER ONE

Why the *Secunda Pars*?

Within the *Summa Theologiae*, Aquinas *explicitly* treats the sacraments in the *Tertia Pars*.[1] To rely solely on the eucharistic theology presented in the *Tertia Pars*, however, is to overlook the sacramental theology of the *Secunda Pars*. The first section of this chapter will provide an example of the problems that can arise if the *Tertia Pars* is isolated from the *Secunda Pars*. Louis-Marie Chauvet's critique of Aquinas's eucharistic theology is an excellent example of the danger that results from focusing too narrowly on the scholastic grammars that permeate the *Tertia Pars*. By then turning to a close reading of the sacramental theology found in the *Tertia Pars*, the remaining sections of the chapter substantiate the claim that the *Secunda Pars* is where Aquinas *implicitly* treats the sacraments insofar as it contextualizes the *Tertia Pars*. Specifically, the *Secunda Pars* offers us a teleological framework (constructed using grammars of grace and virtue) that can be used as the hermeneutical key for understanding the content of the *Tertia Pars*. By using the *Tertia Pars* to define the Eucharist as a sacrament meant to increase charity, this chapter justifies the subsequent chapters' turn to the *Secunda Pars*.

[1] S.T. III.60-90. It should be pointed out that throughout this chapter when I refer to "sacraments," unless otherwise specified, I am referring to the seven sacraments of the New Law.

I. Lamenting the Loss of a Loss[2]

The French theologian Louis-Marie Chauvet has, in more than one instance, critiqued Aquinas's treatment of the Eucharist in which, Chauvet argues, Aquinas essentially "wrings the neck of Aristotelianism" in a quest to objectify the substantial presence of Christ in the bread and wine.[3] The critiques forwarded by Chauvet point out a tendency of Aquinas's eucharistic theology in which the relationship between Christ's ecclesial body and Christ's eucharistic body is made secondary to the relationship between Christ's historical body and Christ's eucharistic body. Put simply, Chauvet laments the loss of a Eucharist of and for the Church.

1. The Deadly Dichotomy

The main critique Chauvet levels at Aquinas is that the lens through which he understands the sacrament of the Eucharist has fundamentally shifted in a way not beneficial to the Church. Namely, the Eucharist is first and foremost seen as a sacrament in which the historical body of Christ becomes substantially present. The Eucharist is fundamentally a sacrament in which the historical body of Jesus becomes substantially present in the species of bread and wine through a moment called transubstantiation. The fact that this is most often the primary way of describing the Eucharist signals a shift away from a eucharistic theology in which the Eucharist is first and foremost seen as sacrament of charity meant to bring about the unity of the Church.

To understand this critique more fully, I begin with a discussion of what Chauvet, following Henri de Lubac, calls the threefold Body of Christ.

> It was common for theological tradition to distinguish a threefold body of Christ: (1) his historical and glorious body; (2) his Eucharistic body which was called "mystical body" up to the

---

[2] This section is largely taken from David Farina Turnbloom, "A Defense of Aquinas' Treatment of the Eucharist," *Studia Liturgica* 43, no. 1 (2013): 93–110.

[3] Louis-Marie Chauvet, "The Broken Bread as Theological Figure of Eucharistic Presence," in *Sacramental Presence in a Postmodern Context*, ed. L. Boeve and L. Leijssen (Leuven: Leuven University Press, 2001), 245.

twelfth century because it is "his body in mystery," that is to say, in sacrament; (3) his ecclesial body, growing throughout history.[4]

The term "body of Christ" was used with equal validity to describe each designation of the threefold body. For clarity's sake, I would like to mention that throughout this chapter and those that follow this threefold body is referred to by using the terms historical body, eucharistic body, and ecclesial body. In his text *Corpus Mysticum*, de Lubac points out that from the early centuries of the Christian tradition there is a fundamental relationship between the eucharistic body of Christ and the ecclesial body of Christ. He begins his text by highlighting this relationship: "In the thinking of the whole of Christian antiquity, the Eucharist and the Church are linked. . . . The Eucharist corresponds to the Church as cause to effect, as means to end, as sign to reality."[5] In other words, the ecclesial body of Christ (i.e., the Church) was an intrinsic aspect of the sacrament of the Eucharist. Or, in Chauvet's words, "For the Fathers, the ecclesial body was the 'truth' of the eucharistic body."[6] For these early theologians, it would not have been possible to speak of the Eucharist without speaking (at least implicitly) about the Church.

The problem, as Chauvet and de Lubac see it, arises in the eleventh century with Berengar of Tours. Berengar, in opposition to the rising obsession with the relationship between the historical body of Christ and the eucharistic body of Christ, began to deny the eucharistic "real" presence in order to fight the loss of focus on the ecclesial body. In other words, in order to pull everyone's eyes away from the consecrated host and return their eyes to the Church, he denied that there was anything to look at in the host. To his overreaction, Christian tradition went on to add its own; the result was what de Lubac calls the "deadly dichotomy" between Christ's ecclesial body and the eucharistic body. To correct the heresy of Berengar, theologians intensified what Berengar had been trying to correct: they not only continued to focus their attention on the relationship between the historical

[4] Ibid., 139.

[5] Henri de Lubac, *Corpus Mysticum: The Eucharist and the Church in the Middle Ages; Historical Survey*, trans. Gemma Simmonds (London: SCM Press, 2006), 13.

[6] Louis-Marie Chauvet, *The Sacraments: The Word of God at the Mercy of the Body*, trans. Madeleine Beaumont (Collegeville, MN: Liturgical Press, 2001), 139.

body and the eucharistic body, but they also began to obfuscate the relationship between the eucharistic body and the ecclesial body in order to avoid any semblance of heresy. Using the words of de Lubac, Chauvet summarizes this shift:

> About this, Henri de Lubac says that from the end of the twelfth century on a "deadly dichotomy" between the eucharistic body and the ecclesial body became firmly rooted. At the same time symbolism became "something artificial and accessory . . . the essential bond that joined eucharistic worship to the unity of the Church disappeared." Thus, "the ultimate reality of the sacrament," that is to say, the unity of the ecclesial body, "that which formerly was its reality and its truth par excellence, is ejected from the sacrament itself." It does remain its finality; but from then on, it does not belong to its "intrinsic symbolism."[7]

The unity of the Church, then, is no longer the truth of the sacrament. For the patristic authors, the Church was the true body (*corpus verum*) given through the eucharistic body (*corpus mysticum*), and both of these were intrinsic to the sacrament. By the thirteenth century, the "truth" of the sacrament has been redefined. According to the Scholastics, the *corpus verum* is the consecrated bread and wine, while the Church is now called the *corpus mysticum*.[8] The Church, then, is excised from the sacrament itself; the true presence of Christ is now to be primarily sought, not in the lives of the members of the Church, but upon the altar and in the hands of the clergy.

As a result of this development in eucharistic understanding, what Chauvet calls an "ultra-realist" approach to understanding the Eucharist was given more and more validity. The flesh of Christ was seen as hidden "in there somewhere." It is this development that incited the theological treatises that sought to objectify the intelligibility of holding this belief, the most famous of which is Aquinas's theory of transubstantiation. While there is no need to rehearse this theory here, it must be said that while Aquinas pushed the limits of his intellectual powers in order to demonstrate the objectivity of

---

[7] Ibid.

[8] Louis-Marie Chauvet, *Symbol and Sacrament: A Sacramental Reinterpretation of Christian Existence*, trans. Patrick Madigan and Madeleine Beaumont (Collegeville, MN: Liturgical Press, 1995), 294.

Christ's "real" presence in the Eucharist, he was a far cry from the ultra-realism so prevalent at the time in which he was writing. Chauvet points out that

> the novelty [of the language of transubstantiation] consists in the fact that compared with the theology of the pre-scholastic period, the ontological expression of the presence can be understood only as outside any physicalism and any more or less gross representation. Transubstantiation thus has a meaning diametrically opposed to the one often attributed to it.[9]

This is to say that, for Aquinas, claiming that Christ is substantially present in the Eucharist does not mean that Christ is present in the way that something is present in a particular location. In fact, Aquinas explicitly denies this manner of understanding Christ's real presence. "Christ's body is not in this sacrament in the same way as a body is in a place, which by its dimensions is commensurate with a place; but in a special manner which is proper to this sacrament."[10] While one might defend Aquinas from being labeled an ultra-realist, it is harder to save him, however, from the accusation that he stresses the relationship between the historical body and the eucharistic body. In the following chapters (especially chap. 5) I take pains to illustrate that Aquinas does not ignore the relationship between the ecclesial body and the eucharistic body, but for now it must not be denied that Aquinas is guilty of focusing intently on the relationship between the historical and eucharistic bodies of Christ. His extensive treatment of transubstantiation is clearly a symptom of the "deadly dichotomy" that had developed in reaction to the good-intentioned, if imprudent, Berengar.

2. Consequences of the Deadly Dichotomy

For Chauvet, this "deadly dichotomy" is perhaps most clearly visible not in Aquinas's construction of transubstantiation but in his claim that the sacrament is completed with the consecration of the host. "The sacrament of the Eucharist is completed [*perficitur*] in the

---

[9] Ibid., 386.
[10] S.T. III.75.1.ad3.

very consecration of the matter, whereas the other sacraments are completed in the application of the matter for the sanctifying of the individual."[11] After the ordained minister has recited the dominical words, whose power brings about the twofold miracle of transubstantiation and the providential maintaining of the bread and wine's quantity, the sacrament is complete.[12] That is to say, in Aquinas's theology the sacrament of the Eucharist is perfect before it is received by the faithful. More so than the inordinate amount of text devoted to the metaphysics of transubstantiation, this "completion before use" is symptomatic of the fundamental shift in which the fact that Christ is present in the consecrated host becomes more important than why he is present. In other words, this shift leaves us preoccupied with a presence understood as a "being" and not as a "being-for." Or, in Aquinas's own words:

> The difference between the Eucharist and other sacraments having sensible matter is that whereas the Eucharist contains something which is sacred absolutely, namely, Christ's own body; the baptismal water contains something which is sacred in relation to something else, namely, the sanctifying power: and the same holds good of chrism and such like.[13]

Aquinas is careful to distinguish the eucharistic presence from other sacramental presence. For Aquinas, presence is "real" regardless of its destination.

Before briefly touching on how Chauvet believes eucharistic presence should be understood, I must mention the two problems he sees as resulting from the deadly dichotomy. Here, it will be beneficial to quote Chauvet at length.

> In speaking of the "full realization" (*perfectio*) of the Eucharist in the consecration of the matter, inasmuch as the latter contains "in an absolute manner" the *esse* of Christ, one runs the risk of

---

[11] S.T. III.73.1.ad3. See also III.80.12.ad2.
[12] Cf. S.T. III.77.1. Here we see that Aquinas invokes divine providence twice to describe the eucharistic change: first, to change the substance of the species into the substance of Christ (i.e., to cause the *sacramentum et res*) and, second, to sustain the accidental dimensive quantity of the bread and wine (i.e., to maintain the *sacramentum tantum*).
[13] S.T. III.73.1.ad3.

minimizing two capital elements that are linked together. On the one hand, one does not take into account the human destination that is implied by the *materia* in question, the bread and the wine. On the other, one loses sight of a fundamental aspect of the mystery: the Christ of the Eucharist is the *Christus totus*; the "head" cannot be isolated from the "body," the Church which still remains completely distinct from it.[14]

Both of these "capital elements" are concerned with the *purpose* of Christ's presence in the Eucharist. In other words, Chauvet is concerned with what he sees as a presence that is meaningful strictly as presence and not as presence *for the Church*. When Aquinas says that the sacrament is completed by consecration, he removes the reason for the consecration from the sacrament. This is especially evident when he makes it clear that the only words necessary for consecration are "This is my body" and "This is the chalice of my blood."[15] The whole narrative of the eucharistic prayer in which the reason for Christ's presence is expressed becomes unnecessary. What is important is that the bread and wine are now truly the body and blood of Christ. Eucharistic presence has become a question of being (*esse*) as opposed to being-for (*adesse*).

According to Chauvet, sacramental presence (especially eucharistic presence) should be understood as a "being-for." The word "presence" denotes not simply existence but relation. In describing Aquinas's theory of eucharistic change, Chauvet points out that "[presence] is isolated then as a thing in itself, and is being thought in the sole register of 'substance.' In this way, the 'ad-' implied by the notion itself of presence (*ad-esse*) is put in parentheses to the profit of the sole substantial *esse*."[16] This bracketing of the "*ad-*" is a glaring symptom of the deadly dichotomy. To be present is to be present *to something or someone*. Being-for someone puts the focus primarily on the "someone" for whom you are present, in turn defining your own being in terms of that relationship. Something's presence is meaningful only insofar as it is in relation. Or, in Chauvet's words:

[14] Chauvet, *Symbol and Sacrament*, 388.
[15] Cf. S.T. III.78.1c.
[16] Chauvet, "Broken Bread," 250.

> The relational "for" is constitutive of the presence of Christ as
> such. This "for" is not a simple accidental and secondary deriva-
> tion of it, nor a simple extrinsic finality. This point is of course
> capital: the eucharistic *esse* is intrinsically an *adesse*. Consequently
> one can never put this *ad* between parentheses, not even during
> the analysis of the how of the presence.[17]

When Aquinas distinguishes the Eucharist from the other sacraments
in that it is completed after consecration, he has put the "*ad-*" in
parentheses, leaving an *esse* without intention—a reality without
purpose. Of course, this is not to deny that existence is a necessary
aspect of presence but to insist that without the relationality of presence existence is meaningless. To illustrate the point with hyperbole:
that Christ came down from heaven is insignificant; that Christ came
for the salvation of the world is full of meaning. So, without those
for whom Christ becomes present, the eucharistic presence of Christ
is literally insignificant.

When presence is understood as a "being-for," it becomes impossible to claim that the Eucharist reaches its completion without being
used by the Church. To make the ecclesial body of Christ extrinsic to
the Eucharist is to rob the sacrament of its meaning. It is like an un-
wrapped gift. Or, to use the language of Chauvet, to remove the
"being-for" from the eucharistic presence is a symptom of our
"necrotic tendency" (*processus de nécrose*) to try (in vain) to capture
and isolate the Living Christ.[18] That is to say: without an intrinsic
relationship between the eucharistic body and the ecclesial body the
eucharistic body is lifeless.

To conclude this section, we return to its title. The critiques we
have just rehearsed can be summarized as lamentations of the loss
of a loss. In other words, the deadly dichotomy can be seen as the
result of an obsession with possession. Eucharistic theologies that

---

[17] Ibid., 255. This last phrase, "not even during the analysis of the how of the presence," betrays a misunderstanding at the root of so much critique of Aquinas's eucharistic theology. In our post-enlightenment obsession with reductive analysis of
mechanisms, it becomes commonplace to expect foundational sacramental theology
to be carried out through an explanation of the mechanism by which sacraments
work. Hence, the fact that the foundational sacramental theology of signification is
not materially grounding the explanation of eucharistic change is cause for concern
to anyone who expects such a discussion.

[18] Chauvet, *Symbol and Sacrament*, 174.

focus on the substantial presence of Christ in the eucharistic species strive to overcome the fact that Jesus of Nazareth is no longer here. When we succumb to our necrotic tendency to capture the flesh of Christ on our altars, reveling in the knowledge that he is no longer absent, we have lost the blessing of his distance which is our call to be his Church. That is to say, we have lost sight of who we are as Church: the ecclesial body of Christ. When Christ's presence is allowed to be an *esse* that we use as a sacred distraction from our secular lives, we lose the *adesse* that (according to Chauvet) is given as a task to foment our spiritual lives and build the Church that is the presence of the ascended Christ. To make transubstantiation the foundation and heart of eucharistic theology is to surrender the loss on which Christianity stands. To forget that Christ is gone is to forget that we are Christ.

Chauvet shows that Aquinas's preoccupation with the grammar of substance can result in some problematic ways of describing the Eucharist. As I will now argue, however, a careful reading of the sacramental theology in the *Tertia Pars* leaves us with questions that turn us toward the *Secunda Pars*. The depth of Aquinas's sacramental theology cannot be accurately appreciated without broadening our gaze beyond the text of the *Tertia Pars*.

II. The Purpose of the *Summa Theologiae*

While Aquinas began to write the *Summa Theologiae* in Rome in the year 1265, I would argue, with Leonard E. Boyle, that the *Summa* finds its roots in Aquinas's previous experience as lector for his religious community in Orvieto.[19] From 1261 to 1265, Aquinas was charged with instructing his fellow Dominicans, readying them for their primary roles as preachers and confessors. The theological texts available to them, however, focused narrowly on practical theology, often disconnecting it from its dogmatic foundation. These well-established texts, such as Raymond of Pennafort's *Summa de Casibus*,

---

[19] Leonard E. Boyle, "The Setting of the *Summa Theologiae* of St. Thomas—Revisited," in *The Ethics of Aquinas*, ed. Stephan J. Pope (Washington, DC: Georgetown University Press, 2002), 7. "[The *Summa Theologiae*] may have been begun at Santa Sabina in Rome where the *incipientes* were young students of the order, but it was Orvieto and [Thomas's] four years of practical teaching there among the *fratres communes* that had really occasioned it."

were held in high regard by Aquinas and remained a regular source for his own work. However, when given the opportunity to create a curriculum and oversee his own school in Rome (Santa Sabina), Aquinas seems to have shifted his pedagogy. Rather than maintaining the curriculum so prevalent in other Dominican schools, Aquinas was able to focus more on the relationship between dogmatic theology and ethics. As Boyle puts it, "By concentrating on God, Creation, Trinity, and other *dogmatic* or *systematic* areas of theology, he makes it clear that he was breaking away from the customary practical theology of the order."[20] Hence, when he set out to make his own contribution to the body of theological textbooks, he sought to structure the *Summa* in a way that would make the necessary relationship between dogmatic and moral theology explicit.[21] In short, Aquinas "attempted to set the regular training in practical theology in the Dominican Order on a more truly theological course."[22] By developing a dogmatic foundation for his students, Aquinas was emphasizing the intrinsic connection between ethics (i.e., questions regarding the moral quality of the human action) and systematic theology (i.e., questions regarding the dogmatically proclaimed Christian faith). Through the very structure of the *Summa*, Aquinas attests to the fact that "to study human action is . . . to study the Image of God and to operate on a theological plane. To study human action on a theological plane is to study its relation to its beginning and end, and the bridge between, Christ and the sacraments."[23]

While the *Summa* is vast in its breadth, it is a whole unified by its structure. Hence, isolating any part, question, or article of the *Summa* runs the great risk of misinterpretation. By moving to the *Secunda Pars* and examining it as the context of the *Tertia Pars*, I seek to mitigate the risk of such misinterpretation. Methodologically speaking, the role of the present chapter is to extract from the *Tertia Pars* a skeletal framework that we will enflesh in subsequent chapters, using the meat of the *Secunda Pars*. By briefly examining Aquinas's explicit

[20] Ibid., 6.
[21] Jean-Pierre Torrell, *Saint Thomas Aquinas*, vol. 1, *The Person and His Work*, trans. Robert Royal (Washington, DC: The Catholic University of America Press, 1996), 118–20, 144–45.
[22] Boyle, "The Setting of the *Summa*," 7.
[23] Ibid.

treatment of the sacraments, I will highlight some questions that result from such an examination. These questions will be our skeletal framework. As we will see, these questions are not fully answered in the *Tertia Pars*. This lack is the justification of turning to the *Secunda Pars*.[24]

From the outset I wish to emphasize the reason that I am deliberately starting with the sacraments and not with Christology. According to Bernhard Blankenhorn, "Thomas' sacramentology must always be read through his Christology."[25] Admittedly, within the structure of the *Tertia Pars* the relationship between Christ's passion and the sacraments is paramount on both a methodological level and a conceptual level. At the methodological level, beginning with Christology (as the *Tertia Pars* does) determines the grammar within which the examination of the sacraments will occur. Hence, at the conceptual level, the *Tertia Pars* largely defines the sacraments in christological and soteriological terms. However, I am intentionally choosing not to begin with Christology, because Aquinas does not begin with Christology. The *Secunda Pars* comes before the *Tertia Pars*.[26] I do not want us to forget that Aquinas's treatment of Christ and the sacraments is preceded by an ethical context apart from which the *Tertia Pars* cannot be properly understood.

III. Signification and Causality

According to Aquinas, the sacraments are necessary for salvation because by them we are incorporated into Christ, forming one unified

---

[24] It should be noted that this chapter runs the risk of repeating the methodological mistake I am critiquing. I too am starting with the *Tertia Pars*. However, this chapter is not seeking to set up a foundational hermeneutic to be employed in our examination of the *Secunda Pars*. Rather, the questions we will excavate from the *Tertia Pars* in this chapter serve as skeletal framework insofar as they indicate the prior presence of a framework to be found in the *Prima Pars* and *Secunda Pars*. Simply put, highlighting these questions functions to point out that Aquinas is assuming knowledge not present in the *Tertia Pars*.

[25] Bernhard Blankenhorn, "The Place of Romans 6 in Aquinas's Doctrine of Sacramental Causality: A Balance of History and Metaphysics," in *Ressourcement Thomism: Sacred Doctrine, the Sacraments, and the Moral Life*, ed. Matthew Levering and Reinhard Hütter (Washington, DC: The Catholic University of America Press, 2010).

[26] Admittedly, it is also true that the *Prima Pars* comes before the *Secunda Pars*. The relationship between these two will be discussed in the following chapter.

body of his members.[27] Aquinas uses two categories to describe the way the sacraments accomplish this goal: signification and causality. As signs, the sacraments function to make humankind holy by leading us to knowledge of God. Causally speaking, sacraments exist to cause our participation in the life of grace. We turn first to an examination of sacramental signification as it is treated in question 60 of the *Tertia Pars*.

Throughout the opening question of the treatise on the sacraments, signification is discussed in terms of knowledge. "Signs are given to men, to whom it is proper to discover the unknown by means of the known."[28] More specifically, Aquinas tells us that signs are called sacraments when they signify a hidden sanctity.[29] There is, however, an important distinction to be made. Sacramental signification implies sanctification. "Properly speaking, a sacrament, as considered by us now, is defined as being the sign of a holy thing so far as it makes men holy."[30] By the sacraments we do not merely know that which is holy; we are made holy by that knowledge.[31] Sanctification is not the result of a special type of signification but rather the result of that which is signified.[32] In article 3, Aquinas tells us that the sacraments signify Christ's passion (the cause of our sanctification), grace and virtues (the form of our sanctification), and eternal life (the end of our sanctification).[33] Sacraments are said to have sacramental signification because they signify (i.e., offer us knowledge of) the cause, form, and end of our sanctification. In short, we are sanctified through knowledge of the causes of our sanctification.[34]

[27] Cf. S.T. III.61.1sc.

[28] S.T. III.60.2c. See also, a. 4.

[29] S.T. III.60.1c.

[30] S.T. III.60.2c.

[31] It is crucial to note that we are not saying anything yet about what "knowledge" means. Much less have we established how Aquinas understands the relationship between knowledge and sanctification.

[32] S.T. III.60.2.ad1.

[33] S.T. III.60.3c.

[34] According to Aquinas (cf. III.49.1.ad4 and III.61.1.ad3), as a "universal cause," Christ's Passion is "applied" to individuals through the sacraments. There is an implicit, yet acute awareness of the historical nature of salvation at work in Aquinas's thought here. The historical application of the passion will be taken up later in chap. 5.2.

It is the central role of signification that leads Aquinas to place such a high importance on the words used in the sacraments. I will have cause in subsequent chapters to return to the role of language in Aquinas's system. For now, I am content to point out that, according to Aquinas, words are signs *par excellence*, capable of signification in a way that objects and gestures are not.[35] There is an "essential sense" communicated by the words of the sacraments.[36] It is this essential sense of the words, and not the uttered words themselves, that makes sacramental signification possible. The sacramental signification is said to sanctify insofar as the essential sense of the words is believed through faith. So, I can qualify my previous claim: we are sanctified through belief in the causes of our sanctification—causes that are made present and known to us through the sacraments.[37]

With this notion of sacramental signification in mind, we can begin to understand what Aquinas means by sacramental causality. In question 62, Aquinas treats the issue of sacramental causality within the context of examining grace as the principal effect of sacraments. Aquinas points out that any instance of being incorporated to Christ is the result of grace.[38] Insofar as the sacraments are ordained to such an end, Aquinas feels that he is required to say (*necesse est dicere*) that the sacraments may be said to cause grace in some way (*per aliquem modum*). In article 1, he goes on to explain this inherited language by first saying what sacramental causality is not. Sacraments are not principal efficient causes; rather, they are always (even when Christ is substantially contained in the sacrament) separated instrumental efficient causes of grace. "The instrumental cause works not by the power of its form but only by the motion whereby it is moved by the principal agent: so that the effect is not likened to the instrument but to the principal agent."[39] Aquinas uses the relationship between carpenter, axe, and couch as a metaphor for understanding the distinction between principal cause and instrumental cause. This metaphor functions to highlight the fact that the effect (i.e., the couch) shares a likeness to the principal cause (i.e., the carpenter's mind)

---

[35] S.T. III.60.6c.
[36] S.T. III.60.8c.
[37] Cf. S.T. III.60.7.ad1.
[38] S.T. III.62.1c.
[39] Ibid.

and not the likeness of the instrumental cause (i.e., the axe). Before using the instrumental cause, the carpenter has in her mind an image of what she wants to create. The resultant couch shares a likeness to the thoughts of the carpenter (assuming the carpenter is not incompetent) but it does not share a likeness to the axe.

The principal effect of the sacraments is grace, and grace "is nothing else than a participated likeness of the Divine Nature."[40] Without unpacking what is positively meant by "a participated likeness in the Divine Nature" (a task that will be given much treatment in the following chapter), here we are concerned only with saying that grace shares a likeness, not to the sacraments, but to God. So, according to Aquinas, the sacraments cause grace the same way that an axe causes a couch. Likewise, the sacraments contain grace the same way that an axe contains a couch.[41] If we are to give a Thomistic answer to the question "What causes grace?" we must first point out that the question is flawed. The proper question is, "*Who* causes grace?" After answering that more fundamental question, we are then free to inquire about the ways God has deemed it fitting to cause grace.

As we have seen, Aquinas spends most of his time qualifying the traditional claim that sacraments cause grace. God uses sacramental signs to draw us into a participation in the Divine Nature. Put differently, God uses sacraments to cause grace. To contextualize Aquinas's incredibly nuanced exposition of sacramental causality, it is helpful to recall the *Summa*'s genre. It is an introductory textbook. Much like any good teacher of beginners, Aquinas is presenting the tradition as fairly as possible. Aquinas must tell his students that sacraments cause grace, so he tells them that sacraments have no causal power by nature of their form (i.e., the misunderstanding that allows *ex opere operato* to degenerate into hermeticism), but rather they are said to have causal power insofar as by means of signification God causes us to participate in the Divine Nature. Notice what Aquinas has done here: he has taken traditional grammars of causality and constructed a sacramental theology that aligns easily with a grammar of signification and participation. By defining grace in terms of participation he situates any understanding of sacramental causality within that framework.

---

[40] Ibid.
[41] Cf. S.T. III.62.3.

Understanding the relationship between causality and signification is important so as to avoid misunderstanding the role of the sacraments in the sanctification of humankind. The sacraments are not shower handles that, when properly turned, cause grace to shower down upon us from on high. Rather, the sacraments all function together to bring us to faithful participation in the Divine Nature. The enumeration of the sacraments, in Aquinas's treatment, results from the varying roles each religious ritual plays in the sanctification of humankind. That is to say, each sacrament helps us live the graced life in its own specific manner according to our various needs. All seven sacraments of the New Law serve the unity of Christ's body, the Church, by signifying our sanctification in different ways. When we say that the sacraments cause grace, we must avoid imagining seven different rituals causing the same homogenous grace in seven different ways. Rather, it is crucial to remember that each sacrament has its own *res tantum*, its own grace. Remembering that causality is a function of signification, we must look to the way the sacraments bring us to belief in our sanctification. Each sacrament sanctifies by virtue of its distinct form of signification. So, rather than shower handles, sacraments are like a series of letters you receive from a distant loved one, each treating a different aspect of your relationship. In reading a letter that expresses forgiveness after having hurt your beloved, you are drawn more deeply into that relationship with a renewed sense of friendship. A love letter that poetically celebrates a shared desire for one another intensifies the love that was already present. Similarly, sacraments signify God's actions in our lives. They cause grace by bringing us into that divine life.

Any examination of the *Tertia Pars* alone, like the one above, should leave the examiner with questions about the grammar Aquinas employs. As we have seen, through signification the sacraments bring us to belief in the source of our sanctification and, in so doing, we are made to participate in the Divine Nature. Put simply, through the sacraments, we are graced. Based on this discussion of sacramental signification, we have seen that the concepts of grace, participation, and belief are essential to Thomas's treatment of the sacraments. If we want to fully understand the sacraments we must first understand the relationship between grace, participation, and belief. Based on the exposition above, it should be clear that the sacramental theology found in the *Tertia Pars* does not sufficiently develop these terms and their relationship to one another. This is because the *Tertia Pars* is assuming knowledge. In the following chapter, then, we will focus on the relationship between grace, participation, and belief as it is treated in the *Secunda Pars*. Together these terms make up the heart of the grammar of grace that this book is seeking to retrieve from the *Secunda Pars*.

IV. Baptism and Penance: Infusing Charity

Before we move to an examination of individual sacraments, we must briefly treat Thomas's categories of "sacrament only, sacrament and reality, and reality only" (*sacramentum tantum, sacramentum et res*, and *res tantum*, respectively). Each sacrament can be described using these categories. Understanding the relationship between them helps us better understand the relationship between sacramental significa-tion and grace. Simply put, the grace of a sacrament is the reality at which it aims, or its end. Thomas calls this end the *res tantum*. For example, as we will discuss further in the following section of this chapter, the purpose and *res tantum* of the Eucharist is the unity of the ecclesial body of Christ.[42] In the first article of question 73, Aquinas points out that the grace bestowed by the Eucharist is this *res tantum*.[43] Hence, eucharistic grace is identified with the unity of the Church. While each sacrament is ordained toward an end (i.e., its grace), the *sacramentum tantum* and the *sacramentum et res* of each sacrament play the vital role of signifying the sacrament's end. As I have already pointed out, grace is the result of sacramental signification. The *sac-ramentum tantum* and the *sacramentum et res* sanctify us by signifying the causes of our sanctification so that we might believe in that sanc-tification. In the Eucharist, the bread and wine (the *sacramentum tan-tum*) and the eucharistic body of Christ (the *sacramentum et res*) signify the Church's identity with Christ. It is important to note that, accord-ing to Aquinas, the *sacramentum tantum* and the *sacramentum et res* work *together* to cause the *res tantum* through signification.[44] This is very different from saying that the *sacramentum tantum* causes the *sacramentum et res*, which in turn causes the *res tantum*. This point is of particular importance for a proper understanding of the Eucharist.

---

[42] S.T. III.73.3c.
[43] S.T. III.73.1.ad3.
[44] S.T. III.84.1.ad3.

The unity of the Church is not the result of the substantial presence of Christ. It is a result of both the ritual itself and the substantial presence of Christ. In every sacrament, the *sacramentum tantum* and the *sacramentum et res* work together to sanctify us insofar as they are both signs that point beyond themselves to a particular manner of participation in Divine Life, that is, a sacramental grace. Aquinas's use of these three categories allows us to see, again, the foundational role of signification in his sacramental theology. All sacraments are ordered toward a *res tantum*, a particular grace. For Aquinas, it is by virtue of these graces that the sacraments are rightly enumerated as seven individual sacraments.

Having focused on how the sacraments are the same, the remainder of the chapter will focus on what makes the Eucharist different from the sacraments of baptism and penance. As I mentioned above, the Eucharist is ordered to nourishing the unity of the Church. While it is the main focus of this book to examine exactly how the Eucharist attains this end, the present chapter is concerned with offering a simple explanation: *the Eucharist increases charity in subjects.* By way of substantiating that claim, I would like to say what the Eucharist is not. Before I return to an examination of what it means to say that the Eucharist nourishes unity by increasing charity, I will begin by drawing the distinction between increasing charity and infusing charity. Remembering that the sacraments are distinguished by their ends, I will look at the ends of baptism and penance. By examining the relationship between charity and these two sacraments, I will highlight what the Eucharist does not do, namely, infuse charity.

In question 66, article 1, Aquinas points out that inward justification is the *res tantum* of baptism. The water and its use are the *sacramentum tantum*, and the baptismal character is the *sacramentum et res*. Together, the ritual and the baptismal character both signify the justification of the person who is baptized. Expanding on this particular grace of baptism, Aquinas cites John of Damascus who "also set down two things pertaining to the ultimate reality of the sacrament—namely, regeneration which refers to the fact that man by being baptized begins the new life of righteousness; and enlightenment, which refers especially to faith, by which man receives spiritual life."[45] So,

---

[45] S.T. III.66.1.ad1.

when Aquinas says that the very nature of baptism is "a regeneration unto a spiritual life" he is defining the *res tantum* of baptism.[46]

The grace of baptism is regeneration so that the baptized person "may be incorporated in Christ."[47] The relationship between justification and incorporation in Christ will be more closely treated in chapter 3. For now, I want to emphasize that justification is our spiritual regeneration into the life of Christ because through the forgiveness of sins we are "born again in Christ."[48] There is a radical newness to this spiritual life that leads Aquinas to call the sacramental grace of baptism "the grace of newness."[49] Through baptism, we are said to be justified insofar as we receive "a certain rectitude of order in [our] interior dispositions."[50] This ordered interior is accomplished through the infusion of the theological virtues.[51] The *res tantum* of baptism, then, is God's reordering of our dispositions by the infusion of faith, hope, and charity. All this is to say that the sacrament of baptism *infuses* charity where there previously was no charity.

Once we have charity, we can lose it completely and in an instant. Aquinas notes that the character received in baptism is indelible, but the justification we receive can be lost.[52] Through mortal sin, the presence of charity in the subject is destroyed.[53] To remedy such loss, we then need the re-infusion of charity that accompanies penance. For Aquinas, it is clear that through mortal sin we do not lose our other virtues; in a state of mortal sin we can still act justly, we can still have faith, and we can still be prudent. We do lose the form of those virtues, however, and therefore the possibility that they are meritorious. The theological virtue of charity forms all the virtues making them "strictly true" virtues. For instance, faith that is not formed by charity is lifeless faith. Lifeless faith is still a theological virtue, but its fruit is servile fear (i.e., the fear of punishment) as opposed to the fruit of living faith, filial fear (i.e., the fear of separation

---

[46] S.T. III.66.3c.
[47] S.T. III.68.1c.
[48] S.T. III.84.5c.
[49] S.T. III.69.8c.
[50] S.T. I.II.113.1c.
[51] S.T. I.II.113.4.ad1.
[52] S.T. III.66.1.ad1.
[53] S.T. II.II.24.12c.

from God).[54] When forming virtues, charity unites its end with the end of the formed virtue. Charity's end is the unity of deeper friendship with God.[55] While the end of justice is to give each person his or her due, when formed by charity, the end of justice is to give each person his or her due for the sake of friendship with God. Formed by charity, all virtuous ends become means to friendship with God.

The formal relationship between charity and the other virtues is destroyed by mortal sin. This disordered state is the occasion for the sacrament of penance.[56] Without going into excess discussion of penance, I want to highlight its similarity to baptism in that penance is the result of God's action in us whereby we are re-infused with charity. Aquinas distinguishes between internal and external penance.[57] Internal penance is a virtue whereby we deplore the sins we have committed. External penance consists of the external acts of religion necessary for the sacrament of penance. Together, internal and external penance make up the sacrament of penance. According to Aquinas, internal penance is the *sacramentum et res* of the sacrament of penance, without which the forgiveness of sins (i.e., the *res tantum*) is not achieved.[58] This necessary internal penance requires charity because "the act of the virtue of penance is directed against sin, through the love of God."[59] In the absence of charity that results from mortal sin, the sinner cannot come to true penance. True penance that is formed by charity is only had through re-infusion "by God immediately without our operating as principal agents."[60] This infusion of charity where there previously was no charity leads Aquinas to say that the sacrament of penance "belongs to the state of beginners, of those, to wit, who are making a fresh start from the state of sin."[61] Like baptism, penance is a sacrament of new beginnings in the life of charity.

---

[54] S.T. II.II.7.1c.

[55] S.T. II.II.23.1c.

[56] S.T. III.84.2.ad3. In the following discussion of penance I am referring to penance as remedy for mortal sin. To be sure, the sacrament of penance can be a remedy for venial sin, but it "was instituted chiefly for the blotting out of mortal sin."

[57] S.T. III.84.8.

[58] S.T. III.84.1.ad3.

[59] S.T. III.85.6c.

[60] S.T. III.85.5c.

[61] S.T. III.84.8.ad2.

In Aquinas's treatment of baptism and penance, we see that infusion of the theological virtues is the beginning of our spiritual life. Taken on its own, this discussion of baptism and penance leaves us with questions about the relationship between grace, the theological virtues, and justification. Again, Aquinas is using a grammar that is not sufficiently contextualized by the *Tertia Pars*. To fully understand the sacraments, we need to understand how we come to be subjects of the theological virtues and the effects those virtues have in our lives. The answers to these questions are not found in the *Tertia Pars*. Hence, we will need to turn to the *Secunda Pars*'s treatment of the relationship between grace and the theological virtues. This relationship will be the focus of chapter 3.

V. The Eucharist: Increasing Charity

Earlier, I said that my main goal in this chapter is to define the Eucharist as a sacrament that is meant to increase charity. To help enflesh this definition, I am juxtaposing the inaugural character of infusing charity with the active and dynamic character of increasing charity. At the beginning of the previous section, I pointed out that, according to Aquinas, the Eucharist exists to nurture the unity of the ecclesial body of Christ. We can say this because such unity is the *res tantum* of the Eucharist. Just as the purpose of baptism is the justification of the baptized, so the purpose of the Eucharist is the unity of the Church.

In question 79, article 1, of the *Tertia Pars*, Aquinas discusses the effects of the Eucharist. Pointing out that "the spiritual life is the effect of grace," Aquinas says that we can be assured that the Eucharist bestows grace because the Eucharist is ordained toward the nourishment of the spiritual life.[62] Throughout this article, Aquinas repeatedly speaks of the effects of the Eucharist in terms of "life," using the synonymous terms "spiritual life" and "graced life." In considering the relationship between the Eucharist and the spiritual life, Aquinas offers four perspectives from which we might consider the way in which the Eucharist effects its *res tantum*, the unity of the Church.

First, just as the Word became incarnate so that the world might have life, so Christ becomes present in the Eucharist so that we might

[62] S.T. III.79.1sc.

have spiritual life. In Aquinas's words: "By coming sacramentally into man, [Jesus] causes the life of grace." Second, as a sign of Christ's passion, the Eucharist represents the forgiveness of sins that is offered in the Paschal Mystery.[63] Third, because Christ is given as food, the Eucharist "does for the spiritual life all that material food does for the bodily life, namely by sustaining, giving increase, restoring, and giving delight."[64] Finally, in the bread and wine we are given a sign of the Eucharist's effect because they represent unity. Both bread and wine are composed of many grains/grapes that are formed into one bread/wine.[65] These four perspectives function as possible ways to understand the relationship between the Eucharist and its *res tantum*. It would be a mistake to view this exposition as a dissection of the sacrament whereby Aquinas has isolated aspects of the Eucharist and named each part's corresponding result, effectively reducing the Eucharist to a sum of its parts while simultaneously reducing its effect to a sum of these effects. Rather than reduction, we ought to see this article as a meditation on the Eucharist, a meditation that moves from one perspective to another, offering different ways of articulating the Eucharist's relationship to the unity of the Church. From each perspective, Aquinas is discussing the relationship between the Eucharist and its *res tantum*.

In this article, Aquinas is unpacking the significance (strictly speaking) of the Eucharist and its parts. To better illustrate what he is doing in this article, it is helpful to think of the Eucharist as a sentence. Each word in a sentence is an individual sign. Each word signifies something beyond itself. The word "tree," when heard or read, will instantly signify something in the mind of the hearer or reader. When we use multiple signs, however, they affect one another's signification by mutual contextualization. For example, the significance of the word "tree" is altered via contextualization when it is preceded by the word "family." Likewise, the significance of the word "family" is affected in being followed by the word "tree." On their own, words have meaning due only to the context we project on them. But when

---

[63] Aquinas's understanding of Christ's sacrifice and its connection to the Eucharist will be treated in chap. 5. At this point, I wish to simply point out that Aquinas is not equating the Eucharist with baptism or penance.

[64] S.T. III.79.1c.

[65] Ibid.

words accompany one another they provide each other with context that dictates their significance. The words are no longer subject solely to the arbitrary projections of the hearer's desired context. Although made up of two individual signs, together they are a single sign, irreducible to its parts. Similarly, a sentence is a still more complex yet irreducible sign.

Consider the following sentence: "Studying my family tree makes me feel blessed by the past and responsible for the future." This sentence is a single sign. It communicates a single idea, even while being composed of a number of irreducible signs (e.g., words, phrases, modified nouns, etc.). Carrying this thought process further, a particular sacramental celebration (e.g., the 9:00 a.m. Mass on June 30, 2013, at St. Ignatius parish in Chestnut Hill, Massachusetts) is like a sentence. On its own, bread can signify just about anything. When contextualized by an institution narrative (an irreducible sign), bread (another irreducible sign) takes on a particular significance. Made up of many individual signs, the Eucharist is a composite yet irreducible sign with a single *res tantum*: the unity of the ecclesial body. In question 79, article 1, Aquinas is considering various irreducible signs that together make up the irreducible sign of the Eucharist. He is, however, considering them in light of the single *res tantum* of the Eucharist. The effects he enumerates are all descriptions of the single *res tantum* of the Eucharist. This article points out that the spiritual life of the Church and its development are the concrete manifestation of the Church's unity.

In the fifth chapter, I will return to this article in order to examine the link between Christ's sacramental presence, Christ's sacrifice, and the Eucharist's *res tantum*. Before I can adequately carry out that examination, however, it is necessary to understand what Aquinas means when he refers to the spiritual life. When he speaks of the effects of the Eucharist in terms of "life" he is not speaking of an abstract concept. Rather, his use of the term "life" refers to a concrete and historical reality. The body may be mystical, but its unity is not. The unity of the mystical body of Christ is the unity of a Church that lives the spiritual life in its members. The degree to which the mystical body of Christ lives out its spiritual life is the degree to which it is united.

There is an assumption undergirding Aquinas's discussion of the nurturing nature of the Eucharist. Namely, in describing ecclesial unity in terms of the spiritual life, Aquinas is assuming the presence of charity. As I noted in the previous section, the infusion of charity is the beginning of the spiritual life. Hence, any effect brought about by the Eucharist assumes the presence of charity in the subject. The textual proof that Aquinas thinks of the Eucharist not as a moment of infusion but rather as a celebration of preexistent charity can be found when he points out that union with Christ is a consequence of charity. In article 5 of question 79 Aquinas is discussing whether the punishment due to sin is forgiven by receiving the Eucharist.

> Through the power of the sacrament it produces directly that effect for which it was instituted. Now it was instituted not for satisfaction, but for nourishing spiritually through union between Christ and his members, as nourishment is united with the person nourished. But because this union is the effect of charity, from the fervor of which man obtains forgiveness, not only of guilt but also of punishment, hence it is that as a consequence, and by concomitance with the chief effect, man obtains forgiveness of the punishment, not indeed of the entire punishment, but according to the measure of his devotion and fervor.[66]

Union with Christ is an effect of charity. The union with Christ offered in the Eucharist is not a matter of metabolizing a divine substance. Nor is any individual's union with Christ (much less the mere presence of Christ) the purpose of the Eucharist. Christ's presence is a means to the union which is a means to increasing the unity of the mystical body of Christ. All this is to emphasize the fact that the Eucharist needs preexistent charity. Aquinas puts it bluntly in article 7 of question 79:

> As Christ's Passion benefits all, for the forgiveness of sin and the attaining of grace and glory, whereas it produces no effect except in those who are united with Christ's Passion through faith and charity, so likewise this sacrifice [i.e., the Eucharist], which is the memorial of our Lord's Passion, has no effect except in those who are united with this sacrament through faith and charity.[67]

---

[66] S.T. III.79.5c.
[67] S.T. III.79.7.ad2.

While Aquinas presupposes preexistent charity, he also sees fit to redefine the Eucharist's *res tantum* in terms of charity. In article 4 of question 79 he states that "the reality of [the Eucharist] is charity, not only as to its habit, but also as to its act, which is kindled [*excitatur*] in this sacrament."[68] When Aquinas says that the reality of the sacrament is the habit and act of charity, he is saying that an increase in the unity of the ecclesial body, insofar as it is the *res tantum* of the Eucharist, is synonymous with an increase in the presence of the community's *active* charity. The Eucharist begins with charity by which the individual is united to Christ. This sacramental union is meant to increase charity and its acts in the subject. When such an increase of charity and its acts occurs throughout a community, the unity of that ecclesial body of Christ is said to have been nourished and increased. The theological virtue of charity is both the source and summit of the Eucharist. It is both prerequisite and purpose. Hence, the Eucharist is a moment not of infusion but of increase.

While baptism and penance effect justification insofar as they infuse the theological virtues, the Eucharist effects sanctification insofar as it increases charity in the subject. In other words, the Eucharist deepens the spiritual life of the Church. The unity of the ecclesial body of Christ, the grace toward which the Eucharist aims, is an increase in the formally active presence of charity in that communal body. This treatment of the Eucharist leaves us with questions about what it means for a subject to increase in charity and how, practically speaking, that increase relates to the unity of the mystical body of Christ. The purpose of the fourth chapter will be to examine the relationship between increasing in charity and deepening one's spiritual life.

Unlike the infusion of theological virtues accomplished through the sacraments of baptism and penance, increasing in active charity necessarily involves human action. By distinguishing between the individual's union with Christ and the unity of the ecclesial body, Aquinas has made (what today we might call) the horizontal aspect of the spiritual life an essential aspect of eucharistic grace. The unity of the Church cannot be reduced to multiple and simultaneous unions with Christ. For example, my right hand and my left hand are not

---

[68] S.T. III.79.4c.

part of my body simply because they are each united to my head. Rather, they belong to one body because by virtue of their union to my head they are then able to work together according to their nature. The unity of my body does indeed depend on the union between my parts and my head, but the unity of my body cannot be reduced to the sum of those unions. The Church is not a body by virtue of each Christian's connection to Christ alone; rather, it is a body by virtue of the formal effect those unions have on the body's ability to function as one. The spiritual life is not a state of having charity; the spiritual life is actions that are formed by charity. Simply put, *my* union *with* Christ is inseparable from and ordered toward the *community's* unity *as* Christ. It is this necessary horizontal aspect of the ecclesial body's unity that gives rise to what will be the focus of our fourth chapter. Having spent the second and third chapters examining the relationship between grace and the theological virtue of charity, the fourth chapter will examine the role of the moral virtues in this relationship. Put differently, the fourth chapter will seek to understand what role human action plays in the spiritual life.

VI. Unanswered Questions

Too often, readers of Aquinas pick up a copy of the *Summa Theologiae*, begin reading, and assume they know the meaning of the words they are reading. We fail to recognize that words are always contextualized by their grammars. We see words that are readily recognizable to us (e.g., "grace," "cause," and "participation"), and we are too quick to interpret them based on a modern grammar we anachronistically project onto them. The work of the present chapter has been to convince the reader that language being used in the *Tertia Pars* is part of a grammar that has its foundations constructed in the *Secunda Pars*. The unanswered questions I have listed throughout this chapter, then, are the result of a lack in context.

In light of Aquinas's discussion of sacramental signification and causality, we were left with questions about the relationship between grace, belief, and participation. In the next chapter, I will retrieve the grammar of grace that Aquinas constructs primarily in the *Prima Secundae*. This grammar will give us the context to answer questions about the relationship between grace, belief, and participation. In light of Aquinas's treatment of the infusion of theological virtues in baptism and penance, we were left with questions about the relationship between grace, the theological virtues, and salvation. Likewise, in light of the treatment of the Eucharist as increasing charity, we were left with the question, how does the Eucharist increase charity? Turning to the *Secunda Secundae*, I will retrieve the grammars of virtue that allow us to contextualize and properly answer these questions. Finally, building on the examinations of grace and charity in chapters 2 and 3, the fourth chapter will look closely at how the moral and intellectual virtues aid our increase in charity. We will see that the grammars of grace and virtue that contextualize Aquinas's treatment of the Eucharist necessarily include these moral virtues. In short, the next three chapters of this project are essentially the retrieval of grammars that will contextualize our inquiry into the relationship between the Eucharist and its *res tantum*. Without the context of the *Secunda Pars*, we simply cannot comprehend the *Tertia Pars*.

These grammars of grace and virtue will make it clear that, contrary to the claims of Chauvet, Aquinas has not removed the Church from his eucharistic theology. On the contrary; the spiritual life of the Church is the context without which Aquinas's eucharistic theology cannot be understood.

CHAPTER TWO

Grace as the Embodied Spiritual Life

Through these he has given us his very great and precious promises,
so that through them you may participate in the divine nature,
having escaped the corruption in the world caused by evil desires.

—2 Peter 1:4

We begin with questions. Our discussion of sacramental signification in the previous chapter left us with questions that are unanswered
by the *Tertia Pars*. Specifically, we were left with questions about the
relationship between grace, participation, and belief. In the *Tertia
Pars*, Aquinas tells us that grace is "nothing else than a participated
likeness of the Divine Nature."[1] The purpose of this chapter is to
unpack this classically brief Thomistic definition. Understanding
what this definition means will give us an insight into what exactly
the Eucharist functions to achieve. In essence, this chapter intends to
show that Aquinas does not see grace as a reified object that can be
produced. Rather, in this definition, grace is understood in terms of
action insofar as it leads the human person to know, will, and move
(i.e., it leads to moral/human action).[2] In the *Prima Secundae*, Aquinas

---

[1] S.T. III.62.1c.

[2] Throughout this chapter I will refer to "human action" regularly. Unless otherwise
noted, I am using this term to refer to the moral action that moves toward the Final
End through knowledge and love. For a brief exposition of how Aquinas understands
humanis actibus, see Georg Wieland, "Happiness," in *The Ethics of Aquinas*, ed. Stephan
J. Pope (Washington, DC: Georgetown University Press, 2002), 58–59.

constructs a theology of grace in which grace is an external principle of human action. In other words, grace is intrinsically related to human action as the condition for the possibility of human action.[3] The context of the *Prima Secundae*'s discussion of grace nullifies any attempt to divorce grace (insofar as it is considered in relation to the spiritual life) from human action. From the perspective of the spiritual life, grace and human action are intrinsically united.

This chapter will proceed in four sections. First, I will discuss the overarching structure of the *Summa*, which acts as the broad context for Aquinas's discussion of grace. This contextualization allows us to see that any discussion of grace presupposes its role in the spiritual life. Again, grace has a function that dictates the parameters of Aquinas's investigation into the nature of grace. Hence, we must begin by understanding this function and the implications it has on Aquinas's ensuing constructive exposition of grace. Second, I will turn to an examination of what Aquinas means by "a participation in the Divine Nature." Here, I will show that knowledge and love of God are constitutive of graced participation. Third, based on the previous chapter's discussion of sacramental signification as the primary mode of causing our participation in the Divine Nature, I will discuss the role of belief and signification in graced participation. While saving the more in-depth examination of the theological virtues for the following chapter, this section will briefly gesture toward the role of signification in belief so as to highlight the embodied nature of participation. Finally, I will conclude by discussing the cooperative nature of graced participation.

I. The Teleological Nature of the Spiritual Life

Before considering what Aquinas means when he uses the word "participation" we must begin to understand the foundations of the grammar he uses to contextualize his considerations of "participation." The *Prima Secundae* is part of a whole. Therefore, to more fully understand its content (and to avoid misinterpretation), it is necessary to examine the relationship between the whole and this part.

---

[3] Theo Kobusch, "Grace," in Pope, *The Ethics of Aquinas*, 209–11.

1. *The Structure of the* Summa Theologiae

Oceans of ink and countless bits of binary code have been used discussing the structure of the *Summa*.[4] While there are many ways one might organize this great text, most of them agree on the fact that there is a teleological structure to the *Summa*. Broadly put, the *Summa* is concerned with the union between God and Creation. This union has its foundations in the causal relationships between God and Creation. I say "relationships" because God is the efficient cause of Creation as well as the final cause of Creation.[5] Creation is *coming from* God, and Creation is *going to* God. This famous and much commented upon *exitus et reditus* structure of the *Summa* is, in essence, an account of the spiritual life: Creation's pathway from and back to God.

In order to avoid superfluous discussion of the possible textual divisions that could manifest the *Summa*'s structure, I will focus on a single piece of textual evidence for the claim that the *Summa*'s structure is teleological: the prologue to the *Prima Secundae*.

> Since, as Damascene states, man is said to be made in God's image, insofar as the image implies "an intelligent being endowed with free will and self-movement": now that we have treated of the exemplar, i.e. God, and of those things which came forth from the power of God in accordance with His will; it remains for us to treat of His image, i.e. man, inasmuch as he too is the principle of his actions, as having free will and control over his actions.[6]

Within the *Prima Pars*, Aquinas examines God and God's act of creation: *exitus*. In what remains of the *Summa*, Aquinas examines Creation's (re)union with God. We can call this action *reditus* based on the inaugural question of the *Secunda Pars*: Of Man's Last End. Briefly summarized, the last end of authentic human action is attained

---

[4] I will not survey the history of this discussion. For a wonderfully succinct summary of the major movements, see Jean-Pierre Torrell, *Saint Thomas Aquinas*, vol. 1, *The Person and His Work*, trans. Robert Royal (Washington, DC: The Catholic University of America Press, 1996), 150–53.

[5] S.T. I.44.1&4.

[6] S.T. I.II.pr.

by knowing and loving God.[7] The unity of the *Summa* is rooted in this teleological structure.

In a careful consideration of the *Prima Pars*, there are various ways to superimpose organizational structures onto its content. As I am only concerned here with a demonstration of the larger teleological structure of the entire *Summa*, my comments regarding the *Prima Pars* will focus briefly on Aquinas's description of God's act of Creation. According to Aquinas, to say that we are created is to say that we participate in Being (*esse*).[8] All things that exist do so insofar as they participate in the Being that is God. It is significant that the first analogy Aquinas uses to describe the action of God's Creation is "participation" (*participant*). In the *Prima Pars*, however, the consideration of participation can be said to have an archeological structure as opposed to a teleological structure. That is to say, participation is seen as a relationship between Creation and its source or beginning (*arche*). As Jean-Pierre Torrell suggests: "One should not imagine creation as an isolated act that occurred in a distant past; rather, it is a present reality."[9] To be is to participate in God. In other words, the ontology of a creature is always actively relational. We will have cause to return to this archeological treatment of participation later on; for now, it suffices to say that we are always emanating from God through participation in God's *esse*.

In the first article of the *Secunda Pars*, Aquinas tells us that humankind is, by its nature, directed toward God as to its end.[10] Aquinas has been restating this fact since the first article of the first question of the first part. Human beings naturally have a supernatural end. "This treatise considers how the person either reaches or falls short of the proper human end through his or her actions."[11] The *Secunda Pars*, then, is an examination of human action (i.e., actions that come from free will and reason).[12] Working from general considerations (*Prima Secundae*) to particular considerations (*Secunda Secundae*),

---

[7] S.T. I.II.1.8c.

[8] S.T. I.44.1c.

[9] Jean-Pierre Torrell, *Aquinas' Summa: Background, Structure, and Reception*, trans. Benedict M. Guevin (Washington, DC: The Catholic University of America Press, 2005), 24.

[10] S.T. I.II.1.1c.

[11] Wieland, "Happiness," 57. In this quote, the author is referring to the treatise on happiness (qq. 1–5), but it is just as easily said of the entirety of the *Secunda Pars*.

[12] S.T. I.II.1.1c.

Aquinas describes human action in terms of the last end, as both the source and completion of human action.[13] In short, the *Secunda Pars* describes the *reditus* in terms of human action.

In the unfinished *Tertia Pars*, Aquinas discusses Christ and the sacraments. Another way of describing the *Tertia Pars* is to say that it treats of God's instrumental activity in Creation. As we saw in the previous chapter, Christ and the sacraments are instruments of God's salvific activity. Because humankind has been created with a supernatural end, we need divine assistance to achieve that end. The activity of God in Creation, which is carried out with humankind's cooperation, is the external principle of human action. As with the *Secunda Pars*, the *Tertia Pars* is a description of the *reditus*. Specifically, it is a description of the means of our return to God. Insofar as these means are an external principle of human action toward our supernatural end, they are called salvific. If the *Prima Secundae* is a description of the *reditus* in terms of general human action, and the *Secunda Secundae* is a description of the *reditus* in terms of particular human action, then the *Tertia Pars* can be called a description of the *reditus* in terms of salvation history.[14] As christologically founded, the *Tertia Pars* is still a consideration of particular human action. The actions of Christ, even if they are divine instruments, are human actions. Likewise, the sacraments, even if they are divine instruments, are human actions.[15]

To close this consideration of the *Summa*'s structure, I wish to point out that this structure is simultaneously teleological and archeological. It is *exitus* et *reditus*, not *exitus* tunc *reditus*. At the beginning of this section I said that the foundation of the union between God and Creation is the causal relationships between the two. Considered from the perspective of God, there is but one relationship between God and Creation. Considered from the perspective of Creation, we can conceptually distinguish a plurality of relationships between God and Creation insofar as God is said to be both final and efficient cause. When the perspectives of these different relationships dictate the way participation is explained, we end up with archeological and teleological treatments of participation.

---

[13] Torrell, *Aquinas'* Summa, 29.

[14] Or, perhaps less anachronistically, the *Tertia Pars* describes what Jean-Pierre Torrell has called the *reditus per Christum*; cf. Torrell, *Saint Thomas Aquinas*, 152.

[15] This, of course, is not a denial of their status as divine actions.

Another way of understanding this structure would be to see *exitus et reditus* as two distinct grammars employed in the description of the relationship between God and Creation. The grammar of *exitus* is founded on seeing God as the source of Creation. Conversely, the grammar of *reditus* is founded on seeing God as the goal of Creation. The *Secunda Pars* and *Tertia Pars* are constructed using a grammar of *reditus*. As such, they have a distinctive teleological structure. However, if we bear in mind that these grammars are essentially analogical and are being used to describe the same relationship, then we must also say that such teleological structure is necessarily translatable to an archeological structure if we were to switch to a grammar of *exitus*. In other words, any description of Creation's return to God is simultaneously a description of our procession from God.

After our consideration of the role of the *Prima Secundae* in this teleological structure of the *Summa*, the remainder of this chapter will be spent explaining that grace is the description of God's relationship to Creation when considered in terms of human action. As we will see, the *Prima Secundae*'s description of grace is largely dictated by the grammar of *reditus* that Aquinas employs throughout the *Secunda Pars* and *Tertia Pars*.

2. *The Place of the* Prima Secundae *in the* Summa

Within the larger *exitus et reditus* structure of the *Summa*, the *Prima Secundae* is where the *reditus* is described in terms of teleological human action. The *Prima Secundae*'s inquiry is organized into general examinations of the ends and means of human action. The examination of ends is accomplished briefly in questions 1–5. God is the Final End of human action. Specifically, our Final End is union with God through knowledge and love. The examination of the means considers the internal principles of human action (powers and habits in qq. 6–89) and external principles of human action (the law in qq. 90–108 and grace in qq. 109–14).[16] For our purposes I will focus on the significance of the placement of the treatise on grace.

---

[16] In reality, for Aquinas there are only two external principles of human action: the devil who moves us toward evil (treated in S.T. I.114) and God who moves us toward good. As the prologue of S.T. I.II.90 points out, God is the external principle insofar as God instructs us through law and assists us through grace.

Metaphysical inquiry tends to be concerned with first principles. This holds true for the *Prima Secundae*'s metaphysics of human action. In organizing the *Prima Secundae*, however, Aquinas does not put first things first. Quite the opposite is true. Admittedly, Aquinas begins the *Prima Secundae* by treating the last end of human action. Nevertheless, this consideration of God's role in human action does not describe God in terms of a first principle of human action.[17] Rather, it is at the very end of his metaphysics of human action that Aquinas describes God in terms of an external, first principle of human action. This divine action is called grace. As Theo Kobusch points out: "The doctrine of grace is thus not an accidental addition to the doctrine of act, but substantially necessary for the metaphysician of morals or anyone wishing to trace human action to its root."[18] Grace is considered metaphysically, not as to its ontology, but as to its role in human action. As we will see in the following section, grace is the necessary condition for the possibility of human action.

In the previous chapter we saw that the spiritual life is the life of union with God. If our final end is union with God through knowledge and love, then any description of human action toward its Final End is a description of the spiritual life. To close this section, I will to reiterate the fact that the description of God's relationship with Creation that uses a grammar of *reditus* is marked by a teleological structure insofar as it is primarily concerned with the role of human action. With that in mind, we can say that the spiritual life, as it is described throughout the *Summa*, is teleological in nature. Therefore, any discussion of the relationship between grace and the spiritual life (including the *Tertia Pars*'s sacramental theology) will bear the marks of this grammar.

II. Grace and the Spiritual Life

Having examined the teleological nature of the spiritual life, we now examine the role of grace in that life. As I stated above, the

---

[17] Any description of God as last end implies a relationship to the intellect in which God is known by the intellect. When described in terms of "grace," however, God's relationship to human action is prior to the intellect's knowledge of God as last end. Hence, in the metaphysics of human acts, grace is the first principle.

[18] Kobusch, *The Ethics of Aquinas*, 209.

purpose of this examination is to more fully understand what Aquinas means when he says that grace "is nothing short of a partaking [*participatio*] of the Divine Nature."[19] I begin this examination with reference to a passage of particular import from the *Prima Pars*. Here, Aquinas is discussing what it means to say that humankind is made in the image of God:

> Wherefore we see that the image of God is in man in three ways. First, inasmuch as man possesses a natural aptitude for understanding and loving God; and this aptitude consists in the very nature of the mind, which is common to all men. Secondly, inasmuch as man actually and habitually knows and loves God, though imperfectly; and this image consists in the conformity of grace. Thirdly, inasmuch as man knows and loves God perfectly; and this image consists in the likeness of glory. Wherefore on the words, "The light of Thy countenance, O Lord, is signed upon us" (Psalm 4:7), the gloss distinguishes a threefold image of "creation," of "re-creation," and of "likeness." The first is found in all men, the second only in the just, the third only in the blessed.[20]

By this "image of creation," humankind "possesses a natural aptitude for understanding and loving God." In other words, we are "intelligent beings endowed with free-will and self-movement" capable of moving toward our last end.[21] The "image of re-creation" that "consists in the conformity of grace" is, in essence, the active spiritual life. The difference between these two images is the difference between potency and act. In the remainder of this section, I argue that the difference between the image of creation and the image of re-creation is the same as the difference between a *share* in the Image of God and *participation* in the Divine Nature. Understanding how a human person moves from the potential image of creation into the active image of re-creation will help us to understand grace as a participation in the Divine Nature. As such, we will have gained insight into the role of grace in the spiritual life.

---

[19] S.T. I.II.112.1c.
[20] S.T. I.93.4c.
[21] S.T. I.II.pr.

1. Grace Actualizing the Image of God

Returning to the prologue of the *Prima Secundae*, we see that we are said to be made in the Image of God insofar as we are intelligent beings with free will and self-movement. What, then, does it mean for such an image to move toward its final end? As we will see, grace is the external principle of that movement insofar as grace moves the intellect to know God and moves the will to love God. What remains for us to examine is exactly why grace is necessary and how grace achieves this movement.

In questions 79–83 of the *Prima Pars*, Aquinas examines the powers of the human person. "The intellectual soul approaches to the divine likeness, more than inferior creatures, in being able to acquire perfect goodness."[22] The soul accomplishes this acquisition through the exercise of intellectual and appetitive powers.[23] With respect to the intellectual power, the "reason, intellect, and mind are one power."[24] Through the exercise of reason, the intellect comes to understand truths.[25] When, through the exercise of this intellectual power, we use reason to grow in understanding, our share in the Divine Image is active. As Aquinas reminds us in question 109, however, "Higher intelligible things the human intellect cannot know unless it be perfected by a stronger light."[26] While we may naturally be capable of some limited knowledge regarding God's existence (e.g., the *quinqae viae* and other forms of general revelation), this knowledge is neither necessary nor sufficient for knowing God as the Final End of human existence. This presents us with a problem.

We recall that human action is concerned with the last end: God. We attain our last end (i.e., perfect goodness is acquired) through knowledge and love of God. This union with God is called happiness. In an article where Aquinas discusses whether this happiness is an operation of the intellect or the will, he cites Augustine: "Love ranks above knowledge in moving, but knowledge precedes love in

---

[22] S.T. I.77.2.ad1. Note the language of "likeness" in conjunction with language of potency, "able."

[23] It is this exercise, the movement from potency to act, that constitutes the shift from sharing in image to participation in nature.

[24] S.T. I.79sc.

[25] S.T. I.79c.

[26] S.T. I.II.109.1c.

attaining: *for naught is loved saved what is known."* [27] Hence, according to Aquinas, happiness consists primarily in an act of the intellect. But, as Aquinas constantly reminds us, it is seemingly impossible for a human being to be happy. Due to the immaterial nature of our last end, our material nature precludes any natural ability to know our last end as such. With regard to our happiness, human beings are naturally impotent. In other words, the internal principles of human action (i.e., powers and habits) are insufficient for happiness.

Similarly, the appetitive power, the human will, is impotent when it comes to naturally attaining its supernatural end. First, as Aquinas points out in question 3 of the *Prima Secundae*, what is not known cannot be loved.[28] Therefore, if the intellect is naturally impotent with respect to knowledge of its last end, then the will is left without an object to move toward through love. Second, even with graced knowledge of God, the will needs the assistance of grace to move it to love. In the second article of question 109, "On the Necessity of Grace," Aquinas points out that even prior to the corruption of our nature, humankind was not capable of performing meritorious works. "But in the state of integrity, as regards the sufficiency of the operative power, man by his natural endowments could wish and do the good proportionate to his nature, such as the good of acquired virtue; but not surpassing good, as the good of infused virtue."[29] Without grace, even in a prelapsarian state of integrity, a human person would be unable to act meritoriously toward his or her final end. All the more, then, is corrupt human nature incapable of loving its last end without assistance: "In the state of corrupt nature man falls short of [loving God as the last end] in the appetite of his rational will, which, unless it is cured by God's grace follows its private good, on account of the corruption of nature."[30] Based on the impotence of our human nature intensified by its corruption, we know that grace is necessary if we are to move toward our final end. If we are to have our share in the Image of God actualized (i.e., if we are to know and love God), then we require the help of grace. It now remains for us to examine, at

[27] S.T. I.II.3.4.ad4.
[28] Ibid.
[29] S.T. I.II.109.2c.
[30] S.T. I.II.109.3c.

least initially, what it means to say that grace is the external principle of this actualization.

In article 9 of question 109, Aquinas begins by pointing out that God's help can be spoken of as twofold: as a habitual gift and as God's moving us to act. "First, [grace can be spoken of as] a habitual gift whereby corrupted human nature is healed, and after being healed is lifted up so as to work deeds meritorious of everlasting life."[31] This habitual gift heals our corrupted nature (i.e., justifies us) and aids that newly justified nature in actively moving toward its final end. Second, in addition to the language of "habitual gift," we can speak of grace in terms of God moving us to act. This second way of speaking about grace is first discussed in relation to *preparation* for receiving the infused habitual gift whereby we are justified. In article 6 of question 109, Aquinas points out that "every form requires a disposition." In other words, habits (formal causes of human action[32]) can only be present in a power that is rightly disposed.[33] Speaking of this prerequisite disposition, Aquinas is very clear that this predisposition must be accomplished by the free will of the person receiving the habitual gift. He is equally clear, however, that "free-will can only be turned to God when God turns it."[34] Grace, then, is spoken of as God's movement of the human will so as to prepare the person to receive the habitual gift. In addition to speaking of this second type of divine help as preparation, Aquinas examines how God's moving us to act might be spoken of in relation to the habitual gift that has already been received. Specifically, he says that, after having received the habitual gift of grace, we need the continued assistance of grace in order that we might persevere (i.e., be "guided and guarded" so as to be "moved by God to act righteously").[35] "The gift of habitual

---

[31] S.T. I.II.109.9c.

[32] S.T. I.II.110.2.ad1.

[33] We will return to an in-depth discussion of dispositive preparation for habits in the following chapter. For now, I simply want to emphasize that grace, even when spoken of in terms other than "habitual gift," is still concerned with human action. As divine help, grace is an external principle of human action.

[34] S.T. I.II.109.6.ad1. While this vexing passage seems to a modern eye a clear provocation, for now I must put off any further discussion of *liberum arbitrium*. Suffice it to say that when Aquinas writes *liberum arbitrium* he means something quite different than when the modern writer, so influenced by the enlightenment, writes "free will."

[35] S.T. I.II.109.9c.

grace is not therefore given to us that we may no longer need the Divine help; for every creature needs to be preserved in the good received from Him."[36] So, not only is grace spoken of as the habitual gift that forms our intellect and our will so as to be capable of moving toward our final end; grace is also spoken of as the movement of God in us whereby we are prepared for God's formation and helped to persevere in that movement toward our final end. To speak about this twofold divine assistance is to speak about grace as the external principle that actualizes the Image of God in us. Nevertheless, to avoid reifying these distinctions, I now turn to a passage that is crucial for understanding the relationship between all of these various ways of speaking about grace.

Having laid out this twofold manner of speaking about divine assistance to human movement, in the reply to the second objection of article 9, Aquinas provides us with perhaps his simplest explanation of what it means to say that grace is an external principle that actualizes the Image of God: "The operation of the Holy Ghost, which moves and protects, is not circumscribed by the effect of habitual grace which it causes in us; but beyond this effect He, together with the Father and the Son, moves and protects us."[37] While Aquinas here is defending his rhetorical distinction between the twofold nature of divine help, this passage is crucial for understanding the simplicity of grace. That is to say, while Aquinas is perpetually restating that grace can be considered in two ways, he is not implying that God "dispenses" two types of help. Rather, the Holy Spirit's operation in us can be named variously, depending on the perspectives and the mode of inquiry through which we examine it. Regardless of how many distinctions we invent to describe this pneumatological operation (cf. question 111), it is perpetually simple. Therefore, when we take a step back and ask what it means to say that grace is the external principle that actualizes our Image of God, thereby moving us to participate in the Divine Nature, we can see that it is "the operation of the Holy Ghost" that accomplishes this actualization.

For example, when considering the meritorious actions that are the result of grace insofar as grace is considered in relation to actual human movement, Aquinas points out that such action may be con-

---

[36] S.T. I.II.109.9.ad1.
[37] S.T. I.II.109.9.ad2.

sidered in two ways. First, it may be considered insofar as that movement proceeds from the movement of the free will. Second, it may be considered insofar as "it proceeds from the grace of the Holy Ghost moving us to life everlasting."[38] What I emphasize here is that these are not two different types of meritorious action. Rather, all meritorious action (i.e., all graced human action that is our participation in the Divine Nature) is the result of the operation of the Holy Spirit within us.

We will spend the remainder of this and the following chapter providing the thus-far-avoided description of this pneumatological operation in terms of the habitual gift called the theological virtues. For now I point out that, as the external principle that actualizes the Image of God in us, moving us to know and love God, the Holy Spirit's operation in us is nothing other than our participation in the Divine Nature.[39]

2. The Spiritual Life Conforming to Grace

Thus far in this chapter, my aim has been to show that it is not possible to speak of grace without simultaneously (even if indirectly) speaking about human action. Examining grace in terms of actualization is helpful when trying to understand the active nature of the graced spiritual life (i.e., in its historical particularity). However, we are left with a difficult question: is grace the external principle that causes our participation, or is grace the participation itself? In order to answer this we must speak briefly about the limitations of grammars and analogy. Theo Kobusch points out that Aquinas relies quite

---

[38] S.T. I.II.114.3c.

[39] This is an important point because it stops us from reifying habits. The language of habits is a metaphor for explaining the mysterious work of the Holy Spirit's life in our lives. Question 110.4.ad4 is a great example of this. Grace (i.e., the operation of the Spirit) is not in our powers but in the essence of the soul. The Spirit relates to who we are at our most fundamental, not to our accidents, which might be lacking (e.g., through mental disability). Therefore, if, due to the lack of capacity, the Spirit's life does not manifest in action that we would call virtuous, we do not ascribe that to lack of grace (i.e., the absence of the Spirit). Rather, the Holy Spirit relates to who we are. Hence, Aquinas's insistence that all things are capable of loving God (cf. I.II.109.3c). While the use of *caritas* in describing the love expressed by an inanimate creature would make little sense insofar as a habit needs a power, such love is still the Holy Spirit working in what is present.

heavily on analogies of motion in constructing this treatise on grace.[40] The problem with speaking metaphorically about God and God's relationship to Creation is that we humans can easily fall into the trap of univocity. While Aquinas is merely emphasizing the dynamic nature of grace, the analogical use of motion implies chronological order. When imagining the relationship between grace and human action in terms of motion, it is difficult not to see God's action as the first domino that externally acts upon the domino of our own action. In short, we are confronted with a chronology that leads us to ask if grace is prior to our participation or if grace *is* our participation.

If we return to Aquinas's description of the image of re-creation found in the *Prima Pars*, we can see a way of talking about grace and the spiritual life that does not rely on the metaphors of motion. Specifically, Aquinas tells us that the image of re-creation consists in the conformity of grace. In other words, participation in the Divine Nature is tantamount to being formed by grace. If God's relationship to us is one, this conformity is not chronologically prior to our knowledge and love of God. Much like the grammar of creation, which defies the constraints of chronology (i.e., God's act of creation is not an event in the past), so the grammar of grace cannot be fully understood in terms of spatial movement. That is to say, the external principle of human action is not the first domino that starts the process of moving. Rather, it is the underlying possibility of our movement insofar as it provides the order and movement of our soul. From one perspective grace forms the spiritual life (i.e., actualizing the Image of God). From another perspective, the spiritual life conforms to grace. Human action is not subsequent to grace. Human action is simultaneous to grace, manifesting it. In a way, we can speak of human action as a necessary condition for *the experience of* grace. As such, human action is the sacrament of God's action.

III. Belief and Signs

Having spent the majority of this chapter showing how Aquinas relates grace and human action, I now turn to some preliminary and brief considerations of the role of belief in graced participation. I want to point out, however, that in this section I will limit my comments

---

[40] Kobusch, *The Ethics of Aquinas*, 214.

to a consideration of the relationship between signification and belief. I will leave a consideration of the relationship between faith and charity until the following chapter. The current section aims solely at providing a preliminary gesture toward the developed sacramental theology that will be explicated in the fifth chapter.

Thus far, I have explained Aquinas's presentation of grace in terms of an actualized Image of God through which we are said to participate in the Divine Nature. As we saw, it is through the infusion of a habitual gift that grace justifies us and makes us capable of performing meritorious deeds. In a particularly helpful passage from question 110, article 4, Aquinas offers some insight into what exactly is meant by "habitual gift" (*habituale donum*). "For as man in his intellective power participates in the Divine knowledge through the virtue of faith, and in his power of will participates in the Divine love through the virtue of charity, so also in the nature of the soul does he participate in the Divine Nature, after the manner of likeness through a certain regeneration or re-creation."[41] The habitual gifts that are responsible for the movement of the intellect and the will are faith and charity, respectively. It is through these theological virtues that we are said to participate in the Divine Nature. I will have much to say about the relationship between faith and charity in the following chapter. But since we are here concerned with the role of signification and belief in graced participation, I now turn to an examination of the interior act of faith: belief (*credere*).

To begin this examination of belief, I would like to reiterate that faith is necessary if humankind is to move toward its Final End. As I pointed out above, in question 109, Aquinas says that humans can naturally know some truth without the grace of God. We are naturally bestowed with "intelligible light, which of itself is sufficient for knowing certain intelligible things."[42] However, "higher intelligible things the human intellect cannot know, unless it be perfected by a stronger

---

[41] S.T. I.II.110.4c. To reiterate, these are not three different moments in which the human person is said to participate in the Divine Life. Rather, they are three ways of speaking about the relationship between God and human action. Grace is participation through an actualized Image of God. Through knowledge and love of God, we are said to participate in the Divine Nature. While we can and will, like Aquinas, speak at length and with myriad distinctions about grace, all of that speech can be simply summed up: grace is nothing else than a participation in the Divine Nature.

[42] S.T. I.II.109.1c.

light, viz., the light of faith or prophecy which is called the *light of grace*, inasmuch as it is added to nature."[43] Here, we must point out that this light of grace is not an increase in potency (i.e., we are not given the ability to see by some superhuman mode). Rather, this light of grace, insofar as it is the extrinsic principle of the intellect's movement toward its supernatural end, is called the infused habit of faith.[44] Faith is said to perfect our nature (specifically, our natural intellectual powers) insofar as it is a principle of our act of knowing God. To perfect a power is to move it to act. With regard to the last end of the intellect, an extrinsic principle is needed in order to achieve knowledge of (i.e., union with) that end.

Faith moves us toward this union with God insofar as it is a habit that inclines us to believe. When examining the nature of belief, Aquinas, following Augustine, says that to believe is to think with assent (*cum assensione cogitare*).[45] More specifically, "belief" refers to "the movement of the mind while yet deliberating, and not yet perfected by the clear sight of truth."[46] That is to say, "thinking with assent" describes a mode of thinking that is similar to the certain knowledge we acquire through demonstrations (i.e., what Aquinas calls *scientia*) insofar as belief "cleaves firmly to one side," but dissimilar to *scientia* insofar as "[belief's] knowledge does not attain the perfection of clear sight."[47] Simply put, the difference between saying "she knows" and "she believes" is that belief is certain knowledge of an *unseen* object.

Faith is called a *theological* virtue because its unseen object is God.[48] That is to say, faith is the virtue whereby the intellect is inclined toward belief in God. When considering the knowledge and love of God that constitutes our participation in the Divine Nature, the faithful act of belief is union through knowledge whereby our intellect participates in the Divine Nature. To properly understand what it means to say that God is the object of faith, however, we must take

---

[43] Ibid.
[44] Kobusch, *The Ethics of Aquinas*, 210.
[45] S.T. II.II.2.1.
[46] S.T. II.II.2.1c.
[47] Ibid.
[48] S.T. I.II.62.1c.

the time to understand the embodied process that constitutes belief in God.

While faith's object is unseen (God), this unseen object is known through objects that are seen.

> Accordingly the object of faith may be considered in two ways. First, as regards the thing itself which is believed, and thus the object of faith is something simple, namely the thing itself about which we have faith. Secondly, on the part of the believer, and in this respect the object of faith is something complex by way of a proposition.[49]

Put differently, faith has a complex object insofar as "the thing known is in the knower according to the mode of the knower. Now the mode proper to the human intellect is to know the truth by synthesis and analysis."[50] Faith needs to be provided with the complex objects through which God is known. Without unnecessary examination of Aquinas's theory of human cognition, it will suffice to say that the faithful act of believing is not exempt from the limitations of the human body. These limitations are attested to in question 12 of the *Prima Pars*, where Aquinas is discussing human knowledge of God:

> Although by the revelation of grace in this life we cannot know of God "what He is," and thus are united to Him as to one un-known; still we know Him more fully according as many and more excellent of His effects are demonstrated to us, and accord-ing as we attribute to Him some things known by divine reve-lation, to which natural reason cannot reach, as, for instance, that God is Three and One.[51]

According to Aquinas, our union with God through our faithful belief is our union to a known unknown. There is always a mediacy and an absence[52] that marks our intellectual union with God. For example,

---

[49] S.T. II.II.1.2c.

[50] Ibid.

[51] S.T. I.12.13.ad1.

[52] To be sure, the absence of God here is a function of our naturally impotent ex-perience and not of God's withdrawal. Nothing can exist without participating in the presence of God.

when discussing the object of faith, Aquinas spends much time examining the necessity of expressing faith in collections of propositional articles called symbols (i.e., creeds). These symbols are necessary so that the complex objects of faith (i.e., the propositional articles of faith) "might the more easily be proposed to all."[53] The faithful act of belief is directed first toward what is seen and known (i.e., the signs and symbols of revelation) so that it might ultimately be directed toward what is unseen and known as unknown (i.e., God). The historical and embodied nature of belief is further emphasized when we consider that, in addition to the need for signs and symbols, those complex objects need to be "proposed" to those who might believe in them.

Hence, Aquinas attests to the embodied and historical nature of belief and signification when he points out that "Divine revelation reaches those of lower degree through those who are over them."[54] Implicit in this theory is an emphasis on the historical nature of revelation. The human mode of knowing requires particular and complex objects through which God is known. This leads Aquinas to posit a cause of faith beyond the infusion of the habitual gift.

> First, that the things which are of faith should be proposed to man: this is necessary in order that man believe anything explicitly. . . . Those things which are of faith surpass human reason, hence they do not come to man's knowledge unless God reveal them. To some, indeed, they are revealed by God immediately, as those things which were revealed by the apostles and prophets, while to some they are proposed by God in sending preachers of the faith.[55]

---

[53] S.T. II.II.1.9c.

[54] S.T. II.II.2.6c.

[55] S.T. II.II.6.1c. Here, I will not engage in a discussion of the nature of immediate (i.e., personal) revelation. Nevertheless, I would suggest that such revelation is not accomplished independently of the historical particularity of the individual. For example, the confession of St. Peter in Matt 16:18 (despite Jesus' insistence that "flesh and blood has not revealed this to you, but my Father in heaven") was still dependant on both Peter's particular experience of the Incarnate Word, as well as his entire psycholinguistic development up to that point. Hence, even immediate revelation is accomplished in cooperation with the symbolic.

For those of us not numbered among the apostles and the prophets, God chooses to communicate with us through the mediation of preachers (broadly understood as anyone who proclaims the Word of God). Our participation in the Divine Nature through the faithful act of belief is essentially tied to evangelization.[56] Human action, then, in all of its historical and embodied particularity, is rightfully described as the *beginning* of participation in the Divine Nature insofar as through the formulation and proclamation of symbols and signs (i.e., the complex objects of faith) human action mediates the presence of God that is a prerequisite for faithful belief in God. With this role of evangelization in mind, we finally turn to an explicit examination of the relationship between belief and sacramental signification.

While I leave a more in-depth discussion of the role of the Eucharist in the graced movement of the Image of God until chapter 5, I must briefly return here to the material from the first chapter regarding sacramental signification. I pointed out that, for Aquinas, sacramental causality is a function of signification.[57] In other words, if we want to know what it means to say that sacraments cause grace, we must first understand the relationship between grace and signification. As I noted, sacramental signification provides faith with its object.[58] Specifically, the sacraments offer us knowledge of Christ's passion (the cause of our sanctification), grace and virtues (the form of our sanctification), and eternal life (the end of our sanctification).[59] Sacraments are said to have sacramental signification insofar as they signify (i.e., offer us knowledge of) the cause, form, and end of our sanctification. Keeping in mind that the object of faith, when considered from the perspective of the believer, is "something complex by way of a proposition," we can see that sacramental signification makes the object of faith present to the believer. Put differently, sacramental signification manifests the known to the knower in a mode

---

[56] I will refrain from a discussion of the role of faith in revelation. Suffice it to say that the external act of faith (i.e., confession) is the manifestation of the evangelization whereby the signs and symbols of faith are formulated and proclaimed.

[57] Cf. chap. 1.III.

[58] It should be noted that this is obviously not a role exclusively held by the sacraments of the New Law. The object of faith is free to be present to the human intellect in any way God deems fitting.

[59] S.T. III.60.3c.

proper to the human intellect.[60] While Aquinas's treatment of the virtue of faith tends to emphasize the role of words in belief, he clearly has a place for nonverbal communication. For example, in the first question of the *Secunda Secundae*, Aquinas tells us that "things concerning Christ's human nature, and the sacraments of the Church, or any creatures whatever, come under faith, in so far as by them we are directed to God, and inasmuch as we assent to them on account of the Divine Truth." By means of sacramental signification, the sacraments propose the complex objects of faith to us so that, through the mediation of their words, matter, and actions (i.e., sacramental signs), we might believe in God as the source of our salvation.

In this brief section I have tried to gesture toward the importance of sacramental signification for our participation in the Divine Nature. Quite clearly, these preliminary considerations demand further exploration. Specifically, how does belief in God relate to love of God? If it is through both knowledge and love of God that we are said to participate in the Divine Nature, then speaking of belief is not sufficient for understanding grace. With these questions in mind, the following chapter will provide a more in-depth discussion of what it means to say that we participate in the Divine Nature through faith and charity. Specifically, we will take up the question of the relationship between salvation and grace, describing that relationship in terms of justification and sanctification. Those considerations will allow us to develop an understanding of the spiritual life as a process of striving to increase in charity. The purpose of this section, though, in addition to an explanation of belief and signification, has been to show that, even when considered solely in terms of belief (i.e., the

---

[60] Again, grace does not add potency to human nature, thereby making us capable of knowing in superhuman modes. One might argue that Aquinas defends the reality of immediately acquired knowledge (i.e., knowledge gained independently of synthesis and analysis) in his discussion of prophecy. Most notably, in S.T. II.II.171.1.ad4 Aquinas says "It is requisite to prophecy that the intention of the mind be raised to the perception of Divine things." However, insofar as "this raising of the intention is brought about by the motion of the Holy Ghost," Aquinas is not postulating a different mode of knowing. Rather, the elevation of the mind is the inspiration (*inspiratio*) of the Holy Spirit that allows the prophet to apprehend revealed truths. This inspiration is clearly distinct from the revelation "in quo perficitur prophetia." All this is to say that grace perfects our nature insofar as it moves us to more perfectly know in a mode proper to human beings. We must still "know the truth by synthesis and analysis."

internal act of faith), participating in the Divine Nature is an embodied and historical event. In short, this section reiterates the thesis of the whole chapter: grace cannot be separated from particular human action.

IV. Conclusion: Cooperative Participation

In this chapter I focused primarily on grace as participation and the role of belief and signification in that participation. In the previous chapter, I pointed out that if grace is "nothing else than a participated likeness in the Divine Nature," then understanding the role of belief and signification in that participation is necessary for properly understanding the role of the sacraments in our lives. This grammar of grace provides us with a particular way of talking about God's relationship with humankind. Based on the location of the treatise on grace within the larger structure of the *Summa,* we must say that any use of the word "grace" entails a reference to God's effect on the active spiritual life. As such, this grammar of grace emphasizes authentic human action. If grace is "nothing else than a participation in the divine life," then it is a cooperative participation insofar as it is inherently connected to human action. What exactly *cooperative* participation looks like is a question I leave for the following two chapters to flesh out. In this chapter, I treated the graced action of the intellectual power: faithful belief. The following chapter will examine what it means to say that grace acts upon the appetitive power of the will.

At the heart of this chapter is a desire to avoid the reification of grace. Conforming to God's will is not the same as being the next domino in a sequence begun by God. Rather, grace is a dynamic relationship between God and Creation. I use the word "dynamic" because human action is essential to grace. "What is substantially in God becomes accidental in the soul participating in Divine goodness."[61]

Perhaps the clearest condemnation of what we might call a "grace productionist" view of the sacraments in which grace is reified into a created substance is the following passage from the treatise on grace: "No accident is called being as if it had being, but because by

---

[61] S.T. I.II.110.2.ad2.

it something is; hence it is said to belong to a being rather than to be a being." [62] God has being and, in a different way, humans have being. Grace, on the other hand, does not have being but belongs to human beings when God wills what is good for them. When God wills the good for humankind, our share in the Image of God becomes active as, through knowledge and love of God, we conform to and are formed by grace. By that conformity we are said to cooperatively participate in the Divine Nature.

Grace, then, begins with human action (the historically mediated proclamation of revelation) and culminates in human action (the active participation that constitutes the embodied spiritual life). [63] Simultaneously, grace begins with divine action (the self-communication of God) and culminates in divine action (the operation of the Holy Spirit within us). "When the same effect is attributed to a natural cause and to the divine power, it is not as though the effect were produced partly by God and partly by the natural agent: but the whole effect is produced by both, though in different ways, as the same effect is attributed wholly to the instrument, and wholly also to the principal agent." [64] Cooperative participation is embodied. The spiritual life in which we journey toward God is as corporeal as it is spiritual. Our participation in the Divine Nature is not a mystical union that occurs on some spiritual plane of existence, separate from the finite and messy world of created matter. Through Christ, God chose to live with us, and, through the Holy Spirit, God chooses to live within us.

> *By this we know that we abide in him and he in us,*
> *because he has given us of his Spirit.*
>
> —1 John 4:13

---

[62] S.T. I.II.110.2.ad3.

[63] For example, when discussing infant baptism, Aquinas points out that grace is present only as habit, not as action, until later cooperation; cf. S.T. III.69.6.

[64] St. Thomas Aquinas, *Summa Contra Gentiles* III.70.8.

CHAPTER THREE

The Theological Virtues Founding
the Embodied Spiritual Life

We love, because he first loved us.

—1 John 4:19

In the previous chapter I examined how Aquinas describes the embodied spiritual life in terms of grace. The present chapter will examine how he describes that same spiritual life in terms of the theological virtues. This chapter is meant to show that when Aquinas writes about acts of charity he is using a grammar of virtue to describe the embodied spiritual life. As Aquinas describes them, acts of charity are also the Holy Spirit's activity in us (or, better, the Holy Spirit moving us from within). In the previous chapter we saw that Aquinas also uses a grammar of grace to describe the embodied spiritual life insofar as grace is the Holy Spirit actualizing our share in the Image of God. Hence, Aquinas is employing two grammars to describe the same reality. As I will point out, grace is not exhausted by the concept of charity and the acts formed by charity; the distinction between grace and the virtues is not merely a rhetorical distinction. This grammar of virtue allows Aquinas to move away from the general grammar of grace to a more particular grammar of virtue. As Aquinas says in the preface to the *Secunda Secundae*, general considerations of morality are less helpful insofar as human actions are always concrete and particular.[1] Returning once again to the questions from our first

[1] S.T. II.II. Preface.

chapter, I will focus on how, according to Aquinas, we become subjects of the theological virtues and what effects those virtues have in
our lives. Insofar as I can retrieve the answers to these questions from
the *Secunda Secundae,* I will have retrieved a grammar of virtue that
can be used to describe the embodied spiritual life.

While this chapter will treat all three of the theological virtues, its
primary focus will be the virtue of charity. The overarching thesis of
the chapter is that the spiritual life of the wayfaring Christian is the
process of striving to increase in charity. In order to support this
thesis, I will proceed in four sections. First, I will describe the theological virtues by focusing on their roles in moving the intellect and
the will. It is due to these roles that the theological virtues are said
to be necessary for our participation in the Divine Nature. The second
and third sections will describe the roles of the theological virtues in
soteriological terms. Namely, the second section will describe the
theological virtues from the perspective of their generation. That is
to say, we will examine their role in our justification. The third section, then, will describe the theological virtues from the perspective
of their perfection. That is to say, we will examine their role in our
sanctification. The purpose of focusing our attention on soteriological
language is to emphasize the fact that our salvation (i.e., our justification and sanctification) is the process of growing in union with God.
Sanctification will be presented as the process of moving from union
with God to deeper union with God. Finally, by way of transition to
the fourth chapter, I will suggest that this retrieved grammar of the
theological virtues implies a pneumatological soteriology of *theosis.*

I. The Theological Virtues: Orders and Degrees

To move from the natural aptitude for knowing and loving God
(i.e., the image of creation) to actually and habitually knowing and
loving God (i.e., the image of re-creation) is the movement that
Aquinas refers to as participation in the Divine Nature.[2] The previous
chapter was devoted to describing grace in terms of this movement.
Participation in the Divine Nature (i.e., grace) is God's movement of
the intellect to knowledge of God and of the will to love of God. The

---

[2] Cf. chap. 2.II.

present section will be an examination of the roles the theological virtues play in this participation.

1. Faith, Hope, and Charity

In order to be moved toward their final end, the intellect and the will need assistance. Insofar as the purpose of a virtue is to incline a power to move from potency to act,[3] the theological virtues move the intellect and the will toward the final end.[4] As was stated in the previous chapter, the supernatural character of the final end renders our natural principles impotent to attain the final end.[5] "Hence, it is necessary for man to receive from God some additional principles, whereby he may be directed to supernatural happiness."[6] The three theological virtues that constitute these supernatural principles are called faith, hope, and charity (*fides, spes, et caritas*). A brief description of these virtues is offered in an article where Aquinas examines whether faith, hope, and charity are rightly called theological virtues:

> First, as regards the intellect, man receives certain supernatural principles, which are held by means of a Divine light: these are the articles of faith, about which is faith. Secondly, the will is directed to this end, both as to that end as something attainable—and this pertains to hope—and as to a certain spiritual union, whereby the will is, so to speak, transformed into that end—and this belongs to charity.[7]

Hence, faith is the virtue that perfects the intellect with respect to its movement (i.e., assent of belief) toward its final end: First Truth.[8] Hope is the virtue that perfects the will with respect to its attainable yet unattained final end: Eternal Happiness.[9] Finally, charity is the

---

[3] S.T. I.II.55.1c.
[4] S.T. I.II.62.1c.
[5] Cf. chap. 2.II.1.
[6] S.T. I.II.62.1c.
[7] S.T. I.II.62.3c.
[8] Cf. S.T. II.II.1.1.
[9] Cf. S.T. II.II.17.2.

virtue that perfects the will with respect to its attained final end: the spiritual union of friendship with God. Insofar as these virtues move the intellect and the will toward God, they are rightfully called the supernatural principles through which the image of creation is actualized into the image of re-creation. Put differently, the theological virtues are rightfully called principles of our participation in the Divine Nature.

Clearly, much more could be said about these virtues individually. Rather than isolate each virtue for description, however, I will describe them in terms of their relationship to one another. Specifically, I will emphasize their constitutive dependency. The purpose of this method is to avoid the reification of these virtues in the same way that the previous chapter sought to avoid the reification of types of grace (e.g., cooperative and operative). In the end, describing the complex activity of the theological virtues should be seen as a description of the simple activity of the Holy Spirit in the human person, just as any description of various types of grace is a description of the Holy Spirit's single action in us.

2. Orders of Generation and Perfection

In describing the relationship between the theological virtues, Aquinas utilizes the term "order." In question 62.4 of the *Prima Secundae*, Aquinas distinguishes between two orders in the theological virtues: the order of generation (*ordine generationis*) and the order of perfection (*ordine perfectionis*).

In the order of generation, faith precedes hope, and hope precedes charity. It is important to emphasize the fact that the order of generation is a description of the *acts* of the virtue.[10] In other words, "generation" is meant only chronologically with regard to the *acts* of faith, hope, and charity (i.e., belief, hope, and friendship, respectively) and not with respect to the presence of the virtue in the subject.[11] Aquinas says quite clearly that the theological virtues are all infused simulta-

---

[10] S.T. I.II.62.4c.

[11] For example, when discussing infant baptism, Aquinas points out that grace is present only as habit (i.e., infused theological virtues), not as action, until later cooperation; cf. S.T. III.69.6.

neously.[12] We will return to a discussion of how Aquinas is using the word "infusion" later in this chapter. For now I will focus on what the following description of the order of generation tells us about the relationship between the intellect and the will.

> For the movement of the appetite cannot tend to anything, either by hoping or loving, unless that thing be apprehended by the sense or by the intellect. Now it is by faith that the intellect apprehends the object of hope and love. Hence in the order of generation, faith precedes hope and charity. In like manner a man loves a thing because he apprehends it as his good. Now from the very fact that a man hopes to be able to obtain some good through someone, he looks on the man in whom he hopes as a good of his own. Hence for the very reason that a man hopes in someone, he proceeds to love him: so that in the order of generation, hope precedes charity as regards their respective acts.[13]

Faith precedes hope and charity because faith is the virtue that allows us to know God as the object of hope and charity. Hence, Aquinas cites Augustine: "Love ranks above knowledge in moving, but knowledge precedes love in attaining: *for naught is loved saved what is known.*"[14] The knowledge of faith (i.e., belief) presents the will with an object toward which to move. Insofar as God is habitually and actually known through faith, hope is able to move toward God as attainable (but unattained) Eternal Happiness. In other words, hope allows the will to desire God as The Good. Insofar as hope desires God as a good to be attained, charity is able to recognize and love God as a good in and of God's self. Hence, hope leads to the love of charity. The order of generation clearly shows that, regarding the acts of the theological virtues, the actual movement of the intellect toward God must chronologically precede the actual movement of will in hope and love. Again, this is different from saying that the presence of faith in the subject precedes the presence of hope and charity.

In the previous chapter, I stopped short of explicitly discussing the order of generation insofar as I did not consider the relations of the virtues within an individual. Rather, the chapter looked indirectly at

---

[12] S.T. I.II.62.4c.
[13] S.T. I.II.62.4c.
[14] S.T. I.II.3.4.ad4.

the order of generation insofar as it considered faith alone; specifically, we discussed the role of belief and signification in our participation in the Divine Nature. The act of faith (i.e., belief) comes first. As we saw, in coming to belief, faith must be provided with the objects of revelation (i.e., the articles of faith). Faith then moves the intellect to assent. At this point there is a union with God as the True. Insofar as the act of belief is the beginning of our *actualized* participation in the Divine Nature, we are describing faith as it fits in the order of generation. Through the act of faith, the intellect provides the will with an object toward which it moves. So, in the order of generation, we have a description of the will's dependence on the intellect.

After describing the order of generation, Aquinas briefly addresses the order of perfection: "In the order of perfection, charity precedes faith and hope: because both faith and hope are quickened by charity, and receive from charity their full complement as virtues. For thus charity is the mother and the root of all the virtues, inasmuch as it is the form of them all."[15] Here, I must take the time to offer an initial explanation of charity's formative role insofar as it elucidates the relationship between the intellect and the will. Charity "directs the acts of all other virtues to the last end, and which, consequently, also gives the form to all other acts of virtue: and it is precisely in this sense that charity is called the form of the virtues, for these are called virtues in relation to 'informed' acts."[16] Charity is the virtue whereby the human person desires to be virtuous for the sake of deepening friendship with God. By moving the will to love God, charity is the virtue through which we strive to be united to God *as a friend*. Put differently, when charity forms faith, the movement of the intellect depends on the movement of the will. Or, in the words of Aquinas: "Charity is called the mother of the other virtues, because, by commanding them, it conceives the acts of the other virtues, by the desire of the last end."[17] Aquinas uses the word *vivificare* ("to make live," often translated as "quicken") to describe the relationship between charity and the other virtues. Friendship with God gives life to all other virtues, insofar as all actions are done for the sake of friendship

---

[15] S.T. I.II.62.4c.
[16] S.T. II.II.23.8c.
[17] S.T. II.II.23.8.ad3.

with God. We will return to the formative role of charity in much greater length in the following chapter. For now, I simply wish to emphasize the fact that, in the order of perfection, we have a description of the intellect's dependence on the will.

By employing these two orders, Aquinas is maintaining a tension. In the order of generation, the intellect moves the will: faith generates charity. In the order of perfection, the will moves the intellect: charity perfects faith. Rather than simply describing a five-step process from faith to charity and back again, it seems to me that Aquinas is maintaining a tension insofar as he is using these two orders to describe the relationship of codependence that exists between the will and the intellect.

As moral theologian and Thomistic scholar James F. Keenan has pointed out, one of the great problems of scholastic thought was the relationship between the will and the intellect.[18] In question 9 of the *Prima Secundae*, Aquinas maintains the will's autonomy by naming God as the final cause of the will's movement. Or, as Keenan puts it, "by God's creative act, this inclination [toward God] is already in the will, and thus the final cause is already in the will prior to any presentation of an object by reason."[19] In an article where Aquinas is treating the relationship between faith and charity, he notes that, unlike prudence, which "moderates the appetitive movements pertaining to the moral virtues, faith does not moderate the appetitive movement tending to God, which movement belongs to the theological virtues: it only shows the object. And this appetitive movement towards its object surpasses human knowledge."[20] As we will see in our examination of justification, the autonomy of the will and its relationship to the intellect is described only with difficulty. By using these two orders of generation and perfection, however, Aquinas is able to speak about the relationship between the intellect and the will in a manner that maintains the tension of their codependence in their movement toward God. In considering whether faith is the first of the theological virtues, Aquinas makes it clear that the order of generation cannot be isolated from the order of perfection:

---

[18] James F. Keenan, *Goodness and Rightness in Thomas Aquinas's* Summa Theologiae (Washington, DC: Georgetown University Press, 1992). See, in particular, chaps. 2–3.

[19] Ibid., 44.

[20] S.T. I.II.66.6.ad1.

"Faith without charity cannot be the foundation of the spiritual life."[21] In this way, it is not faith alone that begins the spiritual life but perfected faith on which the edifice of the spiritual life stands. In this life, the theological virtues simply cannot be separated. Insofar as the theological virtues are considered in terms of the spiritual life, they are essentially relational.

3. Three Degrees of Charity

As the principles of our participation in the Divine Nature, all three theological virtues unite the human person to God. However, the unions created through faith and hope are distinct from the union of charity insofar as faith and hope "adhere to God as to a principle wherefrom certain things accrue to us," whereas "charity makes us adhere to God for his own sake, uniting our minds to God by the emotion of love."[22] Hence, the union of charity is said to be more perfect than the union of faith or hope. While charity is a union attained, however, that does not mean that the union is static. On the contrary, according to Aquinas there are three degrees (*gradus*) of charity.[23] For Aquinas, the spiritual life is a dynamic process of striving to deepen one's union with God.

At the outset, we must note that the three degrees of charity are rhetorically attributed so as to emphasize the dynamic nature of charity. The degrees are not to be understood as levels of God's love for us. Rather, as Aquinas puts it, "the diverse degrees of charity are distinguished according to the different pursuits to which man is brought by the increase of charity."[24] As charity increases (i.e., as friendship with God deepens), that friendship will manifest itself in various ways depending on its depth. Aquinas describes these "different pursuits" as follows:

> For at first it is incumbent on man to occupy himself chiefly with avoiding sin and resisting his concupiscences, which move him in opposition to charity: this concerns beginners, in whom charity has to be fed or fostered lest it be destroyed: in the second place

---

[21] S.T. II.II.4.7.ad4.
[22] S.T. II.II.17.6.c.
[23] S.T. II.II.24.9sc.
[24] S.T. II.II.24.9.c.

man's chief pursuit is to aim at progress in good, and this is the pursuit of the proficient, whose chief aim is to strengthen their charity by adding to it: while man's third pursuit is to aim chiefly at union with and enjoyment of God: this belongs to the perfect who "desire to be dissolved and to be with Christ."[25]

As we will see in the following two sections, infusion of theological virtue does not make one perfect (or proficient) in charity. In most human lives, charity is received by patiently struggling to deepen our union with God. As Aquinas points out, the primary pursuit of a beginner in charity is to resist sin. Those who are proficient in charity, on the other hand, strive to increase in charity. As with any habit, the strength of the inclination toward its end is subject to change. We will examine the process of increasing in charity more closely in our third section. For now, I want to emphasize that Aquinas's description of the three degrees of charity is meant as a description of charity seeking increase in charity, of union seeking deeper union.

This section's examination of the orders and degrees of the theological virtues is meant to emphasize the fact that Aquinas sees the spiritual life as a *dynamic process*. Hence, the Christian is called a "wayfarer." In order to see how the theological virtues (and charity in particular) relate to the embodied spiritual life, I now turn to a consideration of salvation. In the following sections we will see that processing through the degrees of charity can be described in terms of the generation of the theological virtues and in terms of the perfection of the theological virtues.

II. Falling in Love with God[26]

To talk about salvation in terms of the spiritual life, we return once again to Aquinas's discussion of the Image of God found in the *Prima*

---

[25] Ibid.

[26] Before I enter into a soteriological discussion, I would like to address the glaring lacuna that will mark the next two sections: there will be no mention of Christ. That discussion is in chap. 5 when the grammars of grace and virtue that are retrieved from the *Secunda Pars* will be connected with the Christology and sacramental theology of the *Tertia Pars*. Focusing on these grammars of grace and virtue before treating Christology ensures that Aquinas's implicit pneumatology (i.e., the theology of divine action that undergirds his discussion of grace and the theological virtues) will not be subsumed by his much more explicit Christology. This will ensure that any

Pars. There we saw a threefold Image of God.[27] As I pointed out in the previous chapter, the image of re-creation is the active Image of God that manifests the spiritual life. As I will argue throughout the remainder of this chapter, speaking about justification and sanctification are two different ways of describing the relationship between the theological virtues and their effects on the spiritual life. Speaking in terms of justification is an archeological (as opposed to teleological) way of speaking about the theological virtues that generate us as subjects of the theological virtues. Put differently, we fall in love with God.

1. Justification

In an article where Aquinas treats the distinction between grace and the theological virtues, he succinctly sums up his theology of justification: "It is in respect of receiving this [divine] nature that we are said to be born again sons of God."[28] To share in the image of re-creation (i.e., to be a born-again child of God) is to participate in the Divine Nature. Here, I will examine how Aquinas describes this participation in terms of being generated as a subject of the theological virtues.

In question 113 of the treatise on grace, Aquinas discusses justification as an effect of grace. The term "justification" is used in order to denote "a certain rectitude of order in the interior disposition of man in so far as what is highest in man is subject to God."[29] This reordering of the human mind is a matter of "movement [*motus*] from one contrary to the other, and thus justification implies a transmutation from the state of injustice to the aforesaid state of justice."[30] As Aquinas puts it, "The order of nature can only be restored, i.e. man's will can only be subject to God, when God draws man's will to Himself."[31] Ultimately, this reordering of human nature away from sin

---

interpretation of the Christocentrism in the *Tertia Pars* does not degenerate into Christomonism. Again, the relationship between the *Secunda Pars*'s pneumatological soteriology of *theosis* and the christological soteriologies of the *Tertia Pars* will be treated at length in chap. 5.

[27] S.T. I.93.4c.
[28] S.T. I.II.110.3.c.
[29] S.T. I.II.113.1c.
[30] Ibid.
[31] S.T. I.II. 109.7c.

and toward God is called justification. At this point, it is worth noting that speaking in terms of reorientation frames justification as a relationship. Any understanding of justification as an ontological status must be conceived as a function of relationship with God. Hence, as I will now show, speaking of justification as the infusion of a habitual gift is always a description of participation in the Divine Nature (i.e., the indwelling of the Holy Spirit).

Aquinas lists four things required for justification: "the infusion of grace, the movement of the free-will towards God by faith, the movement of the free-will [away from] sin, and the remission of sins [*culpae*]."[32] Aquinas is clear that the remission of sins is called a requirement for justification only insofar as "every movement has its species from its term."[33] Put differently, rather than being the final step leading to justification, the remission of sins *is* justification.[34] Regarding the role of the free will in justification, Aquinas says that the movement of free will toward sin is detestation of that which is contrary to God. Likewise, the movement of free will toward God by faith is love for God.[35] The free will's movement away from sin and toward God is the reorientation/transmutation of the human mind toward its Final End. Here, we must pause to highlight the role of the free will in this process. According to Aquinas, "God does not justify us without ourselves, because whilst we are being justified we consent to God's justification by a movement of our free-will."[36] This consent (*consentimus*) is constituted by our detestation of sin and desire for God.[37] We must ask, then, what is it that moves the free will?

Hence, we come to the first of Aquinas's prerequisites for our justification: the infusion of grace.[38] Here, we are primarily concerned with the infusion of the habitual gift (i.e., the theological virtues). We must take time to note, however, that "infusion of grace" denotes

---

[32] S.T. I.II.113.6c. The English translation by the Fathers of the English Dominican Province renders *motus liberi arbitrii in peccatum* as "the movement of the free-will towards sin." However, I have chosen to substitute "towards" with the term "away from" to make the use of the orientational metaphor more consistent.

[33] S.T. I.II.113.6.ad1.

[34] S.T. I.II.113.1.sc.

[35] S.T. I.II.1113.5c.

[36] S.T. I.II.111.2.ad2.

[37] S.T. I.II.113.7.ad1.

[38] S.T. I.II.113.7c.

more than the gift of the theological virtues. In the previous chapter,
I pointed out that Aquinas speaks of God's help as twofold: as a
habitual gift and as God's moving us to act. "First, [grace can be
spoken of as] a habitual gift whereby corrupted human nature is
healed, and after being healed is lifted up so as to work deeds meritorious of everlasting life."[39] This habitual gift heals our corrupted
nature (i.e., reorientation, transmutation, justification) and aids that
newly justified nature in actively moving toward its final end. Second,
in addition to the language of "habitual gift," we can speak of grace
in terms of God moving us to act.[40] This second way of speaking
about grace is first discussed in relation to *preparation* for receiving
the infused habitual gift whereby we are justified. In article 6 of question 109, Aquinas points out that "every form requires a disposition."
Speaking of this prerequisite disposition, Aquinas is very clear that
this predisposition must be accomplished by the free will of the person receiving the habitual gift. He is equally clear, however, that
"free-will can only be turned to God when God turns it."[41] In an
article where Aquinas discusses whether faith is the first of the
virtues, he says that "some act of the will is required before faith, but
not an act of the will quickened by charity."[42] As I pointed out above,
this noncharitable act of the will is attributed to grace, because, "by
God's creative act, this inclination [toward God] is already in the will,
and thus the final cause is already in the will prior to any presentation
of an object by reason."[43] In short, grace prepares the human mind
for the theological virtues insofar as God has oriented the free will
toward its Final End. Being so graciously predisposed, the powers
of the mind (i.e., the intellect and will) are capable of receiving the
theological virtues.

The first aspect of "the infusion of grace" necessary for justification,
then, is the preparatory movement of the free will by grace. I turn now
to the second aspect of this necessary "infusion of grace:" the habitual
gift. Here, I want to call attention to the fact that Aquinas uses the
virtue of faith to describe the free will's movement toward God. After
establishing the necessary role of the free will in justification, Aquinas

[39] S.T. I.II.109.9c.
[40] Ibid.
[41] S.T. I.II.109.6.ad1.
[42] S.T. II.II.4.7.ad5.
[43] Keenan, *Goodness and Rightness*, 44.

points out that the mind's turning toward God is through an act of faith.[44] This is not a claim that excludes other acts.[45] However, when we recall that, in the order of generation, the act of faith is prior to the acts of hope and charity, we see why Aquinas describes the justifying movement of the free will toward God in terms of faith. The movement of the free will toward God must be toward God, not as toward an object known through natural means, but as toward the "object of beatitude."[46] In other words, belief in the historically mediated articles of faith (specifically, the Mystery of Christ[47]) must be the foundation for the free will's movement toward God. Hence, when Aquinas says that the free will moves toward God "by faith" (*per fidem*), he is emphasizing the role of the symbols and articles of faith through which God's revelation is known by the human mind. While the movement of the free will is accomplished by the infusion of all the theological virtues (a single gift), Aquinas's emphasis on the foundation of faith betrays a preoccupation with the operation of the exterior sources of our justification. In short, as far as I can tell, speaking of salvation in terms of justification is a way of speaking about salvation with the order of generation in mind. *Converto*,[48] *sano*,[49] and *infundo*[50] are metaphors about beginning/inauguration. The habitual gift is infused, and we are generated as subjects of the theological virtues: that is, Christian wayfarers. Hence, as with the order of generation, when speaking of justification, faith is the theological virtue that takes the place of (grammatical) primacy.

2. Infusion

I now highlight the fact that justification is no more a moment in the past than creation is a moment in the past. As we saw in the previous chapter's discussion of Aquinas's treatment of God's creative

---

[44] S.T. I.II.113.4c.

[45] Cf. S.T. I.II.113.4.ad1. The acts of hope and charity are necessary for justification. The movement of the free will is still an act of charity. However, Aquinas is emphasizing the dependence of this charitable movement on faith's movement of the intellect.

[46] S.T. I.II.113.4.ad2.

[47] Cf. S.T. I.II.113.4.ad3.

[48] Cf. S.T. I.II.109.6.c.

[49] Cf. S.T. I.II.109.9.c.

[50] Cf. S.T. I.II.110.3.c.

act, participation is seen as a relationship between Creation and its source or beginning (*arche*). To reinvoke Torrell's words: "One should not imagine creation as an isolated act that occurred in a distant past; rather, it is a present reality."[51] To be is to participate in God. In other words, the ontology of a creature is always actively relational. The same is true of justification. Justification is an archeological way of speaking about the generation of the theological virtues in the human person. When Aquinas speaks about how faith leads to hope, which leads to charity, he is speaking about the (re-)creation of a Christian wayfarer. Hence, Aquinas says that, as with the act of creation, "God is always working man's justification."[52] The ontology of a justified person is always actively relational. When he says that "the justification of the ungodly is not successive,"[53] we must be careful not to interpret *non est successiva* as "is completed in a single moment." Rather, according to Aquinas, "the common and wonted course of justification is that God moves the soul interiorly and that man is converted to God [i.e., the image of re-creation], first by an imperfect conversion, that it may afterwards become perfect."[54] What is meant by *non est successiva* is that God's action in us is simple.

Hence, the four prerequisites for justification are all ways of describing God's efficacious love for the human person. When describing the remission of sins, Aquinas says that "sin is remitted to us, when God is at peace with us, and this peace consists in the love whereby God loves us."[55] Grace, the movement of the free will, and the forgiveness of sins are all descriptions of God's efficacious love. To be justified (i.e., to become a subject of the theological virtues) is to be loved into loving God.

When speaking about the generation of subjects of the theological virtues, we are ultimately speaking about the gift of Christian identity. Hence, the habitual gift whereby we are justified is the gift of self. The movement of our intellect and our will toward God is tantamount to God holding us in Christian existence; the image of re-creation is

[51] Jean-Pierre Torrell, *Aquinas' Summa: Background, Structure, and Reception*, trans. Benedict M. Guevin (Washington, DC: The Catholic University of America Press, 2005), 24.

[52] S.T. II.II.4.4.ad3.

[53] S.T. II.II.113.8.c.

[54] S.T. I.II.113.10.c.

[55] S.T. I.II.113.2c.

synonymous with being a born-again Child of God. Speaking about justification is a way of speaking about the role of the theological virtues in the spiritual life. Specifically, justification is a way of speaking about this role in terms of the source of our subjectivity. As such, speaking about justification is an archeological way of speaking about the generation of theological virtues in the human person. We are saved when God turns us toward God's self with an offer of friendship. We fall in love with the One who loves us.

To close this section on justification, I would like to briefly point out what it means to say that the theological virtues are a *single* habitual gift. An important word to understand when describing the generation of the theological virtues is "infusion" (*infusionem*). The first and most crucial thing to understand about infusion is that it is less a noun and more an adjective. By this I mean that the metaphor of "infusion" that Aquinas uses to describe the generation of the theological virtues is always used as a way of distinguishing them from the acquisition of human virtues that is connatural to human nature. For example, when discussing the cause of charity's presence in us, Aquinas says that, due to our lack of natural capacity to acquire the virtue of charity, it is in us "by the infusion of the Holy Ghost, Who is the love of the Father and the Son, and the participation of Whom in us is created charity."[56] Similarly, when Aquinas is speaking of the generation of faith, he says that the movement of belief "must needs accrue to him from some supernatural principle moving him inwardly; and this is God."[57] "Infusion" is a word used by Aquinas to deny the natural and affirm the supernatural source of the theological virtues. Put differently, infusion is not only a description of *how* the theological virtues (i.e., the habitual gifts) are given. Rather, infusion is meant to signify that the theological virtues are a gratuitous gift. It is crucial to realize that "infusion" is not invoked to signify an unmediated, ahistorical, instantaneous divine intervention, as much as it is meant to signify the primacy of divine action. It is even more crucial to resist the temptation to use words like "inject" or "absorb" as synonyms for infusion.

Why is this important? Because we must avoid seeing our salvation as a passive relationship between a moved object and an efficient

---

[56] S.T. II.II.24.2.c.
[57] S.T. II.II.6.1.c.

cause.[58] This perception leads to seeing the spiritual life through a deistic lens whereby God makes the clock (injects us with theological virtues) and watches us go. Rather, the infusion of the theological virtues needs to be understood as the formally effective indwelling of the Holy Spirit who is perpetually actualizing our share in the Image of God. Hence, the spiritual life is seen as a dynamic and co-operative process of increasing in charity. As we will see, to say that we have the theological virtues is to say that the Holy Spirit is present within us. Hence, the habitual gift is not a threefold object (faith, hope, and charity) given by God to the human person. The habitual gift, then, is the single gift of a dynamic relationship insofar as it is God's participation in the human person. Put differently, we fall in love with God.

III. Growing in Love for God

I now turn to a consideration of the role the theological virtues play in our sanctification. According to Aquinas, "The special sanctifica-tion of every creature consists in resting in God [*in Deo requiescit*]."[59] Simply put, to say that something rests in God is to assert the exis-tence of a union between the creature and God. Because I am primar-ily concerned with the theological virtues, I will focus my attention on what it means to say that a *human person* rests in God. What follows is an examination of this union that constitutes holiness.

1. Sanctification

To begin, I would like to point out that, for Aquinas, both justifica-tion and sanctification are about being made holy (*sanctus*). Justifica-tion makes us pleasing to God, heals us, converts us, reorients us, etc. Nevertheless, these ways of speaking about the *generation* of the theological virtues places an emphasis on being (becoming a subject as opposed to operating as that subject). On the other hand, we can also speak of being made holy in a way that emphasizes the *operation* of our healed nature. From the outset, I want to be clear that justifica-tion and sanctification are two ways of speaking about the same thing.

[58] Cf. S.T. II.II.23.2c.
[59] S.T. I.73.3c.

While justification focuses on the *state* of the healed mind as a *consequence* of union with God, sanctification focuses on the *movement* of the healed mind that *constitutes* union with God. The difference between sanctification and justification is a difference in emphasis: justification emphasizes *attaining* union (i.e., generation of the theological virtues) and sanctification emphasizes *deepening* union (i.e., perfection of the theological virtues).

Obviously, these are not mutually exclusive. As we have seen, justification involves reference to the movement of the free will. The *acts* of faith and charity are intrinsic to justification. To believe in God, to desire God, and to detest sin are all part of justification. The way Aquinas chooses to speak about justification, however, tends to emphasize the orientation (i.e., the being) of the generated subject (i.e., the Christian wayfarer). As we have seen, Aquinas prefers the language of healing, conversion, and reorientation when describing justification. On the other hand, it is also possible to speak about the role of the theological virtues in a way that emphasizes their operation. It is the thesis of the current section that such a grammatical shift constitutes a shift from speaking about salvation primarily in terms of justification, to speaking of salvation primarily in terms of sanctification. As I will argue, speaking in terms of sanctification is a teleological way of speaking about the operation of the theological virtues whereby we grow in love for God.

As I pointed out in the previous section, being generated as a subject of the theological virtues is tantamount to falling in love with God. To understand how this love for God grows, we must first say something about the union that constitutes our love for God. According to Aquinas, the love of friendship is "that love which is together with benevolence, when, to wit, we love someone so as to wish good to him."[60] He says that this particular selfless love (i.e., a love not based on concupiscence) is called friendship because it entails a mutuality based on communication. "Since there is a communication between man and God, inasmuch as He communicates His happiness to us, some kind of friendship must needs be based on this same communication."[61] Recalling the order of generation, the reception of this divine self-communication through friendship depends on

[60] S.T. II.II.23.1c.
[61] Ibid.

the prior acts of faith and hope. Through the habitual gift, we accept the gift of God's self-communication by loving God for God's own sake. Aquinas says that in friendship we love the beloved as another self.[62] The difference between friendship among humans and the friendship of charity is that, with charity, we love God as the Thou of whom we are an image. We love God as a self that is higher than ourselves. Therefore, when, through friendship with God, there is a union of mutual indwelling, our nature is elevated through participation in the Divine Nature. To rightly consider how this union of friendship might grow, we must move from considering it as a static orientation (which is always a conceptual construct) to considering its operation. To that end, we now move to a consideration of action that is done out of this union. Such activity is called the life of holiness. In this actualized union of friendship, we know and love God as the Thou in whose image we exist. In other words, we see God as another self insofar as we learn to see in ourselves an image of divinity.

2. Increase

Once we are generated as subjects of the theological virtues (i.e., once we fall in love with God), that love becomes the source of the steps we take as Christian wayfarers. Put differently, the actions that constitute the spiritual life spring forth from our union with God. According to James Keenan:

> The point of departure, or the *terminus a quo*, for charity distinguishes it from and makes it the most excellent of the theological virtues. Further, the end it seeks, or *terminus ad quem*, because it is not God's truth or a share in happiness, but God's very self, also distinguishes charity from and makes it the most excellent of the theological virtues. Thus, charity seeks its own perfection, that is, actual union, and therefore its relationship to the last end is simple: out of union with the last end, it seeks greater union. Charity seeks no other end.[63]

---

[62] S.T. I.II.28.1c.
[63] Keenan, *Goodness and Rightness*, 126.

First, I wish to discuss what it means to say that we move "out of union with the last end." Having established what it means to call charity a commanding form of the other virtues, I will then turn to a discussion of what it means to say that charity seeks greater union.

As we saw in the above discussion of the order of perfection, charity is the mother of all other virtues insofar as it "directs the acts of all other virtues to the last end." Aquinas uses the term *impero* (command) to describe this directive relationship. Specifically, Aquinas says that "by commanding them, [charity] conceives the acts of the other virtues, by the desire of the last end."[64] Here, commanding is a function of the will's movement of desire. Hence, through the will's desire, the ends of other virtues (e.g., the knowledge sought by faith) are made proximate to the final end of union with God. Put differently, the objects of all the virtues are desired on account of our desire for God. Hence, the acts of the virtues that are commanded by charity are acts of charity, not essentially, but formally. As the commanding form of the virtues, charity is rightfully called the *terminus a quo* of the spiritual life. It is important to understand this formative role of charity because acts of charity have a vital role in the increase of charity.[65] Before describing the role of charitable acts, however, we must first examine the mode of charity's increase, namely, radication.

In articles 4-7 of the *Secunda Secundae*'s twenty-fourth question, Aquinas discusses the ways in which one can say that charity increases in the human mind. To begin with, Aquinas says that *caritas viae* (the charity of the wayfarer) can increase. He quotes St. Augustine in order to describe how exactly *caritas viae* increases: "For we are called wayfarers by reason of our being on the way to God, Who is the last end of our happiness. On this way we advance as we get nigh to God, Who is approached, 'not by steps of the body but by the affections of the soul': and this approach is the result of charity, since it unites man's mind to God."[66] He goes on to say that this movement toward God by affection is an increase in the "virtual quantity" of

---

[64] S.T. II.II.23.8.ad3.

[65] In the following chapter, we will return to a discussion of the acts of charity insofar as there is a distinction between elicited and commanded acts of charity. For our purposes in this chapter, however, acts of charity are simply understood as acts that seek the Final End.

[66] S.T. II.II.24.4c.

charity, which increases by the "intensity of the act, namely whether a thing is loved more or less."[67] Simply put, to increase in charity is a matter of loving God more deeply and this deeper love constitutes the steps by which a Christian wayfarer approaches her Final End. Hence, the increase in charity (i.e., growing in love for God) is a teleological movement.

But the question remains: what does it mean to love God more deeply? In article 5, Aquinas eliminates any description of increase by way of addition. Because charity is a single form with a single object, it cannot be increased through addition. Rather, "since charity is an accident, its being is to be in something. So that an essential increase of charity means nothing else but that it is yet more in its subject, which implies a greater radication in its subject."[68] Aquinas goes on to explain this radication in terms of participation: "This is what God does when He increases charity, that is He makes it to have a greater hold on the soul, and the likeness of the Holy Ghost to be more perfectly participated by the soul."[69] Insofar as our participation in the Divine Nature is perfected, we are said to love God more deeply. Hence, Aquinas avers that there is no limit to charity on account of the infinite nature of the Holy Spirit: "For charity itself considered as such has no limit to its increase, since it is a participation of the infinite charity which is the Holy Ghost."[70]

Finally, we must ask what role the acts of charity play in this process of radication. Simply put, because charity is a participation in the Divine Nature, there is no human act (i.e., an act of charity) that can necessitate an increase in charity. The presence and depth of charity is always a gratuitous gift from God.[71] Aquinas says, however, that acts of charity dispose us to such an increase "in so far as one act of charity makes man more ready to act again according to charity, and this readiness increasing, man breaks out into an act of more fervent love, and strives to advance in charity, and then his charity increases actually."[72] We will return to a consideration of this disposi-

---

[67] S.T. II.II.24.4.ad1.
[68] S.T. II.II.24.4.ad3.
[69] S.T. II.II.24.5.ad3.
[70] S.T. II.II.24.7c.
[71] Cf. S.T. II.II.24.3c.
[72] S.T. II.II.24.6c.

tive role of the acts of charity in the following chapter. For now, I want to highlight the fact that our ability to seek deeper union with God is always a gratuitous gift. We cannot necessitate an actual increase in charity, but when we act out of charity toward deeper union, we necessitate a potential increase in charity. This potential increase in charity is, according to Aquinas, an "advance on the way to God."[73] Hence, as we will see in the following chapter, these dispositive acts of charity constitute the embodied spiritual life insofar as they strive to grow in love for God.

At the beginning of this section I pointed out that, for Aquinas, "the special sanctification of every creature consists in resting in God [*in Deo requiescit*]."[74] This rest is the union of friendship with God (i.e., charity). The more deeply we love God, the more we are said to be at rest in God. Hence, we are sanctified (i.e., we become more holy) insofar as we are actually and habitually in union with God through the movement of our intellect and will. Living a life formed by friendship with God is to live a life of holiness. Or, as Aquinas puts it, "Sanctification is effected by all the virtues, by which also sins are taken away."[75] Holiness, sanctity, friendship, rest, and conformity are all terms to describe the spiritual life in terms of the Christian wayfarer's participation in her Final End. As such, sanctification is a teleological way of describing the role of the theological virtues in the spiritual life. As far as I can tell, speaking of salvation in terms of sanctification is a way of speaking about salvation with the order of perfection in mind.

The purpose of this section has been to show that being perfected as a subject of the theological virtues is tantamount to being sanctified by God. While this section focused on the virtue of charity, this chapter is not called "*Charity* and the Embodied Spiritual Life" because I want to avoid any desire to isolate and separate the theological virtues from one another. Friendship with God, in this life, is accomplished through the *single* habitual gift of the three theological virtues. At no point is a Christian's friendship with God independent of faith and hope. Maintaining the relationships between the theological virtues will prove important when this grammar of virtue is used to

---

[73] S.T. II.II.24.6.ad3.
[74] S.T. I.73.3c.
[75] S.T. I.II.70.3.ad1.

examine Aquinas's sacramental theology. Specifically, any tendency to isolate and separate the theological virtues easily leads to a separation of the sacraments (e.g., baptism is the sacrament of faith and the Eucharist is the sacrament of charity) that should never be considered apart from one another.

IV. Being Saved by Love

The spiritual life of a Christian wayfarer is a life of dynamic friendship with God. As I have tried to show in this chapter, this dynamic friendship is a participation in the Divine Nature through the movement of the theological virtues. Hence, speaking about the role of the theological virtues in the spiritual life is tantamount to speaking about the salvific action of the Holy Spirit. Insofar as the theological virtues are descriptions of the Spirit's re-creation of our nature through participation, we can say that Aquinas's description of salvation in the *Secunda Pars* is a pneumatological soteriology of *theosis*.

One reason that Aquinas gives for asserting the superiority of charity will prove helpful in understanding the theology that grounds this pneumatological soteriology: "Now in things that are above man, to love them is more excellent than to know them. Because knowledge is perfected by the known being in the knower: whereas love is perfected by the lover being drawn to the beloved. Now that which is above man is more excellent in itself than in man: since a thing is contained according to the mode of the container."[76] Here, Aquinas speaks of charity as the principle by which we are drawn toward God.[77] Similarly, as I pointed out above, Aquinas chooses to describe sanctification as "resting in God." I would submit that when Aquinas describes justification and sanctification in terms of the generation and perfection of the theological virtues, we see a Thomistic account of *theosis*. As a participation in the Divine Nature, the spiritual life that embodies the theological virtues seeks to deepen its participation in the Divine Nature. Hence, the spiritual life is *theosis*.

To clarify this theotic form of participation (and to avoid any tendency to read Aquinas through a Pelagian lens), it is helpful to recall that Aquinas says, "A certain nature may be ascribed to a certain thing

[76] S.T. I.II.66.6.ad1.
[77] Cf. S.T. I.II.109.7c.

. . . by participation, as kindled wood partakes of the nature of fire: and thus, after a fashion, man becomes a partaker of the Divine Nature."[78] Our *theosis* (i.e., the spiritual life we soteriologically refer to as salvation) is a process likened to burning. We cannot set ourselves on fire, and yet firewood exists to burn. We can, however, cooperate with the fire by embracing it. Acts of friendship with God dispose us for a deeper friendship with God.

The life of the theological virtues is rightly described in the soteriological terms of salvation, sanctification, and justification because it is movement toward authentic human existence. Any soteriology must answer the question: From what are we saved? To answer this question using grammars of grace and theological virtue, I would argue that we are saved from nonexistence (i.e., death). Participation in the Divine Nature manifested by the effects of the theological virtues is authentic and active human existence. The gift of faith, hope, and charity is the gift of self. When we (are) move(d) away from sin (i.e., the perceived good of an imperfect end) and toward our Final End, our essence is perfected. We exist more fully as authentic human beings. Sin, on the other hand, is the suicidal undoing of God's creation, deactivating (or, better, refusing) our existence. One might summarize this soteriological description of the theological virtues with the words of Romans 6:23: "The wages of sin is death, but the gift of God is eternal life in Christ Jesus our Lord." In the end, I would argue that this pneumatological soteriology of *theosis* can be summarized by saying that we are loved into existence. And insofar as we cooperate with that love, we are saved by God's love. Put in the simplest terms, "We love, because he first loved us" (1 John 4:19).

> *God's love has been poured out into our hearts through the Holy Spirit that has been given to us.*
>
> —Romans 5:5

---

[78] S.T. I.II.62.1.ad1.

CHAPTER FOUR

The Moral Virtues Manifesting the Embodied Spiritual Life

I know your works—your love, faith, service, and patient endurance.
I know that your last works are greater than the first.

—Revelation 2:19

In the first chapter, I pointed out that the embodied spiritual life is not simply a state of having charity. Rather, the spiritual life consists of actions that are formed by charity.[1] As a single body, the Church is not merely a group of unrelated people who are all friends with God. The journey to God that constitutes the spiritual life cannot be properly or adequately understood as the journey of an individual. Rather, by examining moral virtues, we will see that human beings, as a consequence of their embodied nature, necessarily approach God communally. Any description of a personal union with God (i.e., the love of charity) necessarily implies the manifestation of community through the exercise of moral virtue. Simply put, *my* union *with* Christ is inseparable from and ordered toward the *community's* unity *as* Christ. It is this necessary horizontal aspect of the mystical body's unity that constitutes the focus of the present chapter.

The thesis of this chapter, then, is that the moral virtues make up the shape of the unity of the ecclesial body of Christ, as well as the particular shape of the individual paths of Christian wayfarers. In

---

[1] Cf. chap. 1.V.

the exercise of moral virtue, we find the historical manifestation of charity that, through its extension to others, becomes the gratuitous grace whereby we cooperate in the justification and sanctification of humankind. In order to better understand this crucial role of the moral virtues, this chapter will comprise three main sections. First, I will examine how Aquinas defines moral virtue. Special attention will be given to the codependence of the virtues that makes them *all* necessary forms of any good operation. The second section will consider the relationship between the theological virtues and the moral virtues. By focusing on the dispositive role of moral virtue, we will see that friendship with God is not adequately described solely in terms of charity but necessarily includes actions of moral virtues that serve the individual's relationship with God and with other human beings. Finally, by way of conclusion, I will offer a brief recap of the grammars of grace and virtue carried out in these first four chapters.

I. Moral Virtues

In defining virtue, Aquinas is happy to adopt a definition taken from Peter Lombard's use of St. Augustine: "Virtue is a good quality of the mind, by which we live righteously, of which no one can make bad use, which God works in us, without us."[2] In place of the word "quality" (*qualitas*), Aquinas prefers the more specific "habit" (*habitus*). A habit "implies a disposition in relation to a thing's nature, and to its operation or end, by reason of which disposition a thing is well or ill-disposed thereto."[3] As a habit, a virtue is a disposition of human nature (specifically, the human mind) to act toward its end. Hence, the definition uses the phrase "by which we live righteously" because, as Aquinas points out, a virtue is an *operative* habit. That is to say, "the end of virtue . . . is operation."[4] As I have emphasized in the last two chapters, the spiritual life (i.e., living righteously) is habitually and actually knowing and loving God. When Aquinas speaks about virtue, there is an emphasis on the dynamic operation of the human mind, as opposed to its static being. When describing the

---

[2] S.T. I.II.55.4.arg1.
[3] S.T. I.II.49.4c.
[4] S.T. I.II.55.4c.

spiritual life, the emphasis is placed on operation because "as God's substance is His act, the highest likeness of man to God is in respect of some operation."[5] It is through virtuous operation that a person most fully participates in the Divine Nature.

According to Aquinas, "For a man to do a good deed, it is requisite not only that his reason be well disposed by means of a habit of intellectual virtue; but also that his appetite be well disposed by means of a habit of moral virtue."[6] Hence, in order to understand how a human person carries out such good deeds, we must take the time to understand the relationship between intellectual virtue and moral virtue.

1. The Codependence of Moral Virtues

In an article where Aquinas treats the necessity of prudence, he elaborates on why both moral and intellectual virtues are necessary for good deeds. Here, it will be beneficial to quote Aquinas at length:

> For a good life consists in good deeds. Now in order to do good deeds, it matters not only what a man does, but also how he does it; to wit, that he do it from right choice [*electionem rectam*] and not merely from impulse or passion. And, since choice is about things in reference to the end, rectitude of choice requires two things: namely, the due end, and something suitably ordained to that due end. Now man is suitably directed to his due end by a virtue which perfects the soul in the appetitive part, the object of which is the good and the end. And to that which is suitably ordained to the due end man needs to be rightly disposed by a habit in his reason, because counsel and choice, which are about things ordained to the end, are acts of the reason.[7]

Simply put, a good deed is always the result of a right choice. In order that a person does a good deed out of right choice, there must be an act of the reason (through use of intellectual virtue) as well as an act of the appetite (through the use of moral virtue).

---

[5] S.T. I.II.55.2.ad3.
[6] S.T. I.II.58.2c.
[7] S.T. I.II.57.5c.

1.1 Prudence

First, I turn my attention to the role of the reason in choosing to do a good deed. According to Aquinas, for a person to make a choice, there must be something for that person to choose. "In choice [*electione*] there are two things, namely, the intention of the end, and this belongs to the moral virtue; and the preferential choice [*praeacceptio*] of that which is unto the end, and this belongs to prudence."[8] Simply put, prudence dictates the goal of our choices by providing the end; prudence determines what is to be done. As such, Aquinas relies on Aristotle to define prudence as "right reason applied to action."[9] As a virtue of the practical reason, then, prudence is necessary for choosing to do a good deed because it provides knowledge of the goal.[10] Knowing what one is doing is a prerequisite for choosing that action. For example, planting a tree is a good deed only if I *knowingly* intend to plant a seed in the ground. If I simply throw my apple out the window of my moving car as a means of getting rid of the core, and the discarded core happens to grow into a tree, I did not choose to plant a tree. Prudence is the virtue whereby our practical reason is inclined to discern those actions that ought to be done. As such, Aquinas says that prudence is the first principle of movement insofar as it provides the end to which the appetite is meant to conform.[11]

If the appetite is going to intend the end provided by reason, then it needs a virtue to incline it to that end. These virtues that move the appetite to conform to reason (i.e., obey reason by seeking the goal it provides) are called moral virtues. Aquinas quotes Aristotle in order to define moral virtue: "Hence the definition of moral virtue (Ethic. ii, 6) states that it is 'a habit of choosing the mean appointed by reason as a prudent man would appoint it.'"[12] Therefore, before treating these moral virtues individually, it is necessary to briefly examine what it means to say that prudence appoints a mean (*medium*). If moral virtue chooses the mean, then this mean is the end provided by prudence.

---

[8] S.T. I.II.56.4.ad4.
[9] S.T. II.II.47.2.sc.
[10] S.T. II.II.47.2c.
[11] S.T. I.II.58.2c.
[12] S.T. I.II.59.1c.

When Aquinas says that prudence provides the mean as the object to be intended by moral virtue, he is appealing to the contextualized nature of that end.

> In actions and passions the mean and the extremes depend on various circumstances [*diversas circumstantias*]: hence nothing hinders something from being extreme in a particular virtue as to one circumstance, while the same thing is a mean in respect of other circumstances, through being in conformity with reason. This is the case with magnanimity and magnificence. For if we look at the absolute quantity of the respective objects of these virtues, we shall call it an extreme and a maximum: but if we consider the quantity in relation to other circumstances, then it has the character of a mean: since these virtues tend to this maximum in accordance with the rule of reason, i.e. "where" it is right, "when" it is right, and for an "end" that is right. There will be excess, if one tends to this maximum "when" it is not right, or "where" it is not right, or for an undue "end"; and there will be deficiency if one fails to tend thereto "where" one ought, and "when" one ought.[13]

In determining what ought to be done, prudence moves the practical reason to scrutinize the particular context (i.e., the "various circumstances") of an action. For example, at times, prudence will determine that an act of fortitude is necessary. Imagine being mugged in a dark alley. In order to combat the fear that arises, prudence must determine what degree of fortitude is required. Not all muggings are the same. Prudence must attend to the particular circumstances of the moment. Am I being mugged by a four-year-old child wielding a plastic spoon? Or am I being mugged by four men who just exited a bar after celebrating their rugby team's victory? These various circumstances of the situation are the possibility of prudently discerning a virtuous response. A refusal to acquiesce to the toddler's demands may be courageous, while that same resolve misses the mean when surrounded by the inebriated rugby players. Depending on the circumstance, fortitude quickly degenerates into brashness, leading the person to miss the goal of surviving.

---

[13] S.T. I.II.64.1.ad2.

Through prudence, the practical reason attends to a particular context without which a mean could not be determined. Therefore, as we will see, one cannot properly describe the exercise of moral virtue without reference to context. If fortitude is to avoid being cowardly and avoid being brash, prudence needs to provide the mean as a goal. Moral virtue needs an end to seek, and, as a mean, that end must be determined by prudence through careful consideration of particular context. Hence, prudence is the practical reason's ability to relate to a particular context (i.e., the "various circumstances" in which virtuous action takes place). Insofar as prudence accurately determines the mean to be sought, the resultant act is called a right action. Making the right choice requires that one pay attention to the context of a decision.

1.2 Justice

Once prudence has determined the mean, it is up to moral virtue to move the appetite to choose that mean. "Moral virtue is properly a perfection of the appetitive part of the soul in regard to some determinate matter: and the measure or rule of the appetitive movement in respect of appetible objects is the reason. But the good of that which is measured or ruled consists in its conformity with its rule."[14] Having established that prudence determines the mean to be sought by the moral virtues, we can see that moral virtue is said to participate in reason insofar as it conforms to the command of prudence. Put differently, when the appetite actually chooses the mean provided by prudential reason, the resultant choice is said to be virtuous.

In order to make such virtuous choices, a person requires moral virtues that move the appetite to choose the mean provided by prudence. Now, the appetite is composed of three parts: the concupiscible appetite, the irascible appetite, and the rational appetite. Together, the concupiscible and the irascible appetites constitute what Aquinas calls the sensitive appetite, and the rational appetite is called the will. I will begin with a consideration of the will's relationship to the prac-

---

[14] S.T. I.II.64.1c.

tical reason. Here, I am concerned with how justice responds to the command of prudence. According to Aquinas:

> It belongs to human virtue to make man good, to make his work accord with reason. This happens in three ways: first, by rectifying reason itself, and this is done by the intellectual virtues [e.g., prudence]; secondly, by establishing the rectitude of reason in human affairs, and this belongs to justice; thirdly, by removing the obstacles to the establishment of this rectitude in human affairs.[15]

When Aquinas speaks of "establishing the rectitude of reason in human affairs," he is describing the action of justice. As the "perpetual and constant will to render to each one his right," justice intends the external operations whereby a person relates to others equitably.[16] Hence, "it is proper to justice . . . to direct man in his relations with others." Through prudential reason and a just will, the human person is oriented toward that which is external to itself. Hence, in order that a good operation be done, prudence moves the reason to attend to a particular context, discerning what operation ought to be done. Then, justice moves the will to obey the command of prudence, actually carrying out the operation prescribed by reason. Prudential reason commands and a just will obeys. Hence, justice "establishes the rectitude of reason in human affairs" by willing the vision of prudence into reality. A prudent person may know that the hungry should be fed, but it takes a just person to feed the hungry.

1.3 Temperance and Fortitude

Through justice, then, the rational appetite (i.e., the will) intends the end provided by prudent reasoning. The role of the sensitive appetite, however, remains to be described. For our purposes here, I will offer a brief description of how the movements of the sensitive appetite (i.e., the passions) affect the will's ability to act justly. As Aquinas points out, some moral virtues help a person do good deeds

---

[15] S.T. II.II.123.1c.
[16] S.T. II.II.58.1.arg1.

"by removing the obstacles to the establishment of this rectitude in human affairs." He continues:

> Now the human will is hindered in two ways from following the rectitude of reason. First, through being drawn [*attrahitur*] by some object of pleasure to something other than what the rectitude of reason requires; and this obstacle [*impedimentum*] is removed by the virtue of temperance. Secondly, through the will being disinclined [*repellit*] to follow that which is in accordance with reason, on account of some difficulty that presents itself. In order to remove this obstacle fortitude of the mind is requisite, whereby to resist the aforesaid difficulty even as a man, by fortitude of body, overcomes and removes bodily obstacles.[17]

Aquinas frames these hindrances to the will's rectitude in terms of disordered passions. The concupiscible appetite "pursues sensible and bodily goods," while the irascible appetite "flies from sensible and bodily evils."[18] The obstacle (*impedimentur*) that temperance removes is an attraction (*attractus*) to an end that contradicts the end provided by prudence. Prudence may dictate that one should get out of bed at six o'clock in the morning and begin working on his manuscript, while the concupiscible appetite would rather stay in bed until ten thirty watching television. The concupiscible appetite may on occasion be moved toward the imprudent end through attraction. In these circumstances, the concupiscible appetite is said to be disordered due to a lack of conformity to reason. Hence, Aquinas says that temperance is charged with "removing the obstacle" so that the will might more readily choose to conform to the command of prudence.

It must be emphasized, however, that the passions of the sensitive appetites are not necessarily obstacles that hinder the movement of the will. Aquinas is clear that passions are not in and of themselves bad.[19] On the contrary, passions can aid the will in its ability to move toward the reasonable good. Hence, when Aquinas says that temperance removes obstacles, this removal is not adequately understood in a purely negative fashion (i.e., as solely mitigating the adversarial

---

[17] S.T. II.II.123.1c.
[18] S.T. II.II.141.3c.
[19] S.T. I.II.24.2c.

role of disordered passions). Rather, temperance removes obstacles by ordering the passions. More specifically, by inclining the concupiscible appetite to be drawn toward the good determined by reason, temperance inclines the concupiscible appetite to support the will. Put differently, a temperate person takes pleasure in what is reasonable. Hence, Aquinas says that "the passions of the soul, in so far as they are contrary to the order of reason, incline us to sin: but in so far as they are controlled by reason, they pertain to virtue."[20]

Insofar as it is charged with ordering passions that can either hinder or support the will, fortitude is similar to temperance. Rather than being charged with ordering desires and sorrows of the concupiscible appetite, however, fortitude is charged with ordering the hopes and fears that occur when the irascible appetite encounters the difficulties that arise when a person seeks to obey prudence. For example, the irascible appetite may become fearful of an end that is perceived as concomitant with the end commanded by reason. A young child may know he needs to begin a load of laundry; however, his fear of the basement is enough to repel him from following through on this duty. When disordered, this fear of difficulty causes the will to reject the judgment of prudence. But it is the task of fortitude to incline the irascible appetite to quell fear, for "it behooves one not only firmly to bear the assault of these difficulties by restraining fear, but also moderately to withstand them, when, to wit, it is necessary to dispel them altogether in order to free oneself therefrom for the future."[21] Hence, the fortitudinous person is able to bear the unavoidable difficulties that accompany reasonable operations.

In the end, the sensitive appetites are naturally concerned with the well-being of one's self. When they fail to conform to the rule of reason, the sensitive appetites have the ability to hinder the will's desire to carry out the external operations commanded by prudence. Put differently, seeking pleasure and avoiding fear can stop us from doing what is just. They also have the ability, however, to support the will's ability to obey reason. Together, then, temperance and fortitude ensure that our concern for ourselves does not inordinately affect our ability to will the common good. Rather, temperance and fortitude work together to order the mind's inclinations so that

---

[20] S.T. I.II.24.2.ad3.
[21] S.T. II.II.123.3c.

prudence can accurately determine the goal to be sought and the will can readily obey. In fact, as I will point out now, it is not possible to obey reason and operate justly without the assistance of temperance and fortitude.

In order to carry out a good operation, we need all four of these virtues. They all depend on one another. Without prudence engaging the world around us, we have no particular goal to seek. Without justice, the goal will remain an intellectual exercise. Without temperance and fortitude, the will quickly loses its resolve. In short, there is no such thing as a human operation that lacks the influence of any one of these cardinal virtues.

1.4 Maintaining the Tension of Codependence

Thus far I have described the relationship between these moral virtues in terms of their ability to conform to reason. Put differently, reason moves the appetites.[22] As we saw in the previous chapter, however, the relationship between the will and the intellect is not so easily described.[23] While Aquinas clearly champions the primacy of reason when it comes to describing virtuous operation, he also clearly champions the primacy of the appetite. For instance, in an article where he is discussing the subjects of virtue, he says the following:

> But the subject of a habit which is called a virtue simply, can only be the will, or some power in so far as it is moved by the will. And the reason of this is, that the will moves to their acts all those other powers that are in some way rational, as we have said above: and therefore if man do well actually, this is because he has a good will. Therefore the virtue which makes a man to do well actually, and not merely to have the aptness to do well, must be either in the will itself; or in some power as moved by the will. Now it happens that the intellect is moved by the will, just as are the other powers: for a man considers something actually, because he wills to do so. And therefore the intellect, in so far as it is subordinate to the will, can be the subject of virtue absolutely so called.[24]

---

[22] Cf. S.T. I.II.56.4c.
[23] Cf. chap. 3.I.2.
[24] S.T. I.II.56.3c.

In the end, then, Aquinas holds that it is by an act of moral virtue (i.e., an operation of the appetitive power) that we choose rightly.[25] It is simultaneously true, however, that no choice can be made without an end that is provided by reason.

Here, we need to address a tension in Aquinas's description of the relationship between the intellect and the will. As we saw in our previous chapter's treatment of the theological virtues, Aquinas has different ways of speaking about the relationship between virtues that allows him to maintain the tension of codependency that exists between the intellect and the will. Aquinas says that, by providing the end, "reason is the first principle of human action."[26] On the other hand, in the above block quote, Aquinas also says that "the will moves to their acts all those powers that are in some way rational." Hence, the will is the mover, but it is only virtuous insofar as it is in conformity to reason.

I highlight this tension as a reminder that, as with the theological virtues, we must avoid reifying these virtues. As we have seen, when Aquinas speaks about virtuous operation, he is able to speak in various ways that emphasize the role of a particular aspect of human nature and its relationship to the world in which it acts. In fact, this tension is so fundamental to Aquinas's understanding of the human mind that it allows him to blur the distinction between intellectual virtues and moral virtues. When discussing the intellectual virtue of prudence, Aquinas says that it is rightly called a moral virtue. "Now it belongs to prudence, as stated above, to apply right reason to action, and this is not done without a right appetite. Hence prudence has the nature of virtue not only as the other intellectual virtues have it, but also as the moral virtues have it, among which virtues it is enumerated."[27] The virtues and the powers they move are not entities that work together to render a human act. Unlike internal organs that can be neatly distinguished and assigned their individual tasks, the moral virtues provide us with various ways of describing the complexity of a single human action.

This grammar of moral virtue, then, provides a way to speak of the spiritual life with a degree of specificity that does not concomitantly dissect and compartmentalize morality. According to James Keenan,

[25] S.T. I.II.58.1.ad2.
[26] S.T. I.II.58.2c.
[27] S.T. II.II.47.4c.

"The mutual dependency of prudence and the moral virtues (this is an evolving spiral, not a vicious cycle) incorporates and integrates moral reasoning into an evolving vision of the human person."[28] Through these moral virtues (and all the virtues contained within these cardinal four[29]), the human person accomplishes the operations that constitute the good life. The question remains, what role do these moral virtues play in striving to increase in charity? Before answering this question, I wish to take a moment to describe how the human person acquires and increases in moral virtue.

2. Acquiring and Increasing Moral Virtue

Simply put, virtues that can be acquired are caused by acts.[30] According to Aquinas,

> Everything that is passive and moved by another is disposed by the action of the agent; wherefore if the acts be multiplied a certain quality is formed in the power which is passive and moved, which quality is called a habit: just as the habits of moral virtue are caused in the appetitive powers, according as they are moved by the reason.[31]

For example, when we obey the command of reason, that action influences our appetite, disposing the will to more readily obey reason in the future.

These virtue-causing actions are not innately known. Rather, in order to perform the acts that cause virtue, we need friends to imitate and learn from. According to Aquinas, friendship is required for happiness. We need friends so that we have people to love but also so that we might be helped toward good operation.[32] As we will see in the following section, it is difficult to overstate the importance of relationships with others when it comes to developing one's virtues. In an article that treats the need for prudence, Aquinas takes up the

---

[28] James F. Keenan, "The Virtue of Prudence," in *The Ethics of Aquinas*, ed. Stephen J. Pope (Washington, DC: Georgetown University Press, 2002), 259.

[29] Cf. S.T. I.II.61.2.ad3.

[30] Cf. S.T. I.II.51.2 and S.T. I.II.65.2.ad3.

[31] S.T. I.II.51.2c.

[32] S.T. I.II.4.8c.

objection that prudence is not necessary because we can lead a good life by following the good counsel of others. When we act according to the good counsel of others (i.e., when we take advice from friends or mentors), that particular act is "not yet quite perfect."[33] To illustrate the point: Because I trust my mother's wisdom, I will visit the sick if she tells me it is the right thing to do. When I act solely out of my trust in her counsel, however, I have failed to operate out of my own prudential reasoning. Hence, my act is imperfect. But when the counsel of others becomes the counsel of our own intellect, we have increased in prudence. Once my intellect gains the experience necessary to independently see visiting the sick as a good to be done regardless of my mother's endorsement, my action will rightly be called an act of virtue simply.

As Aquinas points out, though, a single act is not sufficient to cause a virtue.[34] To say that we need experience in order to follow our own counsel is to say that developing a pattern of virtuous action is crucial to growing in virtue. These ongoing patterns of action are called *exercitia*, a term that "refers . . . to the regular performance or execution of particular acts."[35] James Keenan points out that Aquinas's affinity for this term seems to come from St. Paul's use of this metaphor in describing the Christian life.[36] To exercise moral virtue one must repeatedly choose to do good deeds. For example, Aquinas points out that in order to have prudence, one must have the experience of using one's reason to command the appetite.[37] So it is with the other virtues; if one wants to become more temperate, one must act temperately. Therefore, when these "acts be multiplied, a certain quality is formed in the power which is passive and moved."[38] An

---

[33] S.T. I.II.57.5.ad2.

[34] Cf. S.T. I.II.51.3 and S.T. II.II.24.6.ad2: "Even when an acquired virtue is being engendered, each act does not complete the formation of the virtue, but conduces towards that effect by disposing to it, while the last act, which is the most perfect, and acts in virtue of all those that preceded it, reduces the virtue into act, just as when many drops hollow out a stone."

[35] James F. Keenan, *Goodness and Rightness in Thomas Aquinas's* Summa Theologiae (Washington, DC: Georgetown University Press, 1992), 51. For a thorough discussion of how Thomas uses the term *exercitium* throughout the *Summa*, see also pp. 50–52 and 105–8.

[36] Ibid.

[37] S.T. II.II.47.16.ad2.

[38] S.T. I.II.51.2c.

appetite that has learned to desire what is reasonable is all the more ready to choose the reasonable end. In other words, by developing patterns of good deeds, we continually deepen our disposition toward further virtuous operation.

These *exercitia* constitute the virtuous acts that allow us to acquire and increase in virtue. Increasing in moral virtue is not, however, as simple as isolating a single virtue (i.e., fortitude) and solely focusing on the matter of that virtue. This approach misunderstands the co-dependence of the virtues. Rather, to increase in moral virtue, it is necessary that all the virtues be exercised. As I said above, a good deed can be accomplished only by the simultaneous use of all four cardinal virtues. Due to this fact, a deficiency in any one of the virtues hinders the growth of the others. Hence, Aquinas says:

> If [a person] exercise himself, by good deeds, in all such matters, he will acquire the habits of all the moral virtues. But if he exercise himself by good deeds in regard to one matter, but not in regard to another, for instance, by behaving well in matters of anger, but not in matters of concupiscence; he will indeed acquire a certain habit of restraining his anger; but this habit will lack the nature of virtue, through the absence of prudence, which is wanting in matters of concupiscence.[39]

Again, in Aquinas's discussion of increasing in moral virtue, we see his desire to maintain the tension between them by emphatically asserting their codependence. If we try to separate them, we cease to discuss moral virtue. We cannot rightly speak of a person who is incredibly temperate but lacks all fortitude. To be a triathlete one must be good at swimming, cycling, and running. It does not matter how good at cycling and running a competitor is. If she cannot swim, her cycling performance will suffer due to the fact that she drowned in the first leg of the race. In short, it takes an integrated under-standing of the human person to rightly exercise the moral virtues. To increase in virtue, one must attend to all matters of virtue, without giving undue preference to the matter of a favorite virtue. Obsessing over social justice might easily lead to an intemperate mind that, consequently, is incapable of accurately determining what injustices need attention.

---

[39] S.T. I.II.65.1.ad1.

Moral living is relying on the help of friends to develop a pattern of good operations that will, in turn, help others develop their own patterns. This process requires embracing membership in a community as well as cultivating a willingness to engage one's particular context. With this description of moral virtue in mind, I turn to see how these patterns relate to the theological virtues. In essence, I am trying to articulate how one might rightly call these operations a participation in the Divine Nature. Put differently, how do the moral virtues help us strive to increase in charity?

II. Embodying Friendship with God

As I stated above, the purpose of this chapter is to emphasize the fact that the operations carried out through the moral virtues constitute the particular shape of our friendship with God. Having shown that every human operation requires the use of all the cardinal virtues, I turn now to a description of how Aquinas envisions the role of these virtues in a life lived striving to increase in charity. I will begin by first determining what it might mean to say that one operates out of charity (*ex caritate*). Then, I will turn my attention to what it means to say that the moral virtues are a necessary part of growing in charity.

1. *Operating* Ex Caritate

Operations that constitute the spiritual life are gifts from God insofar as the moral virtues required for such operations are motivated by and in service of God's friendship. When speaking about acts of charity, we can distinguish between charity's *terminus a quo* (the end out of which) and charity's *terminus ad quem* (the end toward which). The difference between these two is the difference between charity's current union being the source of action (i.e., the mode of operation) and charity's everlasting union being the goal of action (i.e., the term of operation). To speak of an operation being done *ex caritate* implies both a particular movement and a particular end. Specifically, it implies that an operation is done out of existing union with God for the sake of everlasting union with God.[40]

---

[40] Cf. Keenan, *Goodness and Rightness*, 126.

Turning first to the *terminus ad quem* of charity, it must be emphasized that charity (in conjunction with the other theological virtues) provides the Final End.[41] Having spent some time discussing this role of charity in the previous chapter, I will not spend much time replicating that discussion. Here, it will suffice to repeat that charity forms the moral virtues by putting all other ends in service of the Final End. All operations done *ex caritate* have proximate ends that help persons move toward their Final End. For example, if done *ex caritate*, almsgiving is an operation that serves movement toward the Final End (i.e., friendship with God). Hence, when formed by charity, prudence is right reason about things to be done for the sake of everlasting union with God.

When we speak about charity's formal role in terms of commanding, we see the emergence of how we might speak of charity as the *terminus a quo* of an operation. By putting all other ends at the service of the Final End, charity is said to command all the other virtues. Prudence is still charged with specifying and commanding the deeds to be done, but charity's antecedent command implies that the object of prudence is always a proximate end. By providing the remote Final End to which all other virtues unite their proximate ends, charity is called the *efficient* form of the virtues.[42] In other words, the efficient form of any operation done *ex caritate* is friendship with God. The essential form of the operation, however, is the moral virtue that specifies the operation. Friendship with God motivates us into specific operations that have the moral virtues as their essential forms. Simply put, when done *ex caritate*, an act of moral virtue has friendship with God as its mode of operation and its term of operation. Hence, to say that an operation is done *ex caritate* is to say that it begins and ends in charity (i.e., union with the Final End). As such, the operation is a manifestation of the Holy Spirit's life within the person.

By speaking of charity as an efficient form that commands, Aquinas makes it clear that charity needs the moral virtues. Just as there are no acts done by a single cardinal virtue, there are no acts done solely by charity. Acts of charity are operations done *ex caritate*. The first part of this chapter emphasized the fact that all four cardinal virtues

[41] S.T. II.II.23.6c.
[42] S.T. II.II.23.8.ad1.

are necessary for carrying out the operations whereby we most fully resemble God.[43] When done *ex caritate*, operations of moral virtue embody friendship with God, giving that friendship a particular shape.

When treating the cardinal virtues in question 61 of the *Prima Secundae*, Aquinas offers a typology that clearly articulates the radical influence that charity has on the moral life while simultaneously emphasizing the necessary role of the moral virtues. Here, it will be beneficial to quote Aquinas at length:

> Since man by his nature is a social animal, these [cardinal] virtues, in so far as they are in him according to the condition of his nature, are called "social" virtues; since it is by reason of them that man behaves himself well in the conduct of human affairs. It is in this sense that we have been speaking of these virtues until now. But since it behooves a man to do his utmost to strive [*trahat*] onward even to Divine things, as even the Philosopher declares in Ethic. x, 7, and as Scripture often admonishes us—for instance: "Be ye . . . perfect, as your heavenly Father is perfect" (Matthew 5:48), we must needs place some virtues between the social or human virtues, and the exemplar virtues which are Divine. Now these virtues differ by reason of a difference of movement and term: so that some are virtues of men who are on their way and tending towards the Divine similitude; and these are called "perfecting" virtues [*virtutes purgatoriae*]. Thus prudence, by contemplating the things of God, counts as nothing all things of the world, and directs all the thoughts of the soul to God alone: temperance, so far as nature allows, neglects the needs of the body; fortitude prevents the soul from being afraid of neglecting the body and rising to heavenly things; and justice consists in the soul giving a whole-hearted consent to follow the way thus proposed.[44]

Here, Aquinas tells us that some cardinal virtues are called "perfecting" due to the fact that they "differ by reason of a difference of movement and term" from those cardinal virtues that are called "social." As we have seen, charity is charged with forming cardinal

---

[43] S.T. I.II.55.2.ad3.
[44] S.T. I.II.61.5c.

virtues so as to direct the person to friendship with God (i.e., the "divine similitude" Aquinas calls the image of re-creation). Put differently, because they operate *ex caritate*, the perfecting virtues have a different mode of operation and a different term of operation than the social virtues. It is by virtue of this relationship to charity (i.e., being elevated toward God) that the moral virtues are called "perfecting."

For Aquinas, when charity forms a virtue's mode and term of operation, that virtue is rightly called a gift. Hence, he expounds upon the difference between social and perfecting virtues by appealing to the familiar language of "infusion."[45] As infused, the perfecting virtues seek a proximate end that surpasses human reason. In distinguishing infused moral virtue from acquired moral virtue, he says:

> Human virtue directed to the good which is defined according to the rule of human reason [i.e., the social type of cardinal virtue] can be caused by human acts: inasmuch as such acts proceed from reason, by whose power and rule the aforesaid good is established. On the other hand, virtue which directs man to the good as defined by the Divine Law, and not by human reason [i.e., the perfecting type of cardinal virtue], cannot be caused by human acts, the principle of which is reason, but is produced in us by the Divine operation alone.[46]

When Aquinas says that infused moral virtue is "produced in us by the Divine operation alone" (*causatur solum in nobis per operationem divinam*), he is not implying that human cooperation plays no role in the generation of infused moral virtue. Recalling the final part of Aquinas's definition of virtue (i.e., "which God works in us, without us"), we can see that, rather than excluding human cooperation from the definition, Aquinas is including charity as a necessary part of the definition. Hence, when discussing the gifts of the Holy Spirit Aquinas says that "wisdom and understanding and the like are gifts of the Holy Ghost, according as they are quickened [*informantur*] by charity."[47] Just as human cooperation is an integral part of the generation of infused theological virtues, human cooperation is necessary for

---

[45] Cf. S.T. I.II.63.3c.
[46] S.T. I.II.63.2c.
[47] S.T. I.II.68.8.ad3.

the generation and increase of infused moral virtues. As I pointed out in the previous chapter, "infusion" does not so much denote the mechanism of generation as it denotes the divine source of a virtue.[48] As formed by charity, the perfecting virtues are infused. As infused, the perfecting virtues are gifts from God.

Operating *ex caritate* is acting out of the perfecting virtues that are, with the theological virtues, a single gift from/of God. The perfecting virtues are the result of God's friendship radically transforming our entire moral lives to the extent that we can speak of moral virtues that are capable of transcending human nature. The infused moral virtues do not receive their object from reason alone but from faith's reasonable assent to God's revelation as communicated through the person of Christ and the life of his Church. Nevertheless, lest we use the language of "infusion" and "gift" to negate the role of human action, it is crucial to emphasize that, just as charity needs the symbolic objects of faith to be in love with God, the gifts of infused moral virtue need the historically mediated content of divine law. As with acquired moral virtue, infused moral virtue needs the life of a community (i.e., divine instruments) through which we are given the "divine things" toward which we strive.[49]

When we operate *ex caritate*, we are "tending toward the divine similitude."[50] As such, the life lived through these perfecting virtues is the action that manifests divine action in our lives. When discussing whether or not the gifts of the Holy Spirit are necessary for salvation, Aquinas invokes a telling metaphor: "That which has a nature, or form, or virtue imperfectly, cannot of itself work, unless it be moved by another. Thus the sun which possesses light perfectly, can shine by itself; whereas the moon which has the nature of light imperfectly, sheds only a borrowed light."[51] Living *ex caritate* is like shining borrowed light. By the Holy Spirit's participation in us, we reflect divinity onto the world. By reflecting divinity, the perfecting virtues also perfect the communities they engage. As I emphasized in the first section of this chapter, all moral virtue, whether acquired or infused, must attend to the particularity of its context. Hence, to

---

[48] Cf. chap. 3.II.2.
[49] S.T. I.II.61.5c.
[50] Ibid.
[51] S.T. I.II.68.2c.

most fully reflect divinity, perfecting virtue must engage the particularity of its community. Put differently, the task of reflecting divinity demands that we take into consideration those who need the light. Hence, in Aquinas's treatment of the perfecting virtues, we have the foundations of a sacramental theology constructed in terms of grace and virtue. Simply put, to operate *ex caritate* is to be a sacrament.

2. Dispositive Acts of Charity

Having established what it means to operate *ex caritate*, I now move to a consideration of how this operation is tantamount to striving toward an increase in charity. I will argue that rather than narrowly defining the spiritual life in terms of charity alone (i.e., "striving to increase in charity"), it is more beneficial to speak of "striving to reflect divinity." I prefer this metaphor because, as I pointed out above, reflecting divinity necessarily implies the operations born of the perfecting virtues. So, to more fully describe what it means to strive to reflect divinity, I would like to spend time examining how the perfecting virtues relate to an increase in charity.

From the first, it is important to reiterate what was said in the previous chapter: charity does not increase by amount but by radication.[52] "This is what God does when He increases charity, that is He makes it to have a greater hold on the soul, and the likeness of the Holy Ghost to be more perfectly participated by the soul."[53] Because charity is the participation of the Holy Spirit in us, to increase in charity is always a gratuitous gift from God. What, then, does it mean to say that the spiritual life is striving to increase in charity?

According to Aquinas,

> Each act of charity disposes to an increase of charity, insofar as one act of charity makes man more ready to act again according to charity, and this readiness increasing, man breaks out into an act of more fervent love and strives to advance in charity, and then his charity increases actually.[54]

---

[52] Cf. chap. 3.III.2.
[53] S.T. II.II.24.5.ad3.
[54] S.T. II.II.24.6c.

Why is it that each act of charity "makes man more ready to act again according to charity"? Short answer: every form requires a disposition. To deepen our conformity to charity (i.e., to more readily be formed by charity), we must have a disposition conducive to receive charity. By developing the essential forms of charity's acts (i.e., the "perfecting" virtues), we ready ourselves to conform to the Spirit's participation. Since, as we've seen, acts of charity are acts of the perfecting virtues, in those actions we increase in the perfecting virtues. Acts of charity, then, dispose us to increase in charity, because they simultaneously make us more virtuous. The more morally virtuous a person the more disposed that person is to act according to charity. When we, out of charity, exercise our moral virtues, we cooperate with God's gift in a way that makes us more ready to receive God. While our virtuous predisposition does not necessitate our righteousness, it opens us up to the One whose participation in us is righteousness.

To offer a thicker description of this dispositive process, it will be beneficial to return to Aquinas's description of the perfecting virtues in question 61 of the *Prima Secundae*. In the reply to the second objection, Aquinas cites Plotinus's description of the perfecting virtues as "uprooting" (*auferunt*) the passions.[55] But he ends the reply by adding a caveat: "It may also be said that here [Plotinus] is speaking of passions as denoting inordinate emotions [*motus*]."[56] Hence, Aquinas frames his discussion of the perfecting virtues largely in terms of their role in reordering disordered passions. The perfecting virtues of infused temperance and fortitude stop the will from being hindered in its inclination to follow the command of infused prudence. A more literal translation of *virtutes purgatoriae* ("perfecting virtues") would be "purgative virtues." These virtues purge us of disordered passions. The more the sensitive appetite is perfected by purgative virtues, the more the will is ready to actually operate out of charity. The more we order our passions, the more we accept the movement of the Holy Spirit within ourselves. Hence, through the perfecting virtues, we are said to receive the gift of cooperating in our salvation.

Put differently, the order of our passions is the disposition needed by charity. Therefore, our movement toward God is reliant on the

---

[55] S.T. I.II.65.1.ad2.
[56] Ibid.

order of our passions. This allows Aquinas to claim that, even though acts of charity do not necessitate an actual increase in charity, dispositive acts of charity are rightly called an "advance on the way to God."[57] Through these dispositive operations done *ex caritate*, we strive to increase in charity so that we might more fully reflect the divinity that moves us. Put differently, our nature becomes more divine and we are thereby more ready to act as such.

This way of speaking about increase in charity allows us to see that the entirety of our moral lives is a gratuitous gift from God. As operations done *ex caritate*, the acts of perfecting virtues by which we seek to dispose ourselves for increase in charity come from an existent friendship with God. Put simply, it is God who moves us to seek God. Hence, when we speak about the perfecting virtues purging us of the disordered passions that inhibit charity's radication, we are utilizing a grammar of justification that allows us to emphasize God's operation in our lives. It is God who calls us into being as pilgrims on The Way. On the other hand, if we speak of the perfecting virtues as striving toward deeper union with God, we are utilizing a grammar of sanctification that allows us to emphasize our cooperative role in the sanctification of ourselves and others. Together, these ways of speaking about the moral virtues allow for a description of *theosis* that refuses to neglect the dynamic and embodied nature of that process.

Having laid out how acts of charity dispose us for an increase in charity, I would like to return briefly to our previous discussion of the degrees of charity.[58] I highlighted Aquinas's treatment of these degrees as a way of showing that the spiritual life is a dynamic process. We recall the following passage:

> In like manner the diverse degrees of charity are distinguished according to the different pursuits to which man is brought by the increase of charity. For at first it is incumbent on man to occupy himself chiefly with avoiding sin and resisting his concupiscences, which move him in opposition to charity: this concerns beginners, in whom charity has to be fed or fostered lest it be destroyed: in the second place man's chief pursuit is to aim at

[57] S.T. II.II.24.6.ad3.
[58] Cf. chap. 3.I.3.

progress in good, and this is the pursuit of the proficient, whose chief aim is to strengthen their charity by adding to it: while man's third pursuit is to aim chiefly at union with and enjoyment of God: this belongs to the perfect who "desire to be dissolved and to be with Christ."[59]

It seems to me that we can thicken this description of the degrees of charity by utilizing Aquinas's description of the perfecting virtues, namely, each degree emphasizes the role of a particular virtue. Since "resisting his concupiscences" is the pursuit of a beginner, charity's command of temperance is particularly important. Put differently, beginners need to give special attention to matters of temperance, striving to order their desires. Similarly, in those who are proficient in charity, charity's command of fortitude comes to the fore. The proficient give special attention to matters of fortitude, striving to order their fears so that they might have the strength to persevere. Taking up one's cross and following Jesus is an experience that demands fortitude. Hence, Aquinas describes those proficient in charity as acting "with one hand doing work and with the other holding a sword."[60] Finally, in those who are perfect in charity, charity's command of justice takes a place of primacy. Because their passions have been rightly ordered (i.e., disordered passions have been uprooted), the perfect give special attention to willing the good presented by infused prudence. The more readily they are able to will this good, the more they are said to be perfect in charity.

To be clear, charity always commands all of these virtues at every degree of charity. I reiterate: the moral virtues cannot be isolated. The emphasis on a particular moral virtue, however, is what manifests the wayfarer's current level of charity. This emphasis is the consequence of the particular matter at hand. The "various circumstances" of our lives may render us beginners in desperate need of temperance. For example, there are few parents who remain perfect in charity

---

[59] S.T. II.II.24.9.c.

[60] S.T. II.II.24.9.ad2. This use of Scripture (Neh 4:17) is telling. "One hand doing the work" implies that temperance has stopped disordered concupiscence from desiring unreasonable ends. Hence, the prudent end is being willed (i.e., "work" is being done). Nevertheless, the other hand needs the sword to defend against those dangers that are concomitant with the work being done. Hence, fortitude is needed to mitigate the fears that would hinder the will from working toward the prudent end.

when confronted with the death of their child. Likewise, few would argue that St. Peter was perfect in charity when fear of harm caused him to deny Christ three times. Hence, the "various circumstances" in which we live must dictate what type of friend we will be to God. At times, we will inevitably be the type of person who struggles in our friendship with God. A cursory glimpse at the lives of the saints will confirm this dynamic character of the spiritual life. Most saints have their "dark nights." Similarly, most sinners have their moments of perfection wherein they are ready to act spontaneously and passionately out of love for God. In short, the degrees of charity are not meant to describe a monolithic trajectory of charity's increase. Rather, appealing to the degrees of charity is a way of describing our dispositive struggle. In the life of a wayfarer, striving to reflect divinity is always a dynamic struggle that requires our willingness to engage our particular contexts. Increasing in charity, then, demands that we utilize the moral virtues to engage various circumstances of our lives.

I argue, then, that the degrees of charity are about how *disordered* passions, when left unchecked, will gradually eradicate the indwelling of the Holy Spirit. The more ordered our passions, the more capable we are of receiving and embodying the movement of the Holy Spirit. I say "capable" because ordered passions do not necessitate an increase in charity. There is a long history of saints who, despite their ordered passions, regularly experienced a lack of union with God. The degrees of charity, then, are also about how *ordered* passions gradually accept the indwelling of the Holy Spirit, allowing our lives to more fully reflect divinity.

To conclude this subsection, I offer a brief clarification regarding the way I am using the term "striving." According to James Keenan, the "strivings, or formal interior acts [of charity], are antecedent to questions concerning specification, that is, they are antecedent to questions of intention and choice, or to questions pertaining to the proximate ends intended and the actual objects realized."[61] Put differently, when trying to describe the goodness of the person, whether or not they are operating *ex caritate* is the criterion by which we judge a person as good. While Keenan uses the word "striving" to denote this antecedent "moral motivation," my use of "striving" is intended

---

[61] Keenan, *Goodness and Rightness*, 142.

to include the role of the "perfecting" virtues. This difference in use of the term "striving" comes from the difference in our projects. Keenan establishes rules for the use of "good" and "right" in describing the moral quality of an individual. On the other hand, I describe the embodied spiritual life in terms of the codependence of the theological virtues and the moral virtues. As such, when I use the term "strive," I denote operations carried out *ex caritate*. Insofar as these operations come from a community and serve a community, striving to increase in charity needs the specification that occurs through the exercise of moral virtue done *ex caritate*. Striving to reflect divinity is an operation born of an embodied struggle. We must wrestle with the passions that are the result of our embodied nature. Further, because this striving is accomplished through the exercise of the perfecting virtues, there is no step we take on the path to God that is not intimately related to the community in which we live. As a community, we strive together. To conclude this section on embodying charity, I turn now to the crucial role of community in the spiritual life.

3. Communal Embodiment of Friendship with God

At the beginning of this chapter, I noted that, due to the ensuing turn to Aquinas's eucharistic theology, I am primarily interested in the role of the moral virtues in the unity of the mystical body of Christ. With that in mind, I return to a consideration of (1) the necessary role of historical mediation in the generation of the theological virtues and (2) the role of human action in the sanctification of others.

In chapter 2, I emphasized the fact that faith works in a human mode.[62] That is to say, the symbols through which God's revelation is presented to the human intellect are always objects proportionate to human reason. Aquinas emphasizes that faith's unseen object (God) is known through complex propositions. In turn, this leads him to place an emphasis on the role of words in sacramental signification.[63] It seems, however, that operations of the perfecting virtues are likewise revelatory. An example from Scripture: "Now when the

---

[62] Cf. chap. 2.III.
[63] Cf. chap. 1.III.

centurion, who stood facing him, saw that in this way he breathed his last, he said, 'Truly this man was God's Son!' " (Mark 15:39). Actions can be revelatory, providing the content necessary for a confession that manifests faithful belief. Therefore, the life of moral virtue formed by charity is a manifestation of God's revelation. Divine Nature is communicated to others through the cooperation of the graced agent's participation (i.e., through operations done *ex caritate*). As such, we can say that a graced human nature is an instrument of God.

Bearing this in mind, we can return to Aquinas's treatment of grace to describe the relationship between a person operating *ex caritate* and that person's community. We recall the following passage:

> And thus there is a twofold grace: one whereby man himself is united to God, and this is called "sanctifying grace" [*gratia gratum faciens*]; the other is that whereby one man cooperates with another in leading him to God, and this gift is called "gratuitous grace" [*gratia gratis data*], since it is bestowed on a man beyond the capability of nature, and beyond the merit of the person. But whereas it is bestowed on a man, not to justify him, but rather that he may cooperate in the justification of another, it is not called sanctifying grace. And it is of this that the Apostle says (1 Corinthians 12:7): "And the manifestation of the Spirit is given to every man unto utility," i.e. of others.[64]

Here, Aquinas describes how the actions of others are the instruments whereby a person is justified (i.e., made pleasing to God through *gratia gratum faciens*). Insofar as our operations done *ex caritate* are the *result* of the operations of others, our operations are the manifestation of *gratia gratum faciens*. On the other hand, insofar as those same operations are the *cause* of the operations of others, our operations are the manifestation of non-sanctifying *gratia gratis data*. Hence, Aquinas provides us with two ways of describing the same operations. These two ways of speaking allow us to acknowledge that our participation in the Divine Nature is both a matter of being operated on and cooperating with God's operation on others. Just as much as God saves individuals through salvation history, that individual's embodied spiritual life manifests the salvation history by which God

---

[64] S.T. I.II.111.1c.

saves the world. So, while I can do nothing to save myself (Aquinas is not guilty of advancing a soteriology of works righteousness), by virtue of my salvation I am responsible for the salvation of others. God saves me through others, and God saves others through me.

When we reflect divinity, we preach the objects of faith in a way that helps those in our communities. Our moral living becomes an instrumental mirror that provides an experience of God to the world. In addition to self-formation, acts of perfecting virtue form our communities. Just as a good preacher takes into account the particularity of her listeners, however, we must take into account the particularity of the community we are engaging when we strive to reflect divinity. The particular shape of our moral lives is an object of faith to those around us. Insofar as we "preach the propositions" of faith through our moral lives, we are mediating the sanctifying grace that moves the free will of our neighbor. Put differently, as a gift of the Holy Spirit, the ethical life of the Church signifies and implements the salvific will of God.

Insofar as the moral virtues constitute the shape of the unity of the mystical body of Christ, as well as the particular shape of the individual paths of Christian wayfarers, we must say that human beings relate to their final end, not simply through their interior desire for God. Actually knowing and loving God involves moral operation done *ex caritate* in the context of a community. The moral virtues make up the shape of the unity of the mystical body of Christ, as well as the particular shape of the individual paths of Christian wayfarers. In the exercise of moral virtue, we find the historical manifestation of charity that, through its extension to others, becomes the gratuitous grace whereby we cooperate in the justification and sanctification of humankind. At the heart of this chapter is the fact that embodiment precludes any isolation and reification of the human person's "interior." I repeat our thesis from this chapter's introduction: The journey to God that constitutes the spiritual life cannot be properly or adequately understood as the journey of an individual. Any description of a personal union with God (i.e., the love of charity) necessarily implies the manifestation of community through the exercise of moral virtue. Simply put, *my* union *with* Christ is inseparable from and ordered toward the *community's* unity *as* Christ. The union of charity that we have with our Final End is always the result of our relationship to the world around us, because God has freely chosen to love us according to our embodied and communal nature. Or, as Pope Benedict XVI has written so eloquently:

> We should recall that no man is an island, entire of itself. Our lives are involved with one another, through innumerable inter-actions they are linked together. No one lives alone. No one sins alone. No one is saved alone. The lives of others continually spill over into mine: in what I think, say, do and achieve. And con-versely, my life spills over into that of others: for better and for worse. . . . Our hope is always essentially also hope for others; only thus is it truly hope for me too. As Christians we should never limit ourselves to asking: how can I save myself? We should also ask: what can I do in order that others may be saved and that for them too the star of hope may rise?[65]

III. Grammars of Grace and Virtue

In these last three chapters, I retrieved two grammars that depend on one another. The grammar of grace that we retrieved in chapter 2 provides a particular pattern of talking about the relationship be-tween God and human action. The grammar of grace is primarily founded on the category of participation. The grammar of virtue, then, allows us to speak about participation in the Divine Nature (i.e., grace) in terms of *particular* human action. By appealing to theological virtues, we are able to talk about the gratuitous nature of that par-ticipation insofar as the emphasis is placed on the operation of God moving the intellect and the will. By appealing to moral virtues, we are able to talk about the cooperative nature of participation insofar as the emphasis is placed on the essential forms (i.e., the perfecting virtues) whereby we might dispose ourselves and our communities to God's friendship.

The purpose of retrieving these grammars is twofold. First, based on Aquinas's treatment of sacramental signification that I treated in the first chapter, thicker descriptions of grace and charity are needed. The retrieval of these two grammars has been in service of the ensu-ing examination of Aquinas's sacramental theology and eucharistic theology. In order to understand Aquinas's treatment of the sacra-ments, we must understand how he is envisioning the spiritual life.

---

[65] Benedict XVI, *Spe Salvi* 48.

Second, I retrieved these grammars to make clear the connection between grace and virtue. At the heart of this retrieval is a desire to emphasize the fact that, at least in Aquinas's treatment, language about grace and virtuous action are descriptions of God's single self-gift. Participation, sanctification, justification, theological virtues, and perfecting virtues are interrelated terms that allow us to describe the single gift of God's self in various ways. These grammars, then, multiply the perspectives from which we can describe God's life in our lives, thereby providing insights that mutually enrich one another.

I chose to treat grace, theological virtue, and moral virtue in that order so as to (1) emphasize the theological foundation of Aquinas's approach to virtue while simultaneously (2) emphasizing the embodied and historical nature of God's self-gift. The more we try to disembody our friendship with God, the more difficult we make it to increase in charity and, simultaneously, the more difficult we make it to cooperate in the salvation of the world. For Aquinas, preoccupation with contextualized exercises of virtue is preoccupation with our relationship with God.

Throughout this book, I use the phrase "the *embodied* spiritual life" because communal moral living done out of charity is the source and summit of the spiritual life. Anyone who, hearing this claim, replies, "I thought the Eucharist was the source and summit of our faith," has created a false dichotomy. As we will see in the following chapters, the Eucharist is itself an act of the perfecting virtues through which we dispose ourselves for an increase in charity.

In the following chapters, I will return to the *Tertia Pars* to examine the role the Eucharist plays in the embodied spiritual life. Specifically, I will describe the unity of the ecclesial body of Christ in terms of grace and virtue. By applying the retrieved grammars to Aquinas's sacramental theology, we will see that the *Secunda Pars* is helpful for contemporary sacramental theology, because it precludes any desire to construct a sacramental theology that would isolate sacraments from moral engagement with the cultural particularities without which sacraments cease to have meaning.

CHAPTER FIVE

The Eucharist Nourishing the Embodied Spiritual Life

Therefore, my friends, since we have confidence to enter the sanctuary by the blood of Jesus, by the new and living way that he opened for us through the curtain (that is, through his flesh), and since we have a great priest over the house of God, let us approach with a true heart in the full assurance of faith, with our hearts sprinkled clean from an evil conscience and our bodies washed with pure water. Let us hold fast to the confession of our hope without wavering, for he who has promised is faithful. And let us consider how to provoke one another to love and good deeds, not neglecting to meet together, as is the habit of some, but encouraging one another, and all the more as you see the Day approaching.

—Hebrews 10:24-25

Having mined the *Secunda Pars* for ways of speaking about grace and virtue, the remaining chapters of this book will return to Aquinas's *Tertia Pars* and his explicit treatment of the sacraments. The thesis of the current chapter is that the eucharistic theology found in the *Tertia Pars* is intimately connected to Aquinas's concerns for the life of the Church. To use the terminology of our retrieved grammars, Aquinas presents the Eucharist as an integral part of the embodied spiritual life insofar as the Eucharist affects the Church's participation in the Divine Nature by increasing the Church's unity.

This thesis will be defended in three steps. First, I will examine the relationship between Aquinas's christological treatise and the pneumatological soteriology of *theosis* that was treated in chapter 3. Specifically, I will argue that, by means of his life, Jesus Christ establishes the possibility of *theosis*. Next, I will turn to Aquinas's sacramental theology to explain how the sacraments work as signs that provoke us to follow the way that is Christ. Finally, I will show how the Eucharist is itself the Church's nourishment for the way.

I. Jesus Establishes the Way

In chapter 1, I quoted Bernhard Blankenhorn as saying that Aquinas's sacramental theology must be understood through the lens of his Christology.[1] The present section will seek to avoid the danger that results from *beginning* with Aquinas's Christology. Namely, I am trying to avoid a christomonistic reading of Aquinas's sacramental theology. Such readings easily degenerate into the types of sacramental theologies rightly bemoaned by de Lubac and Chauvet.[2] It is, however, my hope that, in light of the second and third chapters of this book, the reader will have little trouble envisioning an undergirding pneumatology (i.e., the theologies of grace and virtue we retrieved from the *Secunda Pars*) that makes such christomonistic readings of the *Tertia Pars* impossible.

To begin our consideration of how the Eucharist relates to the spiritual life, I will provide a description of how Christ's presence is salvific. In the current section, I will relate the pneumatological soteriology of *theosis* with the christological soteriologies of the *Tertia Pars*. Contextualizing these soteriologies will provide a trinitarian framework for understanding the following sacramental theology and eucharistic theology. The embodied life of Jesus Christ, particularly in the culminating act of his passion, has opened up for humankind a "new and living way" (Heb 10:20). Subsequently, through the indwelling of the Holy Spirit, we are moved to follow the way established by Christ.

1. Paschal Mystery as Sacrificial Sign of God's Love

In the first article of the first question of the *Tertia Pars*, Aquinas writes the following regarding the fittingness of the incarnation: "It

---

[1] Cf. chap. 1.II.
[2] Cf. chap. 1.I.

would seem most fitting that by visible things the invisible things of God should be made known."[3] From the outset, Aquinas grounds the *Tertia Pars* in a theology of revelation. Put differently, human knowledge of God is always at the heart of Aquinas's christological considerations. Hence, when considering Christ's "manner of living" (*modo conversationis*), Aquinas frames his discussion in terms of preaching the divine truth.

> Christ's manner of life had to be in keeping with the end of His Incarnation, by reason of which He came into the world. Now He came into the world, first, that He might publish the truth [*manifestandum veritatem*]. . . . Hence it was fitting not that He should hide Himself by leading a solitary life, but that He should appear openly and preach in public. . . . Secondly, He came in order to free men from sin. . . . And hence, as Chrysostom says, "although Christ might, while staying in the same place, have drawn all men to Himself, to hear His preaching, yet He did not do so; thus giving us the example to go about and seek those who perish, like the shepherd in his search of the lost sheep, and the physician in his attendance on the sick." Thirdly, He came that by Him "we might have access to God."[4]

In this passage, Aquinas highlights the revelatory character of the reasons for the incarnation. Even the second reason, which might not be immediately recognized as concerned with revelation (i.e., freeing humankind from sin), is described in terms of preaching. As if to avoid unnecessary complications, Aquinas provides a simple summary: "Christ's action is our instruction."[5] Far from reducing the incarnation to the content of Christ's verbal preaching, Aquinas is emphasizing that the entirety of Christ's life communicates divinity. But if we are to avoid idolatry, we must further qualify these claims.

As Aquinas points out when discussing the object of faith, what is seen cannot be believed.[6] Recalling our discussion of belief in chapter 2, the object of faith is always presented in a human mode so that what is believed is made accessible through signs that point beyond

[3] S.T. III.1.sc.
[4] S.T. III.40.1c.
[5] S.T. III.40.1.ad3.
[6] S.T. II.II.1.5c.

themselves.[7] Through signs (e.g., the articles of the Creed, the sacraments, etc.) the Word of God is communicated to humankind. Put differently, Aquinas has a theology of God's transcendence.

While God's transcendence is a function of our natural (in)ability to know God, this theology of transcendence is so fundamental that even the Incarnate Word, Jesus Christ, points beyond his own embodied life to the divine life of the Trinity. Hence, Aquinas says: "Things concerning Christ's human nature, and the sacraments of the Church, or any creatures whatever, come under faith, in so far as by them we are directed to God, and in as much as we assent to them on account of the Divine Truth."[8] Things pertaining to the human nature of Christ (e.g., his body and blood, his speaking, his actions, etc.) are not the final object of faith but rather point beyond themselves. Every aspect of the incarnation points beyond itself to God *as our Final End*. Emphasizing that God is believed in as Final End is important because such an emphasis refuses to disconnect the content of revelation from the dynamic character of the spiritual life. The Word of God is incarnate (i.e., communicated in a human mode) so that we might move toward our Final End. Hence, Aquinas's Christology is rooted in a soteriology of *theosis*.

Before turning to Aquinas's treatment of the passion, I would like to recall the genre of the *Summa* in order to help us make sense of the plurality we find in the *Tertia Pars*. Aquinas presents multiple soteriologies in the *Tertia Pars*. It would be a mistake to assume that these soteriologies are seamlessly systematized into a coherent whole. Recalling that the *Summa Theologiae* is written as an introductory text meant to expose theology students to the depth of the tradition, it is unsurprising to see that Aquinas regularly provides multiple descriptions of a particular issue. For example, in question 46, Aquinas lists five ways "that man was delivered by Christ's Passion."[9] Again, in question 49, he lists three ways that "Christ's Passion is the proper cause of forgiveness."[10] Throughout his soteriological considerations, we find Aquinas stacking up ways in which the Christian tradition has spoken about Christ's salvific efficacy. Aquinas justifies this plu-

---

[7] Cf. chap. 2.III.
[8] S.T. II.II.1.1.ad1.
[9] Cf. S.T. III.46.3.
[10] Cf. S.T. III.49.1.

rality by asserting the superiority of using several ways to bring about a single goal.[11] In essence, Aquinas refuses to limit himself to a single interpretation of the tradition. Therefore, while I will now describe Aquinas's soteriology largely in terms of our retrieved grammars, I do not mean to insinuate that Aquinas denies the validity of other soteriological language. However, here I argue that Aquinas has a preferred grammar for soteriology that runs throughout both the *Secunda Pars* and the *Tertia Pars*.

This preferred grammar for soteriology is one based on the revelatory purpose of the incarnation whereby the Paschal Mystery of Jesus Christ is understood as a sacrificial sign of God's love. Hence, Aquinas notes:

> Even Christ's Passion, although denoted by other figurative sacrifices, is yet a sign of something to be observed by us, according to 1 Peter 4:1: "Christ therefore, having suffered in the flesh, be you also armed with the same thought: for he that hath suffered in the flesh hath ceased from sins: that now he may live the rest of his time in the flesh, not after the desires of men, but according to the will of God."[12]

The passion of Christ points beyond itself to a way of living *ex caritate* through the perfecting virtues. Indeed, Aquinas emphasizes the fact that Christ's passion is only pleasing to God as an act of charity.[13] "But Christ obtained a result from His passion, not as by virtue of the sacrifice, which is offered by way of satisfaction, but by the very devotion with which out of charity He humbly endured the passion."[14] As such, the passion is a sacrificial sign of God's love at work in the world. When Aquinas lists the reasons that Christ's passion is rightly called salvific, first among the reasons is that "man knows thereby how much God loves him, and is thereby stirred [*provocatur*] to love him in return, and herein lies the perfection of human salvation."[15] Hence, as an operation done *ex caritate*, the passion is a sign

---

[11] Cf. S.T. III.46.3.ad1.
[12] S.T. III.48.3.ad2.
[13] S.T. III.48.3c.
[14] S.T. III.22.4.ad2.
[15] S.T. III.46.3c.

of charity that provokes us into a way of living (i.e., an embodied spiritual life) that is "the perfection of human salvation."

2. Provocation as Possibility of Theosis

In question 49, Aquinas points out that the passion of Christ is said to cause our justification because it provokes (*provocantis*) the charitable movement of our will through which "we procure pardon for our sins."[16] As we saw in chapter 3, our justification (i.e., the forgiveness of sins) is a function of being turned and moved toward God.[17] Hence, as an act of perfect charity, the passion causes our justification by provoking the movement of our minds toward God and away from sin. Put differently, the passion causes our friendship with God by provocatively proclaiming God's love for us.

As an act of charity that provokes our charity, Jesus' sacrifice is the cause of our justification. As with all human operations done *ex caritate*, however, Jesus' acts of charity are embodied insofar as they are commanded operations of moral virtue. Disembodied charity does not provoke anyone. In the previous chapter, I emphasized the codependence and inseparability of the moral and theological virtues. Due to this codependence, provoking charity also requires provoking the moral virtues. If Christ's passion provokes our charity, it does so in a specified manner. Hence, Aquinas's second reason that Christ's passion is rightly called salvific: "because thereby He set us an example of obedience, humility, constancy, justice, and the other virtues displayed in the Passion, which are requisite for man's salvation."[18] Through the operations of Christ's moral virtues, his charity is made known to us as an embodied and virtuous way to be followed. Put differently, Christ shows us what it looks like to operate *ex caritate* so that we might go and do likewise.

It remains to be seen, however, exactly how this provocation occurs. Specifically, how is it that the movement of our charity is attributed to the efficacy of Christ's charity? Aquinas provides us with a two-part answer. "Christ's Passion, although corporeal, has yet a spiritual effect from the Godhead united: and therefore it secures its efficacy

---

[16] S.T. III.49.1c.
[17] Cf. chap. 3.II.1.
[18] S.T. III.46.3c.

by spiritual contact—namely, by faith and the sacraments of faith." [19] The spiritual effect of the passion (i.e., the provocation of our embodied love for God) is brought about by "spiritual contact." This demands further explanation. First, Aquinas speaks of this efficacious spiritual contact in terms of application (*applicare*) through faith:

> Christ's Passion is applied to us even through faith, that we may share in its fruits. . . . But the faith through which we are cleansed from sin is not "lifeless faith" [*fides informis*], which can exist even with sin, but "faith living" through charity [*fides formata per caritatem*]; that thus Christ's Passion may be applied to us, not only as to our minds [*intellectum*], but also as to our hearts [*affectum*]. And even in this way sins are forgiven through the power of the Passion of Christ.[20]

As a sign that points beyond itself to God's love for us, the passion provokes our response of faith that is formed by charity. Simply put, "application," "provocation," and "spiritual contact" are ways of speaking about causality based on signification. When, through faith formed by charity, we believe in the truth revealed through the passion, we are justified. That is, we are turned and moved toward our Final End, not solely as the truth to be known (i.e., the isolated act of lifeless faith), but as the good to be done (i.e., the active life lived *ex caritate*).[21]

For those of us who were not firsthand witnesses to the sacrificial consummation of Christ's life, however, some form of mediation is needed. Put differently, we need to be told the Good News. "Since Christ's Passion preceded, as a kind of universal cause of the forgiveness of sins, it needs to be applied to each individual for the cleansing of personal sins. Now this is done by baptism and penance and the

[19] S.T. III.48.6.ad2.

[20] S.T. III.49.1.ad5.

[21] If this description of the efficacy of the passion seems to lack power, consider the consequences of standing in a large crowd and screaming, "Fire!" or "Free money!" There is a reason that inciting a mob is a serious crime. Similarly, there is a reason parents are concerned with the environment of their children. Personalities are forged and formed by the signs that surround a person. The signs we use to communicate are wrought with efficacious power. Hence, we ought not apply the reductive criticism that provocation is merely a soteriology of a moral exemplar. Rather, provocation is fundamental to the way subjectivities are formed.

other sacraments."[22] As signs that provide knowledge of Christ's salvific life, the sacraments apply the passion to us in an efficacious manner. Simply put, sacramental signs signify the unique sacrificial sign of Christ's passion; sacraments are signs of The Sign. Even when communicated through sacramental signification, the passion is still primarily applied through living faith.

This central role of living faith allows us to return to our previous treatment of the theological virtues. This will allow us to describe the passion's efficacy in terms of the Holy Spirit's movement. If this christological soteriology is based on signification that provokes the response of theological virtue, then, based on our retrieved grammars, it is easy to see that the Holy Spirit is intimately active in our salvation. The movement of the theological virtues is the formally effective indwelling of the Holy Spirit who is perpetually actualizing our share in the Image of God. Hence, speaking about the role of the theological virtues in the spiritual life is tantamount to speaking about the salvific action of the Holy Spirit.[23] To say that the passion is applied in faith is to say that through Christ's revelatory life the Christian individual comes to believe in and move toward God as the Final End. The embodied movement of the theological virtues is our response to the sacrificial sign of the passion. Put simply, the sacrificial death of Christ causes *theosis* by way of provocation. On the cross we see an irrevocable invitation to friendship with God. It is the Holy Spirit (i.e., the external principle that actualizes the Image of God in us, moving us to know and love God) who moves us from within to respond to Christ's provocation.[24] Through Christ, we are offered salvation as a way to be walked, and through the indwelling of the Holy Spirit, we follow Christ.

The thrust of this christological section has been to show that the Christomonism often read in the *Tertia Pars* is a result of reading only the *Tertia Pars*. In the *Tertia Pars* we see soteriologies stacked up on top of one another. However, when read through the lens of the pneumatological soteriology of *theosis* that emerges from the *Secunda Pars*, we can see that the provocative role of the incarnation grounds Aquinas's christological soteriology of sacrifice. Speaking about

---

[22] S.T. III.49.1.ad4.
[23] Cf. chap. 3.II.2 and 3.IV.
[24] Cf. chap. 2.II.1.

salvation in terms of provoking charity precludes any charge of Christomonism, because charity is always a movement of the Holy Spirit.
The pneumatology that is the foundation for Aquinas's soteriology
must be maintained. As I said in the preceding subsection, even
Aquinas's Christology is rooted in a soteriology of *theosis*. Now we
can see more clearly that Aquinas's christological soteriologies are
rooted in a pneumatological soteriology of *theosis*. Rather than a
christomonistic, static, hierarchical economy of grace production,
Aquinas's soteriology is a deeply trinitarian, dynamic, communal
drama of graced participation.

Further, reading through the lens of a pneumatological soteriology
of *theosis* ensures the inclusion of human cooperation as a starting
point for the ensuing sacramental theology. Rather than a pseudo-
Anselmian flow chart of reified grace cascading down an ecclesial
hierarchy through sacramental channels, we can envision a *communal*
pilgrimage established by Christ and motivated by the Spirit who
moves us to our Final End. According to Aquinas, the passion is a
provocative sign given for the good of the Church. While provocation
is the possibility of *theosis*, Aquinas is clear that we are called *as a
community* to the "new and living way that [Christ] opened for us":
"To be 'a glorious Church not having spot or wrinkle' is the ultimate
end to which we are brought by the Passion of Christ."[25]

II. Sacraments Show the Way

If Christ is the way of salvation, how do we come to follow that
way? As I said in the previous section, for those of us who were not
firsthand witnesses to the sacrificial consummation of Christ's life,
some form of mediation is needed. We need to be told the Good
News. "Since Christ's Passion preceded, as a kind of universal cause
of the forgiveness of sins, it needs to be applied to each individual
for the cleansing of personal sins. Now this is done by baptism and
penance and the other sacraments."[26] As signs that provide knowledge of Christ's salvific life, the sacraments apply the passion to us
in an efficacious manner. Simply put, sacramental signs signify the
unique sacrificial sign of Christ's passion; sacraments are signs of

[25] S.T. III.8.3.ad2.
[26] S.T. III.49.1.ad4.

The Sign. In this section, I will show that, just as Jesus Christ was a provocative sign that invited us into a way of living *ex caritate*, sacramental signification is a means to making Christ present in a manner that seeks to transform us into Christ.

In order to understand how sacramental signification brings about this transformation, I will focus on the relationship between the sacraments and Jesus Christ, as well as the relationship between the sacraments and the Holy Spirit. To that end, I first turn to the following passage in which Aquinas directly addresses both of these relationships:

> As in the person of Christ the humanity causes our salvation by grace, the Divine power being the principal agent, so likewise in the sacraments of the New Law, which are derived from Christ, grace is instrumentally caused by the sacraments, and principally by the power of the Holy Ghost working in the sacraments.[27]

Sacramental grace is caused principally by the power of the Holy Spirit. This is a crucial passage for properly understanding the trinitarian nature of the sacraments. As with Aquinas's christological considerations, his sacramental theology is also rooted in a pneumatological soteriology of *theosis* wherein we are made to participate in the Divine Nature through the indwelling of the Holy Spirit. The way established by Christ is made known to us through the working of the Holy Spirit.

1. Writing the Signs through Religion

Without going into superfluous repetition of the material covered in the first chapter, here I reiterate that a sacrament is a separated instrument that is used by God to sanctify humankind.[28] Put differently:

> The saving power must needs be derived by the sacraments from Christ's Godhead through His humanity. . . . By His Passion [Christ] inaugurated the Rites of the Christian Religion by offer-

[27] S.T. I.II.112.1.ad2.
[28] Cf. chap. 1.III.

ing "Himself—an oblation and a sacrifice to God" (Ephesians 5:2). Wherefore it is manifest that the sacraments of the Church derive their power specially from Christ's Passion, the virtue of which is in a manner united to us by our receiving the sacraments.[29]

To put this in terms of signification, the separate instrument (sacramental signs) works by means of a united instrument (Christ's humanity) that works by means of the efficient cause (God). The sacraments derive their power from Jesus Christ insofar as a sign's power comes from what it signifies. So, when Aquinas says that the sacraments derive their power from the passion of Christ, this derivation should be understood in terms of signification.

The sacraments signify more than the fact of Christ's passion, however. Just as the passion itself was a consummation of a revelatory life, the sacraments work together to provide knowledge of the way that Christ established through his sacrificial life.

> A sacrament properly speaking is that which is ordained to signify our sanctification. In which three things may be considered; viz. the very cause of our sanctification, which is Christ's passion; the form of our sanctification, which is grace and the virtues; and the ultimate end of our sanctification, which is eternal life. And all these are signified by the sacraments. Consequently a sacrament is a sign that is both a reminder of the past, i.e. the passion of Christ; and an indication of that which is effected in us by Christ's passion, i.e. grace; and a prognostic, that is, a foretelling of future glory.[30]

The sacraments sanctify us by giving us provocative knowledge of the cause, form, and end of the spiritual life. Simply put, they show us the way. At the heart of the way is grace and virtue because, as we have seen in our previous chapters, these constitute the spiritual life of the wayfarer. Included in this signification, however, is also the whence and the whither of the way.

We are left, then, with Aquinas saying that the sacraments derive their power from Jesus Christ. But Aquinas also clearly emphasizes

[29] S.T. III.62.5c.
[30] S.T. III.60.3c.

the fact that sacramental grace is caused "principally by the power of the Holy Ghost working in the sacraments."[31] While it is clear that the relationship between Jesus and the sacraments is a matter of signification, it remains to be seen how the power of the Holy Spirit is at work in the sacraments.

Simply put, the Rites of the Christian Religion are carried out through human operations; the sacraments are acts of moral virtue. Specifically, they are acts of the virtue of religion. Because I will return to a more in-depth discussion of the virtue of religion in our final chapter, here I emphasize that religion is a virtue annexed to justice. In other words, it is a virtue of the will whereby we choose to give to God what God is due. Specifically, religion is a virtue concerned with giving God the worship that God is due.[32] But what is the purpose of this worship?

> We employ words, in speaking to God, not indeed to make known our thoughts to Him Who is the searcher of hearts, but that we may bring ourselves and our hearers to reverence Him. Consequently we need to praise God with our lips, not indeed for His sake, but for our own sake; since by praising Him our devotion is aroused [*affectus excitatur*] towards Him, according to Psalm 49:23: "The sacrifice of praise shall glorify Me, and there is the way by which I will show him the salvation of God." And forasmuch as man, by praising God, ascends in his affections to God, by so much is he withdrawn from things opposed to God. . . . The praise of the lips is also profitable to others by inciting their affections [*affectus provocetur*] towards God.[33]

How, then, does this worship provoke our devotion and affection for God? When this worship consists of the sacraments, it provokes us by signifying the cause, form, and end of salvation, that is, the past, present, and future of the spiritual life called "The Way."

Hence, signification is the purpose of sacramental acts of religion. The sacraments are meant to give us knowledge of the causes of our salvation: the virtues being the formal cause. From the previous chapter's discussion of the increase of charity, it should be clear that the

[31] S.T. I.II.112.1.ad2.
[32] Cf. S.T. II.II.81.2-4.
[33] S.T. II.II.91.1c.

moral virtues are not accidental to our salvation. We owe God the fruitful proclamation of his revelation, the virtues being part of that content. Hence, as operations of religion, the sacraments need to communicate the virtues (theological and moral) so that we might come to know our salvation (i.e., the way of the Lord). In signifying the virtues, the sacraments need to signify in a way that allows us to live *ex caritate*. The sacraments provoke our response *and* show us how to respond. The sacraments teach us to walk just as much as they tell us where we are going and whence we've come. A description of *how* the sacraments accomplish this task will be the focus of the following chapter.

With regard to clarifying the role of the Holy Spirit, the point I emphasize here is that sacramental signification is an operation of the perfecting virtues. As acts done *ex caritate*, the sacraments are manifestations of the Spirit given to the Church unto the utility of others.[34] In titling this subsection "Writing the Signs through Religion," I use the term "writing" to imply embodiment of a sign. As an operation of religion (i.e., an operation of perfecting virtue), a sacrament is writing the Word of God with our bodies. So, one way of describing how the sacraments work principally by the power of the Holy Spirit is to say that they are operations of the perfecting virtues, by which we reflect divinity in a provocative manner. As such, the Church embodies the signs of God's love for the world. We write the sacraments through the virtue of religion, because the Holy Spirit writes the sacraments through our cooperation.

2. Reading the Signs through Faith

As signs written through religion and meant to provoke friendship with God, the sacraments need to be read with a mind moved by the Holy Spirit. Put differently, the theological virtues are the proper disposition of a sacramental reader. Because the passion is always applied through faith (even when mediated through the sacraments[35]), the efficacy of the sacraments is primarily a function of the Holy Spirit moving the minds of those who read sacramental signs. As Aquinas says, the operations of religion are done to provoke our

---

[34] Cf. S.T. I.II.111.1c.
[35] S.T. III.48.6.ad2.

devotion and affection and therefore are said to help us in the spiritual life. As was pointed out in the above discussion of the passion and provocation, however, the provocation of our love for God is always made efficacious through the operation of the Holy Spirit. The movement of the theological virtues is the formally effective indwelling of the Holy Spirit who is perpetually actualizing our share in the Image of God.

Hence, we are provided with another way of describing the role of the Holy Spirit in the sacraments: we read the sacraments through faith. By actualizing our image of creation, the Holy Spirit moves us to know and love God through the mediation of sacramental signification. Put differently, through participation in the Divine Nature, the human person is moved to recognize and respond to God's friendship, an invitation that is offered through the Rites of Christian Religion. Hence, when titling this section "Reading the Signs through Faith" my use of "reading" implies influence on the reader. To read the sacraments is to respond to their signification. Put differently, when we are shown the way, we respond by following it.

In our daily lives, we often read texts by simply passing our eyes over the written words. After thirty minutes of reading this way, we suddenly realize that we have retained nothing. Additionally, we can also read with a hermeneutic of suspicion born of a personal bias that closes our minds to the text's influences. But celebrating a sacrament as a subject of charity is like reading a text with a hermeneutic of charity. We allow the text to form us for the better. We are willing to hear the One who longs to speak to us. With sacraments, this means reading in a way that allows the ritual to provoke our charitable response. Reading the sacraments through faith allows us to reflect the divinity that is seen in the sacraments. Our lives become visibly marked by our reading of the sacraments. When the sacraments signify the virtuous form of our salvation, a sacramental reader will seek to adopt that form.

It must be said that signification need not be instantaneously effective in provoking this response. As with all reading, sacramental reading does not need to happen immediately. One of my high school English teachers made his students memorize poetry. When I memorized and recited these poems, I became a writer who embodied these texts, but I would often come to realize the meaning of these stanzas years later. It took me a long time to become a reader whose life was influenced by the words I was writing. Delayed reading is not less meaningful. This sense of reading is the foundation for properly understanding *ex opere operato* in terms of signification. *Ex opere operato* need not be envisioned as denoting an instantaneous mechanism. The more we write the sacraments the more we are disposed to read them. When we develop patterns of religious actions, we are disposing ourselves to an actual increase in the faithful charity whereby we are sacramental readers who reflect divinity. Simply put, reading is a gratuitous gift.

The biggest problem with sacramental theologies based on *ex opere operato* is our inability, as Pierre Teilhard de Chardin put it, to trust in the slow work of God. Almost all appeals to this iteration of sacramental efficacy are rooted in our desire for instantaneous mechanisms of control, not just of God, but of those who are sanctified.[36] Preoccupation with fidelity to rubrics and sacramental validity is often indicative of wanting to remove the cooperation of the one who is sanctified. Even if we cooperate in the sanctification of others by writing the sacraments, this does not remove the need for their cooperation in reading the sacraments. This is why the Christian tradition has a rich history of mystagogical catechesis. Beginning with the Gospel of John's Bread of Life Discourse and extending throughout Christian tradition, disciples of Christ have needed and received help in reflecting on their experiences of the sacraments so that those experiences might bear fruit in their lives. To borrow the terminology of Louis-Marie Chauvet, we must be patient and let the Holy Spirit verify sacramental grace with our lives. We must trust in the slow work of God. Mysteries are gradually discovered. Love is patiently made. In light of the fact that the efficacy of Christ's passion is applied through faith, the sacraments work principally through the power of the Holy Spirit because it is through the Spirit that the signs are made effective in our lives.

---

[36] Cf. Bruce Morrill, "Sign of Reconciliation and Conversion? Differing Views of Power—Ecclesial, Sacramental, Anthropological—among Hierarchy and Laity," *Theological Studies* 75 (September 2014): 585–612. Here, Morrill provides careful consideration of how disciplinary use of power determines the manner in which sacramental efficacy is imagined.

3. Graced Cooperation

The Holy Spirit's power is at work in the sacraments in two ways. First, as operations of religion, the sacraments are manifestations of the Spirit's work in the life of the Church. As such, the Church reflects divinity to the world. All sacramental celebrations are a gift from the Spirit who moves us. Second, as signs of our salvation, the sacraments provoke the movement of the virtues within us. They move us to better reflect divinity by moving us on the way established by Christ. In my own words, the Holy Spirit allows us to be sacramental writers and sacramental readers. So, we can say that, for Aquinas, the sacraments derive their power from the passion insofar as a sign's power comes from what it signifies. On the other hand, the sacraments derive their power from the Spirit insofar as the Church is moved by the Spirit to both write and read the sacraments. Hence, the pneumatological soteriology of *theosis* grounds this sacramental theology of provocative signification.

The sacraments show the way in a provocative manner. Through operations of religion we embody (i.e., write) God's invitation to friendship that was offered once and for all in Jesus Christ. This is all accomplished through the Holy Spirit; just as any subsequent reading (i.e., operations done *ex caritate*) is also done through the Spirit. Hence, as I said in the second chapter, grace begins with human action (the historically mediated proclamation of revelation) and culminates in human action (the active participation that constitutes the embodied spiritual life). Simultaneously, grace begins with divine action (the self-communication of God) and culminates in divine action (the operation of the Holy Spirit within us).[37]

As we saw in chapter 4, grace can be described as sanctifying (*gratia gratum faciens*) and non-sanctifying (*gratia gratis data*).[38] The former is grace that makes an individual pleasing to God, effecting the personal sanctification of that individual. The latter is grace whereby people cooperate in the sanctification of others. Similarly, the participation in the Divine Nature that is the celebration of the sacraments can also be described simultaneously in these two ways. Hence, sacraments are simultaneously two types of grace. As sacramental

---

[37] Cf. chap. 2.IV.
[38] Cf. chap. 4.II.3.

readers, we are sanctified by the sacraments and are moved to love God more deeply. Hence, the sacraments bring about our salvation and are rightly said to cause sanctifying grace (*gratia gratum faciens*). On the other hand, by embodying the sacraments through operations of religion, the Church is cooperating in the salvation of others. As sacramental writers, we help to move others to friendship with God. As such, sacraments are non-sanctifying grace (*gratia gratis data*). We are called *to* the sacraments so that we might continue to be called *through* the sacraments. We write so that we might read, and we read so that we might write. Both reading and writing the sacraments are the cooperation that manifests our participation in the Divine Nature. We go toward the sacraments to write them with our bodies (to glorify God by proclaiming the Good News), and we come from the sacraments reading them with our lives (to glorify God by living the Good News). God's use of instruments is always cooperative. The grace that causes the spiritual life is salvation history and not an intervention into it.[39]

Sacramental signification, then, is a means to making Christ present in a manner that seeks to transform us into Christ. All the sacraments work together to show us the way who is Christ. To say that we, as a Church, are called to follow Christ is to say that we are called to become Christ. As we will see in the next section, nowhere is this goal more evident than in the celebration of the Eucharist. However, just as the virtues (theological and moral) cannot be isolated, so the sacraments all depend on one another to serve one eucharistic grace. Insofar as they signify our salvation, all the sacraments are about making the Church sinless.[40] Put differently, sacraments form a community that reflects divinity.

> The Church's sacraments are ordained for helping man in the spiritual life. But the spiritual life is analogous to the corporeal, since corporeal things bear a resemblance to spiritual. Now it is clear that just as generation is required for corporeal life, since

[39] Cf. chap. 2.I.1: "The *Tertia Pars* can be called a description of the *reditus* in terms of salvation history. As christologically founded, the *Tertia pars* is still a consideration of particular human action. The actions of Christ, even if they are divine instruments, are human actions. Likewise, the sacraments, even if they are divine instruments, are human actions."

[40] Cf. S.T. III.8.3.ad2.

thereby man receives life; and growth, whereby man is brought to maturity: so likewise food is required for the preservation of life. Consequently, just as for the spiritual life there had to be Baptism, which is spiritual generation; and Confirmation, which is spiritual growth: so there needed to be the sacrament of the Eucharist, which is spiritual food.[41]

For Aquinas, the sacraments are about beginning and sustaining a communal journey.

III. Eucharist as Nourishment for the Way

In the first chapter of this book, I rehearsed Louis-Marie Chauvet's critique of Aquinas's eucharistic theology.[42] In short, Chauvet (following the thought of Henri de Lubac) highlights Aquinas's tendency toward "a deadly dichotomy" wherein the relationship between the eucharistic body of Christ and the ecclesial body of Christ is obfuscated. This dichotomy is the result of an overemphasis on the relationship between the eucharistic body of Christ and the historical body of Christ. By spending so much time constructing a theory of transubstantiation and limiting his focus to the moment of consecration, Aquinas provides a eucharistic theology that seems to ignore the role of the Church in the celebration of the Eucharist.

The main focus of this section will be to present Aquinas's eucharistic theology in a way that, while affirming these critiques, simultaneously highlights Aquinas's concern for the relationship between the Eucharist and the spiritual life of the Church. Simply put, this section will show that, in Aquinas's sacramental theology, the Eucharist exists to serve the unity of the ecclesial body of Christ. Specifically, it does this by making Christ present through signs that provide knowledge of what it means to live as a unified body of Christ. In the final chapter, I will provide a more sustained consideration of *how* the celebration of the Eucharist relates to the Church. Here, *I am concerned solely with clearly establishing the fact that "being for the Church" is essential to the definition of the Eucharist.*

---

[41] S.T. III.73.1c.
[42] Cf. chap. 1.I.

1. Writing Christ through the Eucharist

In the first chapter, I emphasized the fact that all the sacraments have a *sacramentum tantum*, a *res et sacramentum*, and a *res tantum*.[43] According to Aquinas, the reality of the sacrament (i.e., the *res tantum*) is its grace, while the signs (i.e., the *sacramentum tantum* and the *res et sacramentum*) exist to cause that reality. As a sign, the Eucharist is charged with signifying our sanctification (i.e., the passion, the perfecting virtues, and eternal life) so as to bring about the sacramental grace that is our sanctification (the unity of the ecclesial body of Christ). In order to examine how eucharistic sacramental signification provokes the unity of the ecclesial body, I return to the first article of question 79 in the *Tertia Pars*. In this article, we see Aquinas list the various eucharistic signs that signify the causes of the Church's unity. Because the Eucharist (1) contains Christ, (2) represents the passion, and (3) is given through food that is (4) a single whole made from many parts, this sacrament provocatively shows the causes of our salvation so that we might be united as an ecclesial body.

In this article, Aquinas shows us that the various signs that make up the moment of consecration *work together* to bring about the grace to which the sacrament is ordained. The unity of the ecclesial body is a result, not solely of the substance of Christ's body and blood, but of the signs through which this sacrament is embodied. Put simply, the Eucharist is made up of signs that rely on one another. I will return more forcefully to this point in the following chapter. For now, I will address Chauvet's criticism regarding Aquinas's claim that the Eucharist is complete at consecration.[44] Here, it will be helpful to quote Aquinas at length:

> A thing is one in perfection, when it is complete through the presence of all that is needed for its end; as a man is complete by having all the members required for the operation of his soul, and a house by having all the parts needful for dwelling therein. And so this sacrament is said to be one. Because it is ordained for spiritual refreshment, which is conformed to corporeal refreshment. Now there are two things required for corporeal refreshment, namely, food, which is dry sustenance, and drink,

---

[43] Cf. chap. 1.4.
[44] Cf. S.T. III.73.1.ad3 and III.80.12.ad2.

which is wet sustenance. Consequently, two things concur for the integrity of this sacrament, to wit, spiritual food and spiritual drink, according to John: "My flesh is meat indeed, and My blood is drink indeed." Therefore, this sacrament is materially many, but formally and perfectively one.[45]

When speaking about the completion of the Eucharist, Aquinas chooses the language of nourishment in order to express what is necessary for the sacrament's completion. Put differently, the eucharistic body of Christ (i.e., the *res et sacramentum*) derives (at least in part) its completion from the bread and wine in which it is given (i.e., the *sacramentum tantum*). In order for the eucharistic body of Christ to be received as spiritual nourishment, it is given through food and drink. The completion of a sign is a function of its ability to fruitfully provide the knowledge it is ordained to provide. While the eucharistic body of Christ is the spiritual nourishment that unites the Church, it is only known as such because of the other eucharistic signs that provide its context (i.e., the bread and wine, the words of consecration, etc.). Hence, in the Eucharist, Jesus Christ is present as spiritual nourishment through the various signs that rely on one another to bring the Church to knowledge of the One who is the cause of our salvation.

All this is to say that one cannot isolate the eucharistic body of Christ without undoing its completion. Hence, even when we minimize the bread, remove the wine, place the consecrated host in a bejeweled monstrance, and place that monstrance in a room far away from the eucharistic table, the other eucharistic signs (regardless of how much we try to minimize and ignore them) always remain the necessary conditions for that eucharistic body accomplishing its sanctifying purpose. Without knowledge of the external actions of religion that embody the celebration of the Eucharist, one has no eucharistic body to adore. Every consecrated host bears the marks of the signs that surround it, and by those marks that host means something.[46]

---

[45] S.T. III.73.2c.

[46] It must be said that, in a largely self-defeating choice, Aquinas unnecessarily limits the actions of religion that he considers in his treatment of the Eucharist. In other words, Chauvet's critique is quite accurate. By focusing so narrowly on the moment of consecration (the dominical words, the minister, the bread and the wine), he ignores other religious actions that write the presence of Christ. Specifically, he

A meal that has been grown in a family garden and prepared with much care over the course of an entire day is able to nourish more than just the body that eats it; such a meal signifies the love that provides a family with its identity. If you bracket that meal, though, providing no knowledge of its sources, its nourishing power is reduced to the metabolic. Similarly, the celebration of the Eucharist causes grace because, through all its signs, it writes the eucharistic body of Christ that is made present as the nourishment who strengthens us to live as Christ lived. In the eucharistic body of Christ, we see the cause, form, and end of our salvation. We see Christ who lived, died, and was raised. As such (i.e., as Christ), it is the sacramental sign *par excellence*.

The eucharistic body of Christ, then, is not the result of a moment in time. It is the result of human cooperation with the Holy Spirit whereby we, through operations of religion, embody those signs that write the provocative presence of Christ. Writing the eucharistic body of Christ is a moral action carried out by the Church. As such, we celebrate the Eucharist as subjects of charity insofar as, out of and in service to our friendship with God, we embody the eucharistic signs that make Christ present. In the following chapter, I will return to a more in-depth consideration of the moral quality of embodying eucharistic signs. For now, it will suffice to reiterate that, insofar as the eucharistic body of Christ is complete as spiritual nourishment, it takes the religious operation of the Church to embody the eucharistic signs that write the presence of Christ *as spiritual nourishment*. Given the written presence of the eucharistic body of Christ, however, there is still the matter of how it nourishes the Church.

2. Spiritually Eating through Faith

While in the previous subsection I was concerned with the eucharistic signs that exist to provoke the unity of the ecclesial body of Christ, here I am shifting my attention to *how* those signs are made effective. Specifically, I will examine what it means to spiritually eat

---

ignores those actions that relate the eucharistic body of Christ to the celebrating community that manifests the ecclesial body of Christ, most notably the rite of communion. I will return to a consideration of this limitation later on in this chapter and in great length in the following chapter.

124 Speaking with Aquinas

the Eucharist. If the Church writes Christ through eucharistic signs, then it eats Christ by believing through those signs. The eucharistic body of Christ is written as a provocative sign that nourishes us for living out our response. In the previous section, I used the metaphor "reading" to speak about celebrating the sacraments in a way that invites their influence. When applied to the Eucharist, "reading" is better understood as "eating." Employing the term "spiritual eating" is the result of using a grammar that describes the Eucharist as food. Simply put, to read a nourishing sign is to eat food. What, then, is spiritual eating?

In an article titled "Whether the Eucharist Is Necessary for Salvation?" Aquinas sums up in six words what is, for him, at the heart of the Eucharist: "Spiritual food changes man into itself."[47] This intrinsic relationship between the eucharistic body of Christ and the ecclesial body becomes evident in the distinction Aquinas makes between spiritual eating and sacramental eating: "As the perfect is divided against the imperfect, so sacramental eating, whereby the sacrament only is received without its effect, is divided against spiritual eating, by which one receives the effect of this sacrament, whereby a man is spiritually united with Christ through faith and charity."[48] As with the other sacraments, the Eucharist is made effective through faith that is formed by charity. Hence, there is nothing metabolic about spiritually eating the Eucharist. Put differently, the theological virtues are prerequisite for spiritually eating the Eucharist.

To use the language of our previous section, the theological virtues are the proper disposition of a eucharistic eater. If "baptism by desire" is the terminology we use to refer to the justifying action of the Holy Spirit in the mind of someone who has yet to be sacramentally baptized,[49] then "spiritual eating" is the term we use to refer to the sanctifying action of the Holy Spirit in the mind of someone who has yet to sacramentally eat the Eucharist. Spiritually eating the Eucharist is accomplished by only those who are justified (i.e., those who have been generated as subjects of the theological virtues), because spiritual eating is dependent on the prior movement of the theological virtues. The Eucharist does not infuse charity. Rather, it presupposes the presence of charity. Hence, we must say that eating the Eucharist

---

[47] S.T. III.73.3.ad2.
[48] S.T. III.80.1c.
[49] Cf. S.T. III.68.2.

is a gift of the Holy Spirit's movement within us. Put differently, spiritually eating of the Eucharist is the union of charity seeking deeper union. The friends of God come to the Eucharist so that through this meal they might grow in friendship.

Because sacraments are applied through the theological virtues, there is no *need* for sacramental eating.[50] For Aquinas, this spiritual eating whereby the Eucharist is received as effective spiritual nourishment does not require physically eating or drinking the eucharistic species (i.e., the *sacramentum tantum*). Rather, he says that "the effect of the sacrament can be secured by every man if he receives it in desire though not in reality."[51] Spiritual eating is a matter of the Holy Spirit moving us to respond to the provocative presence of Christ. Within the eucharistic theology of Aquinas, anyone who is a subject of charity is capable of eating the Eucharist. Put provocatively, there is no discipline (e.g., exclusion, excommunication, age restrictions, etc.) that can come between Christ and the one who loves him.[52]

This distinction between spiritual eating through faith and sacramental eating with one's mouth allows us to return again to Chauvet's criticism. Aquinas clearly says that the Church's use of the sacrament (i.e., sacramental eating) is not necessary for the completion of the Eucharist.[53] Rather, as I pointed out above, for Aquinas, the Eucharist is completed when all the signs necessary for effecting grace are present.[54] When Aquinas says that the Eucharist is complete at consecration, he is saying that you do not need to eat with your mouth.[55] The consecration of the bread and wine is the completion of the Eucharist not because the eucharistic body of Christ has come into *existence* but because the object of the theological virtues is now *present* to the subjects of charity as their spiritual nourishment.

---

[50] Aquinas is clear, however, that sacramental eating serves a purpose. I will return to this point in the next chapter.

[51] S.T. III.80.1.ad3.

[52] Aquinas's acute awareness of the distinction between spiritual eating and sacramental eating leads him to say that "the non-baptized are not to be allowed even to see this sacrament." Cf. S.T. III.80.4.ad4.

[53] S.T. III.80.12.ad2.

[54] Cf. S.T. III.73.2c.

[55] To be clear, Aquinas clearly states that actually receiving the consecrated species is preferable. Cf. S.T. III.80.1.ad3. I will return to the relationship between sacramental eating and spiritual eating in the following chapter. For now, I wish to emphasize the fact that sacramental eating is not necessary for the perfection of the sacrament. Again, this puts an emphasis on the role of faith.

Bearing Aquinas's definition of perfection in mind, as well as his description of spiritually eating by faith through signs, I would argue that Aquinas's location of the completion of the sacrament is actually indicative of his desire to avoid a eucharistic body of Christ that is simply an *esse* to be possessed. One cannot spiritually eat of the Eucharist by virtue of the substantial existence of Christ. Rather, for Aquinas, the presence of Christ is an *adesse* grasped only through faith. In short, by saying that the Eucharist is completed through the presence of all the eucharistic signs necessary to know Christ as spiritual nourishment, Aquinas has completed the sacrament at the moment when Christ becomes present for the living faith of the Church. Neither the possession of Christ (i.e., the sacramental eating in which we literally hold on to the substance of Christ) nor the nourishment through Christ (i.e., the spiritual eating through which we are provoked by the presence of Christ) is intrinsic to a complete Eucharist.

So, it is possible to defend Aquinas from Chauvet's critique: the eucharistic body of Christ is described as spiritual nourishment that is present to those who need nourishment. Clearly, the life of the Church is foundational to Aquinas's eucharistic theology. Nevertheless, we must also affirm Chauvet's critique, but on the grounds of Aquinas's own sacramental theology. For Aquinas, the Eucharist is complete at consecration because the spiritual nourishment of the Church is present. But Aquinas also clearly states that "grace is . . . principally [caused] by the power of the Holy Ghost working in the sacraments."[56] Spiritual eating is the work of the Holy Spirit in the community that reads the eucharistic presence of Christ. So, on the one hand, the Eucharist is completed when the Church's nourishment is present. But, on the other hand, the Eucharist is complete before the community is actually nourished. In short, Aquinas's definition of a complete Eucharist excludes eucharistic grace.[57] While this phrasing may cause some eyebrows to raise, this is much less problematic in light of what has already been said about reading the sacraments.[58] A written sign does not need to be read immediately to be effective. Put in terms of nourishment, it takes time to digest what has been eaten.

---

[56] S.T. I.II.112.1.ad2.
[57] Cf. S.T. III.73.1.ad3.
[58] Cf. chap. 5.II.2.

In the eucharistic theology I have just rehearsed, Aquinas is self-defeating in two main ways. First, Aquinas is working against himself by overemphasizing the distinction between spiritual and sacramental eating. As can be seen from the preceding presentation of spiritual eating, the result is a description of eucharistic efficacy that is overly individualistic. While Aquinas succeeds in emphasizing the role of the theological virtues (and therefore the agency of the Holy Spirit) in the one who is nourished by the Eucharist, he also ends up presenting spiritual eating as the action of an individual Christian and not of a dining community. The following chapter will address this individualism. My purpose in rehearsing this problematic presentation of spiritual eating has been, however, to show that Aquinas's emphasis on the role of faith highlights the pneumatological foundations of his eucharistic theology. Could Aquinas have better integrated his pneumatological soteriology of *theosis* and his eucharistic theology in a way that better addresses the ecclesial nature of the Eucharist? Certainly. Does Aquinas fail to address the role of the Holy Spirit in his eucharistic theology in a way that completely forgets the ecclesial nature of the Eucharist? Certainly not.

Second, in limiting himself to considerations of the moment of consecration, Aquinas is obfuscating his claim that sacramental signs work together to write a provocative presence of Christ. Chauvet is correct to note that Aquinas impoverishes his eucharistic theology (and those theologies that have followed his lead for many years) by excluding a consideration of the other rites that surround the moment of consecration. The more we limit the rites that write Christ, the less faith has to read. Hence, ignoring the proclamation of Scripture, the recitation of the Lord's Prayer, the communion rite, or the kiss of peace is to ignore aspects of the Eucharist that write the eucharistic presence of Christ as the provocative object of faith that nourishes our charity. Without denying his tendency toward self-defeat, however, the main point of this chapter is that Aquinas has not removed the Church from his eucharistic theology. Could his eucharistic theology have been better formed to address the relationship between the eucharistic body and the ecclesial body? Certainly. Does Aquinas fail to address the relationship between the eucharistic body and the ecclesial body? Certainly not. As I stated at the beginning of this section: Here, *I am concerned solely with clearly establishing the fact that "being for the Church" is essential to Aquinas's description of the Eucharist.*

Taking these tendencies toward self-defeat as its starting point, the following chapter will be a constructive effort. There, I will gesture toward how Aquinas might have better integrated his grammars of grace and virtue with his sacramental theology. The result will be a liturgical theology that seeks to emphasize the provocative nature of sacramental signification and its influence on the embodied spiritual life.

Throughout this section, I have tried to show how the pneumatological soteriology of *theosis* undergirds Aquinas's eucharistic theology. Just as the passion of Christ is the cause of our justification by virtue of provoking the movement of our charity, so the eucharistic presence of Christ is there to provoke the movement of our charity. The essence of spiritual nourishment is not flesh and blood but Christ's sacrifice of charity that excites our charity. Jesus' flesh and blood did not reveal God. Rather, God was revealed in the way in which Jesus' flesh and blood perfectly embodied charity.[59] Spiritual nourishment exists to form the eater into itself. Hence, in the Eucharist, perfect charity turns imperfect charity into itself. Our liturgies need to be events where the perfect charity of Christ is communicated to our faith as the promise of God's love in which we are called to participate.[60] As spiritual nourishment, the Eucharist exists to form the Church into Christ. Insofar as we read the written Christ in a way that helps us conform to Christ, we come to reflect divinity more perfectly. As such, eucharistic grace is the communal moral reality of the Church virtuously living the embodied spiritual life. *My* union

---

[59] It is important to bear this distinction in mind when constructing theologies of the ministerial priesthood. Human persons are able to act *in persona Christi* insofar as they have the type of body capable of embodying sacrifices of charity. Hence, we would want to restrict the ministerial priesthood to human beings who are of an age that they are capable of using their body to operate *ex caritate*. However, it would make little sense to restrict the ministerial priesthood to those sharing the bodily accidents of Christ. For example, if we were to restrict the ministerial priesthood to men of Jewish descent who were under the age of thirty-three, such restrictions would misunderstand the revelatory purpose of Jesus' human nature, choosing to fixate on the flesh rather than the charity it embodies.

[60] Again, Aquinas's narrow focus on the moment of consecration limits the liturgical event's ability to communicate Christ's charity. In the following chapter, I will argue that the more we pay attention to the particular shape of the various rites in our event-full liturgies, the better we are able to be nourished by the provocative charity of Christ.

with Christ (i.e., spiritually eating the eucharistic body of Christ) is inseparable from and ordered toward the *Church's* unity *as* Christ (i.e., the unity of the ecclesial body of Christ).

3. *The Unity of the Church: The Fellowship of Sinful Saints*

In treating the degrees of charity, Aquinas says, "For at first it is incumbent on man to occupy himself chiefly with avoiding sin and resisting his concupiscences, which move him in opposition to charity: this concerns beginners, in whom charity has to be fed or fostered lest it be destroyed [*corrumpatur*]."[61] Feeding and fostering charity is a crucial task the Church carries out in every celebration of the Eucharist. Speaking of the Eucharist as spiritual nourishment that serves the unity of the Church implies that the Church needs nourishment. The experience of being a beginner in charity is the experience of being a sinner, of being disordered. Because we are all regularly beginners in charity, we need spiritual food to nourish our development (i.e., to sanctify us). Provocatively put, without the presence of sinners, the Eucharist has no occasion or purpose.

It is important to begin a consideration of eucharistic grace with a consideration of sin because this helps reiterate the fact that the Eucharist is nourishment for a difficult journey and not the reward at the journey's end. Indeed, the pilgrims who most struggle (i.e., we who are beginners in charity) most need to be nourished. Bearing this in mind, we can describe the unity of the ecclesial body in terms of sin. As a community that embodies charity through operations of the perfecting virtues, the Church's life is a participation in the Divine Nature that reflects divinity onto the world.[62] Insofar as that reflection is imperfect, however, we are a sinful Church. We regularly fail in our mission to reflect divinity. While Christ provides us with the way of living in divine friendship, we do not always follow. The more sinful the Church, the less it is united as Christ, and the less it embodies Christ. Hence, Aquinas is clear that the Eucharist always serves a unity that is imperfect.[63] When he says that the unity of the ecclesial

---

[61] S.T. II.II.24.9c.
[62] Cf. chap. 4.II.3.
[63] S.T. III.79.2c.

body of Christ is the fellowship of the saints,[64] this is not meant to imply a sinless community. In this life, all human members of this *societas sanctorum* are wayfarers.

The fact that the Eucharist is for a sinful Church confronts us with the fact that the Eucharist calls us to a deeper, embodied union with God. The Church always needs to perfect its discipleship. The Eucharist serves the unity of the ecclesial body of Christ by transforming the Church into a community that embodies charity the way that Christ embodied charity. The unity of the ecclesial body, then, is an embodied reality lived out through the virtues. The more we reflect Christ through our discipleship, the more we are a united ecclesial body. Being nourished by the Eucharist (i.e., becoming the Christ we eat) is a matter of ordering ourselves to better reflect divinity. Hence, we consume nourishment that shows us who we are called to be. If the unity of the ecclesial body of Christ is a community of disciples striving to reflect divinity, then the manifestation of eucharistic grace is the fruition of Christ's life: "To be 'a glorious Church not having spot or wrinkle' is the ultimate end to which we are brought by the Passion of Christ."[65]

Recalling that Aquinas speaks of grace as an external principle of human action, we must emphasize that the unity of the ecclesial body of Christ is itself an external principle of human action insofar as the Church's moral life is a participation in the Divine Nature that reflects divinity onto the world. As we saw in the fourth chapter, the life of the Church is the gratuitous grace (*gratia gratis data*) whereby we cooperate in the justification of others.[66] Hence, saying that the unity of the ecclesial body of Christ is constituted by its ability to be a salvific sacrament to the world is tantamount to saying that the unity of the ecclesial body of Christ is the grace of God. As the life of this united community, eucharistic grace is virtuously living the spiritual life.

While the Eucharist is ordered toward the spiritual life of the Church, the celebration of the Eucharist is also part of that spiritual life. Insofar as celebrating the Eucharist is a communal act of religion, the Eucharist is a manifestation of eucharistic grace. Put differently,

---

[64] S.T. III.80.4c.
[65] S.T. III.8.3.ad2.
[66] Cf. chap. 4.II.3.

writing Christ through the Eucharist causes grace *ex opere operato*. When the ecclesial body of Christ, through the movement of the Holy Spirit, writes the eucharistic body of Christ, the unity of that ecclesial body is performed. As such, writing the Eucharist is a participation in the Divine Nature. However, when the ecclesial body of Christ, through the movement of the Holy Spirit, reads the eucharistic body of Christ by becoming Christ more fully, the unity of the ecclesial body is performed through the spiritual life that manifests the *koinonia* of a community.

As operations of religion, the eucharistic signs through which we write Christ are the work of the Holy Spirit who incarnates Christ *through* the flesh of the Church so that Christ might be more perfectly incarnate *in* the flesh of the Church. By the power of the Holy Spirit, Christ is born of human cooperation. This birth, as with the Virgin Birth, is not an end in itself. It is wrought for a purpose: that we might follow the way set forth by Christ and, by following, be divinized. Therefore, we need the Holy Spirit to help us write and eat of this spiritual food that transforms us into Christ, the One who was perfectly full of grace.[67] Hence, as a community we assemble, "not neglecting to meet together," so that we might "consider how to provoke one another to love and good deeds" (Heb 10:24-25). "Encouraging one another" through the celebration of the Eucharist, we become the One who is nourishment for the way he established with his life.

In the opening section of the first chapter, I pointed out that Chauvet's critiques of the "deadly dichotomy" can be summarized as lamentations of a loss of a loss.[68] Based on the preceding exposition of Aquinas's sacramental theology, however, one might claim that, for Aquinas, the substantial presence of Christ in the Eucharist is not the abolition of the absence of Christ. To be sure, Aquinas goes to great lengths to point out that Christ (his body, his soul, and the Godhead) is truly present as the result of the eucharistic signs. When understood through the lens of a pneumatological soteriology of *theosis* wherein the Eucharist is a sacramental sign meant to nourish our spiritual life and move us toward our Final End, however, then the Eucharist cannot be said to destroy the loss of Christ brought about by the ascension. Rather, within Aquinas's sacramental

[67] S.T. III.26.2.ad1.
[68] Cf. chap. 1.I.

theology, we celebrate the Eucharist because Christ is the absent end to which we are ordained. The Eucharist does not overcome Christ's absence; it overcomes our inability to grow continually closer to the Final End who is revealed in Christ. So, while Chauvet laments the loss of the loss of Christ so frequently found in preoccupation with the substantial presence of Christ in the Eucharist, he finds a fellow mourner in Aquinas. In Aquinas's sacramental theology, the Eucharist is a celebration of the loss of Christ's historical body insofar as the Eucharist is a celebration of Christ's ecclesial body. Far from being a distraction from ecclesial identity, the Eucharist is a provocative sign that confronts the Church with a responsibility to live as Christ for the world.

The Eucharist's role in the embodied spiritual life is to serve the historical and bodily life of the Church. As was pointed out in the first chapter, by identifying eucharistic grace with the unity of the ecclesial body of Christ, Aquinas has made the spiritual life of the Church the purpose of the Eucharist.[69] In fact, the Eucharist cannot exist without prior eucharistic grace. As an operation of religion, the Eucharist is a result of the unity of the ecclesial body of Christ. Not only is the Eucharist *for* the Church, it is also clearly *of* the Church. From the religious actions that mediate God's revelation, to our response through the operations done *ex caritate*, the Eucharist is essentially bound to the embodied spiritual life. The Eucharist serves the spiritual life by deepening our participation in the Divine Nature that is nothing other than the Holy Spirit's effective life in our lives. Thus, the eucharistic theology found in the *Tertia Pars* is intimately connected to Aquinas's concerns regarding the life of the Church. To use the terminology of our retrieved grammars, Aquinas presents the Eucharist as an integral part of the embodied spiritual life insofar as the Eucharist affects the Church's participation in the Divine Nature by increasing the Church's unity.

[69] Cf. chap. 1.V.

CHAPTER SIX

A Liturgical Theology of Right Religion

When you come together, each one has a hymn, a lesson, a revelation, a tongue, or an interpretation. Let all things be done for building up.

—1 Corinthians 14:26

The *Tertia Pars* contains sacramental theology that is grounded in Aquinas's concern for the spiritual life of the Church. But the *Tertia Pars* also contains theology that tends to work against the pneumatological soteriology of *theosis* that Aquinas presents in the *Secunda Pars*, using his grammars of grace and virtue. As was mentioned in the previous chapter, the *Tertia Pars* is marked by an individualism and sacramental minimalism that ought not be ignored. The purpose of this final chapter is to use the retrieved grammars of grace and virtue to construct a liturgical theology of right religion that avoids these shortcomings, more fully integrating Aquinas's grammars of grace and virtue into a sacramental theology.

I. A Self-Defeating Tendency

The reason for constructing this liturgical theology of right religion is Aquinas's failure to adequately integrate the *Secunda Pars*'s grammars of grace and virtue with the *Tertia Pars*'s sacramental theology. In the previous chapter, I mentioned that Aquinas has a self-defeating tendency toward individualism and narrowly focuses on the signs he deems essential to the sacraments (i.e., sacramental minimalism).

In this section, I will briefly reflect on these shortcomings that are the occasion for constructing a liturgical theology of right religion.

In the first chapter, I pointed out that Aquinas emphasizes the essential sense of the words used during the celebration of a sacrament. He writes:

> A sacrament may be considered on the part of the sacramental signification. Now Augustine says that "words are the principal signs used by men"; because words can be formed in various ways for the purpose of signifying various mental concepts, so that we are able to express our thoughts with greater distinctness by means of words. And therefore in order to ensure the perfection of sacramental signification it was necessary to determine the signification of the sensible things by means of certain words. For water may signify both a cleansing by reason of its humidity, and refreshment by reason of its being cool: but when we say, "I baptize thee," it is clear that we use water in baptism in order to signify a spiritual cleansing.[1]

In this passage, Aquinas elucidates the relationship between verbal and nonverbal signs. Specifically, words determine the significance of the nonverbal signs by adding greater distinctness to the concepts that are meant to be expressed by the sacrament. If the sacraments exist to communicate provocative knowledge, then words are the most effective aspect of sacramental communication, because they ensure clarity in communication.

Further, Aquinas's preference for words seems to come from an idealized notion of how they function. Throughout question 60, Aquinas turns to considerations of the various ways the words of a sacrament might be spoken. In explaining the efficacy of these words, he appeals to the "essential sense" (*debitus sensus*) that is expressed when a word is used.

> As Augustine says, the word operates in the sacraments "not because it is spoken," i.e. not by the outward sound of the voice, "but because it is believed" in accordance with the sense of the words which is held by faith. And this sense is indeed the same for all, though the same words as to their sound be not used by

---

[1] S.T. III.60.6c.

all. Consequently no matter in what language this sense is expressed, the sacrament is complete.[2]

Without entering into a prolonged discussion of what we might call Aquinas's theories of language and epistemology, I simply point out that, for Aquinas, words are employed to communicate mental concepts.[3] These mental concepts can remain unchanged, however, despite variation in the language used to communicate the essential sense. Put differently, words are used to express mental concepts that are prior to the use of the words. Hence, due to the immutability of a sacrament's essential sense, a baptism celebrated in Latin in the year 1280 accomplishes the same result as a baptism celebrated in Greek in the year 280.

Here, Aquinas appears to misunderstand language on two points. First, his emphasis on words underestimates the efficacy of nonverbal signs, specifically in their ability to help determine the significance of verbal signs. For Aquinas, words are charged with providing clarity to the significance of a sacrament, whereas the significance of nonverbal signs is passively determined by the words.[4] Second, by upholding the immutable "essential sense" of a word, Aquinas fails to acknowledge the relational nature of signs. The notion that there is a universal essential sense undergirding every formulation of a sacrament's form fails to acknowledge the reciprocally formal relationship of language and mental concept (i.e., of sign and signified). Put differently, Aquinas fails to acknowledge the importance of a sign's context.

While Aquinas's sacramental minimalism is clearly influenced by medieval liturgy as he knew it, as well as by the tendency toward reduction that marks the genre of the *Summa Theologiae*, I argue that his preoccupation with words also bears responsibility for limiting the range of data he considers when constructing his sacramental theology. As I pointed out in the previous chapter, in his consideration of the Eucharist, Aquinas's treatment of nonverbal signs is largely limited to those signs immediately related to the dominical words of consecration. Hence, bread, wine, and the minister all receive

[2] S.T. III.60.7.ad1.
[3] S.T. I.85.2.ad3.
[4] Cf. S.T. III.60.7c.

extensive consideration that pertains largely to their relationship to the words of consecration. One might speculate that if Aquinas had a more robust understanding of signification, he would be more likely to include the other aspects of eucharistic celebrations in his considerations. For example, rather than focusing narrowly on the dominical words of consecration, he might offer a more prolonged treatment of the entirety of the eucharistic prayer.

For the remainder of this chapter I use the term "liturgical theology" to denote a tendency toward sacramental *maximalism* that is preoccupied with all aspects of ritual action. This is juxtaposed to Aquinas's sacramental minimalism wherein he tends to reduce his considerations to what is deemed essential to the sacrament. To be clear, Aquinas's sacramental *minimalism* does not mean that he sees no value in what is nonessential. On the contrary, Aquinas has what one might call liturgical instincts. By "liturgical instincts" I mean that Aquinas acknowledges the significance of those religious operations that he would not consider necessary for the completion of the sacrament. Despite his emphasis on words, he clearly has a tendency toward a liturgical theology that has a place for nonverbal signs.

For example, when treating the external acts of religion, Aquinas considers the usefulness of music and chanting. Here, he uses a telling phrase: "It is evident that the human soul is moved in various ways according to various melodies of sound. . . . Hence the use of music in divine praises is a salutary institution."[5] As we saw in chapters 2 and 3, Aquinas emphasizes the mediation of revelation through words (i.e., the symbol of faith) when he discusses the mind's movement toward the Final End by means of knowing and loving God. In this treatment of music, however, there is an awareness of "various ways" that this movement might occur. In fact, Aquinas says that the words being sung do not need to be understood. "The same applies to the hearers, for even if some of them understand not what is sung, yet they understand why it is sung, namely, for God's glory: and this is enough to arouse their devotion."[6] In the preceding passage we begin to see Aquinas move away from his insistence on the need for verbal signification. Aquinas goes on to assert, however, that "to arouse men to devotion by teaching and preaching is a more excellent

[5] S.T. II.II.91.2c.
[6] S.T. II.II.91.2.ad5.

way than by singing."[7] While he is clinging to the supremacy of words, Aquinas is willing to affirm the efficacy of nonverbal signification. He is wrestling with a tension.

In order to examine an example where nonverbal signs are elevated past their passive role, I turn to Aquinas's treatment of sacramental eating. The way Aquinas speaks of the communal act of physically consuming the consecrated bread and wine offers us insight, not only into the significance of nonverbal signs, but also into the moral weight such signification carries. As I pointed out in the previous chapter, Aquinas is primarily concerned with spiritual eating. This concern stems from his understanding of the purpose of the Eucharist: to nourish the Church's spiritual life. Hence, Aquinas focuses on the role of the theological virtues in the Eucharist to the extent that he is able to deny the need for sacramental eating. This does not mean, however, that sacramental eating (or restricting such eating) should be taken lightly. In fact, Aquinas clearly says that spiritual eating with actual reception is better than spiritual eating without reception.[8] For Aquinas, physically eating the consecrated host and drinking the consecrated wine is a significant action.

First, sacramental eating is a sign of incorporation in Christ's ecclesial body. "Whoever receives this sacrament, expresses [*significat*] thereby that he is made one with Christ, and incorporated in His members."[9] Hence, the choice to eat and drink of the Eucharist is a choice to communicate a relationship to those who witness that eating. Put differently, a communion line is a community embodying its fellowship. Through sacramental eating, spiritual eating is done communally. As nonverbal signs, eating and drinking are significant actions that, like music, are capable of moving our minds toward knowledge and love of God.

Second, sacramental eating can be an expression of a reality that is not present. Just as a communion line embodies fellowship, a body excluded from a communion line embodies a lack of fellowship. Therefore, excluding oneself or another person from the Eucharist is

---

[7] S.T. II.II.91.2.ad3.

[8] Cf. S.T. III.80.1.ad3.

[9] S.T. III.80.4c. It is worth noting that, while Aquinas calls the unity of the ecclesial body of Christ the *res tantum* (i.e., the reality not signified), throughout all of question 80 he is considering how this *res tantum* is signified in the celebration of the Eucharist.

an act of religion that signifies a reality. Because sacramental eating is not merely eating a sign but is itself a sign, there are moral dimensions to be considered. Hence, Aquinas says that those who are not justified (i.e., who are not subjects of charity) yet choose to partake of the Eucharist choose to embody a deceptive sign. "Whoever receives this sacrament while in mortal sin [i.e., while lacking all charity] is guilty of lying to this sacrament, and consequently of sacrilege, because he profanes the sacrament: and therefore he sins mortally."[10] The point I want to emphasize is that the nonverbal sign of sacramental eating is an act of religion that is deeply significant.

I forward these few examples as evidence of an inclination, albeit slight, toward liturgical theology in Aquinas's sacramental theology. The sacramental minimalism of Aquinas does not completely stop him from attending to the significance of the nonverbal liturgical actions of the Church. Nevertheless, Aquinas remains a sacramental minimalist. These few examples of Aquinas's liturgical instincts ought not be used to distract us from the self-defeating sacramental minimalism that undeniably marks the *Tertia Pars*. Hence, I now turn to the construction of a liturgical theology of right religion that, by magnifying Aquinas's liturgical instincts, will help us to avoid the minimalism and individualism that mark the *Tertia Pars* but that are so absent in the *Secunda Pars*'s grammars of grace and virtue.

II. Goodness and Rightness

In his work, *Goodness and Rightness in Thomas Aquinas's* Summa Theologiae, James F. Keenan makes a distinction between moral operations that are good and those that are right. Specifically, he argues that Aquinas has two ways of evaluating moral actions:

> The distinction between goodness and rightness could be stated in this form: goodness measures whether out of love one *strives to attain* a rightly ordered self. Charity, for Thomas, is this measure. Rightness, on the other hand, measures whether one *actually attains* a rightly ordered self. Thus, the order of reason determines whether proximate ends and means attain the mean.[11]

---

[10] S.T. III.80.4c.

[11] James F. Keenan, *Goodness and Rightness in Thomas Aquinas's* Summa Theologiae (Washington, DC: Georgetown University Press, 1992), 137–38.

For an act to be called right, it must attain the mean. Recalling our previous treatment of moral virtue in chapter 4, attaining the mean is a result of prudence determining an end, of temperance and fortitude controlling the inhibitory effects of the passions, and justice moving the will to actually choose the end determined by prudence.[12] When prudence is properly formed (i.e., supported by temperance and fortitude), it is able to accurately determine the mean of a virtue, providing the end to the will. Insofar as this prudent end is chosen by the will, the consequent operation is a right act. Or, in Keenan's words, an operation is right when it is the operation of a "rightly ordered self."

Of course, prudence regularly errs when providing proximate ends to the will. Insofar as an operation is the result of a disordered self, that external act is called "wrong." Wrongness does not, however, necessarily imply badness. Rather, as Keenan points out, "badness is not deliberately willing the wrong, but failing to strive for the right, i.e. [failing] to grow in virtue."[13] As we saw above, this "striving for the right" is the measure of goodness. Hence, even when prudence misses the mean, that does not imply a failure on the will's part. One can be wrong while still being good. But what does it mean to *strive* for rightness?

Simply put, when we act *ex caritate*, our acts are morally good. Insofar as charity is a union with God that seeks greater union, it can also be described in terms of striving for rightness. Hence, when a person acts out of love for God so that they might more deeply love God, that person acts in a good way. In the end, we have two ways of evaluating moral acts: "External acts must be measured both as *ex caritate* and as fitting to reason. Measuring the same act with two distinct measurements is, as far as [Keenan] can see, the distinction between goodness and rightness."[14]

"Thomas argues that in all external activity there are two measures. Therefore, as every act bears two descriptions, the distinction between goodness and rightness is not between person and act, but between the heart and reason."[15] This striving is "antecedent to questions concerning intention and choice, or to questions pertaining to proximate

---

[12] Cf. chap. 4.I.1.
[13] Keenan, *Goodness and Rightness*, 139.
[14] Ibid., 131.
[15] Ibid., 143.

ends intended and the actual objects realized."[16] In other words, while goodness does require specific choice and intention, the specific shape of the action (i.e., *what* is chosen and *what* is intended) is a matter of rightness, not goodness.

Ordered reason is required for being a morally good person who operates rightly. In the fourth chapter, I argued that operating *ex caritate* constituted a person's ability to reflect divinity to others.[17] Hence, while goodness may be an authentic form of *theosis*, rightness perfects this reflective potential of a moral operation because it brings the operation's specification into consideration. Disembodied charity never provokes anyone. Rightly embodied charity is, however, a better provocation than charity embodied through a disordered reason. When we see a person do the wrong thing, we can still acknowledge that they were trying. Their striving in a difficult situation can still be a reflection of divinity despite their disorder. In their goodness, we have an example of striving that inspires our own goodness. On the other hand, when we see a person do the right thing in the face of adversity, their reflection of divinity provides more than an example of striving. Their rightness provides an example of embodied virtue that ought to be emulated. In other words, the person who is right *and* good reflects what divinity *ought* to look like when incarnated in the graced life of a human being.

III. Religious Signification

Before we begin a consideration of right and wrong religion, I want to discuss how the virtue of religion relates to sacramental signification. I briefly touched on this topic in chapter 5, but I revisit it here to add depth to the previous discussion.[18] While, there are many external acts of religion, here I am interested in the Sacraments of the New Law. Specifically, I will highlight what it means to say that the sacraments are the result of our obligation to signify the salvation of the world.

Because religion is a moral virtue annexed to justice, it implies obligation (i.e., giving what is due). Specifically, religion is the virtue

---

[16] Ibid., 142.
[17] Cf. chap. 4.II.
[18] Cf. chap. 5.II.1.

by which we are obliged to give God worship from our devotion.[19] In the celebration of the sacraments, the virtue of religion elicits communal action in order to offer God praise. According to Aquinas, however, the sacraments need to offer signs of the cause, form, and end of our salvation.

> A sacrament properly speaking is that which is ordained to signify our sanctification. In which three things may be considered; viz. the very cause of our sanctification, which is Christ's passion; the form of our sanctification, which is grace and the virtues; and the ultimate end of our sanctification, which is eternal life. And all these are signified by the sacraments. Consequently a sacrament is a sign that is both a reminder of the past, i.e. the passion of Christ; and an indication of that which is effected in us by Christ's passion, i.e. grace; and a prognostic, that is, a foretelling of future glory.[20]

Throughout chapter 5, I emphasized what it means to say that the sacraments signify "the very cause of our sanctification, which is Christ's passion." For our current purposes, I draw attention to how the sacraments signify the form of our sanctification, that is, grace and the virtues. Because the sacraments are operations of religion, we are obligated to signify the virtues through which God's grace is manifested. We are charged with showing the world how to live as Christ lived.

Recalling the codependence of the virtues, it is not possible to signify charity without signifying a moral virtue. Hence, we are obliged to sacramentally signify the perfecting virtues (i.e., the moral virtues formed by charity) through which we are said to participate in the Divine Nature. By this sacramental signification, we fulfill our obligation to signify the virtues and the grace that constitute the form of our sanctification. I emphasize, however, the fact that there is no universal form of our salvation. While it is tempting to point to faith or charity as the form of salvation, there is no isolating the theological virtues from one another, and there is no isolating the moral virtues from the theological virtues.[21] Hence, if they are obligated to signify

---

[19] Cf. S.T. II.II.81.2-4.
[20] S.T. III.60.3c.
[21] Cf. chap. 4.II.

the form of our sanctification, then the sacraments must signify all of these virtues. For example, if the Eucharist is meant to signify charity, it must do so by signifying the perfecting virtues through which charity is embodied.

The sacraments, then, are communal operations of religious signification wherein the Church uses signs to provide knowledge of the way we are called to live like Christ. As Aquinas points out, this religious signification is our obligation because human beings need help:

> Yet such is the weakness of the human mind that it needs a guiding hand, not only to the knowledge, but also to the love of Divine things by means of certain sensible objects known to us. Chief among these is the humanity of Christ, according to the words of the [Preface for Christmastide], "that through knowing God visibly, we may be caught up to the love of things invisible." Wherefore matters relating to Christ's humanity are the chief incentive to devotion, leading us thither as a guiding hand, although devotion itself has for its object matters concerning the Godhead.[22]

Through the sacraments we signify the virtues that allow us to live as Christ lived, thereby moving on the way toward our Final End. Christ's provocation is the possibility of our *theosis*. Because the virtue of religion is a moral virtue, however, the specification of its operations requires prudence. Put differently, determining precisely *how* to carry out this provocative religious signification is a matter of right reason commanding religion.

IV. Right Religion

In this section, I assume the goodness of religious operation. That is to say, in the considerations that follow, all operations of religion are assumed to be carried out *ex caritate*. This is not meant to imply that all operations of religion actually are formed by charity. As a moral virtue, religion is perfectly capable of operating without charity. It is not hard to imagine religious action done for nefarious reasons that contradict friendship with God. Those particular acts of

---

[22] S.T. II.II.82.3.ad2.

religion, however, are not considered here. Rather, good religion (i.e., religion done *ex caritate*) seeks to serve the union with God that is both religion's occasion and purpose. The fact that good religion is done *ex caritate* means that all such operations are the result of the Holy Spirit's prior movement within the members of the religious community. But we must ask, what does it mean to say that the Holy Spirit uses right reason as an instrument to increase charity? How does right reason help the religious signification of our salvation?

1. Religious Prudence

If prudence is right reason about things to be done, then religious prudence is right reason about worship to be given to God. In terms of sacramental signification, religious prudence is right reason about sacramental signs to be embodied. Hence, religion that follows the command of right reason results in an operation of right religion. As I pointed out in chapter 4, prudence is tasked with attending to particular context (i.e., the various circumstances of our lives) so as to accurately determine the proximate end to be willed and the mean of the virtues needed to achieve that end.[23] Religious prudence, then, is tasked with attending to the various circumstances of the worshiping community so as to accurately determine the form of sacramental signification to be embodied. Put simply, religious prudence must determine the form of the sacraments by scrutinizing the particular context of the religious act.

For example, when a pastor with religious prudence sets out to write a sermon, she will take stock of the particular audience that will hear the sermon. The pastor will take into account the congregation's temporal location (e.g., Easter, Advent, etc.), their geographic location (e.g., vernacular language), and their cultural location (e.g., education level, current events, etc.). On the other hand, a pastor lacking religious prudence will write the sermon for the congregation she wishes she had, giving no consideration to their particularity. We will return to our imprudent pastor shortly; for now let me stress that religious prudence seeks to celebrate sacraments that embody *effective* (that is to say, truly provocative) signs of God's love.

---

[23] Cf. chap. 4.I.1.1.

When utilizing this notion of right religion to consider the formation of sacraments, it must be emphasized that prudent evaluation of the community's needs and capabilities is paramount. If the sacraments are to fruitfully signify the form of our sanctification, then religious prudence must take the worshiping community into account. Every community has different potential. As sacramental writers, different congregations may have different liturgical abilities. Some communities may be more capable of a prolonged liturgy that utilizes lengthy musical pieces and learned sermons. Another congregation may be capable of celebrating multilingual liturgies as a way of providing for a culturally diverse community. As sacramental readers, different congregations need to hear different messages (i.e., read different signs). Some communities may need to hear a message that emphasizes justice. Other communities (e.g., elementary schools) may need simplified messages. All of these various capabilities are the concern of the religiously prudent person. The words, postures, timing, gestures, materials, art, and architecture that constitute our religious actions should be determined by religious prudence in order to yield operations of right religion that in turn yield communities that reflect divinity.

Bearing in mind that sacraments exist to signify the virtues through which Christians manifest grace, right religion must elicit sacraments that properly signify the *particular* form of the *particular* community's salvation. Simply put, it is necessary to prudently determine which moral virtues to emphasize through our sacramental signification so as to properly signify the embodied charity that is most needed in that community. In other words, our sacraments must show us how to live in the way that will allow the Church to fall more deeply in love with God.

2. Striving for Right Religion

What happens, then, when a religious community and its leaders lack religious prudence? To answer this question, I first turn to Aquinas's treatment of superstition. In discussing the vices against religion, Aquinas speaks about superstitious observances:

> Now the end of divine worship is that man may give glory to God, and submit to Him in mind and body. Consequently, what-

ever a man may do conducing to God's glory, and subjecting his mind to God, and his body, too, by a moderate curbing of the concupiscences, is not excessive in the divine worship, provided it be in accordance with the commandments of God and of the Church, and in keeping with the customs of those among whom he lives. On the other hand if that which is done be, in itself, not conducive to God's glory, nor raise man's mind to God, nor curb inordinate concupiscence, or again if it be not in accordance with the commandments of God and of the Church, or if it be contrary to the general custom—which, according to Augustine [Ad Casulan. Ep. xxxvi], "has the force of law"—all this must be reckoned excessive and superstitious, because consisting, as it does, of mere externals, it has no connection with the internal worship of God.[24]

Here, I would like to draw attention to the fact that acts of religion are to be carried out "in keeping with the customs of those among whom [the worshiper] lives." Without projecting our theory of religious prudence and right religion onto Aquinas, it is clear that the particular modes of religious operations are intimately connected to contingent cultural location.

Aquinas is clear, however, that the mode of worship can fail to conform to local custom while still being an act of devotion to God.

Accordingly the species of superstition are differentiated, first on the part of the mode, secondly on the part of the object. For the divine worship may be given either to whom it ought to be given, namely, to the true God, but "in an undue mode," and this is the first species of superstition.[25]

It is possible to worship God in an undue manner while still worshiping God. Again, it is not my desire to anachronistically project a concern for cultural plurality back onto Aquinas. Rather, I refer to these passages for two reasons. First, for Aquinas, the mode of worship given to God is influenced by the particularity of the worshiping community. Second, worshiping the true God out of devotion and for the purpose of deepening that devotion does not suffice for a

---

[24] S.T. II.II.93.2c.
[25] S.T. II.II.92.2c.

nonvicious operation of religion. I highlight these two points because it helps cast a light on the moral quality of worship. That is to say, worship requires that prudence dictate its mode by assessing the various circumstances of the particular context. In worship, as with all acts of human virtue, the moral virtues cannot be isolated. An operation of right religion is always the fruit of prudence, temperance, fortitude, justice, faith, hope, and charity.[26]

Reverting to our terms, it is possible have *good* acts of religion that seek to foment charity but that do not meet the criteria for *right* religion. How, then, are we to distinguish between acts of religion that are good but wrong and those acts that are good and right? By examining the relationship between the religious operation and its particular context it is possible to determine the degree to which religious prudence was involved in that act of religion. If cultural context had no influence on the form of the sacrament, then religious prudence was not involved in that act of religion. For example, if a community is being regularly oppressed through violent racism, it is imprudent to celebrate a liturgy that emphasizes the virtues of obedience and humility while ignoring the community's need for fortitude and justice. While such acts of religion fail to signify the form of sanctification that is needed by the community, that does not mean that the act was not good, nor does it mean that the act cannot be efficacious.

When acts of religion fail to conform to reason, but nonetheless are done out of charity, we have what I call a good act of wrong religion. On the surface, this good act fails to reflect divinity as sacramental signs are intended (i.e., by providing knowledge of the virtues through which a community responds to God's love). If, however, a community is aware of the charitable motivation of the religious act, then that act can still be recognized as the work of the Holy Spirit. As I said above, those who strive and fail still inspire others to strive.

It is an all too common occurrence to see one religious community belittling the liturgical practices of another community. Particularly when it comes to ecumenical relations, liturgical norms are often the occasion for denigration. Roman Catholics have a tendency to proclaim (in a deeply erroneous way) that Protestants do not believe in

---

[26] Again, I am assuming the presence of charity. It is possible to have an imperfect act of right religion that lacks charity.

the real presence of Christ. Similarly, Roman Catholics are often accused of Pelagianism as a result of their sacramental practices. Even within Roman Catholic communities it is not uncommon to hear someone bemoan the use of guitar music in postconciliar "folk Masses," or to see people roll their eyes at the use of chant during a Mass. If a bishop chooses to wear pontifical gloves and a *cappa magna*, one can expect to hear derisive laughter (usually occurring somewhere behind his back). If a bishop chooses to wash the feet of a woman during a Holy Thursday Mass, that bishop's competence will often be questioned publically and impatiently. These examples are a few unfortunate drops in a bucket filled with the crimes of the so-called Liturgy Wars. Clearly, it is crucial to engage in ongoing discussion regarding liturgical practice; that is the main point of the current chapter. But it is crucial to begin these discussions with an affirmation of the goodness of these liturgical practices. This affirmation will go a long way to ensuring that discussions about liturgy are carried out as charitable conversations and not vitriolic arguments. Acknowledging and affirming the goodness of religious action that is wrong/imprudent/superstitious is essential to the spiritual life of the Church. When we affirm the goodness of wrong religion, we affirm our community's status as a *pilgrim* community that perpetually strives to grow in religious perfection.

A group of good Christians does not, however, suffice for a salvifically efficacious ecclesial body of Christ. Moral rightness is also necessary. Insofar as a worshiping community continually lacks religious prudence when determining the shape of religious acts, that community fails (if not completely) to reflect divinity to the world. In the fifth chapter, I said that the Church's unity is a function of its ability to reflect divinity to the world.[27] Hence, wrong religion, even when done *ex caritate*, hinders the Church's ability to grow in unity as the ecclesial body of Christ.

To conclude this consideration of right religion, I want to emphasize a point that is often too obvious to be noticed: right and wrong are not exclusive categories. Rather, they are the idealized poles of a sliding scale. Just as there are no acts of authority that avoid violence, there are no liturgies that avoid idolatrous superstition. This is why

[27] Cf. chap. 5.III.3.

Keenan's notion of striving is so important. Striving implies affirming our obligation to seek perfection while recognizing an inability to avoid imperfection.

Striving for right religion, then, is a process of perpetual liturgical reform. It is a *perpetual* process, because careful attention must be given to the ever-changing context of each unique sacramental celebration. Because the spiritual life of the Church is a community's dynamic pilgrimage toward God, the sacraments must serve that pilgrim Church in all its various circumstances and particular imperfections. Beginners in charity need food, but not all hunger is the same. I began this section by asking what it means to say that the Holy Spirit uses right reason as an instrument to increase charity. Through the cooperation of the Church's sacraments, the Holy Spirit signifies the form of our sanctification, teaching us how to deepen our friendship with God. Through the use of religious prudence, however, that provocative lesson is personalized for our time and place.

V. Writing a Diverse Christ for a Plural World

In this final section, I will show that a liturgical theology of right religion allows the Church to attend to the sacraments as moral obligations that require ongoing reform if they are to be effective in the spiritual life of the Church. To this end, I will first briefly describe what it means to say that Christ is present in a eucharistic act of right religion. Here, I will emphasize the fact that the eucharistic presence of Christ is a diverse reality. Then, by way of illustration, I will briefly gesture toward ways this liturgical theology of right religion might be applied to the Eucharist.

1. Prudently Writing Christ

In the fifth chapter, I described the sacraments as rituals that signify the charity of Christ in a way that provokes the Church into participating in that charity.[28] The Eucharist was described as signifying Christ's charity as food that perfects our imperfect charity by turning us into Christ. In this section, I want to answer the following ques-

---

[28] Cf. chap. 5.I.1.

tion: Into which Christ are eucharistic eaters transformed? I suggest that religious prudence dictates how Christ is represented and, therefore, dictates the Christ into which the worshipers are formed. If the community is formed into the Christ that lives the way Jesus Christ would have lived *for that community's time and place*, then that eucharistic celebration was an act of right religion.

The Eucharist signifies Christ's provocative life so that we might be provoked into discipleship. Insofar as the Eucharist is a representation (i.e., a sign) of Christ's sacrificial life, the way in which that representation occurs will dictate the way in which our charity is provoked. When we look at Jesus' sacrifice as the cause of our justification, we are looking at an act of charity that provokes our charity by which sins are remitted. Like our charity, however, Jesus' acts of charity are visible because they are embodied through moral virtue. Hence, the particular moral virtues that are emphasized in our christologies and soteriologies greatly impact the way the Eucharist will signify Christ and, therefore, greatly impact the transformation of the ecclesial body's unity.

For example, if Jesus' cross is an act of solidarity with the oppressed, then that act of charity provokes our charitable solidarity by which we seek to serve those who are marginalized. Similarly, if Jesus' cross is an act of obedience, then that act of charity provokes our charitable obedience by which we seek to curb our passions. Of course, Christ's cross is both of these and much more. The existence of multiple christologies and soteriologies allows the Paschal Mystery to speak to the various circumstances of a world deeply marked by plurality. At times we may need to hear and see Christ signified in one way and in another way at a different time. We recall that, through the sacraments and the faith that believes through them, Christ's Paschal Mystery is applied to the Church.[29] Hence, the way we signify Christ is the historical application of his passion as the cause of our salvation.

The sacramental signs we choose to embody are the mediation through which faith knows the God who loves us. Simultaneously, those signs are the mediation through which God calls us to participate in that love. Hence, by acts of right religion we come to actually know and love God. In light of this fact, the importance of religious

---

[29] Cf. chap. 5.II.

prudence cannot be overstated. The knowledge that the sacraments provide is the presence of Christ for a particular community. By signifying Christ's virtues in a way that is influenced by the particular needs of a community, that community is provoked into discipleship *of a particular form*. Hence, the form of their sanctification will differ from that of another community. In other words, the embodied *theosis* of one community is never identical to the *theosis* of another community. In this spiritual life, there is no universal form of salvation.

Religious prudence, then, is tasked with determining how Christ will be written in the Eucharist. Striving for right religion means patiently determining the eucharistic signs that will embody the eucharistic body of Christ.[30] Hence, the Real Presence of Christ is not always the same. In fact, the opposite is true. The eucharistic body of Christ is different in every writing of the Eucharist. When the Eucharist is an act of striving for right religion, Christ is present for that particular community's needs. This point becomes less controversial when we think about how Jesus related to those he loved. Each person came to Jesus with particular needs and those needs dictated the Christ they met. For example, Jesus treated tax collectors differently than he treated religious leaders. He treated lepers differently than he treated merchants in the temple. Jesus' prudence dictated the unique manner by which he was present to each person. Likewise, the religious prudence of worshipers needs to dictate the unique manner that Christ is present for the community that longs to become Christ. The sacraments need to show us how to be Christ *for our time and place*. In short, right religion seeks to write a diverse Christ for a plural world. Through right religion, the provocative invitation to God's friendship is personalized. Hence, in the Eucharist, we are able to meet Christ as the One who listens to our own needs and walks with us as a friend.

2. How Do We Write Christ?

What we have, then, is a way of seeing liturgical action that needs to attend to its context to appropriately communicate the necessary virtues. This approach to liturgical reform celebrates plurality. There

---

[30] Cf. chap. 5.III.1.

is no end to the variety of liturgical forms that can be utilized. Hence, this liturgical theology of right religion is best understood as a method for understanding and reforming worship. For the remainder of this section, I will offer a few examples of how this method might be applied to eucharistic celebrations.

First, and perhaps most obvious, is our previous example of preaching. Sermons are vitally important liturgical signs that allow the eucharistic body of Christ to speak. Recalling our past treatment of the degrees of charity, the "various circumstances" of our lives may render us beginners in desperate need of temperance or fortitude. When a community tragedy occurs, it is necessary to reform that day's liturgy to address the particular needs of the community. A prudent preacher will ask if the community's anger has grown into hateful desire for retribution or if their sadness has developed into despair. Beyond preaching, these needs can also be addressed in the prayers of the faithful and music selection. To ignore these particular needs out of fear of backlash from parishioners or superiors would be to fail in right religion and, therefore, hinder that community's ability to be the united ecclesial body of Christ.

Beyond the rapidly changing daily issues of sermons, music, and prayers, we can also apply a liturgical theology of right religion to nonverbal signs of the liturgy that tend to change less often. For example, during the eucharistic prayer, the congregation will embody certain postures. Depending on cultural location, this posture is usually standing or kneeling. It is often the case that some members of a congregation will stand while some are kneeling. The point I emphasize is that these postures help write the eucharistic presence of Christ. Religious prudence must take into account this difference in signification and work to determine which posture is most appropriate for that congregation. Should the congregation emphasize kneeling as a way to signify solemnity and reverence to Christ? Should the congregation emphasize standing as a way to signify joyful hope and respect for Christ? Should the congregation emphasize maintaining a collective posture (i.e., discouraging some from kneeling while others stand and *vice versa*) whereby the entire congregation signifies a Christ who is present to a community as opposed to a divided group of individuals? When and for what reasons should these postures be changed? All of these postures are uniquely significant and deserve the consideration of religious prudence so that the congregation might continue striving toward the right religion through which God speaks in a unique way.

This being a discussion of the Eucharist, I would be remiss to not spend some time discussing how bread is used in liturgies. For example, in contemporary Roman Catholic eucharistic celebrations, we tend to use mass-produced communion wafers. Religious prudence needs to attend to the *significant* difference between these edible discs and bread. If a communion wafer is placed in front of random human beings, asking them to name what they saw, it would be a rare occasion to hear a response of "bread." Rather, responses would range from the specific "communion wafer" to a "cracker." The point is, the communion wafer is not recognizable as bread. Hence, our contemporary eucharistic celebrations have substituted bread with a sign for bread.

Without going into a superfluous consideration of why this substitution has occurred, I want to highlight the loss of significance that results when food is no longer used as a eucharistic sign to write Christ. On the night he was betrayed, Jesus did not take "something made out of water and wheat." He took bread. If the Church desires to write a Christ who is spiritual food, then, as Aquinas emphasizes, the use of food is necessary for such signification.[31] Using actual food as a sign to write Christ helps to write a Christ that is a source of nourishment. In other words, if a community needs to learn that God is the source of their life, then actual food speaks that truth more effectively than individual communion wafers. If a community needs humility, then using food to signify their relationship to God may be a more effective act of religion.[32]

Beyond the significance of using actual food, the shape of the food that is eaten is significant and deserving of consideration. If, as Aquinas points out, the Eucharist is meant to signify our unity as a community, then eating a fragment of a whole loaf that was blessed and broken is a different sign from eating a communion wafer that was consecrated at an earlier Mass and retrieved from a tabernacle. When members of a congregation eat unique fragments of a single

---

[31] Cf. chap. 5.III.1.

[32] Obviously, this is not meant to imply that a lack of food renders the Eucharist ineffective. Communion wafers are signs that undeniably write the eucharistic body of Christ.

loaf, God is speaking to them about who they are as a community. In short, eating broken bread signifies solidarity and responsibility to one another. Deciding to celebrate the Eucharist this way is an act of religious prudence that is seeking to signify the Christ who calls us as a united community.

The significance of the food's shape becomes most crucial when taking Communion to those who were absent from the liturgy. Opening a gilded pyx to reveal a perfectly whole circle that we have agreed to call "bread" is not the same as offering a chunk of food that was clearly part of a whole but has been broken for those who are not at the altar. That fragment of bread, eaten in a nursing home room, is the liturgical undoing of the communicant's spatial and temporal absence and the affirmation of her unity in Christ. To argue that it is not the bread or its shape that causes unity but rather the substance of Christ that underlies the inconsequential accidents is to fundamentally misunderstand sacramental signification and therefore the sacraments. Religious prudence knows that sacramental signification writes Christ. Hence, the prudent pastor seeks to *effectively* write Christ in the Eucharist.

Finally, beyond the shape of the food that is eaten, there are significant differences in the way that food is eaten. While Aquinas is clear that we eat the Eucharist spiritually through faith, sacramental eating is a sign that helps write the Christ who is spiritually eaten. There are many ways to eat this sacrament: while kneeling, while standing, on the tongue, in the hand, from an extraordinary eucharistic minister, from an ordinary eucharistic minister, etc. Religious prudence seeks to understand the difference in these signs and put them to the service of the community. For example, receiving the Eucharist on one's tongue is a particularly powerful sign of humility. Depending on the culture and the individual communicant, being passively fed can provide an experience of God's operation in our lives. Put differently, this way of eating can signify temperance and humility. On the other hand, using one's own hands to bring the food to our mouths can provide an experience of responsibility and cooperation. This way of eating can be a sign of fortitude and justice. The prudent worshipers will scrutinize their needs and embody the signs that provocatively teach them who they are called to be.

From all these considerations of applying religious prudence, one important point comes to the fore. It is not possible to prudently form a liturgy without intimate knowledge of the particular worshiping community. Any system of liturgical reform that creates space between the reformers and the worshiping community is doomed to fail. Religious prudence knows that it must attend to the various circumstances of the particular community. Hence, using the principle of subsidiarity, the prudent pastor (especially the pastors who find themselves either moving from one community to another or overtasked with administrative duties) will be sure to appoint committees of liturgists and worship planners who can carry out the perpetual liturgical reform that every community needs and deserves. Knowing one lacks the ability to prudently form worship is itself an act of religious prudence that serves right religion.

As I said above, we are called to the sacraments so that we might continue to be called through the sacraments.[33] In the end, a liturgical theology of right religion asserts that, in cooperation with the Holy Spirit, we must choose what the unity of the Church will look like by choosing the Christ we will write in the Eucharist. This religious action is not accomplished by simply repeating the actions of Christ at the Last Supper. Jesus celebrated the Last Supper the way he did because of his particular context. He was a Jew observing the Passover with other Jews in a time of political upheaval and uncertainty. If we are called to simply mimic Jesus, we have been failing for two thousand years. Rather, by proclaiming Christ through diverse signs that reach out to a world marked by plurality, the Church does what Jesus did: make God present as the One who comes to meet the needs of those God loves.

---

[33] Cf. chap. 5.II.3.

CONCLUSION

Speaking with a Lost Voice

Throughout this book, I have retrieved grammars of grace and virtue as a means to facilitate contemporary discussion about eucharistic theology. The preceding liturgical theology of right religion is rooted in the theology of St. Thomas Aquinas. The grammars of grace and virtue out of which Aquinas beautifully articulates his vision of the embodied spiritual life have, here, been put to use in articulating a vision of how the liturgical worship of Christian communities serves their embodied spiritual life. In essence, I have tried to integrate his grammars of grace and virtue into a sacramental theology that maintains the ecclesial concerns of the *Secunda Pars*. This liturgical theology of right religion should not be taken simply as interpretation of Aquinas's sacramental theology. I have used Aquinas's grammars in a way that has clearly changed his voice. In the previous chapter, more than anywhere else in this book, I used Aquinas's voice in a way that seeks to make it my own. Recalling the phrasing I used in the introduction, in constructing a liturgical theology of right religion, I am speaking with a lost voice in a way that addresses contemporary concerns.

What I have done throughout this book is try to use Aquinas's grammars of grace and virtue in a similar way to how Henri de Lubac and other *ressourcement* theologians sought to use the theology of patristic authors.[1] I am not trying to absolutize Aquinas's grammars

[1] Cf. introduction.IV.

155

of grace and virtue, nor am I implying that a liturgical theology of right religion is how Aquinas himself would use them. I do believe, however, that using the grammars of virtue and grace in this way allows us to have conversations that simultaneously seek to be grounded in Tradition while honestly addressing contemporary contexts and the questions they generate. In the end, I am seeking to provide a way of speaking that should be used when it is helpful and curbed when it is not.

Throughout this book, I have emphasized the importance of rightly writing the sacraments so that the Church might live the spiritual life of friendship with God as a pilgrim community. In choosing this emphasis, I risked burdening the Church and its human weaknesses with an impossible task. Cooperating with God is difficult. So I wish to close with this assurance: the beauty of sacramental signification (and all cooperation with God) is that it need not be understood as such in order to function successfully. In fact, the majority of Catholic Christians tend to understand the sacraments in a way that is reminiscent of ancient magic (i.e., moving earthly elements and speaking the correct words will provoke divine intervention). We tend to think we are provoking God when the exact opposite is true. It is God who provokes us. As daunting as cooperation may be, it is God who is operating, and a merciful God at that. Despite our misunderstandings of the sacraments (and there are no doubt some examples in the preceding pages), God will continue to cooperate with human beings as images of divinity that are made to reflect the love of God into all of Creation.

Bibliography

Ambrose, Glenn P. *The Theology of Louis-Marie Chauvet*. Burlington, VT: Ashgate, 2011.

Anderson, E. Byron, and Bruce T. Morrill. *Liturgy and the Moral Self: Humanity at Full Stretch before God; Essays in Honor of Don E. Saliers*. Collegeville, MN: Liturgical Press, 1998.

Aquinas, Thomas. *Disputed Questions on Virtue: Quaestio Disputata De Virtutibus in Commune and Quaestio Disputata De Virtutibus Cardinalibus*. Edited by Ralph McInerny. South Bend, IN: St. Augustine's Press, 1998.

———. *On Charity (De Caritate)*. Edited and translated by Lottie H. Kendzierski. Milwaukee, WI: Marquette University Press, 1960.

———. *The Summa Theologiae of Saint Thomas Aquinas, Latin-English Edition*. Scotts Valley, CA: NovAntiqua, 2008.

Baldovin, John F. *Bread of Life, Cup of Salvation: Understanding the Mass*. Lanham, MD: Rowman & Littlefield Publishers, 2003.

———. *Reforming the Liturgy: A Response to the Critics*. Collegeville, MN: Liturgical Press, 2008.

———. *The Urban Character of Christian Worship: The Origins, Development, and Meaning of Stational Liturgy*. Rome: Pont. Institutum Studiorum Orientalium, 1987.

Beaton, Rhodora E. *Embodied Words, Spoken Signs : Sacramentality and the Word in Rahner and Chauvet*. Minneapolis: Fortress Press, 2014.

Berger, David. *Thomas Aquinas and the Liturgy*. Naples, FL: Sapientia Press of Ave Maria University, 2005.

Bordeyne, Philippe, and Bruce T. Morrill. *Sacraments: Revelation of the Humanity of God; Engaging the Fundamental Theology of Louis-Marie Chauvet*. Collegeville, MN: Liturgical Press, 2008.

Brunk, Timothy M. *Liturgy and Life: The Unity of Sacrament and Ethics in the Theology of Louis-Marie Chauvet.* New York: Peter Lang, 2007.

Cessario, Romanus. *The Moral Virtues and Theological Ethics.* South Bend, IN: University of Notre Dame Press, 1991.

———. *The Virtues, Or, the Examined Life.* New York: Continuum, 2002.

Chauvet, Louis-Marie. "Are the Words of the Liturgy Worn Out? What Diagnosis? What Pastoral Approach?" *Worship* 84, no. 1 (January 2010): 25–37.

———. "The Broken Bread as Theological Figure of Eucharistic Presence." In *Sacramental Presence in a Postmodern Context,* edited by L. Boeve and L. Leijssen, 236–62. Louvain: Peeters, 2001.

———. "Causalité et Efficacité: Enjeux Mediévaux et Contemporains." *Transversalités* 105 (2008): 31–51.

———. "Parole et Sacrement." *Recherches de Science Religieuse* 91, no. 2 (2003): 203–22.

———. "Ritualité et Théologie." *Recherches de Science Religieuse* 78, no. 4 (1990): 535–64.

———. *The Sacraments: The Word of God at the Mercy of the Body.* Collegeville, MN: Liturgical Press, 2001.

———. *Les Sacrements: Parole de Dieu au Risque du Corps.* Paris : Les Editions de l'atelier/Les Editions ouvrières, 2003.

———. "Le Sacrifice Comme Échange Symbolique." In M. Neusch, ed., *Le Sacrifice dans les religions.* Paris: Beauchesne, 1994, 277–304.

———. *Symbol and Sacrament: A Sacramental Reinterpretation of Christian Existence.* Collegeville, MN: Liturgical Press, 1995.

———. *Symbole et Sacrement: Une Relecture Sacramentelle de l'Existence Chrétienne.* Paris: Cerf, 1987.

———. *Du Symbolique au Symbole: Essai Sur Les Sacrements.* Paris: Éditions du Cerf, 1979.

Cipolla, Richard G. "Selvaggi Revisited: Transubstantiation and Contemporary Science." *Theological Studies* 35, no. 4 (1974): 667–91.

Crownfield, David. "The Seminal Trace: Presence, Difference, and Transubstantiation." *Journal of the American Academy of Religion* 59, no. 2 (1991): 361–71.

Dewan, Lawrence. "St Thomas, James Keenan and the Will." *Science et Esprit* 47, no. 2 (1995): 153–76.

Duffy, Mervyn. *How Language, Ritual and Sacraments Work: According to John Austin, Jürgen Habermas and Louis-Marie Chauvet*. Rome: Editrice Pontificia Universita Gregoriana, 2005.

FitzPatrick, P. J. *In Breaking of Bread: The Eucharist and Ritual*. Cambridge: Cambridge University Press, 1993.

Häring, Bernhard. *The Law of Christ: Moral Theology for Priests and Laity*. Westminster, MD: Newman Press, 1966.

Henninger, Mark Gerald. *Relations: Medieval Theories, 1250–1325*. Oxford: Oxford University Press, 1989.

Holmer, Paul L. *The Grammar of Faith*. San Francisco: Harper & Row, 1978.

Hughes, Kathleen. *Saying Amen: A Mystagogy of the Sacrament*. Chicago: Liturgy Training Publications, 1999.

Hutter, Reinhardt, and Matthew Levering. *Ressourcement Thomism: Sacred Doctrine, the Sacraments, and the Moral Life; Essays in Honor of Romanus Cessario, O.P.* Washington, DC: The Catholic University of America Press, 2010.

Jordan, Mark D. *Ordering Wisdom: The Hierarchy of Philosophical Discourses in Aquinas*. Notre Dame, IN: University of Notre Dame Press, 1986.

———. *Rewritten Theology: Aquinas after His Readers*. Challenges in Contemporary Theology. Oxford: Blackwell, 2006.

Keenan, James F. *Goodness and Rightness in Thomas Aquinas's* Summa Theologiae. Washington, DC: Georgetown University Press, 1992.

———. *Virtues for Ordinary Christians*. Kansas City, MO: Sheed & Ward, 1996.

Kilmartin, Edward J. *The Eucharist in the West: History and Theology*. Collegeville, MN: Liturgical Press, 1998.

———. "Sacramental Theology: The Eucharist in Recent Literature." *Theological Studies* 32, no. 2 (1971): 233–77.

Kubicki, Judith M. "Recognizing the Presence of Christ in the Liturgical Assembly." *Theological Studies* 65, no. 4 (2004): 817–37.

Laporte, Jean-Marc. "Dynamics of Grace in Aquinas: A Structural Approach." *Theological Studies* 34, no. 2 (1973): 203–26.

Lawler, Michael G. *Symbol and Sacrament: A Contemporary Sacramental Theology*. New York: Fordham University Press, 1995.

Levering, Matthew, and Michael Dauphinais. *Rediscovering Aquinas and the Sacraments: Studies in Sacramental Theology*. Chicago: Hillenbrand Books, 2009.

Levering, Matthew. *Sacrifice and Community: Jewish Offering and Christian Eucharist*. Malden, MA: Blackwell, 2005.

Lindbeck, George A. *The Nature of Doctrine: Religion and Theology in a Post-liberal Age*. Louisville, KY: Westminster John Knox Press, 1984.

Lonergan, Bernard. *Grace and Freedom: Operative Grace in the Thought of Saint Thomas Aquinas*. Toronto: University of Toronto, 2000.

Lubac, Henri de. *Corpus Mysticum: The Eucharist and the Church in the Middle Ages; Historical Survey*. Edited by Laurence Hemming, Susan Paul, and Frank Parsons. Notre Dame, IN: University of Notre Dame Press, 2007.

MacIntyre, Alasdair C. *After Virtue: A Study in Moral Theory*. Notre Dame, IN: University of Notre Dame Press, 2007.

Macy, Gary. "A Re-Evaluation of the Contribution of Thomas Aquinas to the Thirteenth-Century Theology of the Eucharist." In *Intellectual Climate of the Early University*, edited by Nancy Elizabeth van Deusen, 53–72. Kalamazoo, MI: Western Michigan University, 1997.

———. *The Theologies of the Eucharist in the Early Scholastic Period: A Study of the Salvific Function of the Sacrament According to the Theologians, c. 1080–c. 1220*. New York: Clarendon Press, 1984.

———. *Treasures from the Storeroom: Medieval Religion and the Eucharist*. Collegeville, MN: Liturgical Press, 1999.

Mawson, Michael. "Understandings of Nature and Grace in John Milbank and Thomas Aquinas." *Scottish Journal of Theology* 62, no. 3 (2009): 347–61.

Mazza, Enrico. *The Celebration of the Eucharist: The Origin of the Rite and the Development of Its Interpretation*. Collegeville, MN: Liturgical Press, 1999.

McCue, James F. "Doctrine of Transubstantiation from Berengar through Trent: The Point at Issue." *Harvard Theological Review* 61, no. 3 (1968): 385–430.

Meyer, Hans Bernhard. *Eucharistie: Geschichte, Theologie, Pastoral*. Edited by Irmgard Pahl. Regensburg: F. Pustet, 1989.

Miller, Vincent J. "An Abyss at the Heart of Mediation: Louis-Marie Chauvet's Fundamental Theology of Sacramentality." *Horizons* 24, no. 2 (1997): 230–47.

Morrill, Bruce T. *Anamnesis as Dangerous Memory: Political and Liturgical Theology in Dialogue*. Collegeville, MN: Liturgical Press, 2000.

———. *Divine Worship and Human Healing: Liturgical Theology at the Margins of Life and Death.* Collegeville, MN: Liturgical Press, 2009.

———. *Encountering Christ in the Eucharist: The Paschal Mystery in People, Word, and Sacrament.* New York: Paulist Press, 2012.

Morrill, Bruce T., and Bernard J. Cooke. *Bodies of Worship: Explorations in Theory and Practice.* Collegeville, MN: Liturgical Press, 1999.

Morrill, Bruce T., Joanna E. Ziegler, and Susan Rodgers. *Practicing Catholic: Ritual, Body, and Contestation in Catholic Faith.* New York: Palgrave Macmillan, 2006.

Mudd, Joseph C. *Eucharist as Meaning: Critical Metaphysics and Contemporary Sacramental Theology.* Collegeville, MN: Liturgical Press, 2014.

Noble, Ivana. "From the Sacramentality of the Church to the Sacramentality of the World: An Exploration of the Theology of Alexander Schmemann and Louis-Marie Chauvet." In *Charting Churches in a Changing Europe,* edited by Tim and Ivana Noble, Martien E. Brinkman, and Jochen Hilberath, 165–200. New York: Rodopi, 2006.

Pickstock, Catherine. *After Writing: On the Liturgical Consummation of Philosophy.* Oxford: Blackwell Publishers, 1998.

———. "Thomas Aquinas and the Quest for the Eucharist." *Modern Theology* 15, no. 2 (1999): 159–80.

Pope, Stephen. *The Ethics of Aquinas.* Washington, DC: Georgetown University Press, 2002.

Porter, Jean. "Desire for God: Ground of the Moral Life in Aquinas." *Theological Studies* 47, no. 1 (1986): 48–68.

———. "Moral Rules and Moral Actions: A Comparison of Aquinas and Modern Moral Theology." *Journal of Religious Ethics* 17, no. 1 (1989): 123–49.

———. "Salvific Love and Charity: A Comparison of the Thought of Karl Rahner and Thomas Aquinas." In *The Love Commandments,* edited by Edmund N. Santurri and William Werpehowski, 240–60. Washington, DC: Georgetown University Press, 1992.

———. "The Subversion of Virtue: Acquired and Infused Virtues in the *Summa Theologiae.*" *Annual of the Society of Christian Ethics* (1992): 19–41.

Robinette, Brian DuWayne. *Grammars of Resurrection: A Christian Theology of Presence and Absence.* New York: Herder & Herder, 2009.

Rubin, Miri. *Corpus Christi: The Eucharist in Late Medieval Culture*. Cambridge: Cambridge University Press, 1991.

Sauer, Stephen J. "Naming Grace: A Comparative Study of Sacramental Grace Language in Edward Kilmartin, S.J., and Louis-Marie Chauvet." STD Diss. Catholic University of America, 2007.

Schillebeeckx, Edward. "Transubstantiation, Transfinalization, Transfiguration." *Worship* 40, no. 6 (1966): 324–38.

Schwartz, Regina M. *Sacramental Poetics at the Dawn of Secularism: When God Left the World*. Stanford, CA: Stanford University Press, 2008.

Sherwin, Michael S. *By Knowledge and by Love: Charity and Knowledge in the Moral Theology of St. Thomas Aquinas*. Washington, DC: The Catholic University of America, 2005.

St. John, Hal. *The Call of the Holy: Heidegger–Chauvet–Benedict XVI*. London: Bloomsbury T&T Clark, 2012.

Stout, Jeffrey, and Robert MacSwain. *Grammar and Grace: Reformulations of Aquinas and Wittgenstein*. London: SCM, 2004.

Tillard, Jean-Marie-Roger. *Flesh of the Church, Flesh of Christ: At the Source of the Ecclesiology of Communion*. Collegeville, MN: Liturgical Press, 2001.

Torrell, Jean-Pierre. *Aquinas's* Summa: *Background, Structure, and Reception*. Washington, DC: The Catholic University of America Press, 2005.

———. *Saint Thomas Aquinas*. Washington, DC: The Catholic University of America Press, 2003.

Vollert, Cyril. "Transubstantiation and the Encyclical." *Continuum* 3, no. 3 (1965): 388–90.

Wadell, Paul J. "Growing Together in the Divine Love: The Role of Charity in the Moral Theology of Thomas Aquinas." In *Aquinas and Empowerment*, edited by G. Simon Harak, 134–69. Washington, DC: Georgetown University Press, 1996.

Wawrykow, Joseph Peter. *God's Grace and Human Action: "Merit" in the Theology of Thomas Aquinas*. Notre Dame, IN: Notre Dame Press, 1996.

Wilkins, Jeremy D. "Trinitarian Missions and the Order of Grace According to Thomas Aquinas." In *Philosophy and Theology in the Long Middle Ages*, edited by Ken Emery Jr., Russell L. Friedman, and Andreas Speer, 689–708. Leiden: Brill, 2011.

Index

absence, 43, 131–32
Aristotle, 76
Augustine, 35, 42, 53, 67, 74, 134, 145

Baldovin, J., xxiii
baptism, 6, 16–20, 24–26, 48, 70, 109,
  111, 120, 124, 134–35
Benedict XVI, 100
Blankenhorn, B., 11, 104
body
  of Christ, xxiii–xxv, 2–9, 20–25, 73,
    97–99, 106, 120–32, 137, 147–54
  physical human body, 43, 89, 101,
    118–19, 128, 137, 149–50
Boyle, L., 9–10

cardinal virtues, 82–90
charity
  degrees of, 56–57, 94–96, 129, 151
  form of virtues, 18–19, 54–56, 87–92
  increasing in, 20–26, 46, 64–69,
    92–97
  infused, 16–20, 37, 52, 60–64
  moral goodness, 96, 138–40
  orders of, 52–56, 61, 65, 67, 69
  union with God, 23, 57–70, 97–100
Chauvet, L.-M., xxi, xxvi, 1–9, 26, 104,
  117, 120–32
choice, 75–78, 83, 96, 139–40
Christology, 11, 57, 104, 106, 111
church, xxv–xxvi, 2–9, 16–17, 20–26,
  103–4, 118–32, 147–54

communion, community, *koinonia*,
  24–25, 73, 91–92, 97–101, 123, 127,
  129–31, 137, 144, 146–53
creation, 29–33, 40, 61–62, 71
creed, 44, 106
culture, xxi–xxii, 153

de Lubac, H., xxiii–xxvi, xxix, 2–4, 104,
  120, 155
death, 71, 110
disposition, 18, 37, 58, 60, 74, 86, 93,
  115

Eucharist
  bread and wine, xxiii–xxvii, 2, 4,
    6–7, 16, 21–22, 122, 125, 135, 137,
    152–53
  consecration, xxiii, 5–8, 120–28,
    135–36
  eating, 123–29, 137–38, 152–54
  presence of Christ, xxii–xxxii, 2–9,
    17–24, 104, 121–32, 148–54
  transubstantiation, xxii, xxv–xxviii,
    2–6, 9, 120
evil, 32, 80

faith
  belief, xxi, 13–16, 25, 40–47, 51–54,
    61, 63, 98, 105, 149
  theological virtue, xxv–xxviii, 51–64,
    97–99, 109–10, 115–17, 123–28, 149
fortitude, 79–82

grace, 11–16, 33–48, 57–71, 98–101,
    118–19, 129–32, 141
grammar, xvii–xxxii, 11, 14–16, 25–26,
    32–33, 49–50, 94, 100–101, 133,
    155–56

habit, 37–39, 57, 60–64, 74–76, 82, 84,
    86
Holy Spirit, 38–39, 46–48, 49, 52, 59,
    64, 68, 70, 88, 90–93, 96, 99, 104,
    110–18, 123–27, 131–32, 143, 146
hope, 51–56, 61–64, 100
humility, 108, 146, 152–53
Hütter, R., xxii

identity, xv, xxvi, 16, 62, 123, 132
idolatry, 105, 147
Image of God, 34–41, 48, 57–58, 64
incarnation, xx–xxi, 104–7, 110
infusion, 16–20, 23–25, 52–53, 59–64,
    90–95
instrument, 13–14, 31, 48, 91, 98–99,
    112–13, 119

Jesus Christ, 104–11, 128, 147–54
John Paul II, xxiii
justice, 19, 78–79, 82, 89, 139, 144, 146,
    153
justification, 17–18, 20, 24, 37, 41, 46,
    58–65, 70–71, 98–101, 108–9, 124,
    130, 138, 149

Keenan, J., 55, 60, 66, 83–87, 96–97,
    138–39, 148
kenosis, 50, 70–71, 94, 104–11, 118,
    127–28, 131, 140, 142
koinonia. *See* communion

language, xx–xxxi, 135
Lindbeck, G., xxii–xiv
liturgy, 135, 144–54
Lombard, P., 74

MacIntyre, A., xxix
merit, 36–41

Morrill, B., 117
music, 136–37, 144, 147, 151
Mysterium Fidei, xx–xxiii, xxvii

participation, 14–17, 25, 27–31, 39–48,
    50–54, 69–71, 91–93, 100–101,
    118–19, 129–32
passion, of Christ, 11–12, 21–23, 45,
    104–13, 141
passions, 77, 79–81, 93–97
Paul VI, xx–xxi, xxiv
penance, 19–20
pneumatology, 38–39, 50, 57–58, 70–71,
    104, 110–12, 127–28
powers, 35–37, 41–42, 47–48, 82–85
preaching, 105, 136, 151
presence, xxii–xxv, 2–9, 17–18, 22–24,
    121–23, 125–32, 147–51
priesthood, 128
prudence, 75–89, 139, 143–54

Raymond of Pennafort, 9
religion, 19, 112–16, 118–23, 130–32,
    133–54
revelation, 35, 43–48, 54, 61, 91, 97–98,
    105–6, 115, 118, 132, 136
ritual, xxvi, 15, 136, 148
Robinette, B., xvii–xviii

sacraments, 11–16, 31, 45–46, 92,
    100–101, 103–4, 111–32, 134–38,
    140–54
sacrifice, 107–14
salvation, 11–12, 70–71, 98–99, 108–24,
    140–44
sanctification, 12–16, 45–46, 50, 64–66,
    69–71, 97–101, 112–13, 117–19,
    141–42
Schillebeeckx, E., xxv–xxviii
Scripture, xxiii, 127
Second Vatican Council, xvii, xxiii, xxv
sin
    in general, 71
    mortal, 18–19

subject, subjectivity, xiv, xxvi, 22–24, 58, 61–66, 68–69, 82, 109, 123–24

Tillard, J.M.R., xxv
transubstantiation, xxii, xxv–xxviii, xxxii, 2, 4–6, 9, 120

virtue
   moral, 73–100, 108, 114, 140–44
   theological, 18, 20, 24–26, 39–42, 49–71, 100–101, 110, 124–27

will, 36–38, 51–55, 59–67

When
AMERICA was
GREAT

When
AMERICA was
GREAT

THE FIGHTING FAITH OF POSTWAR LIBERALISM

KEVIN MATTSON

ROUTLEDGE
New York • London

Published in 2004 by
Routledge
270 Madison Avenue
New York, NY 10016
www.routledge-ny.com

Published in Great Britain by
Routledge
2 Park Square
Milton Park, Abingdon
Oxon OX14 4RN, UK
www.routledge.co.uk

Library of Congress Cataloging-in-Publication Data
Mattson, Kevin, 1966-
When America was great : the fighting faith of postwar liberalism/Kevin Mattson.
    p. cm.
Includes bibliographical references and index.
ISBN 0-415-94775-8 (alk. paper)
1. Liberalism—United States—History—20th century. I. Title.
JC574.2.U6M33 2004
320.51'3'097309044—dc22   2004006006

For Joseph,
May his future be bright

Table of Contents

Acknowledgments ix

Introduction 1
Endings and Beginnings

Chapter 1   Characters 26
The Unspoken Virtues of Liberalism

Chapter 2   Enemies 52
The Integrity of Liberal Anticommunism

Chapter 3   Values 86
The Pay-Offs and Problems of Pluralism

Chapter 4   Loves 110
The Nation as Beloved Community

Chapter 5   Hopes 140
Liberalism and the Quality of Public Life

Chapter 6   Tragedies and Conclusions 172

Notes 181

Index 220

Acknowledgments

First, for the dough. Thanks to those at Ohio University who granted me an OURC grant. I am especially indebted to Roxanne Male-Brune who helped me navigate the bureaucracy to find this helpful batch of money. Thanks also to the Gilder-Lehrman Foundation, which gave me support to visit New York City and consult the archives at Columbia University. Ohio University also bought the papers of Americans for Democratic Action (ADA) on microfilm, which made my research that much easier.

Second, a round of thanks to those who provided me with a place to stay on my many travels. In New York, Mark Schmitt, Ron Hayduk, David Dysegaard-Kallick, and Sarah Ritchie put me up. In Chicago, my heartfelt thanks go to David Raskin and his family and my *Baffler* friends. Thanks to John Summers for his ascetic retreat in Cambridge, Massachusetts, and to John McMillian for drinking much-needed beer. Thanks to Richard Ford and to Leah and the young 'un for a place to crash in D.C. Finally, to Danny Grobani and my cousin Dan and his wife Nina for places to sleep, plus so much else.

Then there are those who read this manuscript and gave me help that was crucial. The typical caveat applies: all the mistakes made herein are mine, not theirs. Thanks especially to George Cotkin and Neil Jumonville. Both were incredibly helpful, more than they can know.

At Routledge, I was fortunate enough to have this project (literally) fall in the lap of Robert Tempio who took it on with commitment and zest.

He provided not only helpful editorial advice but also an amazing knowledge of post-war intellectual history. I was also helped by Dave McBride, not just a friend but someone whose editorial acumen I appreciated even more after this project was done. Thanks also to Mimi Williams.

My two oldest and dearest friends, Jeff Boxer and Richard Ford, helped me out, as they always do.

Finally, there's my family. My mother read the manuscript and provided keen insights that only a mother can provide. She's also a damn good mother. My wife Vicky helped not by reading the manuscript but by putting the ideals of this book into practice. I love her for that and so much more. In closing, I dedicate this book to the coolest kid in the world, my son Joseph.

* * *

For allowing me to utilize archives and manuscript collections, I would also like to thank Yale University Library's Manuscripts and Archives Department (for the C. Vann Woodward Papers); the University of Chicago's Special Collections Library (for the Congress for Cultural Freedom Papers); the Stanford University Special Collections Department (for the Bernard DeVoto Papers); the Wisconsin Historical Society (for the James A. Wechsler Papers); Columbia University's Rare Book and Manuscript Division (for the Lionel Trilling Papers); Daniel Bell for allowing me to explore the Americans for Cultural Freedom (ACCF) Papers at the Taminent Library of New York University; the Library of Congress Manuscript Division (for the Reinhold Niebuhr Papers); and finally, John Kenneth Galbraith, Arthur Schlesinger, Mark DeVoto, and Nancy Wechsler for allowing me to quote from the manuscripts consulted for this book.

Our times require greatness as well as bigness—and greatness is a matter, not of the arsenal or of the pocketbook, but of the spirit. We will win the world to an understanding of our . . . purposes not through the force of our arms or the array of our wealth but through the splendor of our ideals.

Arthur Schlesinger, Jr., 1962

INTRODUCTION
ENDINGS AND BEGINNINGS

BEGINNING WITH THE END

The year was 1988, and there he was, his visage beaming to television audiences across the country, as it had for eight years. He held the mantle of national leadership, ready to pass it on to his vice-president. This was his moment at the Republican Party convention, a national performance replete with placard waving and cheers from the floor. The anointed were gathering energy for what hoped to be an upcoming slaughter like the last presidential election. And here he was at the center of it all, literally and metaphorically, as the great messenger. Having received a political education from the staunch conservative Barry Goldwater back in the early 1960s, having lambasted student protestors in the state of California during the late 1960s (a state he returned to "law and order"), having chipped away at the welfare state as best he could during the 1980s (although not as deeply as he wanted), Ronald Reagan now stood before his brethren and explained why Americans should continue his legacy. The answer came in three mean words that he pinned on his opposition: "liberal, liberal, liberal." There it was—a term dripping with venom—and that came to be known in the words of Reagan's vice-president as the "L word." From that moment on, a term once worn with pride became *dirty*.[1]

Conservatives had long dreamed of a day when liberalism could become a term of derision. William Buckley, the "patron saint" of conservatives, certainly beamed in 1988. When he began the *National Review* back in 1955, at the ripe age of 30, Buckley had fixed his magazine's sights on liberalism, attacking it for being too permissive, too secular, too meddling in the economy, and too soft on communism.

Liberalism was not just wrong, but, from Buckley's perspective in 1955, liberals "run this country." Holding together a quirky collection of writers at his magazine, he sought out a strong political leader who could give voice and power to his views. He watched as his political heroes, Joe McCarthy, the Red-hunting senator from Wisconsin, and Barry Goldwater, the libertarian presidential candidate for the Republicans in 1964, fell to defeat. Reagan was the only one who could scream at liberalism the way Buckley did while appealing to broad numbers of Americans. And so, after twenty-five years of waiting, Buckley found the messenger who could successfully take out liberalism.[2]

An irony emerges here, for a similar discontent with liberalism came from the left, not just the right. Like Buckley and Reagan, student leftists during the late 1960s started to hurl bombs at liberalism. There were leaders within Students for a Democratic Society (SDS), the central organization of left-leaning students calling for "participatory democracy" and an end to the Vietnam War, who chastised "establishment liberalism" in tones remarkably similar to Buckley's (although their solutions were different). Even before the Vietnam War heated up, there were certain intellectuals connected to the civil rights and peace movements of the 1960s, the harbingers of a New Left that became more vocal as the decade heated up, who argued that liberalism was elitist and technocratic by nature and thus unworthy of support from the left. They attacked "corporate liberalism," which in their minds was little more than a palliative for exploitation, a "system of political ideas," as an editor of the New Left publication, *Studies on the Left*, wrote, "consciously developed to strengthen the system of large-scale corporate capitalism." Liberal reform was little more than shadow boxing, simply a new way to preserve the interests of an elite, meaning liberalism had become the New Left's enemy as much as it was conservatives'. Animosity toward liberalism made increasing sense to student protestors and organizations like SDS because the "liberal establishment" and politicians moved slower than hoped on the cause of civil rights and because Vietnam looked like a "liberals' war," having been heated up by Lyndon Baines Johnson, the very same president who committed America to building a stronger welfare state in the guise of the "Great Society."[3]

Conservatives never stopped attacking liberalism after the 1960s; nor did the left. As the 1960s crashed and burned and the New Left retreated to academia during the 1970s, a new intellectual trend, "post-structuralism," rekindled the essential core of the New Left critique of liberalism. Now, the cast of sins was wider, including not only liberalism but the Enlightenment tradition and rationalism itself. The French intellectual and radical Michel Foucault, for instance, wrote an entire book about liberal prison reform. Instead of telling a tale of liberal reformers making criminal prosecution more humanitarian and enlightened, he exposed new forms of social control, seemingly more pernicious than those of the past. Where there was once physical torture of prisoners (bloody, cold, and brutal), now prisoners submitted to the regimentation of becoming morally upright. Sure, Foucault suggested, the modern prison no longer physically assaulted its subjects; instead, it imposed something much worse, a regime of self-control via the internalization of conscience, something this libertarian from the left hated. Liberal reform—no matter its claims—was now suspect. And so, imagine, if you will, student protestors of the New Left, Michel Foucault, Ronald Reagan, and William Buckley gathering for drinks and bonding around a shared hatred of liberalism. Intellectual and political life could come full circle this way, with the left meeting the right, even if none of these activists or intellectuals could agree on what should be done once liberalism was wiped out. Liberalism found itself boxed in from both sides, from both ends of the political spectrum.[4]

The intellectual beatings did not stop in the 1970s; the cast of critics just continued to grow. Liberalism gasped and then arose in the 1970s to confront more punches. There were "neo" or new conservatives who felt "mugged by" the "reality" of the 1960s, cursing liberalism's ethic of tolerance for "evil" things such as the counterculture, drugs, and the breakdown of traditional authority (the things that some New Leftists and Foucault embraced). Communitarians of the 1980s lambasted liberalism for being too individualistic and inattentive of shared values and religious belief. Here was a double whammy, for old-style conservatives, working alongside what were often left-leaning communitarians, continued to malign liberalism, pushing a new theme, that the liberal welfare state was too paternalistic.

Tolerant, individualistic, and paternalistic as it supposedly was, liberalism limped along only to face the wrath of a new generation, more cynical than any before. Younger political critics and pundits, coming of age in the wake of the Reagan era and facing the heady go-go days of the 1990s, started to kick the dead dog. So for Michele Mitchell, a young journalist at the *New York Times*, her generation rejected the naiveté and "bleeding heart" nature of 1960s liberalism, which she associated "with crumbling housing projects, holier-than-thou attitudes, and 'wouldn't it be great if' theories." Mitchell's assessment, echoed by many other Generation-X pundits, symbolizes just how beaten up liberalism had become by the late 1990s. It now appeared downright silly, doomed to exit the American political lexicon via the trash bin of American forgetfulness and conservative ridicule.[5]

The loudest of our political pundits today continue the assault, even if liberalism seems defunct and perhaps even powerless. Their message? That liberalism is "treasonous," capable of betraying the country at just about every moment in American history. So says Ann Coulter, the pundit turned historian, in *Treason: Liberal Treachery from the Cold War to the War on Terrorism* (2003). More respectable conservatives were quick to condemn the book, but the accusation of treason and the book's popularity shows just how far the right's culture wars have gone. There's a real political and intellectual insanity to all of this. It was liberals who defended this nation against communist threats long before Coulter's hero, Joe McCarthy (who was also William Buckley's hero), tried to boost his career by smearing his enemies as communist. It was liberals who invoked the memory of Abraham Lincoln and wanted to hold this country together in the face of Southern talk of secession during the civil rights movement of the 1950s and 1960s. It was liberals who spoke most boldly of the American promise, the hope that this nation could become a great world leader if it recognized its potential. Of course, understanding this depends on a good grasp of history, something not in abundant supply in today's sound-bite society.[6]

Some have tried to scream back at conservative pundits. Indeed, Al Franken and Michael Moore, both from the left, have tried to counterpunch for progressive causes, sometimes at the expense of honesty and veracity. Rarely do these counterattacks spell out any positive vision that could counteract conservatism, even if they sometimes successfully challenge conservative stereotypes of liberalism. In general, though, liberals have a hard time defending themselves, and for good reasons inherent in liberalism itself. Arthur Schlesinger pointed out fifty years ago that liberalism was a democratic faith that negated "passion." "Democracy, by its nature," Schlesinger claimed, "dissipates rather than concentrates its internal moral force. The trust of the democratic faith is away from fanaticism; it is toward compromise, persuasion and consent in politics, toward tolerance and diversity in society. . . ." And therefore, liberals have a hard time screaming back and defending themselves; the liberal ethic cuts against such a thing. As the poet Archibald MacLeish, put it during the 1950s, a "liberal is by nature a disinterested man—a man who is more concerned with the human truth than with the partisan advantage of some preconceived opinion. But precisely because we [liberals] see more clearly what must be done, we are reluctant, or so it seems, to do it." Liberalism embraces complexity and nuance over simple sloganeering; it is a foreign language to the shouting world of pundits. And here we get to the purpose of this book: to explain the promise of liberalism, believing that a better understanding of liberalism can improve current political discussion.[7]

To acquire this better understanding, I suggest a historical voyage of sorts, not too far back but far enough to get inside a different political world from ours, to clear the air so to speak. Go back to the years following World War II, a time of massive change for America as it moved out of four years of exhausting military battle to the prolonged and drawn-out conflict of the Cold War. This was a time, I argue, that liberal intellectuals and activists understood the potential of American greatness. They embraced their country's promise—the "American creed" of equality and democracy—but never allowed themselves to become pure celebrants of the American way of life or lose sight of their role as critics. They knew America was great but that it could become greater. To say such a thing about these thinkers and activists runs against not just the conservative pundits of today but a New Left historical interpretation, an even weightier inheritance for anyone that writes from the left. One narrative about "Cold War liberal" intellectuals dominates: they *acquiesced*. Intellectuals during the postwar years, this academic mantra goes, witnessed "embourgeoisement," busy as they were "making it" as middle-class eggheads in fat and prosperous America. They were therefore "deradicalized," moving out of the leftism that dominated Depression-era America during the 1930s into the center and sometimes careening rightwards during the affluent 1950s. And so we have, in the words of Jackson Lears, a "dreary saga of accommodation among a self-constituted critical elite" of intellectuals. If we are to believe this narrative, liberal intellectuals got caught up in the hype of national celebration that constituted so much of America's Cold War culture. The word on the street today would have been that they "sold out."[8]

So the existing histories of liberal intellectuals tell stories about acquiescence. We learn from the history books that their movement was "slow" and they spoke a dangerous language of "gradualism" on the issue of equal rights for African Americans. Liberal intellectuals were too stodgy to embrace the activism of civil rights protestors as they hit the streets and seized their rights. Their anticommunism made them dupes of the Central Intelligence Agency (CIA), their ideas becoming manipulative tools for the powerful, or so histories of the Congress for Cultural Freedom (CCF) argue. Because anticommunism bled into McCarthyism, liberal anticommunists are blamed for that as well. To add insult to injury, historians have castigated liberal intellectuals from the past as snobs and elitists, as out of touch with the ordinary people they should have tried to reach. Historical research therefore confirms what New Leftists and critics of liberalism have been saying since the 1960s: liberalism is defunct and rightfully so because it's the wrong place to look for vibrant political ideas.[9]

I don't see liberalism as a story of acquiescence or selling out. Nor is it what conservatives like Coulter or Buckley make it. Instead, I argue that liberalism is a public philosophy that demands citizens think of themselves as members of a national community committed to greatness. Instead of understanding liberalism as a separate set of policy plans generated by policy wonks or activists (i.e., health care reform, regulation of the economy, support of labor unions), I depict it as a humanist project committed to pushing people to think beyond the interests of the self. Liberalism demands that citizens think of public purposes and improve the quality of collectively shared resources. Liberalism, contra conservative critics, is a strong tradition in American political thought that stands at the center of this country's history. It stems from the framers of our Constitution and the thinking done in the *Federalist Papers*, from Abraham Lincoln's commitment to national unity in the face of Southern secession and the Civil War, and from the political vision represented in Teddy Roosevelt's Progressive Era presidency and Franklin Delano Roosevelt's leadership during the New Deal. As evidenced shortly, and closer to the time this book focuses on, liberal political thought was jumpstarted by World War II. This transformative event opened Americans up to a new phase of their collective history and pushed them to consider the demands of national greatness.

Liberalism, as my story tells it, demanded public thinking on the part of citizens while holding to a realist outlook on human nature. Human beings, from a liberal perspective, are naturally self-regarding and prone to foibles. This makes the variant of liberalism I'm tracing out here distinct from other strains of progressive thought that are more optimistic about human nature and therefore more hopeful about the future. Nonetheless, liberalism as I discuss it here is not pessimistic or cynical, because it believes in the ability of human beings to acquire key characteristics or virtues that can make them fulfill their responsibilities as citizens in a democratic society, that is, engaged in public questions and able to think beyond the needs of the self (although ideally not at the expense of privacy and an individual's well-being), equipped with a sense of humility, pragmatic rather than ideological, and committed to a dispassionate attitude that avoids fanaticism (in other words, to hold an "ironic" disposition).

These are the core liberal virtues spelled out here, and they were expected from individuals as well as the nation as a whole. As Americans looked outward to the world, throughout history, they have always faced absolutist and tyrannical powers opposed to their own way of life. This is a reality of international existence and has been diagnosed by many, not just liberals. Liberals, however, believe that national humility is a necessity in dealing with enemies of liberal democracy. Hubris is always a tendency to be avoided. So liberals uphold an ethic of irony and humility in the nation's and the individual citizen's life.

As much as opponents of liberalism have characterized it as a political ideology that encourages meddling in the economy and civil society and strengthening the state at the expense of local power, it has actually upheld the core values of pragmatism and pluralism. On a philosophical and political level, pluralism upholds the belief in divided power, that different interest groups, many themselves national entities (labor unions, business associations, etc.), vying for influence, serve as the best source for a healthy democracy. Liberalism has always placed faith in a vibrant civil society of voluntary associations, but at the same time, has balanced this aim against the need for a national and public interest transcending a plurality of interest groups and associations. As a form of political thought, liberalism is essentially a balancing act, one that recognizes the importance of political freedom and association but also the realities of nationhood. For instance, national purposes can legitimately counteract the wishes of citizens at the local level, be they citizens who want to deny citizenship to others or be they those who want to place economic motives ahead of common purposes. Liberalism takes seriously the ideal of a national community while also embracing pluralism and thereby holds key values in tension.

THE CAST AND THEIR IDEAS

To understand liberalism better, we must reassemble not just a set of ideas but a group of writers and scholars. We must listen in on the conversations that intellectuals were having with each other after World War II, with ideas and values they inherited from the past, and dialogues with public leaders, essentially, an older world of argument and thought displaced today by shouting pundits. Central to this book is the belief that ideas from the past need not be boring or dry. Nor should ideas from the past be disconnected from the present. In fact, ideas can live past their point of origin and tell us something about how we live and could live differently today. And at certain special moments in history, ideas can cohere into a "worldview," the reconstruction of which is the historian's responsibility. So this book has two purposes: to reconstruct the worldview of "Cold War liberalism" in its own context and evaluate it from the perspective of the present.

The thinking of one person does not constitute a worldview. A biography of a lone writer can never convey the energy that builds from collective thinking. In this book, therefore, intersections between ideas and different thinkers will matter more than singular thoughts. So too does the interaction between ideas and historical context. After all, ideas never live in a vacuum; they rub up against the important events of the day, becoming shaped and sometimes (although more rarely) shaping them. As a key character in this book once put it, "the pressure of world events" did more to influence his political thought than the pile of books lying on his desk as he wrote. Sometimes, the thinkers studied here tried to shape events as activists; sometimes they pulled back from the world to get a better perspective. But whatever their mode of operation, they developed a vision known as liberalism, one that is recoverable and capable of correcting the current misunderstandings perpetrated by conservative intellectuals and younger pundits.[10]

Much like a play or novel, this work of history has a central cast. The four key actors are the world-renowned theologian Reinhold Niebuhr, the Pulitzer Prize–winning historian Arthur Schlesinger, Jr., the best-selling economist John Kenneth Galbraith, and the newspaper editor James Wechsler. All were united around anticommunist ideals by 1945, winding up in the Congress for Cultural Freedom (CCF), the most important international group of intellectuals during the Cold War. All were members of Americans for Democratic Action (ADA), the leading liberal organization after World War II. Each one had the ear of Adlai Stevenson, crafting his speeches, giving him advice, and pushing this two-time presidential loser to be more liberal and principled. And there can be no doubt that all were "men of ideas" and "intellectuals" who led truly interesting lives, intertwining their thinking with the events of the day. I therefore trace their thinking and biographies as they reacted to a changing world, without reducing ideas to the times in which they developed.

There is a narrative structure in this book, one that follows events during a time when this strain of liberalism was congealing into a worldview, but there's also a thematic approach. Starting by discussing the backdrop of World War II, I move onto the early and frightening stages of the Cold War (1947 to 1949), a time that morphs into the rise of Senator Joe McCarthy to power (1950 to 1954). The chapter on "Enemies" focuses on this period in terms of these thinkers' critique of communism and right-wing anticommunism, and the chapter "Values" examines the positive dimension of their political thought, including pluralism. By following the Cold War's thaw during the second part of the 1950s, I examine these thinkers' conception of qualitative liberalism (which was first evident in the thinking of Bernard DeVoto and C. Vann Woodward, examined in the chapter on "Loves") and their engagement in the Kennedy administration (especially clear in the chapter entitled "Hopes"). At this moment, the political alliances of John Kenneth Galbraith and Arthur Schlesinger became especially important. I then close with the final tragedy of the Vietnam War, a war that threatened the legitimacy and unity of liberalism. Overall, the story here is one of intellectual comrades moving through history, seeking each other out, joining and forming organizations together, and campaigning for ideas and politicians arm in arm, sometimes winning, sometimes losing. Out of their engagement in history and their ideas grew the worldview I believe can teach us something about the deeper meaning of liberalism.[11]

Around this central cast swirled other thinkers. In fact, there's a fair amount of crossover with a group of writers who have received the most attention from historians analyzing post–World War II American culture, namely, the "New York Intellectuals." Indeed, I discuss, briefly, the literary critic Lionel Trilling, the philosopher Sidney Hook, the sociologist Daniel Bell, and the historian Richard Hofstadter. My cast of characters worked closely with this group of thinkers but always remained independent from this wider grouping. Most important, my cast of characters was always much more politically engaged in electoral politics and public policy, giving their arguments a pragmatic heft that was often absent from the work of the New York Intellectuals. Although Schlesinger, Niebuhr, Galbraith, and Wechsler were anticommunists and therefore involved in the Congress for Cultural Freedom, as were many New York Intellectuals, my cast was also deeply involved in Americans for Democratic Action, an organization that not only held fast to anticommunism but tried to carve out a positive philosophical framework for liberal action. My cast desired to go beyond anticommunism, articulate a constructive public philosophy of liberalism, and make their ideas actually effective in electoral politics, and these things made them distinct from other intellectuals of this era. Although some New York Intellectuals might have rejected politics from the 1930s for cultural matters during the 1950s, as many historians have argued, that interpretation simply does not hold for the cast in this book.[12]

Nonetheless, the New York Intellectuals and others enter the story where they help us understand the worldview of liberalism better. It's important to understand that my cast was a gregarious bunch that cast the net of intellectual comradery wide. A sense of that net must be provided to illustrate the influence of their worldview. Think of a play, when words uttered offstage help redirect activity in significant ways. So it is here. Not only do other intellectuals enter, but so too do politicians, especially that new breed coming of age during this period, men of ideas themselves such as Hubert Humphrey, Paul Douglas, and, of course, Adlai Stevenson and John F. Kennedy. At one moment, this book takes a slight detour into the thinking of two intellectuals, namely, the conservationist and popular historian, Bernard DeVoto, and the civil rights historian, C. Vann Woodward. These two make cameos, so to speak, because they help explain the relation between liberal thought and nationalism and its interaction with the challenge of sectionalism in American life and political conflicts of the Eisenhower administration. This should not seem too much of a diversion to any reader who understands the central theme of this book, the interaction between American "greatness" and the liberal tradition.

A cast such as this will be sure to generate complaints, especially its white male character. Where, some will undoubtedly ask, are representatives from underrepresented races and where are women? Let me explain. First, I believe my central cast here has an internal logic to it, one that provides coherence to the story I'm trying to tell. Second, the worldview presented here was antiracist and integrationist to the core, but these thinkers traveled in a world of white men. They listened to African Americans who pressed nobly for their civil rights at this moment in time, but they remained privileged, white, and well-educated themselves. Nonetheless, what's most remarkable was how these privileged men could articulate an inclusive nationalism that black intellectuals such as Ralph Ellison and Martin Luther King used to advance their call to open up the American creed to those descended from slaves and the nasty legacies of racism. These men operated in a world before the modern women's movement; however, they often had strong wives who were intellectuals (Ursula Niebuhr), writers (Kitty Galbraith), and legal activists (Nancy Wechsler) in their own right (Wechsler also worked for one of the most powerful women in New York City, the newspaper publisher Dorothy Schiff). These thinkers listened to women writers of the time; Arthur Schlesinger, for instance, promoted the work of Mary McCarthy and Hannah Arendt. There was room here for powerful women, even if feminism was not yet on the table.

But with this said, we should take these men for what they were, thinkers operating in a day when battles for civic equality for blacks and women were just starting to gain more power and influence. Nothing in their work stood in the way of these burgeoning movements; if anything, they nurtured them (Reinhold Niebuhr's influence on King, for instance, was immense). Certainly, there were limits to the worldview reconstructed here, but we should not allow those limits to plug our ears to what these people had to say or how widely this vision could be seen.

Indeed, the education and privilege of these thinkers garnered them influence. They wrote for widely read magazines such as *Fortune* and *Life* and mass circulation newspapers such as the *New York Post*. They debated on *Meet the Press* and other shows in this first decade of television. Their books appeared amidst the "paperback revolution" of the 1950s, when sophisticated ideas were first bought for cheap. This was, one writer points out, the "golden age" of the newspaper "column." Schlesinger and Wechsler were pros at this style of writing, with its quick muscular synthesis of policy and ideas, capable of being read on trains that jostled back and forth from city to suburb. Politicians took newspaper writers seriously then. This was also a time when intellectuals could write on a broad array of topics in the older tradition of the "man of letters" and when intellectuals felt certain an entry into the world of journalism would not stain their prestige or standing as scholars. Even after winning a Pulitzer Prize for historical writing, Arthur Schlesinger, Jr., for instance, considered a job in journalism (the *Washington Post* and *Fortune* fast in pursuit) prior to accepting a position at Harvard University. When he did accept, Bernard DeVoto explained to a friend that Harvard would "never make" Schlesinger "an academic," by which DeVoto meant a narrow, anemic, specialized scholar who only wrote for his peers. These thinkers, although often scholars, tried to influence public debate and politics rather than staying within the confines of academia. At the same time, they were generalists, essentially scholars with ideas, but not experts or what today we call "policy wonks." All they had were ideas and a desire to make them influence power; they also had the fortune to live in a world that still prized the insights of generalists rather than the work of experts.[13]

But we should not read their influence as *power*. After all, consider the obvious: their conduit of influence, Adlai Stevenson, lost his run for the presidency twice in a row during this period. The 1950s were years of liberal frustration as much as influence, due to an exhaustion on the part of the American populace toward reform (having just come out of the Depression and a world war, Americans sought comfort more than change). Certainly, Republican President Eisenhower did not scrap the New Deal's accomplishments; he strengthened Social Security even while using hard-right rhetoric about the welfare state's "creeping socialism." But Ike's centrist policies hardly signify a "liberal consensus," as witnessed by his own rhetoric (presidents do not typically use words unless they think they resonate with the American public). Still, since Eisenhower's presidency, it has been all too easy to write historical narratives depicting the 1940s and 1950s as years of complacent consensus cemented around a weak welfare state; conflicts seem to emerge only during the tumultuous 1960s.

Writing about a long tradition of reform beginning in the years following the Civil War, the historian Eric Goldman ended his 1952 book, *Rendezvous with Destiny*, with the sort of confidence and consensus about liberal reform that would still hold long afterward: "The country went along, almost as a matter of course, with the belief that government, particularly the federal government, should interfere to protect and advance the standard of living and the status of the more depressed groups." Unfortunately, this overestimation of a liberal consensus often stems from the arguments of the intellectuals studied here. For instance, in 1955, John Kenneth Galbraith could sound the language of consensus when writing, "Social welfare legislation is almost entirely noncontroversial." He was *more* accurate when he recognized that not only did the American right exist (small as it might be) but that it possessed a "near monopoly of articulate objection" to liberalism. Galbraith intended these words to apply to American foreign relations, but they applied just as well to domestic policy. After all, as Galbraith's contemporary, Daniel Bell, pointed out, the "radical right" had a coherent and articulate vision for "dismantling" the "welfare state" and "taming labor unions."[14]

Bell was right. There never was anything like a "liberal consensus" in America during the Cold War. In fact, certain business leaders were hungry to build back power and prestige during the 1950s, feeling they had lost too much during the New Deal. They financed organizations (the National Association of Manufacturers [NAM] and the Chamber of Commerce [CoC]) that were willing to fight for their vision and lobby hard. They won antilabor union legislation with the passage of the Taft–Hartley Act in 1947. Even when they lost that same year, as in the case of their battle against the Marshall Plan (which NAM despised inasmuch as this postwar economic plan provided American aid to "socialist" countries such as Britain and France), their voice never shrank from American political discourse. The libertarian right prepared for a long-term battle by forming organizations such as the American Heritage Foundation in 1947 (William Buckley followed suit with the *National*

Review eight years later). In the meantime, the right could rely on a set of journalists, on both television and nationally syndicated in major newspapers, to articulate a pro-business and antiregulatory vision. Fulton Lewis, Jr., Westbrook Pegler, Walter Winchell—these might not be household names today, but they were widely listened to back then, and all of them trumpeted conservative causes, combining McCarthyism with antiregulatory politics. They would be prepared to see the civil rights movement as a threat to states' rights and tinged with communism.

All of this suggests that liberals were by no means the only voices shaping public debate at this time. Jimmy Wechsler liked to remind people that his paper, the *New York Post*, was the only one that deserved the moniker of liberal in that supposed liberal bastion of New York City (even the *New York Times* endorsed Eisenhower in 1952). By most counts, a liberal consensus during this period is little more than a myth. Following this, I contend that the thinkers studied here were at their best when recognizing this, when they spoke less of their ideas as part of a "consensus" presently reigning in American political culture and more as a "fighting faith" that had to do battles for the hearts and minds of their fellow citizens. That fact, in part, is what makes this tale so interesting. During a conservative period, these liberal intellectuals had to show that their thinking lived up to the best ideals of America. They drew much of their original energy and inspiration from World War II, a conflict that highlighted American greatness.[15]

BEGINNINGS: THE CRUCIBLE OF WORLD WAR II

The war serves as the backdrop to the ideas studied here. Therefore, it's good to end this introduction by explaining the war's impact on intellectual and political life in America. Of course, the primary aim of the war was to prevent the advance of German aggression throughout the continent of Europe and Japanese power throughout the Pacific. But as the bombs rained down on Germany and American boats dodged Japanese bombs and planes, there was a quieter war back "home" that focused on the mobilization of a nation. The war catapulted itself into the consciousness of those on the homefront, as women manufactured munitions and kids crushed cans and prepared for salvage drives. Peoples' everyday experience was crowded out by the war: air raid alarms went off, rationing prevented ordinary shopping, and radio news kept the war in the forefront of people's minds. This war was "total" in the terms of overseas brutality but also in terms of citizen mobilization and the heightening "awareness of" Americans' "common lot."[16]

A central challenge of World War II was to generate a sense of national unity for an international cause, and this bled into the cause of liberalism itself. Throughout the wide expanse of the American continent with its polyglot regions, there needed to be built an "imagined community" of soldiers and citizens who were likely never to meet one another face to face but had to feel a common purpose. Solidarity had to replace private desire; "obligation" and "commitment" had to become operative terms. That there was a liberal essence to this commitment was evident in the enemy to be fought, namely, the ideology of fascism. This is precisely what made World War II a "liberal" war demanding liberal support. Fascism, with its glorification of the state and führer over the individual, its eradication of political pluralism and civil society, and its violent racial hatred, was the clearest antithesis of liberalism's ethic of openness and tolerance.

Add to this broad conflict between liberal and fascist ideologies the war's awakening of Americans to the sinister nature of their own racism. For instance, A. Philip Randolph struck a blow against racial segregation during World War II when he threatened a massive march on Washington unless the government prevented racial discrimination in federal contracts with defense manufacturers. The "hopes" of African Americans increased as Franklin Delano Roosevelt acquiesced to Randolph's demand. Some liberals started to believe that America would no longer be able to square racism with the "American creed." Not only racial oppression but class privilege was challenged during the war. Although America's armed forces remained racially segregated, young men from different socioeconomic backgrounds were thrown together "as equals in a common task." Sacrifice was expected of everyone, not just the poor. The federal government protected the interests of labor alongside those of munitions manufacturers. It is no surprise that FDR, building on the momentum of the New Deal, called for a "second bill of rights" in 1944, one that ensured economic equality as a part of America's national purpose. With this declaration, the case seemed to be clinched: World War II—with its fascist enemy and call to racial and economic equality—was a liberal's fight.[17]

Still, it took a great deal to convince liberal intellectuals that this was *their* war. The problem was that there had already been a world war to "save democracy," and the thing was botched. World War I, which America entered in 1917, had *not* brought democracy to Europe; in its wake, President Wilson could not get the United States to support the League of Nations, the first attempt to govern the world along more democratic and cooperative lines, and Europe went back to carving up the third world into the colonial fiefdoms that predated the war. Some American liberals looked hopefully within their own nation, believing that the federal government might continue to regulate the national economy as it did during the war through agencies like the War Industries Board and the War Labor Board; this way, a national purpose could prevail over private profit in the long term. But those hopes were dashed, as the regulatory mechanisms of World War I collapsed in 1919, followed not only by a growing fear of communism (in the wake of the successful Russian Revolution led by Lenin) but also the conservative and pro-business decade of the 1920s. Add to this that the war had been a slaughter with dead bodies piled up senselessly on the battlefields of Europe, and it became difficult for liberals to believe that war could *ever* be an instrument of good. Pacifism seemed the most legitimate response to future calls for war.

The first thing to do, then, was convince liberals that World War II was *not* World War I. The war had to be seen as something more than just a battle between European countries (a war of "capitalist states" against "capitalist states" as some Trotskyists saw it at the time). The ideological importance of the war needed to be understood. Pleas were made, and sometimes they became histrionic, understandably so because fascism was clearly what Archibald MacLeish called "a revolt against the common culture of the west." The stakes, as anyone who read Hitler's writings would have known, were high. For MacLeish, a thinker who had imbibed the Popular Front ideals of left-wing "Americanism" during the 1930s, opponents of World War II who alluded to the disillusionment of World War I were "irresponsibles."

The "lost generation" of the 1920s—those who had become war weary and alienated from society, moving to Europe to drink away their shattered illusions—could not understand the threat of fascism. They had locked themselves into the past, making memories of World War I permanently etched in their minds against the very different realities of

World War II. MacLeish knew of what he spoke, having enlisted for service during World War I and befriending key figures of the lost generation such as Ernest Hemingway. So too did the American intellectual and cultural historian Lewis Mumford. He had opposed World War I and now found himself ready to send his son off for military battle in World War II (where, in fact, his son would die). For Mumford, post–World War I weariness had induced "emotional anesthesia" that clouded the minds of liberal intellectuals. The critical distance so central to intellectual work now eclipsed the passion necessary to react to the dangers of fascism and the fall of Europe. The problem was, as younger intellectuals such as Arthur Schlesinger, Jr. saw it, these calls to arms from MacLeish and Mumford sounded too strident and belligerent, likely to become susceptible to another round of postwar disillusionment.[18]

That's what made Reinhold Niebuhr's call to arms during World War II so important (and why, in this story, he becomes such a central character at this moment). Niebuhr was just as much a critic of pacifism as MacLeish and Mumford. He too saw the pacifist rejection of war as irresponsible and World War II as a "crisis of civilization." Pacifists, for Niebuhr, ignored the reality of evil found in fascism. Their protest against bombing Germany, for instance, showed off what he called an "inability to understand the tragic necessities of history." Pacifists wanted to retain their "selfish" purity (keeping their hands clean of violence) rather than recognizing the extent of the fascist threat. But Niebuhr made himself distinct from MacLeish and Mumford by being just as frightened by those who saw their fight against the "irresponsibles" as grounded in absolute certitude. Here the liberal conscience with its overtones of ambiguity and sense of limits crept into an area typically thought to be about dark and light. For instance, Niebuhr argued against those who believed the fight against fascism constituted a "holy war." After all, the "weapons we use in this combat are certainly not 'holy.' They are terrible." Here, Niebuhr drew upon Christian ethics but, as he would throughout his career, made them speak to more than just fellow Christians. The condemnation of the "irresponsibles" should not inflate the sense of moral righteousness of antifascists. "The Christian acts," Niebuhr explained, "with an uneasy conscience both because of the ambiguity of his cause and the impurity of his weapons." In other words, "pure holiness" was unavailable to those waging a "just" war against Nazism. When looking back on the war after it had passed, Niebuhr maintained his sense of humility: "The human instruments by which the defeat of tyranny was encompassed were of course themselves tainted with some of the evil which they fought." Here was a liberal defense of America's entry into World War II, both certain of the brutality of fascism, but never belligerent about its own cause.[19]

Liberals, Niebuhr implied, needed to fight without losing sight of their core principles. "Commitment" should recognize its own internal conflicts, inasmuch as the home front had numerous problems (including racism) still needing to be solved. As America was just starting to get involved in World War II, Niebuhr counseled, "Our spiritual task is not an easy one because we must defend a civilization which has been digging its grave for decades and has the right to live only because the alternative is so horrible." Niebuhr's advice seemed straightforward: provide support but be cautious. Take the issue of civil liberties, a central liberal cause. Here, Niebuhr allowed for some curtailment of rights. There was no such thing as "pure liberty," Niebuhr argued, but one must always be aware of previous abuses of wartime hysteria to wipe out nonconformists (Niebuhr cited the crackdown on "subversives" during World War I, much of which was ugly and hysterical-minded). Thus, he condemned the infamous mistreatment of Japanese Americans who had shown themselves loyal to the American cause but were still forced into places that looked eerily like concentration camps. And as he balanced commitment with humility, Niebuhr also balanced "the stability and unity" that "the national community" needed with "the liberty of individuals," without "making either the nation or the state into the idolatrous end of the meaning of all existence." Only this sort of ethical disposition could make World War II a liberal war.[20]

If the war was construed as liberal in this deeper sense, then an intellectual obviously had an obligation to commit to the cause. Our cast of characters did just this. Prior to Pearl Harbor, these thinkers harangued their fellow citizens to join the war. In 1940, Niebuhr formed the organization Union for Democratic Action (UDA) to "crystallize and make interventionist sentiment effective primarily in labor and liberal groups" and started to edit *Christianity and Crisis*, a magazine that counseled Christians to shed pacifism. Arthur Schlesinger, Jr. recounted "a hundred conversations" he had when traveling across country with Bernard DeVoto in 1940, both of them persuading fellow citizens that

World War II was *their* war. Talk turned to action once America entered the war. James Wechsler served a short term in the army; Schlesinger, due to bad eyesight, couldn't serve in the military but did work first for the Office of War Information (OWI) and then the Office of Strategic Services (OSS); John Kenneth Galbraith, too tall to fit into military uniform, worked at the Office of Price Administration (OPA), and Reinhold Niebuhr, too old for service, worked formally with the army on a program that educated soldiers about the purpose of the war and informally with the Office of Facts and Figures (OFF) and OWI.

All of these intellectuals showed an intense desire to be useful. A sense of this is captured in Bernard DeVoto's pressing letters to his friend Elmer Davis who was serving as head of the OWI. DeVoto pleaded almost desperately for "some minute share in the war somewhere." Intellect serving in wartime—this is what these thinkers demanded from themselves. Often, this search taught them about the limits of intellect and the need to be flexible. Galbraith explained to a fellow economist about his governmental service, "An economist in such a post can be very useful and can have a good deal of influence. His influence depends, however, on avoiding a too-stiff-necked attitude." So as much as these intellectuals saw themselves filling a special role, they also learned about the ethic of compromise that both the war and liberalism itself demanded of adherents.[21]

Galbraith's experience at the OPA taught him much more than just flexibility. It showed him the promise of American life, how the country could remake itself through collective action and civic sacrifice. It also showed how local power and national power could work conjointly. Created in 1941, the OPA's chief tasks centered around stabilizing the American economy in order to clinch overseas victory. The OPA monitored economic activity, set prices, ensured that there were enough goods for overseas through rationing, and tried to prevent inflation at home. The impact on ordinary citizens was immense, seeing, as one historian put it, "nearly every item Americans ate, wore, used or lived in was rationed or otherwise regulated." The OPA worked with other important agencies such as the Office of Production Management, War Production Board, and National War Labor Board. Most of Galbraith's work at the OPA was bureaucratic in nature and often thankless. As he wrote ten years after the war, "The regulation of economic activity is without doubt the most inelegant and unrewarding of public endeavors."

Getting people to understand the rationale behind price regulation was difficult in itself, and bureaucratic ineffectiveness and a general lack of coordination within the OPA often drove Galbraith to distraction. He also faced business conservatism that resisted federal meddling in the economy. So why did he stay as long as he did?[22]

Galbraith drew energy from the national sacrifice the OPA generated. Rationing connected the citizen at home to the army overseas (nurturing the "imagined community" of a nation united), and there were additional liberal lessons. As Reinhold Niebuhr put it, "Sacrifices of the war will greatly reduce the inequalities of our economic system." Galbraith concurred. But what was perhaps most remarkable about the OPA's activities was its dependence on citizen activism, not just the directives from bureaucrats such as Galbraith. As the historian Lizabeth Cohen put it, the OPA's success relied upon a "rich soil of community voluntarism." For who was it that checked on stores in local towns and cities to ensure compliance with price regulations and who was it that denied themselves basic comforts? Ordinary housewives who believed that private profit should not be placed above the national interest. Therefore, as Meg Jacobs makes clear, the OPA symbolized not only a "political culture premised on broad participation and consumer rights" but also a vision of "state building from the bottom up." Witnessing the sacrifice of ordinary citizens for the purpose of securing the nation's future had an enormous impact on Galbraith both at the time of his work with the OPA and long after.[23]

The work of the OPA energized James Wechsler as well (his father worked alongside Galbraith). A labor journalist at the left-wing newspaper *PM* prior to serving in the army, Wechsler was supportive of Galbraith's work. He knew how important economic regulation was for the urban working class who suffered the most when prices skyrocketed. He was especially attuned to the plight of labor unions during wartime, knowing that certain labor leaders felt pressure toward accepting unequal sacrifice. On the other hand, he grew perturbed at the leader of the United Mine Workers (UMW), John L. Lewis, who violated a no-strike pledge in the coal industry in 1941 and 1943, jeopardizing labor's standing in relation to government (indeed, the War Labor Board reacted with punitive measures against unions due to Lewis's move). Like Galbraith who grimaced at the refusal of business to comply with price regulations, Wechsler condemned Lewis's demagogic move that put labor's interest over that of the nation's during the emergency of war. At the same time, Wechsler believed the national interest could be balanced against labor's power. All interests had to be taken into consideration if the nation was to unify for war.[24]

While Galbraith helped unify the country around a commitment to fair prices and Wechsler argued for labor's interest alongside that of business, other intellectuals helped the war effort in a way that came naturally, through words and ideas. World War II demanded public support, and although President Roosevelt never felt comfortable with the manipulative tendencies of modern propaganda (especially because the opposition used it all too well), he knew that the war needed to be explained to the American public. So in October 1941, he approved the creation of the Office of Facts and Figures (OFF). Archibald MacLeish, then the Librarian of Congress, oversaw OFF's operations. MacLeish had a particular concern when accepting the job. In 1940, James Wechsler hit upon the trouble that MacLeish would face one year later: "The greatest obstacle to Allied Propagandists in World War II was the propaganda that preceded American entry into World War I." More precisely, the legacy of World War I posed problems for liberal commitment to World War II. In this case, the memory of the Committee on Public Information (CPI), the American government's agency for whipping up public sentiment in favor of World War I, proved sensitive. Headed by the muckraking journalist, George Creel, and employing numerous writers and scholars, the CPI had demonized the enemy through grotesque posters and often resorted to dishonesty by planting stories in newspapers. The cause of truth and the demands of propaganda had clearly conflicted.

MacLeish was painfully aware of this legacy and struggled to ensure that OFF not duplicate the CPI's abdication of truth. Because as Nazi Germany built power through the lies of propaganda, the demand became that much more important. As America entered the war in December 1941, OFF moved from issuing informational pamphlets about the international conflict to motivating a wider audience via radio broadcasts. The radio program *This Is War* was, in the words of John Morton Blum, "much of exhortation, less of interpretation and war aims." MacLeish now found it difficult to preserve truth against more manipulative tactics; or put another way, the intellectual's craft—writing persuasively while taking truth to heart—was being trumped by the cynical tools being developed by Madison Avenue. MacLeish decided to resign and make way for a new organization. So in June 1942, less than a year after its creation, OFF folded, and the Office of War Information (OWI) took its place under the leadership of radio journalist (and liberal) Elmer Davis.[25]

The OWI became a hotbed of liberal writers, including Arthur Schlesinger, Jr. Elmer Davis found these people to be crucial in his work but also difficult to manage at times, and he found himself amidst the same sort of bureaucratic infighting Galbraith faced at the OPA, plus a larger conflict over the role of intellect during war. The OWI did many of the same things as the OFF. It issued pamphlets about the war and tried to get on the radio. But it also pressed in new directions, including the promotion of overseas propaganda and working more closely with Hollywood.

The latter area was rather tricky, seeing as the motion picture industry never thought of itself in the business of truth. The OWI's Bureau of Motion Pictures scrutinized Hollywood's scripts and bemoaned how films stressed fast-paced military action over a more serious explanation of the ideological underpinnings of America's cause. Explosions displaced ideas, and debates surrounding fascism and American democracy rarely graced the silver screen (one exception was *Casablanca*, a movie the OWI supported but didn't think went far enough in explaining the war's aims). Worse yet, films could sometimes resort to racial stereotypes of the Japanese, which prompted the OWI's stern disapproval. "This is not a racial war," one memo from OWI scolded film writers. As the OWI intervened in the world of visceral emotions and entertainment created by Hollywood, it faced the same difficulty that troubled MacLeish in his struggle over radio content, that is, balancing truth against manipulative propaganda. Unfortunately for Davis, this struggle did not manifest itself only in the OWI's work with Hollywood.[26]

When accepting his job, Davis believed that information alone was enough to mobilize Americans to fight World War II. After all, what more was needed to persuade the American people to fight than a realistic description of Hitler's political and racist philosophy and his march throughout Europe? Nonetheless, the same year that the OWI got up and running, the federal government helped nurture the War Advertising Council, and Davis himself felt pressure to employ not just writers but those familiar with the newer techniques of Madison Avenue.

Recognizing the conflict between advertisers and writers, he tried to keep them separate from each other within the organization. Such internal bureaucratic efforts, however, could not prevent those inside the OWI from seeing the work that reached the public. The OWI's "product," so to speak, smacked increasingly of the influence of Madison Avenue. And in 1943, the writers revolted. Arthur Schlesinger complained to Bernard DeVoto in April 1943 that the "advertising men" had taken over the OWI and that the new "primary interest" was now "in manipulating the people." Joined with other writers, Schlesinger complained to Davis, who obviously felt caught in the middle. Schlesinger did battle but finally left for another job at the OSS. Davis concluded, as he continued his work with the OWI, that intellect could never be fully squared with the imperatives of war. What was certain was that truth and persuasion were not easily married.[27]

The OSS suited Schlesinger for the rest of the war. Here he did research and editing that provided intelligence for wartime strategy. We don't know as much about this work as we do about the OWI (for the obvious reason that it was much more secretive). One thing is clear though: it was more technical than ideological and thus much less susceptible to the problems faced at the OWI. But with this said, we should not see the OWI as a closed and shut chapter in Schlesinger's life. It would actually leave behind many long-lasting lessons. First and foremost was that America was not just a country bounded by land and geography or simply a military power; it was an "idea" whose image was increasingly being projected abroad. How that idea became constructed, whether it grew out of the words of writers and intellectuals or out of the images and slogans of advertisers, could be a source of conflict. A central challenge for American liberals originated in the OWI and would live long afterward: how to remain devoted to truth while persuading others of the imperative of one's own values? Any national purpose, as Niebuhr had warned, had to be coupled with a sense of humility. Liberals needed to keep in mind their own nation's proclivity toward evil as much as good. Commitment had to take into consideration its own foibles. So Schlesinger left the OWI, but as the war wound down, he would return to the ideological question of America's values, never finding comfort in the technical world of intelligence temporarily provided by the OSS. He would continue to define America's public purposes at home and abroad.[28]

After the OWI, OSS, and OPA faded into the memory of the war and the military battle came to an end, there was a brief period of exalted celebration. Popular memory conjures up pictures of soldiers listening to cries of "victory" blaring from radios and cheering, with beaming big smiles on their faces, and navy men kissing girls on the streets. But the war itself, as Niebuhr understood so well, had taught tragic lessons not easily displaced by the triumphalism of victory. Intellectuals especially could not help but brood. The political theorist Jeffrey Isaac rightfully calls the period between the Great Depression and World War II a "brutal form of intellectual shock therapy." The years after the war would intermingle celebration with "doubt," that as one cultural historian points out, was "rooted in the forebodings of an age that had witnessed a war that left sixty million persons dead; the murder of six million Jews in the Holocaust; the development and use of the atomic bomb; the Great Depression, which seemed always on the verge of reappearing; and the cold war, which ironically matched the nation against the Soviet Union, its wartime ally." Darkness crept into American culture in the years following the war. Optimism seemed inappropriate, seeing as it would have to rely upon a certain faith in progress that the Holocaust and the tragic choice of using the atomic bomb seemed to negate.[29]

It is not surprising to find American culture, during the 1940s, being marked by doubt and unease, by what Arthur Schlesinger called "anxiety." Painting, for instance, moved away from the strident social realism of the 1930s (especially that of Thomas Hart Benton), with its faith in the common working person, toward the more complex artwork of abstract expressionism and its exploration of subjectivity and contingency. The chance and chaos captured in Jackson Pollock's "drip paintings," which scattered paint across a canvas in seemingly random order, appeared, for some critics and connoisseurs, more appropriate to an era of doubt than paintings of burly workers in factories. Jazz music moved from the sweet sounds of swing, intended to entertain dancers, to a harsher and more complex music known as "bop" more appropriate for intent listeners in smoky bars. "Seriousness" seemed the right attitude in the face of a world grown slightly mad. Existentialism, with its concomitant faith in individual choice and absurdity, came into vogue during the 1940s, with people clutching copies of Søren Kierkegaard's dark and foreboding books. This cultural mood reflected the fact that the World War II generation had witnessed not just national victory but also, in Bernard DeVoto's words, "the delusions that mankind and society could be made perfect and that evil could be eradicated as a force in man's souls and their societies." Although in the past some liberals believed in optimism, now they found optimism impossible to defend.[30]

Liberal intellectuals had another transformation to face in 1945: the death of President Franklin Delano Roosevelt. This event heightened the general anxiety of the time. It seemed at times that liberals believed FDR would live forever, understandable because he had been elected four times straight and had pulled America through the Depression and war. Roosevelt's death freed liberals from hanging their ideals on a single personality but also induced the sort of dread that accompanies freedom. As Arthur Schlesinger wrote in 1947, "The existence of Franklin Roosevelt relieved American liberals for a dozen years of the responsibility of thinking for themselves." Only until his death did liberals "realize to what extent their confidence in the postwar period had rested on one man." Now liberals could think for themselves. The need for a liberal worldview and "vision" could never have been stronger than in 1945. And there were people who belonged to a "new and distinct political generation," people like Schlesinger himself, who were ready to accept the challenge. They knew they had to move beyond the New Deal and FDR's legacy but also ensure that the national promise captured in both the New Deal and World War II would continue to speak to Americans as they headed into the Cold War.[31]

With the death of FDR and the realities of the Holocaust and the destruction of the war, liberalism needed to become "tougher" and develop what Schlesinger called "guts." "Whether you invoke Augustine or Freud or Pareto," Schlesinger argued, "there are moody and destructive impulses in man of which official liberalism has taken no serious account." It was time for the accounting to begin. During the 1940s, thinkers such as Lionel Trilling would start to distinguish between "a false and degenerated liberalism" and a more realistic form of liberalism. Some called this a "liberalism of responsibility" or a "tough minded" and realist type of liberalism. The war and the context of the 1940s demanded such a thing. It was up to liberal intellectuals to define, in light of the lessons they learned, what this meant.[32]

CHAPTER ONE

Characters
The Unspoken Virtues of Liberalism

The history of philosophy is to a great extent that of a certain clash of human temperaments.

William James[1]

EGGHEAD ETHICS: THE PASSIONS OF IRONISTS

World War II opened up the world of public service to liberal intellectuals. Intellect engaged the project of building national unity, and it created busy lives in the process. During the war and immediately afterward, these thinkers tried to balance the demands of service with the necessary independence of mind that made them intellectuals. It was in this balancing act that we get a sense of what they were like as people and a feeling for their political ethics, of what they expected not just from themselves but from other citizens living in a liberal democracy. Getting to know the sort of "characters" these thinkers were during the war and then afterward, we learn more about the liberal view of character that is central to this book. Here I set out the broadest outlines of these characters' biographies while showing what they tell us about political philosophy.

Start with John Kenneth Galbraith, always a very busy man. At the OPA, his days were full of meetings where he faced down lawyers armed with anger, facts, and arguments for their clients' interests against government regulation. There was infighting within the bureaucracy and the difficult (and daily) work that went into monitoring just about every sector of the economy. Read his memos and notes from this period and you'll read about the prices of beer, cigarettes, toilet paper, maple syrup,

26

vegetables, and even admission prices to bowling alleys. Galbraith threw himself into this work with a passion and dedication to public service, working alongside other young idealists who wanted to unite America against its fascist enemies. In return, Galbraith got to hear his name slandered by the conservative pundit Fulton Lewis, Jr. and angry congressmen in committees who disliked the OPA's regulatory power.[2]

Things hardly slowed down when Galbraith resigned from the OPA in 1943. Afterward, he wrote for *Fortune* magazine and then worked with the State Department, eventually assessing the military and economic damage done to Europe and Japan by the war. It was only in 1948 that he settled down (those words should go into quotation marks) and took a teaching position at Harvard (a year after Arthur Schlesinger, Jr. had arrived). Even still, public service beckoned. In addition to teaching full-time, Galbraith encouraged Adlai Stevenson and other leading Democratic Party politicians, in 1953, to create something like the New Deal's "brain trust," that is, a group of intellectuals grounded in different policy arenas who could give advice and help shape upcoming campaigns. Galbraith helped run what became known as the "Finletter Group" (named after Tom Finletter, a former secretary of the air force and ambassador, whose house served as the meeting place). He gathered papers from different people, arranged and facilitated meetings, and tried to craft a vision out of these conversations for Stevenson. He continued this line of work with the Democratic Advisory Council during the later 1950s, writing speeches and thinking up policies for the party's leaders and specific candidates. Galbraith moved in and out of public life, settling back into academia for what were hardly respites, inasmuch as he took the demands of teaching seriously, but also wrote large numbers of articles and books about difficult economic matters that were intended to reach wide audiences.[3]

The climax of his public service came during the Kennedy administration. As an economist, one would expect him to become an economic advisor like his friend Walter Heller. But Galbraith was also deeply interested in third world development, and so Kennedy made him diplomat to India, a country that had a crucial role to play in Cold War international politics because it tried to remain unaligned, threatening to cozy up to Russia while trying to get as much as it could from the United States. At one point during Galbraith's ambassadorship, the United States had cut economic aid, and so India's prime minister threatened to buy Soviet MIGS, prompting Galbraith to scramble in order to secure delay. This sort of stress continued due to heightened tensions and low-grade wars among India, China, and Pakistan. Galbraith's schedule alone gives a good sense of his workload. Listen to him outline his coming days to the president:

> I am starting on a 10 or 12 day tour of the far South; a major speech and honorary degree at one of the southern universities, inauguration of a school feeding program in Kerala, a general show of support for the non-Communist forces in this state, a speech at the Defense College in Wellington, a breathtaking display of horsemanship, a visit to the Maharajah of Mysore and the great religious festival of Dasara, an inspection of two industrial plants in Bangalore.

As if this weren't enough, Galbraith got up at 5 a.m. every day in order to have time to write. Worse yet, there were those embarrassing moments, as when his son locked the keys in the car right before Galbraith had to drive to the airport to pick up Jackie Kennedy, his boss's wife.[4]

Throughout all this, Galbraith combined what might seem two contradictory personal characteristics: passion and irony. He knew the hardest part of being a diplomat was not his schedule but the violation of his intellect, the necessity of sacrificing truth for the job. When accepting his job as diplomat, he wrote in his diary, "To rationalize and explain and cover up as Washington requires will come very hard." He rarely had to do this (although he did at times), inasmuch as he remained a critic even while a member of the Kennedy administration. He protested some of the administration's moves openly, dashing off letters and memos to his friends and the president himself that were as funny as they were informative and critical. His friend Arthur Schlesinger Jr. later reveled in the "supplementary aphorisms, wisecracks, and other pieces of Galbraithina" sent his way. His attitude also shone through in his writing where he sometimes ensured readers that he could not write a "polemic" based on "anger," explaining that he "would like to suppose I do not take myself so seriously." Perhaps the most interesting comment made about his busy life of public engagement came when he looked back in 1981 and explained how he "always tried for a measure of detachment. I've felt that one should hold some part of one's self in reserve, never be completely sure of being right." These words captured the essence of his attitude and a recurring theme throughout Galbraith's life: passion combined with irony.[5]

Schlesinger understood the sentiment well. Indeed, he saw the essence of democratic politics in Galbraith's detached engagement. Schlesinger explained, "Democratic politics, as Orwell has observed, permits the participant 'to keep part of yourself inviolate.'" Galbraith's balance in life therefore personified a classic tenet of the liberal state: "The liberal state acknowledged many limitations in its demands upon men: the total state acknowledges none." Schlesinger himself took to heart Galbraith's ethic, although there seemed more passion here than irony (a "passionate participant" but also a "man of thought" as his journalist friend James Wechsler described him).

Schlesinger became the quintessential "engaged" intellectual; his biography, as we look back on it, is like Galbraith's in that it is capable of being broken down into a series of activist episodes, including his work with the Office of War Information (OWI) and Office of Strategic Services (OSS) during the war, the Economic Cooperation Association (ECA) after the war, the Finletter Group with Galbraith, and finally his role as special advisor to President Kennedy. He believed in a "tough-minded" realism that saw intellect in service to the world of politics, a world of messy compromise and inevitable failures. He chided those who wanted a better world but were unwilling to get their hands dirty. Wechsler praised him "for demonstrating by both word and deed that it is possible to 'act as a man of thought and think as a man of action.'" Schlesinger was an intellectual *engagé*, as the French put it.[6]

Yet Schlesinger never saw his life as the only model for intellectuals. One need not write propaganda, counsel politicians, or become an advisor to the president. There always existed a plurality of modes of being an intellectual as far as Schlesinger was concerned. He believed intellectuals could be "activists," like himself, or "prophets," or even naysaying "gadflies." Indeed, he admired his friend and fellow historian Richard Hofstadter who never became engaged in politics and instead wrote in an ironic detached style about American politics. At another moment he praised one of James Wechsler's colleagues, the journalist Murray Kempton, for writing screeds against those in power and thereby offering an "antidote to the danger that those with influence might take themselves too seriously." That he wrote these words while serving as an advisor to President Kennedy makes them especially poignant. From the mouth of a committed engaged intellectual came the ironic spirit, pluralistic about its ethics and, all the while, willing to laugh at itself.[7]

If Wechsler called Schlesinger a man of action capable of "detachment," Schlesinger said the same about this journalist. The two of them met when Wechsler wrote for *PM*, a liberal newspaper that refused commercial advertisements and became a forum for his pro-labor and anticommunist writing during World War II. Wechsler and Schlesinger maintained their friendship when Jimmy moved on to the *New York Post* in 1946 and when he became chief editor during the late 1940s. During the 1950s, Wechsler got Schlesinger to write columns for him and tried, unsuccessfully, to get Galbraith to do the same. Although Schlesinger had decided on academia rather than professional writing, he retained a love for the newspaper world with its pressure cooker atmosphere built around editorial deadlines or what one writer called the "slam-bang world of metropolitan tabloid journalism." Schlesinger explained:

> Jimmy was first of all a newspaperman. His style in the profession was a happy mingling of modes of the Twenties and the Thirties. There was more than a little in him of *The Front Page*—the hard-drinking, hard-smoking (alas, cigarettes were to kill him), jaunty, iconoclastic scribe who revels in the comedy of life and views authority with sardonic skepticism. One recalls Jimmy at his desk, writing nonstop, a bottle of bourbon by his side and the radio blaring out the baseball game. . . . Jimmy . . . had an irrepressible sense of the absurdities of life and humor eased the tensions of politics without cutting the nerve of responsibility.

Others attested to Wechsler's hectic, chaotic, but always humorous world of editing, remembering how he moved around the *Post*'s office to confer with journalists. He had the "aggressive demeanor of a bantam, which is typical of the way he writes," said one person.[8]

The pressures of a hectic office were just the beginning of Wechsler's challenges. As an editor, he had to make the *Post* committed to both truth-telling *and* entertainment. Right before taking over his editorial responsibility, Dorothy Schiff, the paper's owner and a strong and independent woman with political influence, had almost disbanded operations due to poor sales. She needed a strategy that could ensure a wide readership. Wechsler himself had a residual gloom left from his days at the nonprofit newspaper *PM* and a short stint at the liberal magazine *The Nation* during the 1940s (the same years that Reinhold Niebuhr wrote for that publication). As he explained later, "I was troubled by that ancient disease of liberal journalism—the feeling that we were talk-ing to ourselves, and to those who agreed with us, rather than to the great multitudes who daily received their guidance from . . . the con-servative press lords." So it's not surprising that when examining copies of the *New York Post* from the 1940s and 1950s, you find well-researched stories about important political issues next to splashy titles about Hollywood scandal and gossip about key New York personalities (Wechsler never mixed the two worlds, just ran them side by side, mak-ing sure that politics wasn't taken to be the same thing as entertain-ment). As one reader explained, the *Post*, under Wechsler's leadership, was "earnestly liberal" and "equally concerned with racial integration, disarmament, and Hollywood bust measurements." This strange com-mitment to "entertain and inform" at the same time drew a wide read-ership among the "lower middle" and "middle class" of New York City. Although Schlesinger questioned how well all this worked at times, Wechsler believed the only alternative to providing entertaining gossip alongside rigorous reporting was to cop a "self-righteous" attitude, an attitude too common among liberals and one that would lose him an au-dience and therefore any impact. Truth-telling and effectiveness needed to find a working relationship, as Wechsler believed they did at the *Post*. His newspaper, with its readership ensured, could do what any good paper should do, that is, "comfort the afflicted and afflict the comfort-able," as he himself put it.[9]

Most important, Wechsler did this while retaining a sense of humor like Galbraith's. He was witty and capable of entertaining his employees with quick one-liners. His tone was infectious, spreading throughout the *New York Post*'s offices. Pete Hamill, once a cub reporter at the *Post*, recounts this story about Murray Kempton, although similar ones could probably be told about Wechsler himself: "One election night, Kempton was in his third floor office, sending down his copy one sentence at a time, until it was six thirty in the morning." The night editor wanted to know how much more Kempton was to write and sent a copyboy up to ask Kempton. "Mr. Trow wants to know, how much more?" the copyboy said to Kempton. "Kempton lifted his almost-completed bot-tle of Dewar's and said, 'Oh, about an inch.'" Wechsler could preserve wit like that of a sodden Kempton even under the pressure of Senator Joe McCarthy's inquisition. After writing about his experience coming face to face with Joe McCarthy in *The Age of Suspicion*, he sent a copy to Reinhold Niebuhr. Niebuhr loved the book, describing it as "the apologia of a very robust and witty young man who is also a true exponent of democracy." Democratic wit—these were high words of praise indeed from the godfather of postwar liberalism and they were well applied to Wechsler.[10]

Niebuhr himself would seem the furthest thing from a flippant, hard-drinking journalist. This was a man, after all, who rarely touched alcohol and brooded about the evil nature of humans while safe in the confines of the central tower of Union Theological Seminary. And yet, Niebuhr appreciated Wechsler's humor. He connected humor, rightfully, with "a proper" sense of "humility." "To meet the disappointments and frustrations of life, the irrationalities and contingencies with laughter," Niebuhr explained, "is a high form of wisdom." So Niebuhr laughed, but he was also, like the others here, terribly busy. At least that was so from 1940 to 1952. During this time, he edited two magazines, *Christianity and Society* and *Christianity and Crisis*, founded the Union for Democratic Action (UDA), and then helped transform this group into Americans for Democratic Action (ADA), whose foreign policy statements he crafted. He gave advice to politicians and taught Adlai Stevenson a great deal (so Stevenson himself claimed). Niebuhr was also constantly on the road lecturing. One journalist explained in 1943 that he was "away . . . over weekends, preaching at universities on Sunday mornings, addressing political and liberal groups on Saturday nights and Sunday afternoons." He would do most of his writing on trains back and forth between appointments. Indeed, Niebuhr pushed himself so hard that he collapsed a number of times during his life, finally suffering from a severe stroke in 1952.[11]

The stroke made it clear to Niebuhr that he would have to slow down. It also provided him with a deeper sense of humility, seeing as there's nothing like dealing with the physical limits of the body to nurture this sentiment. He doubted whether "altogether healthy people," as he put it to a friend, could really understand "the final mysteries of grace." Sickness made clear human limits and the often absurd nature of life. So too did those people who came to ask him about his own biographical development. For Niebuhr had already acquired prestige by the 1950s (he appeared as something of a godfather to many liberals, including to some studied here) and people came to seek him out for advice. This always made him feel uncomfortable, in large part because it forced him to consider how wrong he had been in the past.

This came out especially in his correspondence with Schlesinger who wrote an early biographical treatment for a book of essays about him, entitled *Reinhold Niebuhr: His Religious, Social, and Political Thought* (1956). As Schlesinger reminded him of crucial biographical facts, Niebuhr grew alarmed, especially at his slowness in shedding his 1930s radicalism for his present-day liberalism. "I find the records of my travels . . . embarrassing," he explained to Schlesinger. "If you had not given chapter and verse I would not have believed that it took me so long to draw the conclusions from the presuppositions." Looking back, his "negative attitude toward Roosevelt" during the 1930s and early 1940s now appeared a "scandal." He described his intellectual and political maturation as "so tardy that it gives me a good indication of the ephemeral character of one's convictions, at least of my convictions, and of my unreliability." Niebuhr continued to learn the personal lesson of humility throughout the 1950s. As he looked back on his life in 1960, he told his colleagues at Union Theological Seminary, "So many of my certainties of the thirties and the forties and of the fifties have disappeared and all that one has left is I hope a degree of modesty that makes one recognize what a fool one has been, particularly if one has written so much and put his foolishness on paper." Humility—inspired by sickness, humor, and, most obviously, Christian theology—was central to Niebuhr's life.[12]

* * *

What emerges from the brief portraits offered here is a sense of "egghead ethics," the ways in which these thinkers, as intellectuals, saw their work and lives. Journalists coined the term "egghead" during the 1950s, a label that suggested a character type and political leaning (liberal) that was ineffective and effeminate, detached and ethereal by nature. If we move beyond this stereotype, though, we notice the outlines of a character type that held great lessons for liberal political philosophy. Thinkers like Galbraith, Schlesinger, Wechsler, and Niebuhr cared about their "attitudes" and dispositions toward life almost as much as they did about their thinking. They *lived* their values as best they could. Think of some of the characteristics traced here and you get a sense of what sort of people they wanted to see more of in America: those who combined passionate commitment and ironic detachment, recognized the inevitable plurality of values without degenerating into purposeless withdrawal from life, combined a commitment to truth with a commitment to effectiveness, laughed at themselves and each other, and embraced a sense of humility. This understanding of the importance of everyday ethics, how one lived and interacted with others, and how this started to link up to politics (at least in a cultural sense) can best be understood by examining one of the most important novels that came out of liberal circles at this time, Lionel Trilling's *Middle of the Journey*. It was a novel read by these intellectuals and that provides a window into the framework and values that guided their own lives.[13]

A NOVEL APPROACH: THE POLITICS OF BEING IN THE MIDDLE

Lionel Trilling was America's most famous literary critic during the 1940s and 1950s, taking the place of Edmund Wilson. Both Wilson and Trilling had been enamored of Marxism during the 1930s, although Trilling's flirtation lasted for a much shorter period of time and by the 1940s and 1950s he had become a self-professed liberal. He also traveled in the same circles as Wechsler, Niebuhr, and Schlesinger. Teaching across the street from Union Theological Seminary at Columbia University, Trilling and Niebuhr met, perhaps when Niebuhr was out walking his poodles around their neighborhood. The two bonded around a realistic assessment of human evil, although Trilling preferred Sigmund Freud's psychological teachings to Augustine's theology (Trilling was Jewish after all). Trilling also thought Schlesinger to be a great thinker and intellectual ally, and he respected Wechsler's journalism. But he never joined Americans for Democratic Action. "Despite my natural sympathy with much of the program of the ADA," he explained to Eleanor Roosevelt, "I am not ready to make the political commitment that attendance at the [upcoming] convention would imply." Like other New York Intellectuals, Trilling was much more of a cultural figure than a political one when it came to the intellectual history of liberalism, something that made him distinct from the cast of characters that are central in this book. But it's precisely his concern with culture and character that warrants a quick detour through some of his intellectual activity from 1940 to 1950. He laid the groundwork for a postwar liberal view of character.[14]

As a character himself, Trilling personified egghead ethics. His wife remembered how people always liked him for "his quiet, his moderation, his gentle reasonableness." He had a cool demeanor that naturally recoiled at personalities animated by extremes. He spoke of the "moral obligation to be intelligent" and embraced "complexity" in his own approach to life's difficulties. Perhaps one of the best stories told about Trilling came from a conversation between him and Richard Sennett: "'You have no position,' Richard Sennett once upbraided Trilling in a conversation. 'You are always in between.' 'Between,' responded Trilling, 'is the only honest place to be.'" Trilling's temperament naturally drifted to the center—toward nuance and complexity—and away from polarized positions.[15]

Trilling's appreciation of complexity also made him critical of the overly hopeful strain in liberal thinking that Schlesinger and Niebuhr were then attacking, the "need for optimism," as Trilling himself once called it. Trilling saw in Sigmund Freud a potential answer to liberalism's shallow understanding of human nature, stressing not Freud's indebtedness to the Enlightenment (his belief in the ability of humans to master themselves through psychoanalysis) but rather the emphasis he had placed on the tragic conflict between human desire and the social demand for limits. For Trilling, Freud understood the "great tragedy" in human life that grew out of an inevitable conflict between biology and civilization or "free will and necessity." Humans, from this Freudian perspective, were constantly finding themselves limited by the past and doing things counter to their best interest.

Trilling appreciated this view of humans, not so much as someone interested in psychology but in literature. As a literary critic, he believed good novels, like Freudian psychic theory, could deepen liberalism's appreciation of everyday behavior and character. For instance, Trilling loved Nathaniel Hawthorne's writings about the impossibility of "moral perfection." He also loved Herman Melville's short story, "Billy Budd," which told of a ship's captain who tries to ignore the evil treatment another man commits against an innocent sailor. For Trilling, novels like this could show the "tragic" element of life, one not so easily sloughed off by those clinging to a naive faith in progress or optimism about human behavior. Novels did something else as well. They opened up a world of experience not capable of being expressed in political theory, the historical mode of communication that most liberal intellectuals had taken up (from John Locke onward). The novel expressed the "moral imagination," as Trilling put it, and allowed readers to put their own "motives under examination" by examining the world of characters created therein (making moral questions more concrete than philosophical speculation). With this in mind, Trilling decided to write his own novel (he had written numerous short stories already) that came out just as the Cold War was heating up.[16]

The Middle of the Journey told the story of John Laskell, a quintessential liberal if ever there was one. Laskell seemed to be a character out of the New Deal, someone who "had committed himself to the most hopeful and progressive aspects of modern life," namely, the design of "public housing developments," which led to a life full of "long dull meetings" about politics (the character's life here seemed like Galbraith's at the OPA). Laskell was hopeful but growing older and moving away from his youthful naiveté. He suffered his first loss when his girlfriend died. Then he himself fell into a serious illness, the sort that Niebuhr saw as a potential source of humility. To recuperate, Laskell decided to stay with Nancy and Arthur Croom in their country house. The Crooms were not just liberals who believed in "reason," as Trilling pointed out, but were still fellow travelers at this point in the novel, willing to make pacts with communists if it seemed to advance their progressive cause (something that Laskell had decided to reject). They had been approached by a friend of Laskell's, Gifford Maxim, who had been a member of the Communist Party.

Nancy Croom admitted that when Maxim was in the party, she had promised to serve as an accomplice to his covert activities, motivated by a perverse desire for action that might remove her from the slower and more complex world of liberal reform with all of its ambiguity. She claimed to be tired of "liberal shilly-shallying talk. I want to do something real," even if that meant complicity with Stalin's murderous regime. After setting up these characters, Trilling then threw them together. As Maxim appeared on the front door step of the Crooms' house during Laskell's stay, the characters were confronted by serious moral questions prompted by Maxim's decision to break with the Communist Party and embrace religious faith.[17]

Trilling modeled Maxim on the real person of Whittaker Chambers, the ex-communist spy who would come to fame by testifying against Alger Hiss, a New Deal liberal with clear connections to the Soviet Union.

This famous trial would take place just one year after *The Middle of the Journey* appeared. Trilling had known Chambers personally for a number of years and admired his break with the Communist Party, although he worried about the hardened nature of his religious conservatism. Trilling then projected this concern onto the character of Maxim.

In the novel, Trilling described Maxim as "the blackest of reactionaries." But at least, Maxim was more sensitive to tragedy than the Crooms. Nancy always avoided talking with Laskell about his girlfriend's death or his illness. This avoidance defined her character: "The desire to refuse knowledge of the evil and hardness of the world can often shine in a face like a glow of youth." At least Maxim had a sense of responsibility toward the world. He knew that when he had pledged himself to the Communist Party during the 1930s he had pledged himself to the terror done in its name: the purges carried out by a police state. "I am involved in the cruelties I have never seen and never will," Maxim explained. "My hands are bloody because of what I was, because of what I consented to, because of my associations." Nancy saw Maxim as insane, as beyond the realm of reason.

Laskell could not concur, for although he rejected Maxim's absolutist and religious conservatism, he still believed Maxim's sense of guilt was understandable. After all, and as Trilling makes clear in a subplot within this novel, Laskell felt guilty about the way he had treated people in his own life (including a young girl who passes away during the story). And thus, Laskell was in the middle, and because of this, he was a more mature liberal, one who had seen tragedy in his own life and thus rejected those who "wish to deny . . . complexity in life," the way Nancy did, or moved to a "false spirituality," like Gifford. "Between," as Trilling had told Sennett, was the place to be.[18]

THE VIRTUES OF LIBERALISM

Arthur Schlesinger loved *The Middle of the Journey*, reading it numerous times. But he noticed a central problem in the novel: Gifford Maxim was a much more engaging character than John Laskell. Schlesinger wrote Trilling in 1947, as the novel was hitting bookstores, "Curiously enough, Maxim is much more vital and vigorous a creation than Laskell that his questions, rather than Laskell's answers, remain in the reader's— or at least in my—mind. That, I would say, is the weakness of the book—or perhaps a source of unconscious strength." Schlesinger's point might sound like it was simply a question of plotting out a novel, when in fact it captured a broader point about an emerging view of the liberal character. After all, Gifford Maxim was supposed to be Whittaker Chambers, a leading conservative intellectual just about to become famous with the Hiss trial and his best-selling book *Witness* (1952). What made Maxim "vital and vigorous" to Schlesinger is what would make Chambers so compelling a character in American public discourse, namely, his moving between two extremes, pledging himself to communist tyranny during the 1930s and then embracing a conservative religiosity of absolute principles in the 1950s, a classic story of fall and redemption.

With *Witness,* Chambers created one of the most melodramatic books in the history of political writing, dripping, as it was, with moralistic overtones drawn from his terrifying experience of rethinking the crimes done in his name. Chambers admitted to considering suicide and wrote evocatively of recurring nightmares. He wrote in the same vein as he defined the Cold War battles that lay ahead for America. Communism may be humanity's "final experience" in world history, Chambers warned, "unless the free world, in the agony of its struggle with Communism, overcomes its crisis by discovering, in suffering and pain, a power of faith which will provide man's mind, at the same intensity, with the same two certainties [promised by communism]: a reason to live and a reason to die." Chambers, as did Gifford Maxim, believed in the need for an absolutist faith to combat the absolutist faith known as communism.[19]

Schlesinger recognized a certain appeal in Chambers's and Maxim's narrative about good and evil. He wrote a glowing review of *Witness,* seeing it as one of the best political autobiographies in American history (which it most certainly was). But Schlesinger was profoundly disturbed by the absolutist tendencies in Chambers's thought, both in his communist and conservative phases. Absolutism was an effrontery to the liberal character who embraced ambiguity. "When Mr. Chambers demands belief in God as the first credential" for his conservative philosophy, Schlesinger complained, "he is surely skating near the edge of an arrogance of his own."

While Schlesinger penned these stinging words against Chambers's absolutist faith, Niebuhr was concurring that *Witness* was "another revelation of how ex-communists, as well as communists, can still be involved in an either/or option." After making this comment to Schlesinger, Niebuhr wrote publicly, "Of those who have renounced their Communist faith, some have, in the violence of their reaction, embraced the dogmas of the extreme right, thus exchanging creeds but not varying the spirit and temper of their approach." The target here was clearly Chambers and what mattered to Niebuhr was not Chambers's thinking, some of which Schlesinger and Niebuhr agreed with (a sense of limits, the argument for original sin, etc.), but his *attitude* or, put more fancily, characterological disposition for absolutes. Rigidity, no matter the ideology that it produced, was troublesome. And Schlesinger's and Niebuhr's point hit conservatives and their view of character straight between the eyes, be it Chambers or other famous ex-communists that moved to the right like Elizabeth Bentley, the "blond spy queen" as she came to be known, or Will Herberg, another thinker who embraced religious certitude after breaking with communism.[20]

For a liberal intellectual like Schlesinger or Niebuhr, complexity and nuance promised a more profound attitude toward life than the search for absolutes. They also knew that the right's offerings provided a sense of certitude that might appeal to some Americans (hence, the fear that Maxim was more interesting than Laskell in *The Middle of the Journey*). After all, they wrote with the legacy of fascism's rise in Germany and the consolidation of Soviet totalitarianism in the forefront of their minds. Many social scientists, some of them transplants from fascist Germany, wrote worrisomely during the 1940s and 1950s about the "authoritarian personality," that is, a human susceptibility to absolutist claims for loyalty. And liberals like Niebuhr and Schlesinger worried that the Cold War's conflict between communism and democracy might lead to a crude reaction on the part of ordinary Americans. Richard Hofstadter spoke of a "conservative pseudo-revolt" in 1955 that spurred simplistic (often conspiratorial) accounts of politics.

At the same time Hofstadter worried about the new right, Reinhold Niebuhr bemoaned the popularity of Billy Graham, the most popular evangelical preacher during the Cold War. For Niebuhr, Graham's "simple pietistic version of the Protestant faith" denied the inherent "complexity" of life. All of these liberal intellectuals worried about the stern moralism and talk of absolutes coming from John Foster Dulles, the secretary of state under Dwight Eisenhower, who called for the moral necessity of "rolling back" communism rather than simply containing it (a view articulated by the ex-Marxist and conservative intellectual James Burnham). Cold War simplicity prompted fear among these thinkers who were partial to nuance and complexity and to the realities of a world that would not necessarily bend to their wishes.[21]

Here we get to one of those keywords of American culture during the 1950s, "anti-intellectualism," a term directly wedded to the post-war definition of the liberal character. Richard Hofstadter first worried about anti-intellectualism in 1953, writing that "everywhere in America, intellectuals are on the defensive," threatened by "populistic democracy." Continuing in Hofstadter's vein, David Riesman, the sociologist and author of the now classic *The Lonely Crowd*, depicted "American politics" in the mid-1950s as "intelligence without force or enthusiasm facing force and enthusiasm without intelligence" because intellectuals ran fearfully from the public sphere. Generally, social critics believed Eisenhower's America to be intellectually deficient, enamored of cheap entertainments rather than the life of the mind. President Eisenhower was known to enjoy reading pulp fiction himself. In reaction, though, the logic of Hofstadter and Riesman might be to elevate the urbane thinker above the unruly masses who seemed too susceptible to simplicities, demagoguery, and authoritarianism. Mark Krupnick, the literary critic, suggests as much when analyzing Lionel Trilling's social thought during the 1950s: "The self-divided intellectual, who had been the butt of communist ridicule in the thirties, now replaced the revolutionary proletarian as possible redeemer of society." The intellectual as savior was always a dangerous possibility in postwar liberal thought.[22]

On this count, these writers inherited a snobbery and elitism that seemed, at times, a natural part of intellectual work itself. It was an inheritance especially evident in American cultural life during the 1920s. During that decade, an intellectual giant overshadowed others, influencing just about every aspect of social thought. Banging out some of the fiercest and meanest social criticism imaginable at the *American Mercury*, H.L. Mencken dominated intellectual life, pushing writers to take aim at the small-town businessman with his petty conservatism and religious evangelicalism (symbolized most evocatively in Mencken's biting commentary on the infamous "Monkey Trial" where William Jennings Bryan defended creationism against evolution in 1925). Mencken wrote in funny and poignant ways, and his barbs against business culture could charm some latter-day liberals. But fundamentally, Mencken was an antidemocratic, misanthropic snob. When writing on education, for instance, he argued that the teacher's call to "spread enlightenment" was an impossibility inasmuch as "thinking is precisely the thing that the great masses of plain people are congenitally and eternally incapable of." This grinding of America's problems deep down into the recesses of democracy led to a general alienation and withdrawal from national life on the part of intellectuals during the 1920s. Those who read and admired Mencken often found themselves so alienated that they literally left the country in an act of expatriation during the 1920s.[23]

So when Hofstadter spoke of "anti-intellectualism" growing from the seedbed of "populistic democracy," Mencken's ghost seemed to hover. When liberal intellectuals fretted about the "authoritarian personality" or the simplicity of Billy Graham during the 1950s the way Mencken did about William Jennings Bryan during the 1920s, there appeared a recurrence. Fortunately, liberal intellectuals also had a sense of history and recognized Mencken's legacy, both its strengths and its weaknesses. Schlesinger, for instance, praised Mencken's writing, his important merging of literary and journalistic styles and his brilliant wit. For Schlesinger, Mencken possessed a "superb polemical style" and an "uproarious contempt for the business culture" that dominated the culture of the 1920s. At the same time, though, Schlesinger explained, "What began as an alienation from business culture was ending in some cases as an alienation from democracy itself."

This was the danger of intellectual snobbery, and it was one that Schlesinger's mentor and friend, Bernard DeVoto, personally witnessed, having published one of his first pieces of social criticism in Mencken's *American Mercury* and regretting it fairly soon thereafter. In 1943, DeVoto called his 1926 article on "Utah" in the *American Mercury*, "ignorant, brash, prejudiced, malicious" and written by a "young buck, intoxicated with the newly achieved privilege of publication." For DeVoto looking back, the lesson in 1943 was clear: "In the 1920s writers withdrew from the national life as a consciously superior caste, and that withdrawal was at once ignorant, arrogant, and dilettante." The result was that liberalism became deracinated and ineffectual. Any desire to use "anti-intellectualism" as a means to justify alienation from society during the 1950s would not seem a live option for people like Schlesinger who had never done so in the first place or DeVoto who had. They knew they needed to communicate to as wide an audience as possible in meaningful ways.[24]

When they wrote about the virtues in one another's attitudes toward life—a sense of humor, humility, and understanding of complexity and nuance—these thinkers did not elevate themselves above the unruly masses, the way Mencken did during the 1920s. After all, intellectuals could just as easily lack these virtues. There were plenty of intellectuals who had no sense of humor, as these thinkers knew all too well from personal experience. Besides, even if intellectual life were conducive to irony and detachment, the intellectual should not recoil from a world gone berserk. Rather, the intellectual must reform society, humanize it if you will, in order to encourage a wider dispersal of liberal virtues. The lives and values of those studied here had to spill over into the institutions of which they were a part. If politics were done appropriately, then a better character type would emerge. That is, better institutions could create better people, and better people could create better institutions even if they could never eradicate selfishness or obtain perfection. That was the liberal idea of building character: perfection was doubted due to a sense of innate selfishness on the part of humans but at the same time, a faith in key virtues such as humility was upheld. In other words, liberals possessed a sense of virtue. Although conservatives today complain that liberals are amoral relativists, this certainly does not seem the case when we examine the characters studied here.

So let us recall here some of these virtues detached from individual biographies and state them a bit more boldly, seeing where they head in terms of political action. There was humility or what Niebuhr called "a humble recognition of the limits of our knowledge and our power." Although he was a critic of the optimistic side of John Dewey's philosophy, Niebuhr certainly embraced the pragmatic tradition's argument in favor of fallibilism. Niebuhr also embraced a sense of humility, believing that this virtue quelled any belief in closure or a "bogus claim of finality." There was also a necessary tolerance of pluralism as when Schlesinger appreciated different modes of intellectual being, the gadfly as opposed to the "responsible" intellectual, or when Galbraith spoke of a British intellectual he knew and admired throughout the 1950s because of his "open-minded concern for the ideas of other people."

This sort of tolerance, Niebuhr argued, was not "a virtue of people who don't believe anything. It is a virtue of people who know that they are not quite right in their beliefs, or that their beliefs are not absolutely true." As we have seen, this was a belief in complexity and nuance that did not negate a passionate commitment to social justice. Perhaps Schlesinger summed up these virtues best when he wrote: "To denounce dogmatism and avoid a sense of one's own infallibility without letting detachment shrivel the will or skepticism cut the nerve of action: this is indeed a model for our contemporary liberalism, which has so often erred in the direction of self-dramatization, priggishness, and maudlinity."[25]

Perhaps the word that sums up these different characteristics best and one used throughout the 1950s was irony. If there was one character disposition central to liberal politics, this was it. Trilling defined irony as "awareness with acceptance of the breach between spirit and the world of necessity." Niebuhr, who wrote an entire book that applied irony to America's role in the world, distinguished the concept from tragedy. The latter dealt with having to do evil in a world of predetermined events, whereas irony was about wisdom facing its own contingency and limits (tragedy was an ancient approach to life, whereas irony was modern). Irony was about accepting the principle of unintended consequences, of actions resulting in something very different from what was hoped. As Niebuhr put it, irony was not just about "laughter" but "a nod of comprehension beyond the laughter" that the world was never controllable.

Ironists were smart people capable of rejecting the absolute certitude of conservatives and then living with the consequences. Irony put strength into one's soul or intellect (the root of the word being iron), the sort necessary to deal with the tribulations of life. This made the attitude similar to what the liberal sociologist David Riesman called the "nerve of failure," that is, "the courage to face aloneness and the possibility of defeat in one's personal life or one's work without being morally destroyed." This nerve of failure could manifest itself only within autonomous individuals capable of resisting social pressures, and, not surprisingly, irony required distance from social institutions in order to laugh at them (and oneself). Irony was therefore directly linked to a virtue of an older, eighteenth-century variant of liberalism, namely, individualism. Niebuhr explained, "The conflict between the conscience of the individual and the community must not be abolished, for it is a source of wisdom and grace for both the individual and community." But this was not an individualism of self-interest alone, the sort glorified by the market, but an individualism that engaged in the cooperative work demanded by civil society and politics. An ironist who retained freedom from institutions with an eye toward changing them for the better was the ideal liberal character type.[26]

If postwar liberals were to become ironists, they also had to pledge themselves to what can be called an ethic of reform. Too often the term "reform" is thought of in strictly narrow political terms, when in fact it should conjure up values and cultural norms. "The liberal belief in working for change," Schlesinger explained, "does not mean that he regards human reason as an infallible or incorruptible instrument, or that he thinks utopia is just around the corner." As an historian, Schlesinger knew how reform movements animated so much of American history, the abolitionist, suffrage, and civil liberties movements as well as the movement for public schools and labor equity during the Jacksonian Era, the former achieving success, the latter living on into the twentieth century. Looking back on this tradition of reform, Schlesinger reflected, "Our democratic tradition has been at its best an activist tradition. It has found its fulfillment, not in complaint or in escapism, but in responsibility and decision." That's what made reform so important and such an ethical conception for these liberals. It combined idealism with realism, irony with passion. Schlesinger was probably hoping, with his fellow historian Richard Hofstadter, that the New Deal had modernized reform in America, ridding it of purist or moralizing tendencies (witnessed in prohibitionism, etc.). Whatever the case, Schlesinger believed the American reformer combined "tough-minded" ethics with "tender-hearted" desires, the essential character disposition of anyone effective at making the world a better place to live. That was reform's essence.[27]

These liberal intellectuals celebrated this reform ethic—with its faith in the efficacy of partial achievements rather than utopianism or withdrawal from the messy realities of the world—and believed it worked well within America's representative political system. Compromise was at the heart of American politics, as these thinkers saw it. So too was complexity. As Galbraith observed, "The good citizen has to operate in and on an inordinately complex environment." The modern political system could never be expected to bend to the whims of individual initiative. Nor, as Schlesinger learned from his friend and British political theorist Isaiah Berlin, could modern politics require complete devotion from its citizens; it could not see political action in the public sphere as the highest good, the way Aristotle and ancient political theorists had seen it. Rather, politics was a necessity for achieving social justice.

The expectations of political action that reform incurred, realistic and tempered, seemed in line with the realities of America's representative politics. And when these liberals started to think about what *they* could do to improve the political state of America, to create a system not entirely perfect but more conducive to liberal virtues, they too began as reformers, as realists, as those who understood the inherent limits placed on them. In 1948, looking ahead to the coming years of liberal activism, James Wechsler wrote, "Whether we like it or not, non-Communist liberals are compelled to engage now in a campaign of limited objectives." Just how to commit to reform themselves became a key challenge in the work of these thinkers. They were ironical reformers, certainly, but this did not answer the question of what this entailed. How could you achieve a liberal political culture that took the virtues outlined in this chapter seriously? How could you retain liberal virtues such as truth and complexity while trying to change institutions?[28]

PUSHING AND PULLING: THE CHARACTER OF POLITICIANS, THE CHARACTER OF NATIONS

To make America a better country—both politically and culturally— depended on throwing oneself into the fray of political conflict. It meant moving beyond the divide that typically exists between intellect and power and accepting the challenges of electoral politics in America. Schlesinger knew there was an intellectual predisposition to see political engagement as compromised and thus impure. He learned firsthand of the realities of this problem when at the OWI. But he held out an ideal and acted upon it, namely, his belief that it is "possible to deal with practical realities without yielding inner convictions; it is entirely possible to compromise in program and action without compromising in ideas and values." So the passionate ironist sought out power.[29]

Just how much power prompted debate. Americans for Democratic Action (ADA), for instance, was an independent organization that issued platforms, tried to push the Democratic Party to the left (most famously in 1948 when Hubert Humphrey scored a more militant plank on civil rights for blacks), and endorsed political candidates. The organization became home to Schlesinger, Niebuhr, Wechsler, and Galbraith. It was an organization that pushed beyond anticommunism, a place where these thinkers could articulate what they wanted, not just what they opposed. But neither they nor the organization's members could settle on just how independent the organization should remain from politicians as it articulated a positive public philosophy. If it divorced itself too much, it might become ineffective, and if it got too close to politicians, it would lose its identity as a critical and independent voice.

"Politics" clashed with "vision," as the historian Steven Gillon points out in his book on the ADA. For instance, Wechsler pleaded with Schlesinger in 1954 to make the ADA more independent from the liberal senator from Minnesota (and future vice president), Hubert Humphrey, who was then, along with Illinois Senator Paul Douglas, one of the leading politicians within the ADA. "To put it simply," Wechsler explained, "if we are to have simply a political organization which operates according to the laws of Humphrey expediency, let us scrap ADA and join the Democratic Party where we can be indignant with the leadership without being thoroughly ashamed of ourselves." Wechsler's attempt to swing Schlesinger to his point of view here showed that there were debates over levels of compromise these thinkers were willing to make toward power. There were disagreements about the issue. For instance, Niebuhr thought that Schlesinger wanted "to be on the play of power at close range" whereas he himself "liked politics at long range precisely because the power motive was so strong." Schlesinger was clearly the most persistent in getting into the halls of power, Galbraith came pretty close to Schlesinger, and Wechsler and Niebuhr stayed independent. But all agreed: power was necessary but needed an ironic judge to be kept in check.[30]

This required assessing the character of a politician. This did not mean the private life of an elected official but rather the character glimpsed when a politician made judgments or projected a certain manner or style in public. It meant championing politicians who understood their role as cultural as well as political leaders. A politician could elevate the quality of national life if thoughtful and effective enough. The most popular liberal model was, of course, FDR, even though liberals were trying to move away from their association with him during this period of time. Nonetheless, Schlesinger would become famous, in part, for writing histories of the New Deal, in which FDR's character was as important as the policies he championed. Schlesinger described him as "a man without illusions," "clear-headed and compassionate," and attuned to "the frailty of human striving." Just as important, he led the nation by educating and elevating it but also by compromising and getting his hands dirty. Schlesinger argued that FDR could practice "the high politics of education and persuasion" as well as the "low politics of pressure, manipulation, and intrigue." Both things were necessary from a liberal standpoint. Truth and effectiveness had to walk hand in hand.[31]

This measurement of politicians is captured in these thinkers' assessment of two key political leaders in postwar America. First, there was Henry Wallace, once secretary of agriculture and then vice president under President Roosevelt. After the war, Wallace veered left and decided to run against Harry Truman for president on the Progressive Party ticket. The ADA's attack on Wallace's campaign is taken as the founding event for Cold War liberalism. And rightfully so: Schlesinger and Wechsler defined their own vision of liberalism as an alternative to Wallace's famous 1948 campaign. They ridiculed the candidate's naïve estimation of the Communist Party's influence on the Progressive Party and the motives of communists whom Wallace saw as "just another variety of indigenous American insurgence" (he would often equate the American with the Russian Revolution in a simplistic and historical manner). Wechsler and Schlesinger lampooned Wallace's ignorance about Soviet expansion during the early stages of the Cold War. They saw the Progressive Party as disastrous because of not just communist influence within its ranks but also its "insistence on running candidates against outstanding liberal incumbents or aspirants to Congressional office."

This was poor political judgment indeed, being both unrealistic and dangerous. But at the same time, when Wechsler covered Henry Wallace's campaign for the *Post*, he did not just tear into Wallace's ignorance about the Soviets or chide the Progressive Party for running candidates against liberals like Hubert Humphrey and Helen Gahagan Davis but spoke openly of the *tragedy* of the venture, even praising the candidate's desire to educate the American public. When Wallace decided to go south, for instance, Wechsler followed and reported on repeated eggings of the candidate by "fiery adolescents who appear alternately exuberant and sadistic." He wrote admiringly of Wallace's decision to challenge racism by refusing to stay in segregated hotels or to speak to segregated audiences. Where Wallace deserved it, Wechsler gave him praise, never allowing his criticism to turn into invective.[32]

After debunking Wallace, these liberal intellectuals sought leaders and increasingly turned to Adlai Stevenson throughout the 1950s. When it came to this governor of Illinois who ran unsuccessfully for president in 1952 and 1956, these thinkers often emphasized his character over his actual policies. This was obviously a way of evading their disagreement with him on key issues but also reflected a real appreciation of his character. Stevenson was himself an egghead, a man of ideas who went into politics, and someone who embraced liberal virtues. As early as 1949, for instance, Schlesinger, before becoming his advisor, praised Stevenson for his "wit" and "charm," two characteristics that would be used again and again to describe him. Stevenson spoke openly in political speeches of America's need for "cold-eyed humility" and a recognition that "our wisdom is imperfect and our capabilities . . . limited." Therefore, it's no wonder that when looking back on his support for Stevenson, Wechsler made him sound like a soul brother of Niebuhr, with his "sense of imperfectability of man, the limitations of what one can achieve on earth, an almost religious sense of humility about man's capacity—without minimizing what one man should try to do."

Nor is it surprising to hear Niebuhr call Stevenson "intellectually and morally the most exciting candidate." After all, Stevenson was ironic, possessing a sense of humor capable of getting him through the demands of campaigning. Wechsler told the story of how Stevenson was campaigning in the Midwest at a factory, shaking hands with workers early in the morning. One worker asked, "Governor, what the hell are you doing up at this hour?" As Wechsler recounted it: "Stevenson said, 'I just responded automatically, 'I'm damned if I know.'" For Wechsler, this showed Stevenson's appreciation of the "comic as well as the cosmic aspect of politics." It certainly marked him as an ironic egghead.[33]

But Stevenson was also seeking public office and often violated core liberal principles in doing so. Although he opposed McCarthy and was strong on welfare policies, Stevenson was weak on civil rights for blacks. This bothered the cast of characters here, especially Wechsler who recoiled in 1955 when Stevenson was silent about the murder of the young black boy, Emmet Till, and Martin Luther King's Montgomery Bus Boycott. Stevenson's silence prompted not just anger but also pressed these thinkers to think about the role of intellect in politics. Could an intellectual remain committed to the truth while having political impact? These thinkers certainly thought so. Wechsler berated

Stevenson on civil rights both in personal letters and editorials. Schlesinger echoed Wechsler's moral diatribes but also came armed with statistics about electoral returns that showed that taking a tougher stance on civil rights might actually help shore up northern votes even if it lost southern states. Here intellect pushed while also conciliating. It never allowed morality to be sacrificed, seeing as that would negate the entire purpose of intellect entering politics in the first place, that is, to elevate it.[34]

There was a great deal more to be done. On the heels of Stevenson's loss in 1952, Galbraith suggested "some organization in or adjacent to the Democratic Party to promote the formulation and discussion . . . of the policies on which our candidates can stand." Out of this came the aforementioned Finletter Group that tried to put intellect to the service of electoral politics. Going into the 1956 election, the group suggested that Stevenson press to get rid of the antilabor union legislation known as Taft–Hartley, attack the Republicans' laxness on a wealth tax, stick up for the civil rights of blacks, increase public spending, and prevent a public lands giveaway.

The last point came from a western conference that Schlesinger wanted to organize, essentially an attempt to get western states to articulate an environmentally sound set of policies for their future. Although it never came to fruition, it was partially realized when Bernard DeVoto arranged a meeting in Montana with Stevenson, educating the candidate about public land management and watershed policy (see Chapter 4). This sort of activity would last beyond the Finletter Group and DeVoto's death in 1955. It found its spirit again in the Advisory Council of the Democratic National Committee, and it continued, to a certain extent, in the Hickory Hill seminars held during the Kennedy administration, when intellectuals and politicians would discuss broad policy issues and ideas. In all of these backstage initiatives, intellect tried to shed its purism in order to elevate politics without losing sight of truth.[35]

Intellect came directly onstage as these thinkers crafted speeches for politicians. Schlesinger penned an anti-McCarthy speech Stevenson gave in Miami. Wechsler wrote one for an appearance at a Liberal Party gathering in New York City. DeVoto wrote several on public lands and the need to manage watersheds more wisely. All of them found Stevenson reworking these speeches to make them his own. Galbraith also did many not just for Stevenson but for other politicians (such as William Benton from Connecticut), leading him to comment that his "political life is ingloriously identified with a typewriter in a bathroom," writing as he did on the road within hotel rooms.

Speechwriting was tricky business, especially for someone like Galbraith. Thinking back on the words he had put in politicians' mouths during the 1950s, he came to pessimistic conclusions. After all, he was an ironist and saw a certain amount of what today we would label "spin." He explained in 1959, "Speeches are ordinarily made memorable by a combination of three ingredients. These are foolish prophecy, ridiculous exaggeration or false heroics." Worse yet, speeches were often little more than rationalization for bad policies. Language could be corrupted when put to bad use. What Galbraith called "the wordfact" made "words a precise substitute for reality," for instance, when a speech turned foreign dictators into "bulwarks of the free world." So in writing speeches, Galbraith tried to embrace irony and honesty, stripping language of its flighty rhetoric, making it simpler and thus more direct. For instance, he counseled JFK on his inaugural speech to shed "pretentiousness" while retaining seriousness, a challenge apropos for a passionate ironist like himself (Schlesinger would describe Kennedy as an ironist more than a moralist). Honesty, lack of pretentiousness, an awareness of the audience's ability to see through puffed up rhetoric—this was the style that these thinkers sought when crafting words to be uttered in public. Here is where the *character* of American liberal leadership could be heard.[36]

If the words of a nation's leaders could be made more ironic, then perhaps the nation itself could become more ironic. Or at least Americans could be reminded of their challenge to avoid hubris and arrogance. These liberals hoped that America's greatness, confirmed by victory during World War II, could become more subtle and self-introspective as it faced what Henry Luce called the "American century," a time when the United States was becoming a "dominant power in the world." What Niebuhr counseled for individuals and societies, he also counseled for the American nation: "The pride and self-righteousness of powerful nations are a greater hazard to their success than the machinations of their foes." The irony of American power was that "our nation has, without particularly seeking it, acquired a greater degree of power than any other nation of history." This sudden power placed a special burden on America, to embrace humility and become virtuous rather than grandiose and bellicose. After all, it seemed to "many Europeans that a nation as fortunate as ours could not possibly be virtuous." If an individual had to accept humility and limits, so too did the American nation. The attitudes cultivated in a liberal's daily interactions—a sense of humor, passion, and irony—needed to be projected upward and outward until they became a part of the American nation as a whole.

This was the liberal project, this cultivating of American greatness mixed with humility. Although individuals should acquire certain character traits and although intellectuals needed to make their nation more humanistic and liberal, the nation itself faced a new enemy during the Cold War and thus a new challenge. Communism required America to rethink its sense of greatness, to redefine it in new ways, and make it appropriate to changed circumstances. This was the first task of the liberal project during the Cold War: to come to terms with communism and to explain how Americans could pledge themselves against it without embracing absolutist principles (and thereby corrupting liberal virtues). It is to this crucial part of the liberal project that we now turn.[37]

CHAPTER TWO

Enemies
The Integrity of Liberal Anticommunism

I do not claim that all the acts of my life have been acts of superior and unquestioned wisdom. I do assert on the basis of a public record that I yield to no one on the issue of fighting Communism in the manner that I believe to be the effective way of fighting it.

James Wechsler to
Senator Joseph McCarthy, 1953[1]

THE MAN WHO MET MCCARTHY

In 1953, the year he faced down James Wechsler, Senator Joe McCarthy was at the height of power. Only three years ago in 1950, right after China had fallen to communism, the Soviet Union had exploded an atomic bomb, and Alger Hiss had been convicted of perjury during a high-profile espionage case, this little-known senator from Wisconsin got up to speak in Wheeling, West Virginia. He waved sheets of paper in front of reporters, asserting that they listed the names of communists in the State Department. Famously, the numbers of people McCarthy accused changed in speeches following the Wheeling performance. But this did not stop him from persevering. Nor did the Tydings Committee in the Senate which found McCarthy's accusations baseless. McCarthy went to the media directly, whipping up a buzz, and befriended important figures in the Republican Party, including Eisenhower, who tried to ignore him but by doing so only allowed him to continue. McCarthy also exploited the anxiety surrounding the Korean War. If things were bad enough for America to commit militarily to this little-known area in Asia, then maybe there really were spies in high places giving advice and secrets to foreign communists.[2]

Three years after his Wheeling speech, McCarthy chaired the Government Operations Committee (GOC) in the Senate, making a fiefdom of the Permanent Subcommittee on Investigations. He continued his search for communists at home by holding public hearings, still not turning up anything new or earth-shattering, and then dared to take his case international. He started to investigate the Voice of America and the State Department's International Information Agency, both of which took up where the OWI had left off. McCarthy sent his assistants, Roy Cohn and David Schine, to Europe in order to investigate the books the State Department had shipped to foreign libraries. The search smacked of potential censorship (the European press alluded to book burnings). It would seem that McCarthy was beginning to "overreach." Wechsler, in the pages of the *New York Post*, argued that Cohn and Schine's investigation "disgraced and dishonored America." This was not the first time Wechsler criticized McCarthy. And it was more than this comment that made Joe McCarthy decide to call him to testify before his subcommittee soon after Cohn and Schine returned from Europe.[3]

Supposedly, some of Wechsler's own books had been found overseas. Because Wechsler was once a communist, this could mean the State Department was subsidizing—through taxpayers' money—communist literature abroad. This at least served as a pretense for Wechsler's testimony, but the pretense quickly broke down. During his testimony, Wechsler asked McCarthy which books had been found but never got an answer. As Wechsler pointed out, he had authored four books by the time he appeared in front of McCarthy, and two of them were written while a communist, two while an anticommunist. *Which* books were found overseas would therefore seem to be an important part of the case.

But Wechsler had stepped into a strange world, something more than a straightforward investigation. Consider this: When Wechsler had broken with the newspaper *PM* due to its softness on communism and had pledged himself to battling communists within the leading newspaper union (started by one of his heroes, the reporter Heywood Broun), McCarthy was, as Arthur Schlesinger pointed out, "accepting Communist support in his primary fight against Bob LaFollette in Wisconsin." Three years before Joe McCarthy waved his infamous papers in Wheeling, James Wechsler was writing articles with titles like "How to Rid the Government of Communists." Before McCarthy had taken up the anticommunist cause, Wechsler wrote in support of Chambers's testimony against Hiss (receiving a thank-you letter from Richard Nixon for doing so). So when Wechsler walked into that room with McCarthy, he was facing a man more interested in building his own career than in an anti-communist crusade with integrity.[4]

It was not just Wechsler's books that fed McCarthy's decision to call him to testify. After all, Wechsler had been a member of the Young Communist League during the 1930s; he might have dirt on other communists, the sort that Whittaker Chambers and Louis Budenz (once the editor of the Communist Party's newspaper, the *Daily Worker*) had shared. There was also the entanglement Wechsler had with the gossip columnist turned journalist, Walter Winchell, a friend of Joe McCarthy. Wechsler had attacked Winchell's rise to fame, arguing he blurred the line between journalism and gossip and fell prey to right-wing anti-communism. Winchell retaliated against a series of articles Wechsler wrote about him by calling Wechsler's paper "the Compost," "Postitute," and, most evocatively, playing on the anticommunist term pinko, "Postinko." But Winchell went further, personally attacking Wechsler by suggesting he was still a communist, never having broken with the party during the late 1930s. This ludicrous accusation, nothing more than a smear, would actually emerge again when McCarthy scrutinized Wechsler, showing Winchell's direct influence on the senator. In the end, Wechsler would sue Winchell successfully for libel and would win a rare thing, an apology from Winchell. Nonetheless, in 1953, it would seem that Winchell had floated ideas out there with which McCarthy ran.[5]

There was a more personal reason for McCarthy to go after Wechsler. In 1951, Wechsler had arranged one of the hardest hitting exposures of McCarthy in the *New York Post*. Written by Oliver Pilat and William Shannon, two young reporters, the series was entitled "Smear Inc." As with much else in the *Post*, the reporting was factual but no-holds-barred when it came to opinion, labeling McCarthy a "buffoon assassin" and "party hack." The series documented how McCarthy talked up his military background when it was actually quite lame. It discussed McCarthy's tax return problems, sleazy lobbying connections to the real estate industry, and penchant for demagoguery. There were the unpleasant alliances McCarthy had built with American anti-Semites and fascists. One point Pilat and Shannon made should have given Wechsler some pause: they took note of how McCarthy had cowed the press (Wechsler would gamble otherwise on this one). Wechsler was probably hopeful about the sentiment expressed toward the end of the series, a belief that McCarthy's days were numbered: "Like a drunk at a party who was funny half an hour ago but now won't go home, McCarthy is camped in America's front room trying to impress everybody."[6]

There were thus plenty of reasons for McCarthy to call Wechsler to testify. There were also plenty of reasons for Wechsler to go. He was armed with wit and intelligence, those central virtues of the postwar liberal, and hoped to bring McCarthy down by exposing his shenanigans. Once he arrived in Washington, D.C., Wechsler met with his attorney, drank a martini at lunch, paced around for a few hours waiting for the proceedings to begin, and then faced his foe. Anyone who has attended a public hearing or who has testified in court will know what a strange experience it can be. Things shift upon entry. Time can stand still. One thing for Wechsler is certain: he had entered a much more surreal world than that of a standard testimony or trial. This was to be a battle of wits, of differing philosophies ramming into one another. Wechsler's fellow writer at the *New York Post*, Max Lerner, rightfully called the meeting "one of the most dramatic clashes of personality and views in the history of Congressional hearings."[7]

The hearing got off to a strange start. Having heard that this was a closed meeting, at least to the press, Wechsler asked why McCarthy had Howard Rushmore, a journalist, sitting at his side. No answer. There then came a clash between personalities, one boorish and single-minded, the other witty and ironic. When Wechsler discussed his exposé of Communist infiltration in Henry Wallace's Progressive Party as proof of his anticommunist credentials, McCarthy stated, "Is it not the truth that you knew that the Wallace party had no possible chance of winning that election [in 1948], but that you were afraid if they picked up enough of the votes of the type that you appealed to, the left-wingers, the party liners, that perhaps it would mean a defeat and an exposure of the old Acheson crowd that had been so thoroughly infiltrated by Communists?" There it was: an equation of liberals and Communists (Acheson had been Truman's secretary of state). Wechsler quipped, "Senator, the Communists up and down the line were supporting Wallace. If you are accusing me of a subjective conspiracy to elect a Democratic President, we have certainly widened the scope of this inquiry and that perhaps affects other Senators on the committee."

At one point, Wechsler was asked about certain communists by name, and he answered the questions. Then McCarthy asked, "Do you know Bernard DeVoto?" "I trust this is not a sequitur" was Wechsler's response. "Pardon?" McCarthy asked, as if stumped by the word. "I trust this is not a sequitur," Wechsler said, as if playing upon McCarthy's fumbling. "It is a question," McCarthy said. And then they proceeded like boxers in a ring. When asked about Cohn and Schine's trip to Europe, Wechsler called it "one of the most absurd and fantastic wastes of taxpayers' money in history, because I do not believe that the presence of one book on one shelf is going to be a decisive issue in the battle against Communist ideas." McCarthy asked about Bill Jenner, a fellow Republican anticommunist. "You think he is a dangerous man," McCarthy insisted. Wechsler quipped, "Senator, I give you *a priori*ty in this field." And so it went, intellectual and ironic punches thrown at a bully scurrying around on what Wechsler called a "fishing expedition."[8]

But nothing Wechsler said could break McCarthy's bizarre line of inquiry. McCarthy traveled far away from the original motive of his investigation, those books that supposedly sat on overseas libraries' shelves. Instead, he took a tip from Winchell, concocting a fictional scenario that seemed to please him: "If I were a member of the Communist Party and I were the bright newspaper man that Mr. Wechsler is, if I wanted to aid the Communist Party, I would not stay aboveground and say I was a member of the Communist Party, I would say I deserted the Communist Party and then I would do exactly as Mr. Wechsler has been doing." McCarthy had no evidence for this, just a persistent desire to convince himself.

When Wechsler tried to establish his anticommunist bona fides by presenting Communist Party statements and a resolution that excoriated his liberal politics and him personally, McCarthy reached a new height of surreality. "Did you have anything to do with the passage of that resolution? Did you take any part in promoting the passage of that resolution?" McCarthy was asking whether Wechsler had concocted a statement against himself, as if years ago he had the foresight to prepare for his defense against McCarthy. "Is that a serious question?" was the only response Wechsler could muster. McCarthy then asked whether anyone on the staff of the *Post* had anything to do with the resolution.

And this really got to the heart of the matter: McCarthy was attacking a liberal newspaper and a liberal newspaperman, not books in overseas libraries. There's an alarming moment in the investigation when McCarthy admits as much, slipping into a creepy third-person voice: "As I have said before, Mr. Wechsler, if the *New York Post* or Jim Wechsler started to praise McCarthy when I exposed Communists, I would be certain that I was hanging an innocent man." The liberal journalist and retired head of the OWI, Elmer Davis, concluded that "in [McCarthy's] opinion a Communist is anybody who criticizes McCarthy." That was the surreal world into which Wechsler walked.[9]

Having entered it, Wechsler found it hard to maneuver. For McCarthy turned the screw and asked him to name names of fellow members of the Young Communist League during Wechsler's brief, youthful stint there. Should he answer? What was the morally right thing to do in this case? Wechsler explained in his memoir, "It was wrong to expose others to McCarthy's wickedness, but it was equally wrong, in my judgment, to embrace the principle that a former communist should tell nothing to anyone." This was a dilemma peculiar to a liberal who refused to plead the Fifth Amendment (the amendment that protected people against giving self-incriminating testimony), believing that silence was an admission of guilt (about five hundred people decided to take the Fifth during this time). This was the dilemma of someone who believed in representative government and democratic principles. Wechsler explained, "Any citizen called before a committee in the proper exercise of its function has a duty to talk." As he put it another time, "It is a citizen's responsibility to testify before a Senate committee whether he likes the committee or not."

The literary critic Leslie Fiedler reflected on Wechsler's case in the wider context of testifying and argued he had done the responsible thing: "Between the evasion of the non-cooperators and the over-cooperation of the confessors lies a troubled and difficult course: what seems to me the truly liberal one." The course was not to go silent but to condemn McCarthy while not lying about one's past. Fiedler knew this course would be difficult (it was like Trilling's ethic of being "between"), because it provided no absolute moral clarity. Those on the right would call any attack on McCarthy antipatriotic, and the response from the left would be just as bad: "When he identifies for the investigators the utterest scoundrel in the pro-Soviet camp, he finds himself scorned and ostracized by the kind of 'sincere' liberal who gasps horrifiedly: 'He named names!'—as if to rat were the worst of crimes. It is not, however, really the boys' code of not squealing which is at stake, but the whole dream of an absolute innocence." Wechsler concurred by accepting the fate of this decision.[10]

He named names with a deep sense of tragedy, accepting the result of democracy's bad decisions (after all, numerous working-class Catholics from Wisconsin had voted McCarthy into office). He knew the limits of democracy: that the only way to change things was to struggle within existing institutions, condemn evil where one saw it, but never abandon representative government. He tried to limit the damage done by arguing that the names not be released to the public. But his biggest goal was to keep the voice of liberal anticommunism out there, not go silent. And so he told McCarthy that he would get his names: "I have always responded freely to questions asked of me by authorized government agencies and I shall not permit you at this late date to create any impression to the contrary." He demanded that in return for naming names McCarthy make the transcripts of his testimony public, for all to see and read. Wechsler believed that this was the best he could do under the circumstances. He chose to expose demagoguery even if it meant that those who had made the same mistake as he had in the past—to side with totalitarians—were to be exposed as well.[11]

Could the ironic liberal do battle against a demagogue? Probably not. In the end, Wechsler's strategy had mixed results at best. He called on the American Society for Newspaper Editors (ASNE) to condemn McCarthy's threat to the press (Wechsler kept pointing out that smaller newspapers than his would probably buckle under the pressure he withstood). An ASNE committee was appointed; half of its members agreed with Wechsler, the other half didn't. Prominent journalists took the side of Wechsler, including Bernard DeVoto and Elmer Davis (Schlesinger tried to get Joe Alsop to lend support but failed). But still there was no formal censure coming from the press. So it would seem that Wechsler had failed. Or had he? Wechsler noted, "Although the committee reached no unanimous conclusion as to the extent of the threat to press freedom involved in this proceeding, it is notable that no member of the committee chose to offer a public defense of McCarthy's action, while 4 distinguished editors upheld my view that a very real challenge to the press was presented by the hearings."

Nor did Wechsler back down during the hearing; he pressed his ironic wit against McCarthy the entire time. He showed that a citizen could retain a faith in democracy and oppose McCarthy at the same time, practicing a liberalism without innocence as Fiedler called it. He continued to press his case against McCarthy by making his arguments clearer in *The Age of Suspicion*, marrying anticommunism and anti-McCarthyism. As he told McCarthy at the hearing: "You have done in my judgment serious damage to the battle against Communism by confusing liberals with Communists." To pull his voice out of the national discussion would have been madness, so he kept it in the forefront as best he could.[12]

THE PROBLEM OF ANTICOMMUNISM

Since the time Wechsler had his argument with McCarthy, it has become harder and harder to understand it. The playwright Lillian Hellman became Wechsler's first critic. She argued that he had found a high-minded justification for an essentially base act, the naming of names. She herself refused to name names, invoking the Fifth Amendment when called to testify. Victor Navasky, a historian and editor of *The Nation*, later argued that Hellman's characterization of Wechsler as a friendly witness was unfair, labeling him instead an "unfriendly informer," a term he seemed to think was kinder. The intellectual historian Richard Pells believes Wechsler acted from "distorted idealism." He then goes on to lionize people such as Lillian Hellman and Arthur Miller who refused to name names at all. Perhaps it is no surprise to hear this characterization of Wechsler not as a man of principle but essentially a dupe. We like our heroes pure, untainted by the messy world of conflicted choice. Heroes must be bold, and refusing to name names sounds bold.[13]

It is especially peculiar to hear Hellman lionized. As Stephen Whitfield points out, this playwright had been a key organizer of the pro-Soviet Waldorf Conference in 1949 (an event Schlesinger and others opposed, using it as a chance to form a new organization known as the Americans for Intellectual Freedom, a forerunner of the Congress for Cultural Freedom). Hellman remained a Stalinist throughout the 1950s, denying Stalin's purges and condemning Khrushchev's admission to the crimes done in Soviet history. Ironically, Richard Pells, who champions Hellman, admits that "much of the opposition to McCarthyism was based on the argument that its victims were in fact innocent of any crime, that the Communist 'conspiracy' was a myth. . . ." Such a characterization was obviously false; after all, there really were spies and communists within the U.S. government (even if not as many as McCarthy said).

Instead of lionizing Hellman and Miller for refusing to name names, we should ask serious questions about their political and ethical judgments. Wechsler at least criticized the crimes of Stalin and his apologists while slamming McCarthy. This led to a messier and more complex set of ethics for Wechsler, seeing as it suggested guilt all around. But in retrospect (who today would deny the crimes of Stalinism?) Wechsler's views capture a better sense of judgment than those who denied the crimes. As well, Wechsler's belief that a system of representative democracy required a citizen to testify the way he did should not be dismissed as just a rationalization for his own self-interest. There was political reasoning going on here, not just self-interest. Wechsler, after all, never shut up; instead, he made his arguments known at the hearing itself and long after.[14]

Our inability to understand Wechsler's decision and point of view represents a bigger problem with anticommunism. Part of the reason for this is that as communism has collapsed in the Soviet Union, our memory of anticommunism has become harder to reconstruct. One historian recently pointed out, "It is hard to recall that Soviet communism once offered a serious ideological competitor to liberal capitalism and a fearful military threat." In addition, it is harder for us to see anticommunism as a rational set of ideas. Instead, we take our lead from Arthur Miller's play *The Crucible*, where the seventeenth-century Salem witch trials served as a metaphor for McCarthyism. The irrational search for witches, who clearly did not exist, became the equivalent of a rational search for communists in government, the existence of which is most definite. When we think about anticommunism today, we conjure up a sense of a collective national mania and abject fear, the sort easily labeled a "witch-hunt." Those working in "cultural studies" have argued more recently that anticommunism is nothing more than a form of creating a dehumanized "other," the pilloried communist. Andrew Ross, for instance, draws out this argument and applies it to, of all people, the Rosenbergs, whose guilt seems unimpeachable. To Ross, though, guilt or innocence need not matter; what matters is that the Rosenbergs became villainized victims of Cold War liberals. Ross's interpretation seems popular among leftists in academia.[15]

This mischaracterization of anticommunism also stems from an unfortunate episode in history. During the late 1960s, it was confirmed that the Congress for Cultural Freedom (CCF), an organization Schlesinger helped form in 1950, with Niebuhr as honorary chairman and Wechsler and Galbraith as active members, had received support and money from the Central Intelligence Agency (CIA). Because this group was so strongly identified with anticommunism, critics saw this revelation as evidence that anticommunism represented a sellout of intellectuals to the U.S. government. As Christopher Lasch put it soon after the first definitive exposé of CIA–CCF ties, "The cold war intellectuals revealed themselves as the servants of bureaucratic power." Just a few years ago, Elizabeth Stonor Saunders, in a more elaborate history of CCF than Lasch's short essay on the matter, winds up supporting his major claim. The original title of her book was *Who Paid the Piper?* suggesting (as did many of the stories throughout) that anticommunist ideas were bought and paid for by those at the CIA. Lasch and Saunders make important points about poor judgment on the part of some of these thinkers. But neither spends much time on the ideas that animated these intellectuals' critique of communism. Intellectuals appear merely as shills for government, ideas mere props and rationalizations for power. Such a characterization allows for a moral stance on the part of the critic, but it misses an awful lot of the nuance and balance of liberalism's anticommunism. Essentially it misses the reasons those thinkers were anticommunists in the first place.[16]

WHAT'S SO BAD ABOUT MARXISM?

To understand anticommunism, we must delve first into the philosophy of communism itself. Before there was the Soviet Union, there was a communist movement in Western Europe. Before there was the philosophy of Stalinism there was Marxism. Although these sets of ideas and practices are separated by history, they are also linked. For the intellectuals here, Marxism was an assessment of industrial capitalism and a political theory that delineated how to create a more just society free of exploitation (today Marxism has gravitated toward the academy, especially cultural studies, draining it of its *political* ideas). The thinkers studied here believed that Marxism helped lay the ground for Stalinism; thus, there was an intellectual and rational basis for their anticommunism. They saw other problems with Marxism as a theory, separate from the question of Stalinism, that they applied to the thinking of many intellectuals during the 1930s (and that Wechsler applied to himself looking back). Unlike conservatives, though, they did not condemn communism as a moral evil. They believed there were "humane and liberal aspects of Marxism" and even some communists who resisted totalitarianism. Certain members of the Communist Party, Schlesinger was willing to admit, partook in "courageous activity against local injustice and exploitation." But even with this sort of human exception to the rule, Schlesinger saw Marxism reaching dangerous political conclusions that needed to be combated intellectually.[17]

Karl Marx, writing during the 1840s and observing the impact of the British industrial revolution, believed he had settled the big questions of political economy and history. He was a social theorist who worked in the grand tradition and summed up world history by seeing it through the lens of class conflict. "The history of all hitherto existing society is the history of class struggles," the *Communist Manifesto* bellowed. It was not just class conflict but *polarization* that marked historical development. In Marx's time, this meant the increasing size of the industrial proletariat (the working class) and the decreasing size but increasing power of the bourgeoisie (or capitalist class). The proletariat grew in numbers as it watched its social conditions worsen; at the same time, the bourgeoisie watched its wealth amass. Inevitably, the Dickensian characteristics of nineteenth-century capitalism nurtured a revolutionary situation in which the proletariat would find itself needing to overthrow the bourgeoisie and institute a communist society. By making this diagnosis, Marx claimed to read not just history but the future.[18]

Looking around during the 1940s and 1950s, this "catastrophic" view of class conflict appeared inaccurate. Although there was a continued fear that America might drift back into depression after the war, the increasing reality was that the working class was doing well. Marx's theory of "immiseration" did not apply, to put it bluntly, as more and more working-class people moved to the suburbs and bought televisions. Schlesinger argued that capitalism "has reduced the size of the working class and deradicalized the worker." Marxism, as Wechsler pointed out, "underestimated the resilience of American capitalism," especially its ability to overcome class conflict. Indeed, the New Deal had already taught this lesson, as Arthur Schlesinger would point out over and over.

This debunking of Marx's theory of class polarization did not mean these liberals ignored class differences or the realities of class conflict.

Rather, Schlesinger traced out an indigenous and distinctly American way of talking about social conflict that existed throughout history but that also believed in ameliorating it through reform, not revolution. For instance, Schlesinger explained, "The founders of the republic construed politics automatically in terms of classes. No more magisterial summation of the economic interpretation of politics exists than James Madison's celebrated Tenth Federalist Paper." Here Madison discussed social conflicts and their relation to the "unequal distribution of property." During the Jacksonian period, many Americans, even the president, spoke about the struggle between the privileged few and the "common man" (as had the subject of Schlesinger's first book, Orestes Brownson). The difference between talking about class this way and talking about class from a Marxist perspective was that the former believed in reforming the system to lessen (not eradicate) class differences. This view of class seemed a more realistic assessment of American affluence in the postwar years and a means to evade catastrophism and its concomitant faith in revolution.[19]

Marxism also prophesied too much. It denied contingency and predicted the future, a dangerous business as far as these intellectuals were concerned. Marx had studied the German philosopher G.W.F. Hegel who believed in a "history of philosophy," an elaborate mapping out of stages of development from the past to the present and future. Marx believed in stages of history following from one another, antiquity to feudalism, and then from the capitalist present to the communist future. The problem here was first the obvious: Marx's predictions had been proven wrong due to the staying power of capitalism especially in Western Europe (where Marx believed the communist revolution was destined to take place). But there was something beyond these empirical inaccuracies. There was the danger of believing too much in the "order and predictability in history," as Wechsler put it. Contingency and unpredictability were better values than prediction based on iron laws of social development. Teleology abolished the power of human activity and this the liberal mind-set found abhorrent, because it eradicated human freedom and self-determination (the sort that could happen within the bounds of social circumstances).[20]

Marxism's prophesying was tied into its theory of politics. And here is where these intellectuals started to make connections between Karl Marx's thinking during the nineteenth century in Western Europe and the realities of Soviet totalitarianism during their own time. Marx's interpretation of representative government in Western Europe (and the United States) was far too cynical. Because he prioritized economic over political power, Marx saw the state merely as an instrument of economic interests. Schlesinger explained, "A century ago, Marx dismissed the limited state in a somewhat cavalier manner. 'The executive of the modern state,' he wrote in the *Communist Manifesto*, 'is but a committee for managing the common affairs of the bourgeoisie.'" This interpretation ignored the accomplishments of bourgeois democracy, including the element of freedom built into politics—especially the sort that occurred within a representative governmental system based on full suffrage—that could help transform the social system for the better. Government, as Schlesinger argued, has "become an object of genuine competition among classes; it is the means by which the non-business classes may protect themselves from the business community. . . ." Or as Reinhold Niebuhr pointed out, the New Deal "invalidated the Marxist dogma of the inevitable subservience of political to economic power." FDR, a member of America's elite, had turned against his own class's self-interest and implemented reform in order to save capitalism. Government might serve as a tool for the wealthy at times, but in a democracy, it could also become a tool for others. Thus, these thinkers believed history had proven wrong Marx's cynical assessment of "bourgeois democracy."[21]

There's an ironic twist on this point. Although Marx was too cynical about government under nineteenth-century capitalist conditions, he was too utopian about government within his conception of a communist future. Marx condemned what he called "utopian" socialism; however, his vision of a communist future was remarkably naive. He spoke of the state withering away after a communist revolution (as would Lenin later) and the creation of an egalitarian society free of class conflict, that is, an end to history. Niebuhr pounced on this blind side of Marx's political philosophy. Although Marxism was a legitimate reaction against the "excessive individualism of the bourgeois classes," he argued, "it is also in error when it assumes that a frictionless harmony between the individual and community can be established" in the future. Conflict, Niebuhr's realism made clear, could *never* be eradicated from life. There would always be those trying to seize power, and not just economic power but political power (which was happening in the Soviet Union at the time he was writing). Once again, Marx's utopian vision stemmed from his simplistic assessment of human society. "The social substance of life,"

Niebuhr explained, "is richer and more various, and has greater depths than are envisaged in the Marxist dream of social harmony."[22]

Marx's utopianism grew from a black hole in his political theory. He never specified exactly how violent revolution and dictatorship of the proletariat could transform themselves into a more peaceful society, allowing the state to wither away. That remained an open question. The problem was that after Marx died, certain political theorists started to answer it in frightening ways. Marx's faith in a "dictatorship of the proletariat," as Reinhold Niebuhr pointed out, led inevitably to a "monopoly of power." All Lenin had to do was turn the "dictatorship of the proletariat" into a dictatorship of the party, and from here it was a small jump to Stalinist dictatorship. Schlesinger wrote, "Lenin's policy of concentrating all authority and wisdom in the Party leadership and smashing all opposition thus made 'Stalinism' inevitable." In addition, Marx never had any appreciation of political "rights" (or civil liberties). For him, rights served only to justify the bourgeoisie's privilege to property ownership, thus stymieing revolution. Marx had no appreciation of the inherent need for rights and their protection of citizens against the abuse of political power. The Marxist mind-set therefore contained little that would protect against dictatorship. Niebuhr explained that "Communism has no understanding of the value of liberty." In other words, it had no way of resisting the political system called "totalitarianism."[23]

This term entered the American political lexicon during the 1940s, and liberal intellectuals helped put it there by pointing to the lack of any opposition to state power in Marxist theory. Totalitarianism essentially meant nothing standing between a centralized government and an isolated individual living in a mass society, that is, the consolidation of *total* power. There were no oppositional political parties or organizations (churches, independent labor unions, etc.) that could check the state's power. Rather, the individual's conscience was subsumed by the state and controlled via propaganda. These were the political features that the Soviet Union shared with the now defunct fascist state run by Hitler. The most important thinker on totalitarianism, the German émigré Hannah Arendt, conflated Soviet and German totalitarianism. Although Niebuhr and Schlesinger appreciated her insights into the operation of power, they also believed Nazism and Soviet totalitarianism differed. The former was absolutely cynical in its love of power. The second used "ruthless power" but hid "behind a screen of pretended ideal ends." This is what made Soviet totalitarianism much more threatening. It could appeal to those searching for answers to problems of social injustice, especially the poor and downtrodden in the world, whereas fascism embraced power for the sake of power itself.[24]

If communism portended so many bad practices on both an intellectual and political level, what could be done to prevent its spread? This question only increased in relevance as the historical realities of the Cold War grew apparent. In 1946 Churchill warned of an "iron curtain" falling on the world, and America found its Russian ally during World War II quickly becoming its enemy. The Soviet Union was expanding its power throughout Eastern Europe and was optimistic about the growing popularity of communists in Western European countries such as France. It reinvigorated its international work by creating the Cominform (which took the place of the then defunct Comintern). And so liberals faced an international and domestic challenge that would define their work for years to come. But they also faced a more complex and puzzling question: how to prevent the growth of communist ideals without succumbing too much to the dark side of human nature? How to stand fast against communism without losing sight of liberal virtues? Could, in the evocative language of Reinhold Niebuhr, the "children of light" check the power of the "children of darkness?" He knew full well that the children of light had darkness within themselves. He also knew that a "frantic anticommunism can become so similar in its temper of hatefulness to communism itself." This was precisely what made the Cold War so challenging for liberals.[25]

THE ETHICS OF PARSING

Although Arthur Miller might have suggested a parallel between a Cold War search for communists and the Salem witch-hunt in early American history, the thinkers studied here knew that communists existed—both as spies and political activists. All they had to do was look around them: Henry Wallace's campaign in 1948 was littered with communists (see the previous chapter); some high-profile labor unions such as the National Maritime Union, Longshoremen, and United Electrical, Radio, and Machine Workers of America were infiltrated by communists. Schlesinger and Wechsler knew communists operated through front groups, lying about themselves in order to try to gain influence within progressive organizations. Wechsler had had firsthand experience with this sort of miserable experience. For instance, he had been a member of the American Student Union during the 1930s, and when he returned to examine it in 1949, all he saw were communists and "fellow travelers" (those who weren't card-carrying members but faithful to the party's line). He realized just how "a disciplined minority may shape an organization's policy" if it tried the way communists did. In addition, he knew that the end goal of communist organizing was to overthrow democratic institutions.

Finally, Wechsler and Schlesinger believed that communists had infiltrated the federal government. They both believed Whittaker Chambers's charge that Alger Hiss had been a spy, and neither believed the Rosenbergs were anything but guilty. As Schlesinger explained, "There can be no serious question that an underground Communist apparatus attempted during the late thirties and during the war to penetrate the United States Government." No matter how strange ex-communists like Elizabeth Bentley might seem, Schlesinger warned fellow liberals in 1947, there was a "hard substratum of truth" in the "stories" they told "before the federal grand jury." The communist threat was a reality, especially between 1945 and 1949, those first, tension-ridden years of Cold War history.[26]

Even during this frightening time, the liberal was responsible for what I call an ethic of parsing. Care and precision needed to be taken when searching for communists. Schlesinger called for "poise, balance, judgment" when prosecuting enemies of democracy (although he disagreed with the anticommunist philosopher, Sidney Hook, on many other points, he put into practice what Hook had labeled the "ethics of controversy"). The key distinction to be drawn was between ideas and actions: the first posed no danger and needed to be countered via argument; the latter, if they constituted espionage, should be crushed. "Ideas are not the enemy," Wechsler wrote in 1947. He explained, "An awareness of the distinction between communism as an idea and the communist parties as battalions of Soviet espionage and sabotage is essential to any national wisdom." Looking back on the late 1940s, Niebuhr believed liberals drew distinctions between ideas and opinions and the *acts* committed by the Rosenbergs and Hiss, because "these trials involved not opinions but overt acts."

Arthur Schlesinger concurred, adding to this difference between ideas and acts the "clear distinction between the rights of an American

citizen and the rights of a government employee in a security agency."
He also reminded Americans of Oliver Wendell Holmes's earlier declaration of a "clear and present danger rule" when cracking down on freedom. There was a "clear and present danger" with communist spies in
the State Department; there was not with citizens articulating communist ideas within the American public sphere of debate. In the sphere of
debate, civil rights had to win out over fear, if an intellectual took "the
traditional democratic methods of debate" seriously. After all, he
explained, "In our detestation of Communism we must not . . . do
irreparable harm to our American heritage of freedom." The liberal had
to parse ideas and action, sabotage and debate, partisans of political
ideals and spies.[27]

This abstract ethic needed to be applied to the measures taken by
the federal government in prosecuting communists. The first and most
important act here was President Truman's Executive Order in 1947
that created a Review Board to examine the loyalty of government
employees (known, therefore, as the Loyalty Act). In principle, Cold War
liberals agreed with the act. But principle is not the only way to assess
government decisions. The ADA eventually decided to support Truman's
Loyalty Program, even though concerns were expressed about "its pro-
cedures." Wechsler worried about the "loose language in the loyalty
order." It had failed to take up the liberal ideal of parsing. This could
be seen in pragmatic terms as liberals witnessed its misapplication after
its passage. The *New York Post* reported as early as 1947 that the State
Department was dangerously widening the concept of "loyalty" to include drunkenness and "sexual perversion." Two years later, Wechsler
reported how one woman was being prosecuted by the Loyalty Program
because she believed in interracial marriage. In the army, things were
even worse. Here a civilian employee was "denied a hearing or even a
statement of charges until after he is dismissed." This was the furthest
thing from the care and precision Schlesinger and Wechsler had counseled. It allowed the idea of loyalty—a defensible ideal within the setting
of a democratic state—to be mixed up with conformity.[28]

This was not just an ethical mistake but a pragmatic one. These intellectuals moved back and forth between analyzing things in terms of
values and then in terms of consequences. Schlesinger worried that if
the Loyalty Program continued to confuse loyalty with conformity, it
might prevent talented employees from entering the State Department.

In addition, as wiretapping became more of a reality, how could the administration pragmatically ensure that it didn't get the wrong people and engender paranoia among citizens? Schlesinger also worried that loyalty programs might make martyrs out of the wrong people. As colleges started to administer their own loyalty oaths, conflicts started to emerge. Schlesinger was particularly concerned with one case at the University of Washington. Here the administration prosecuted six professors for having lied about their Communist Party memberships. Three professors were fired, and the case drew national attention. Schlesinger believed that the accused professors were guilty of lying but that prosecuting them only gave them more credibility. The president of the University of Washington had "transformed these wretched nonentities into living evidences of the capitalist assault against freedom, now paraded through the Eastern campuses," Schlesinger explained. The pragmatic results of prosecuting communists always had to be kept in mind, in addition to the ethical question of being careful and prudent.[29]

As with any good ethical and pragmatic judgment, this one grew out of historical knowledge. There were precedents here. There had been the "Red Scare" of 1919 in the immediate wake of the Russian Revolution. The Attorney General used his powers to investigate not just pro-Russian communists but just about any left-wing activist during this time and had agreed to illegal deportations of foreigners. More recently, the Dies Committee had formed in 1938 in order to investigate "subversive and un-American propaganda." Headed by Congressman Martin Dies, a Texan who had come to oppose the New Deal, the Special House Committee on Un-American Activities was supposed to examine all anti-American causes, be they from the left or the right. But as Wechsler noted, Dies let the right (including pro-Franco fascists in the United States) off the hook and only attacked left-wing and liberal causes (including the New Deal's Federal Writers' Project). Arthur Schlesinger argued that Dies used anticommunism as a "pretext for attacking liberals and New Dealers." Dies had smeared his enemies and sought out publicity. Wechsler himself called Dies a forerunner to Joe McCarthy. Dies made clear, even before McCarthy waved his papers in Wheeling, that the American right could use anticommunism to pursue its own agenda, that is, attacking liberalism as the evil twin of communism.[30]

Indeed, all of the central characters of this book faced right-wing attack at some point during the 1950s. In 1952, McCarthy insinuated that Schlesinger, then giving advice to Adlai Stevenson, was a communist. Wechsler's 1953 run-in with McCarthy is already well documented. Two years later, after testifying about the problems of the American stock market, John Kenneth Galbraith faced the sting of Senator Homer Capehart (Indiana). Capehart quoted passages of Galbraith's testimony and writings out of context to suggest he was a communist stooge. Galbraith was dignified in his protest against Capehart, describing his own behavior as "tolerably urbane," but nonetheless, the attack was, in his own words, a "heavy drain on my (I think considerable) emotional and physical reserves." To top it off, even the ADA was accused of communism, and thus, by implication, Reinhold Niebuhr. With this retrospective view in mind, it is easy to back up Wechsler's assertion in 1947, that if liberals did not get active in ferreting out communists, there would be those with worse intentions waiting to do so.[31]

All the more reason to increase parsing after 1950. Indeed, by this time, Henry Wallace's campaign had gone south with no chance of returning. Hiss had been prosecuted, and the Rosenbergs brought in. The *New York Post* described the Communist Party in 1949 as "a battered band, hopelessly alien in allegiance, deprived of any authentic roots in the labor movement, cut off from the mainstream of American life." By 1950, Schlesinger believed the scarier elements of the communist threat had been pretty much taken care of. Therefore, communism could be defeated through open and public debate and counterintelligence rather than new legislation, Nonetheless, there were still those who wanted more, and Schlesinger and Wechsler opposed them. Senator McCarran, a conservative Democrat from Nevada, pushed through an act that, in the words of the historian J. Ronald Oakley,

> . . . required all communist organizations and communist-front organizations to register with the attorney general's office, banned communists from working in defense plants, prohibited government employees from contributing money to any communist organization or from being a member of any organization conspiring to set up a totalitarian state in the United States, and gave the government the power to halt the immigration of subversive aliens and to deport those already in the country.

Building on this momentum, Hubert Humphrey, an ally to Schlesinger and Wechsler, proposed the Communist Control Act, an act that outlawed the Communist Party outright. Schlesinger and Wechsler opposed both McCarran and Humphrey. It was time for open discussion rather than legislation that threatened civil liberties and ignored the right to hold "loathsome ideas," and Schlesinger and Wechsler were willing to jeopardize political connections (i.e., friendship with Humphrey) to make the point.[32]

At the same time that these acts were jelling, HUAC was turning its attention away from the State Department and toward the worlds of education and Hollywood. On the question of teaching and communism, the ethic of parsing was even more clearly defined. Drawing on the ethic of prudence and pragmatism at the same time, Wechsler explained to a fellow journalist in 1952:

> I just don't believe that the handful of Communists who may be teaching arithmetic and spelling present as much of a danger as that associated with the attempt to rout them out. The truth is that too many teachers are timid and are rendered more so by these performances. . . . I still think the real Communist threat lies in espionage and sabotage— not in the realm of ideas. . . . If a handful of Communist teachers can produce a lot of communists there is something basically wrong with the other teachers and the educational system of which they are a part.

Schlesinger agreed with this argument but got more specific, arguing that if communists were found to indoctrinate elementary school students, then there might be grounds for firing, not because of their beliefs but because they weren't doing their jobs. Still, membership in the CP was not enough, ipso facto, to lead to the firing of a teacher. Here Schlesinger disagreed with Lionel Trilling and Sidney Hook (author of *Heresy Yes, Conspiracy No*), both members of the ACCF and prominent New York Intellectuals, who argued that communists should be fired from teaching positions across the board (although they wanted this done by schools themselves, not the government).

Here Schlesinger developed a distinct liberal form of anticommunism that went against some of the assumptions of the New York Intellectuals, which have received much more attention in this area. Schlesinger could imagine a communist teaching physics just fine, for example, and he reasoned from this point to make a larger one. It was better to err on the side of civil liberties and the ethic of open discussion than the fear of communist indoctrination in the American classroom.

"The important thing," Schlesinger argued, "is to preserve the right to free discussion. This right includes the right to hold loathsome ideas." Let these be aired in the classroom and allow students to decide for themselves. Besides, he reasoned, "there are negligible numbers of Communists today on college faculties." The real danger would be to create an invasive rule out of proportion to the problem.[33]

When it came to hunting down communists in the world of entertainment, Schlesinger and Wechsler were even more critical. The potential to smear was evident when they learned that *The Best Years of Our Lives*, a film that documented the difficulties of World War II veterans returning home and that won the Academy Award in 1946 for best picture, was accused of promoting communist sympathies (because it showed an American businessman treating a returning GI rudely on a plane). The fact that the famous actor and director Charlie Chaplin was not allowed to reenter the United States due to his communist sympathies seemed silly. Nor did it seem wise to have the HUAC hunt down communist writers in Hollywood. Here Schlesinger explained a fundamental motivation behind the ethics of parsing: the need to resist becoming like the enemy. He wrote to Sol Stein of the ACCF that the group should do nothing on "the Communist Conspiracy in the Entertainment World," again raising distinctions between his own outlook and that of prominent New York Intellectuals. The problem was not "serious enough to justify counter-action by grown people. The Communists themselves never looked sillier than when they were exposing Russian clowns or were detecting 'bourgeois tendencies' in Soviet circuses; and I should hate to see Americans imitating the Soviet Union in this respect." If any pro-communist film were actually made during the mid-1950s (and Schlesinger would have to chuckle at that possibility) allow it to be lambasted in public discussion and critical review, he seemed to suggest.[34]

So as the 1950s played themselves out, liberal anticommunism defined itself increasingly against its right-wing opponent. We often forget this when thinking that anticommunism provided a "consensus" in postwar America. No such consensus existed if you follow the debates at the time. If anything, liberal intellectuals parsed out their own anticommunism and wound up increasingly taking on conservative foes. The central forum for this conflict was the American Congress for Cultural Freedom (ACCF), an organization founded in January 1951 by the anticommunist and pragmatist philosopher Sidney Hook, and it was meant to serve as the national office for the international CCF. Counter to the interpretations provided by New Left historians and the more current writings of Elizabeth Stoner Saunders, anticommunism was neither rigid nor stagnant if we follow the debates within this organization. It moved with the times and took note of shifts in the political winds. And within ACCF liberal intellectuals such as Schlesinger and Wechsler found themselves embroiled in debates about the implications of anticommunism with the likes of Whittaker Chambers, Max Eastman, and James Burnham, all conservative anticommunists, and rethinking their own presuppositions as they did battle.[35]

In his memoirs, Sidney Hook argues that ACCF fell apart during the 1950s due to conflicts with the office of the CCF but mostly because of differing opinions about McCarthy. There's a great deal of truth to this assertion. The ACCF sponsored numerous scholarly and intellectual forums, and, at one in 1952, Max Eastman, once a socialist and friend of the Bolshevik John Reed's but by then an arch-conservative, spoke in favor of Senator McCarthy. There was uproar from James Wechsler, Arthur Schlesinger, and the liberal journalist Richard Rovere. To combat Eastman's view and give voice to an increasing sentiment within ACCF, Wechsler proposed the organization make a statement against McCarthy, showing those outside the membership that the senator posed a threat to cultural freedom in the United States. Wechsler described the result: "The matter was brushed aside, and I found myself feeling like a Trotskyite at a YCL convention [i.e., Stalinist] for having brought up the subject."

But Schlesinger and Rovere remained angry and ready to leave the organization if it did nothing on McCarthy, expressing frustration that an article by Irving Kristol, which was clearly favorable toward McCarthy, had been circulated by the ACCF. This also became personal, inasmuch as Burnham, one of the leading "anti-anti-McCarthyites," to use Rovere's term, had smeared Schlesinger in an *American Mercury* article at the same time as Eastman's blustery remarks at the ACCF gathering. Eventually, the pro-McCarthy faction, James Burnham leading, would leave the organization en masse in 1954, feeling increased hostility.[36]

Although McCarthy might have been the pretext of this conflict, it really centered around the larger issue of differing character dispositions and political philosophies. The central conflict was whether anticommunism should become fixated and hardened or if it should become a starting point to prompt a broader debate about the future of American politics. Burnham's anticommunism hardened, and he grew more willing to justify extreme measures, both nationally and internationally, to rid the world of communism. Burnham's hardening and those of other conservative anti-Stalinists was obvious to those attending ACCF meetings. David Riesman, a liberal and a friend of both Galbraith and Schlesinger, joined ACCF in 1953 (a year before Burnham quit) and he grew alarmed at the tenor of its meetings, which he described as having a "polemical, even fanatical quality." The problem was a fixation on anticommunism. Riesman argued, "There is real lack of balance here—an over-preoccupation with Communists at home and abroad without any preoccupation with 'anti-Communists' (including some of my best friends!) at home and abroad." Schlesinger agreed with Riesman and wanted ACCF to widen its definition of cultural freedom to include McCarthyism. More broadly, he wanted anticommunism to prompt a discussion that would open up a dialogue about America's weaknesses as well as its strengths. He wanted, in other words, for anticommunism to become *liberal*, and, as should be clear by now, the liberal intellectual recoiled at hardness and rigidity of character.[37]

It's probably no surprise that the ACCF eventually disintegrated. Schlesinger and Wechsler left in the belief that there were bigger battles to fight as the 1950s went on. When the ACCF went belly up, Schlesinger would try to recruit its ex-membership into the ranks of the ADA, seeing this organization as the sort that could transcend the limits of anticommunism. The struggles within the ACCF were important because they went beyond traditional personal and intellectual infighting. They represented some very basic differences in political philosophy between liberals and conservatives during a supposed age of consensus and differences with New York Intellectuals who sometimes remained fixated solely on the question of communism. Just as important, these differences emerged when liberal intellectuals were starting to look outside the United States and consider how anticommunism could be made effective in American foreign policy.[38]

THE ETHICS OF THE OXYMORON: REALISM AND IDEALISM

In 1952, Irving Kristol asked Arthur Schlesinger if he would like to debate James Burnham in an ACCF forum. Inasmuch as Burnham had just published an article in which he accused Schlesinger of having communist sympathies, Kristol knew this to be a dangerous invite. "I know that you are not, at this time, in exactly a friendly mood toward Burnham," Kristol wrote in an understated way. To have gotten these two in the same room would have been quite interesting. Their disagreements went deep, and not just about McCarthy. In fact, it was on foreign policy that the deepest disagreements surfaced. Burnham had become a leading figure in calling for an "offensive policy" against the USSR. Schlesinger, on the other hand, believed in containment, that is, checking the expansion of Soviet power, while making sure that America did not turn this initiative into an "ideological crusade." Burnham's views would be taken up by Eisenhower's secretary of state, John Foster Dulles, who would call for a "rollback" of Soviet power and who would become an arch-nemesis of both Schlesinger and Niebuhr throughout the 1950s.[39]

If there's a term for these liberal intellectuals' views on foreign policy, it would have to be realism. Unfortunately, the term is loaded. We tend to think of it as an amoral doctrine, because it takes human beings as they are and not ideally as they should be. Realism suggests a cynical view of human (and nation-state) behavior, as it prioritizes self-interest over any commitment to a wider public good. To a large extent, such a view can be found in these thinkers' writing on foreign policy. For instance, during World War II Niebuhr wrote, "Governments must think in terms of national interests. Governments like nations rarely rise to long-range unselfish action." Schlesinger echoed this sentiment when he warned Americans that "any state which states that . . . its own" action "is motivated by noble moral considerations of universal import risks leaving its audience cold." Niebuhr believed the type of level-headedness that Schlesinger suggested here could nurture "a shrewd calculation of possibilities" in foreign policy decisions.[40]

Realism exhibited itself in Niebuhr's dismissal of the possibilities of "world government." While the United Nations (UN) formed in the years after World War II, Niebuhr gave it support but warned against any utopian conception of its potential. He argued that the UN was animated by a "too simple universalism" that ignored national self-interest. To say that different nation-states could form binding pacts the way citizens within nation-states had (or at least potentially had) reflected an unrealistic assessment of nation-state behavior, or what Niebuhr called an "absurd form of the 'social contract' conception of government."

He explained that "the universal community," an oxymoronic term in many ways, "has no common language or common culture—nothing to create the consciousness of 'we.'" The sad conclusion from all this was that force would have to play a role in foreign policy, because mutual agreement on shared norms at the national or international level was a myth.[41]

This language of realism also suggested an appreciation of "limits" in foreign policy. And here is where characterizing realism as purely unethical gets trickier. "Limits," after all, prompted an appreciation of a nation's hubris in the international realm. So, for instance, one problem with Burnham's "rollback" policy was that it empowered the United States too much and ignored this country's own foibles and faults. This was the ethical imperative suggested by realism. Liberals, for instance, needed to be careful not to overextend their reach, so they argued to focus Cold War initiatives mainly on Europe during the earliest stages of the Cold War. It was John Foster Dulles, General MacArthur (during the Korean War), and James Burnham who wanted to push America toward a policy not of containing communism within its existing borders but of rolling back communism in Asia, especially China and Indochina. In countering this argument, Niebuhr used a realist argument that stressed limits and a sense of American humility. He argued that in Indochina, "frustration must be accepted"; indeed, he went so far as to call frustration a "virtue." This was the same counsel that Niebuhr had given earlier during the fall of China to communists in 1949, that the United States must accept this fact with "folded hands." This was the only realistic thing to do, and beyond that, it taught a sense of limits that corrected belligerence. And so, out of the cold arguments of realism and calculation there grew an ethical system.[42]

Realism suggested other moral guideposts for an American foreign policy. Although Niebuhr might not have trusted the concept of "world government," he rarely questioned the need for building alliances with other countries. Schlesinger believed a realist position recognized "the indispensability of allies." Unilateralism was totally unacceptable to these thinkers. And so too was the concept, a very Burnhamian concept (if such a word exists), of "preventive showdown." Schlesinger argued against the journalist Joe Alsop's use of this term by calling it morally suspect and pragmatically impossible in a day and age of nuclear weapons. Galbraith would reiterate the point to Alsop later on when he argued that the journalist's "unsentimental realism" led him to "embrace the *Walpurgische Nacht*—to accept a future of utter darkness." Preventive war was the highest form of hubris, because it placed faith in America to predict the future and suggested an ugly and bellicose situation in the world. The advocates of preventive war, Niebuhr argued, "assume a prescience about the future which no man or nation possesses." Once again, realism nurtured an ethical viewpoint, one that encouraged introspection and questioning of a nation's motivations, rather than just cold-hearted calculation.[43]

Although liberals believed the focus of the Cold War should be Europe, not Asia, they could at least accept tentatively Truman's initiation of the Korean War. Even if Truman might have been caving in to pressure from the right, the war was the furthest thing from a preventive war, because North Korea had attacked South Korea. In addition, Truman approached the United Nations and got its consent and always kept Britain, a key ally, in the loop. As the war proceeded, and General MacArthur crossed the parallel between North and South Korea, thereby drawing China into the conflict, liberals protested and supported Truman's unpopular decision to oust MacArthur (who, it should be recalled, came home to large parades). They also attacked MacArthur's view of foreign policy as being guided by the principles of "alone-if-necessary, maximum counterforce, and . . . Asia-first." Thus, liberals used their ethics of realism to provide critical support to Truman and were ready to criticize when necessary.[44]

Perhaps the best way to understand these Cold War liberals' views of foreign policy is in relation to others who called themselves realists at the same time. Take the thoughts of Hans Morgenthau, Walter Lippmann, and George Kennan—all prominent realist thinkers in the field of foreign policy. The first two thinkers praised Niebuhr and recognized his influence but differed from him in their assessment of the Soviet Union. They were more *old school* realists who argued that the Soviet Union was motivated by traditional concerns such as protecting its borders and internal security. From this perspective, there was more continuity in Russia's historical behavior than change. Walter LaFeber explains that Morgenthau believed that Lenin's 1917 Revolution and Stalin's consolidation of dictatorship was not much of a break with "traditional Russian national power." Lippmann, a prominent journalist and opinion leader, believed Stalin was similar to past Russian leaders like Peter the Great, because he cared only about the material interests of the Russian nation, not ideological expansion. Although Morgenthau and Lippmann were certainly not progressives soft on communism, it was sometimes hard to distinguish their thought from that of Henry Wallace, who believed America could presuppose a "spheres of influence" approach to foreign policy inasmuch as the Soviet Union was acting like a traditional nation-state.[45]

Niebuhr disagreed with this assessment of the Soviet Union's motivation. He saw ideology, not material interest, as playing a more significant role in the development of Soviet power. "Nations are not just geographic entities but concretions and organizations of collective human vitalities," he explained. In this, he was like George Kennan, who stressed the "nature of the mental world of the Soviet leaders, as well as . . . the character of their ideology" to explain their behavior. Contra Lippmann and Morgenthau, Kennan believed that, in the wake of Lenin's revolution, ideology trumped national self-interest in motivating Soviet power. Niebuhr concurred that ideology mattered. There was no other way to explain the appeal of communism to Asian and third world countries, an increasing reality as the Cold War heated up. The problem with Kennan was not that he believed Soviet communism to be ideologically fanatic, but rather his belief that fanaticism could be checked best by Americans being cold and materialist in calculating where and when to check Soviet power. After all, Niebuhr reasoned, if the Soviet Union was driven by ideology, then ideology, in the better sense of that term, would have to be a part of the battle to defeat it.

Here Niebuhr disagreed with those who conflated fascism and communism within the larger rubric of totalitarianism. Nazism, after all, was only "nihilism," whereas communism held out a certain amount of idealism. Schlesinger and Wechsler concurred with Niebuhr on this point. As Wechsler put it, the "communists have appealed to men's loftiest instincts, while the fascists frankly addressed themselves to man's cruelest impulses." As Niebuhr saw it, "communism" was "not primarily a military but a moral-political force." Therefore, Niebuhr agreed with Kennan's assessment—that the Soviet Union was motivated by ideology—but not his prescription for action—that the United States become realist and solely calculate foreign policy on the basis of self-interest. "Egotism," Niebuhr explained, "is not the proper cure for an abstract and pretentious idealism." The right prescription was a "realism without cynicism," that is, a foreign policy that took ideological and moral issues seriously.[46]

So if the Soviet Union was not just a nation-state but an idea vying for world attention, then the Cold War was not just about "military strength" but "other political, economic, and moral factors." The Cold War was therefore a "moral and political battle," but contrary to attitudes such as those of Dulles and Burnham, America, in doing battle, would have to be realistic and resist hubris. America could not become ideologically fanatical like its enemy. It had to combine idealism and realism in the same breath. The "American way of life," as it was becoming known during the 1940s and 1950s, had to lift itself up in the eyes of the world, and especially the poorer countries. Cold War liberal intellectuals did not assume that, as it existed, the American way of life should triumph around the world due to its superiority. Far from it. They believed America needed to *learn* from the rest of the world while projecting its ideals outward. In fighting this cultural Cold War, America would become, by necessity and outside pressure both, a better country. Liberals saw this as the central challenge of the long Cold War that lay ahead. It made them distinct from conservatives pressing in a different direction.[47]

THE BURDEN OF THE COSMOPOLITAN LIBERAL

America had always been geographically isolated from the rest of the Western world. This fact allowed it to delay entry into World War II and to turn a blind eye to the wreckage left in its wake. But not so for the thinkers studied here. They were inherently cosmopolitan—Americans first, most certainly—but the type of Americans who felt a connection to Europe and an increasing awareness of the non–Western world, too. Sometimes, this was directly personal. Reinhold Niebuhr, for instance, had married a British woman and therefore wound up traveling back and forth from America to England quite regularly. Arthur Schlesinger's work with the OWI and OSS during the war had brought him overseas to England and France, and he found much in common with liberal and anticommunist intellectuals such as Isaiah Berlin and Arthur Koestler. The same was true for John Kenneth Galbraith. It seemed that the world pressed in on these thinkers' consciousness on a very personal level. This cosmopolitan sentiment only grew after World War II ended.[48]

It continued to grow after the war. President Truman called for two immediate responses to Soviet expansion in the years following World War II. The first became known as the Truman Doctrine, which called for military aid to countries battling communist forces. Liberals supported this policy, but warily because it could overextend the American military, support antidemocratic forces in the name of fighting anti-communists (which happened in the case of Greece, the first country to receive support under the doctrine), and suggest "unilateral American action." More in tune with liberal sentiments was the Marshall Plan, which provided economic aid to Western European countries and thereby provided incentives for building back their economies while resisting communism. Schlesinger believed containment (the Truman Doctrine) and reconstruction (the Marshall Plan) could work in tandem. But of the two programs, clearly the Marshall Plan was more conducive to Americans opening up a dialogue with Cold War allies. Or at least it could if liberals pushed.[49]

The European political spectrum was much farther left than America's, and this prompted liberal realists to search for a "Non-Communist Left" (NCL) that deserved American support. Social democratic governments were the perfect candidates and wound up receiving U.S. foreign aid under the Marshall Plan. To a certain extent, the Marshall Plan gained support easily because some Americans remembered how depression after World War I helped spawn fascism. But other Americans, especially those organized around conservative organizations such as the National Associations of Manufacturers (NAM) and the Chamber of Commerce (CoC), protested giving aid to social democracies. After all, these organizations' leaders reasoned, the "American way of life" (equated with free markets and competitive individualism) needed to be championed overseas.

Here again is where the realist disposition of liberals prompted an ethical self-scrutiny, where they believed an appreciation of Europe's tragic destruction during the war offered the young idealist nation of America a lesson about hubris. Niebuhr, for instance, counseled that foreign aid could not become tied to "peculiar and parochial conceptions of democracy." He argued that Americans had too strong a faith in "unrestricted liberty," which came out in the debates around the Marshall Plan as well as the simultaneous dismantling of the Office of Price Administration (OPA). "We are always in danger," he explained, "of making democracy odious in Europe by a too individualistic and libertarian interpretation of it." The Marshall Plan, liberals argued, should teach Americans that the world was pluralist and cosmopolitan, not singular and provincial. This lesson would remain in place as liberals like Galbraith, during the early 1960s, started to formulate a vision of economic aid to countries outside the European orbit.[50]

The Marshall Plan taught America that it had to become a world leader without believing in global domination. Because these liberals were cosmopolitans, they embraced this lesson in cultural and moral terms as well as economic ones. Not surprisingly, a place for this lesson was the CCF. Michael Josselson, a key player in the CCF, was born in Estonia and had lived in Germany before becoming an American citizen in 1936. He became a facilitator of CCF activities throughout the 1950s, and he represented a truly cosmopolitan voice due to his background. He grew increasingly frustrated with the "hotheads" in the ACCF as he called them. For instance, he was incensed when the ACCF, without consulting the CCF, denounced the British philosopher Bertrand Russell who had criticized the U.S. government's decision to keep a witness in the Rosenberg case in jail. The hard-line anticommunism coming from the Americans alienated many Europeans, not just Russell. Nicholas Nabokov, who came to direct many of the CCF's activities and who was an émigré from Russia to Europe, complained to Schlesinger about the ACCF's hard line as well. "It seems to me," Nabokov affirmed as early as 1951, "that some of our friends have veered so far to the right" in America "that soon it will be hard to talk to them." Schlesinger constantly got a sense of just how much hard-lined anticommunism and pro-Americanism could wind up alienating Europeans more than drawing them into joint efforts.[51]

This was slightly ironic, seeing as one of CCF's major objectives was to nurture a more favorable European attitude toward America. There were obvious reasons to do so, as witnessed in the growth of anti-Americanism in Europe (especially France) at this time, something that seemed a direct impediment to the Marshall Plan. There was an awareness on the part of American intellectuals that their country's image abroad was being constructed more and more around images in the mass culture being exported to Europe. Hollywood and Coca-Cola were the two major exports to France, for instance, that gave the appearance that America was superficial and sugary (literally and metaphorically).

Niebuhr worried that Europeans' "conception of us is drawn merely from our movies, which are, if I may say so, a tremendously fruitful source of confusion about the character of American life." Movies and soft drinks were accompanied by the popularity of American literature from the 1920s, the writings of H.L. Mencken and Sinclair Lewis, both of whom portrayed Americans as an uncultivated, provincial, and small-minded people (an intellectual strain these liberals had rejected, as seen in the last chapter). This hatred of America was only confirmed by "the sometimes unfortunate conduct of American tourists," as the ACCF admitted in planning a conference on "Anti-Americanism in Europe."[52]

This anti-Americanism fueled many of the activities of the ACCF and CCF. Nicholas Nabokov pleaded for reports on American life that would be published in the French magazine *Preuves*, a publication financed and published by the CCF. He hoped these reports could stress "the fight in America against prejudice, against racial and color discrimination," inasmuch as the French found American racism so hypocritical in light of the country's fight against fascism. Nabokov also hoped for "articles concerning the upward trend of American society." Obviously, these would help build a better impression of American democracy abroad. If anything, liberal intellectuals in America saw this as an opportunity to deepen Europeans' understandings of their country. This drew inspiration from an older intellectual hope in the promise of a democratic culture growing out of American literary activities (what some called the "American Renaissance" of the nineteenth century), as captured in the writings of Herman Melville, Walt Whitman, and Mark Twain. At the very least, they wanted to challenge a one-dimensional view of America on the part of Europe. When Lionel Trilling edited an edition of *Perspectives*, an American journal distributed in Europe and very much in the vein of the CCF's work, he argued,

> I feel that one of the most useful things we can say to Europeans is that we are not a solid phalanx of opinion, a perfectly organized façade to the world, a single American thing, but that we are divided into groups of opinion, that we scold each other—just like Europeans—and that foreigners don't have to decide whether they like us in toto but may find that they like and sympathize with this group or that.

American intellectuals hoped to deepen the European perception of their culture, thus doing their bit in fighting the Cold War.[53]

There was a troubling side to this sometimes. Trilling himself was quite uncomfortable with the idea of cultural propaganda, especially the sort directly linked to the federal government (*Perspectives*, it should be pointed out, was supported by the Ford Foundation, not the federal government). When William Faulkner asked Trilling to contribute an essay to an initiative of President Eisenhower's to provide a better depiction of America abroad, Trilling declined, explaining: "I feel that it isn't the job of a writer as such to undertake to give a 'true picture' of America to the world—that is the job of the State Department, which might properly consult with individual writers: what I don't like is the idea of the whole profession doing the job seemingly of its own initiative." There was a real threat of prostituting intellect to national propaganda, Trilling argued. This was the strain in anticommunist thought and activism later picked up by critics like Christopher Lasch and Frances Stoner Saunders. In fact, Trilling might have been admitting to an earlier guilt as he himself had succumbed to a bit of self-censorship when considering an article he was writing for *Preuves*. He explained to Irving Kristol, then the executive director of ACCF, that the article he was writing was not suitable for *Preuves* because it "says in effect that American literature has no sense of society, that it rejects the social idea. Now this, as I realized in the course of the work, is no thing to be saying to the French at this moment; it is, indeed, a very bad thing to say to them, and it is likely to be taken up and used in a hostile way." The cultural Cold War, at times like this, seemed to suggest that truth would be sacrificed to the cause.[54]

Fortunately, this was not always the case. In fact, the cultural Cold War seemed to suggest to American liberals the need for a balanced account of their culture and its possibilities, not triumphalism or lies. When Trilling edited *Perspectives*, for instance, he included an article by Mary McCarthy entitled "America the Beautiful." Here this novelist and social critic admitted that American culture was certainly ugly in many ways, but that it also promised the possibilities of a truly democratic culture. It was this mixed impression of America, one that recognized its foibles and shortcomings as well as its "promise," that marked the attitude of liberals' efforts during the cultural Cold War. Niebuhr, for instance, admitted that there was an understandable sentiment behind the French protest against "Coca-colonialism." Unfortunately, though, the critique in Europe became "so sweeping that it condemns our true virtues as well our vices." Niebuhr therefore wanted the cultural Cold War to be about trumpeting virtues and criticizing vices, that is, for Americans to be both cultural ambassadors and critics of their own culture. After all, this would capture the truth of the situation rather than degenerate into propaganda.[55]

Indeed, the cultural Cold War had as much ambivalence about it as triumphalism. Or at least that is what these liberal intellectuals wanted: an *ironic* appreciation of American power rather than Henry Luce's celebration of the "American century." This is something the New Left and critics like Saunders tend to ignore. Liberal intellectuals could take the criticisms they heard about their own culture abroad and turn them into an opportunity for national self-criticism. They also understood that America's power in the world was due as much to contingency as to any inherent national greatness. America's isolation, for instance, meant that it escaped the devastation of World War II; the natural wealth it possessed at the time that European countries had exhausted theirs also gave America an advantage in asserting its power on the world stage. "We are a paradise of plenty suspended in a hell of global insecurity," Niebuhr explained. Therefore, Galbraith, following on Niebuhr's assertions, argued that America's foreign policy should be "humble and open-minded."[56]

This humble disposition had to come into play as liberal intellectuals looked within America's borders. Very often, historians looking back believe that intellectuals simply aligned themselves with the American way of life, having shed their radicalism of the 1930s for the national celebration of the 1940s and 1950s. *Partisan Review*'s 1952 symposium "Our Country, Our Culture" is the standard text taken as evidence of this intellectual shift. The editors of this once-Marxist publication were now much more favorable toward America, and thus were selling out, some suggest, to the status quo. Only Irving Howe, Norman Mailer, and C. Wright Mills (all figures who would have an impact on the American New Left) dissented from the chorus of celebration.

But this overall characterization is false if it pays attention to the strain of thought discussed here. Two of our main characters participated in the symposium and did not speak triumphantly of America. Indeed, Niebuhr argued the exact opposite, that America was too full of "self congratulations about the vaunted virtues and achievements of the 'American way of life.'" Certainly America had lessons to teach the world about the importance of democracy and freedom, but this was no excuse for "complacency." "No intellectual life," Niebuhr explained, "can be at ease with the massive spiritual, moral, and cultural crudities which seek to make themselves normative in a civilization." Schlesinger, the other participant in the symposium, would concur, arguing against McCarthyism and the homogenization of mass culture stifling debate (there was very little that was celebratory about his contribution to the symposium). The situation of the Cold War prompted just as much self-anxiety on the parts of these intellectuals as it did an appreciation of their country's promise.[57]

If anything, the Cold War placed a premium on America improving its cultural and political life in order to persuade the rest of the world that it deserved respect. "When we speak rather idolatrously of the 'American way of life,'" Niebuhr warned, "our friends and critics profess not to be certain whether we are recommending certain standards of political freedom or extolling our living standards." At the least, America would have to do something to improve the status of African Americans within its own borders (the Soviet Union constantly reminded the world that blacks in the South were second-class citizens) and the threat of McCarthyism to political and cultural freedom. Additionally, liberal intellectuals had to wonder if America should be celebrated for its economic prosperity and mass culture. They believed there were better ideals than consumerism and wealth to be projected outward to the world. "Foreign policy," Arthur Schlesinger argued, "must be the projection and expression of what we are like as a national community." But this was not as easy a task as it might sound. It required internal self-scrutiny and debate about what ideals and values Americans should hold dear to their hearts. This was the project these Cold War liberals were demanding of their fellow citizens. And the results provoked interesting assessments of America's strengths and weaknesses.[58]

CHAPTER THREE

Values
The Pay-Offs and Problems of Pluralism

Democracy is a method of finding proximate solutions for insoluble problems.

Reinhold Niebuhr[1]

THE MAN WHO MET HIS SELF

The year 1940 was transforming for Reinhold Niebuhr. During it he began to face the fact that he was no longer a socialist but a liberal by severing his connection with the Socialist Party. This was no small move for a man who had voted for its presidential candidate, Norman Thomas, in 1932 and 1936 and who ran for Congress himself on the Socialist Party ticket in 1930. But by 1940, he found the Socialist Party's pacifist opposition to America's possible entry into World War II "intolerable." Although still hopeful about a third-party alternative to the Democrats and Republicans, he got behind the idea of a pressure group pushing the Democrats to the left, rather than splitting from the party. Late in the year, Niebuhr helped form the Union for Democratic Action. The organization became a "group of dissident socialists who split from Norman Thomas's Socialist Party after unsuccessfully opposing its isolationist tendencies" and that eventually transformed itself into Americans for Democratic Action (ADA). Group members were avidly anticommunist and unwilling to play the role of fellow travelers and were also striving for some form of coherent liberal political vision. Three years into the organization's existence, Niebuhr was outlining its political vision as being somewhere between complete social-ization of property and absolute freedom from state intervention. In other words, he was now no longer a socialist but a liberal.[2]

86

Niebuhr's trek toward liberalism repeated itself in other activists' and intellectuals' lives during the 1940s, a decade that witnessed momentous changes in politics. Consider Niebuhr's choice for president during the 1930s, Norman Thomas, a leading anticommunist socialist throughout the Great Depression (and a man who never seemed to tire of losing his run for the presidency). Soon after Niebuhr broke with his party, Thomas was giving "critical support" to FDR's decision to enter the war, thus ditching his prior pacifism. By the 1950s, Thomas had so questioned collectivism and bureaucracy that he seemed more a liberal than a socialist, and not surprisingly, his anticommunism led him to work within organizations such as the Congress for Cultural Freedom (CCF). Consider also how the one-time Trotskyist Dwight Macdonald, a pacifist during World War II, became so disgusted with the Soviet Union that he too wound up having to "choose the West," as he put it, placing him "in the camp of the Americans for Democratic Action" by 1950, as his biographer recounts. So, too, Irving Howe, the independent socialist who was busy editing *Dissent* magazine during the 1950s and laying the ground for the New Left of the 1960s. As Howe's biographer points out, during the 1950s, he was "arguing for a synthesis of liberalism and socialism" to such an extent that it was hard to see where liberalism stopped and socialism began in his political thinking. The line between liberalism and socialism blurred for numerous prominent thinkers throughout the 1940s and 1950s. Liberalism appeared an increasingly appealing set of ideas to old socialists. Niebuhr was therefore not alone in finding history backing him into a liberal position.[3]

Niebuhr's life and ideas would continue to speak to a wide number of people after the war, quirky as this sometimes seemed. For Niebuhr was a theologian who wrote about the meaning of Christianity, and yet his writings reached many readers far beyond the circle of faithful Christians. He had, in Arthur Schlesinger's words, an "extraordinary appeal to those who [did] not share his overwhelming sense of the existence of God." Schlesinger himself was an "agnostic"; yet, he based a great deal of his thought around Niebuhr's arguments. The philosopher Morton White, who disagreed with much of what Niebuhr said, once quipped that there were numerous "Atheists for Niebuhr" clubs in 1940s America. In part, Niebuhr appealed to nonbelievers because of the times. It was hard to be an optimist about humankind after seeing what the Nazis had done to the Jews or Stalin did to political opponents, and it was hard to live with anything but anxiety in the face of nuclear weapons. Secular people such as Schlesinger and Wechsler could believe in Niebuhr's critique of human pretensions and optimism without necessarily embracing the sources he utilized to make these arguments. That was the power of his thought, its ability to sum up a mood that was in the air at the time—a mood of pessimism tinged with a residual hope in changing things for the better.[4]

Another reason for Niebuhr's appeal was how his biography spoke to broad historical themes in America, especially a blurred line between socialism and liberalism that existed long before the 1940s. This blurred line was due to an exceptionalism in American politics. America after all never developed a strong socialist tradition as did Europe. There were some cities with socialist mayors in the early twentieth century (Milwaukee, for instance) and other pockets that voted for Socialist Party congressmen, but socialism never caught on for numerous reasons. Because America lacked a parliamentary system and proportional representation, any vote for a Socialist became a minority voice that evaporated into thin air (and could potentially "spoil" elections). Once communists started importing the strategies pioneered by Lenin during the Russian Revolution into America in 1919, the socialist tradition that did exist became that much more marginalized. In part, this was because socialist ideals had always worked in tandem with liberalism, prompting one historian to call liberalism "a surrogate socialism." Nonetheless, socialism had a larger import.

One of socialism's more important gifts to liberal thought was its *soft* critique of capitalism. Whereas Marxists pursued a hard scientific critique that argued capitalism would fail due to inherent systemic contradictions (see the previous chapter), many socialists, drawing more from romanticism than the social science of Karl Marx, objected to capitalism because of its ugliness (for instance, William Morris, the British leader of the arts and crafts movement and a soft socialist, objected to capitalism because its factories were churning out shoddy products) and its valorization of selfishness. For some socialists, the teachings of Christ, not the writings of Marx, served as an important critique of capitalism's exaltation of private profit. This criticism of capitalism as a system that encouraged socially negligent behavior, rather than as a system that was doomed to imminent collapse, became one of socialism's most important legacies for postwar liberalism.[5]

Niebuhr certainly took up this legacy. After he shed socialism, his critique of capitalism grew out of his thinking about the perils of the self. This theme remained consistent in his social thought throughout the 1940s. He explained, "Evil is always the assertion of some self-interest without regard to the whole." The individual had an innate tendency toward self-love, exhibited in "human impulses and ambitions." This constituted Niebuhr's definition of sinfulness, and he learned it from the great Christian thinker Augustine, more than from the Old Testament's story about Adam eating an apple from the tree of knowledge and thereby staining humankind from that point onward (the story of original sin). Niebuhr chafed at predestination and the sort of "pessimism" that "asserted the untenable doctrine of man's total depravity." He certainly saw self-love as ingrained in human nature but retained hope by placing his faith in an ethic of love that was also a part of human nature. For in the end, the self could not subsist without others, the social need also being inherent to the human condition. The individual, Niebuhr explained, "cannot fulfill his life within himself but only in responsible and mutual relations with his fellow" humans. "Love is the law of life because the self cannot be truly fulfilled unless it be drawn out of itself into the life of others." In passages like these, Niebuhr seemed to hearken back to the teachings of Christian socialism, the sort found in the "Social Gospel."[6]

The Social Gospel grew in popularity throughout numerous mainline Protestant churches during the early twentieth century. The key exponent of it was a Baptist theologian Walter Rauschenbusch. In *A Theology for the Social Gospel*, Rauschenbusch defined sin as selfishness and argued that Christianity encouraged people to pay attention to social ethics, making the "Kingdom of God" and the Christian ideal of equality of all souls before the eyes of God a reality on earth and in everyday social relations. "We love and serve God," Rauschenbusch explained, "when we love and serve our fellows, whom he loves and in whom he lives." He argued that good Christian employers, for instance, should recognize labor unions and provide workmen's compensation if they were to retain their good standing in the eyes of the Lord. Rauschenbusch went a step further than just socializing Christian principles by arguing that a social ethic was already imminent in history. He drew upon the millennial aspects of Christian thought in order to argue that God was presently working within history and that the Kingdom of God was increasingly becoming a reality in human social relations. Faithful Christians simply had to work to push humankind along the progressive course on which it already was charted.[7]

Niebuhr appreciated Rauschenbusch's teachings but could not believe in the progressive dimension of his thought. What proof was there that existing social relations were becoming more just in the eyes of God? What proof especially after the discovery of the concentration camp and gulag? Self-love, Niebuhr believed, was a permanent condition of humankind, no matter how much he hoped to temper it with an ethic of love. The Kingdom of God stood permanently beyond the reach of human beings. "Man is," Niebuhr wrote, "even in the highest reaches of his transcendent freedom, too finite to comprehend the eternal by his own resources." The self would always revolt against God's teachings, because the self was inherently imperfect. The self rarely transcended its own limitations, but this nurtured creativity as well as destruction; therefore, the self should have only "checks and balances" placed "upon" its "pretensions." This was the lesson that Schlesinger drew from Niebuhr's thought, arguing that it was "the belief in the perfectibility of man which encourages the belief that a small group of men are already perfect and hence may exercise total power without taint or corruption." Conflict and force would constantly be a reality, as far as Schlesinger and Niebuhr saw it, no matter if social relations improved. For Niebuhr, Rauschenbusch was an optimistic progressive whose utopian dreams of progress were no longer intellectually defensible. His Christian teachings of love and justice therefore had to be toughened.[8]

If self-love could not be eradicated and if the idea of progress was indefensible, conflict and tension would have to be accepted as part of the future of human society. This was a necessary lesson for a modern liberal, as far as Niebuhr was concerned. Self-love—a love he saw in himself as much as in others—became the basis of Niebuhr's liberal political philosophy. He still believed in the values Rauschenbusch posited: increased social welfare to foster a society more in line with Christian principles of equality.

But Niebuhr changed the way arguments had been made in the past for social welfare. The provisions created during the Progressive Era, the New Deal, and Truman's Fair Deal were legitimate and just, but their justification needed to be deepened. The welfare state was now not just a correction for the Great Depression but for a universal condition of human sinfulness. Niebuhr approached the problem of welfare politics from a different angle from those hoping to defend the poor (after all, he didn't believe the poor had any special claim to virtue). Rather than emphasize the needs of the poor, Niebuhr emphasized the sins of the rich and well-off. "Those who hold great economic and political power," Niebuhr warned, "are more guilty of pride against God and of injustice against the weak than those who lack power and prestige." When organizations such as the National Association of Manufacturers and Chamber of Commerce demanded less regulation of business activities (such as when they lobbied against the OPA), this revealed "the pathetic capacity of powerful men and groups to prefer their own and their immediate interests to the wider interests of the group and their own long-term interests." So welfare provisions and regulation of private interests relied upon a view of self-love, and humankind's state of sinfulness, as a threat to democracy. Taxation was another policy that became a necessity from this viewpoint, because it "demands more of us than we are inclined to give voluntarily." This idea might sound pedestrian today, but it illustrates an important quality of postwar liberal thought. Niebuhr wanted welfare legislation to find stronger intellectual footing. His dissection of the perils of self-love provided a set of ideas that could do this. He also led by example, arguing essentially that liberals needed to assess their intellectual inheritance, use what they could, and throw out what could not fit the dark times in which they found themselves living.[9]

Those who listened to Niebuhr during the mid-1940s knew they had a long, drawn-out battle ahead of them. The Cold War was assured to be a protracted struggle, with liberals prepared for battle against communists pledged to totalitarianism and conservatives desiring to turn back the accomplishments of the New Deal and Truman's Fair Deal. But liberals also knew their political vision required more than just an attack on their enemies. There had to be a positive dimension to their thought, one that sought out values liberals could uphold for their fellow citizens to see and appreciate. Postwar liberals had to search through their own value systems, explain what they believed in, and enter the world of political argument more sure of themselves. This is what Niebuhr had started to do as he recognized both the limits of previous progressive thinkers and the possibilities of a darker tone to liberalism. It was a course he set for himself and others from 1940 onward.

PREDECESSORS AND TRADITIONS

Liberalism, as it is understood in this book, grew out of a central tradition of political thought in America. The ideas explored here did not appear out of thin air or leap from the minds of Niebuhr or Schlesinger without precedent. The tradition went from the founding fathers to the writers of the American Constitution to certain mid-nineteenth-century figures, including presidential leaders, to Abraham Lincoln to Theodore Roosevelt, and finally, to Franklin Delano Roosevelt. Thus, these thinkers believed that the American past was full of ideas that could help them make their case for a future-minded political vision. Looking back on the intellectual lineage of American liberalism, these thinkers believed that certain ideas could serve them well and that some were destined for the dustbin of history. Historical inquiry was central to all of these thinkers' work, although not surprisingly, Schlesinger led the way in examining the past. He saw historical inquiry as an opportunity to assess the liberal's inheritance, to see where previous political thinkers and politicians working with ideas succeeded and failed. For instance, writing in 1945, he argued that the "world crisis" gave "new urgency to the question of the 'meaning' of democracy" best explored through historical inquiry.

This was a more exciting vision of historical research than treating the past as some sort of antiquarian object with no influence on the present. These thinkers went to the past in order to answer pressing questions for their own day and age. This was no easy task, seeing as the American liberal tradition ebbed and flowed and changed with the times. Nonetheless, its broad outlines were capable of being recovered and were right at the center of history. And the first and most obvious place to start was the origin of the American nation, the constitutional moment that created America. The founding fathers were America's first nationalists who put their ideas into words, and postwar liberals found in their activities and thinking an important precedent.[10]

Not only had the founding fathers created the national political system postwar liberals cherished, they were also men of ideas whose

ideas were connected to pragmatic circumstances, their political philos-
ophizing, for instance, growing out of a need to write a constitution.
When sorting through the founding fathers, it was not surprising to find
Schlesinger drawn to Jefferson as a predecessor to the democratic
egalitarianism that found its way into the Jacksonian era of the 1830s and
1840s. But Jefferson never achieved these thinkers' highest estimation,
especially due to his deism and Enlightenment optimism. Schlesinger
and Niebuhr saw clearer precedents to their thoughts in the political
writings of James Madison, the founding father who argued for a strong
and energetic national government capable of correcting for the natural
tendency of humans toward "self-love" (Madison's own term found in
the famous Paper Number Ten of *The Federalist Papers*). Niebuhr especially was drawn to the Federalists' understanding of the darker side of
"human motives and desires" and Madison's "realism." In fact, Schlesinger
argued that Niebuhr's own liberal philosophy was, in large part, a return
to the original pessimism of American liberal thought found in the
Federalists' political vision, a line of thought that subsequent liberals had
forgotten in their rush to embrace optimism.[11]

The next group of thinkers and activists postwar liberals paid attention to were nineteenth-century reformers who took up the original
Federalist project and also argued for a stronger national government.
But these reformers noted more than just the foibles of human nature;
they started to recognize the increasing problems of economic inequality evident during the early stages of industrialization. Or so Schlesinger
argued as he wrote about the origins of the Democratic Party and
Andrew Jackson's presidency. Here he moved onto shaky ground in part
because he was forced to downplay how much the Democratic Party's
opposition in the Whig Party (the party in which Abraham Lincoln,
one of Niebuhr's greatest heroes, cut his teeth) had actually articulated
the need for a strong federal government to build a public infrastructure capable of unifying economic activity. Schlesinger believed the Whig
Party only wanted to empower the business class through governmental
programs (such as a national bank) and implement "humanitarian reform"
as a cover for economic self-interest. This undervaluation of the Whig
Party was unfair, and it forced Schlesinger to deemphasize President
Andrew Jackson's laissez-faire arguments against government support of
a national bank (something Schlesinger's friend Richard Hofstadter
thought was crucial) and emphasize instead his transformation of

government "from a mild and innocuous agency into an instrument with powers of coercion."

Nonetheless, when Schlesinger stressed Jackson's arguments against "privilege" and his political rhetoric in favor of the small farmer and day laborer—a vision articulated most clearly by Orestes Brownson, another nineteenth-century figure Schlesinger revitalized—he discovered a political language that would continue to play an enormous role in the American debate over ideas long after the Jacksonian era passed away. Although Schlesinger's emphasis might have ignored historical complexities at times, he never considered himself to be an academic historian only but a liberal searching for a usable past to orient present-day action. Indeed, his own scholarly work reflected a desire to balance out engagement with detached reflection, one of the central virtues of liberalism traced earlier. Schlesinger's emphasis on Jackson's democratic message was tied to his view of historical inquiry: "History can contribute nothing in the way of panaceas. But it can assist vitally in the formation of that sense of what is democratic, of what is in line with our republican traditions, which alone can save us."[12]

As Schlesinger pursued this creative reading (and in his critics' minds, misreading) of American history, he struck firmer ground in his historical investigations as his timeline approached the present. His training in intellectual history served him well in his search, and he saw a great fruition of liberal thought during the Progressive Era. Herbert Croly's classic work of political theory, *The Promise of American Life* (1907), developed the "new nationalism" President Teddy Roosevelt would embrace, a political philosophy that tried to preserve individual rights while building a stronger federal government capable of regulating the economy for a common good (Hamiltonian means to suit Jeffersonian ends as Croly sometimes described it). Croly was pioneering a massive transition in the intellectual history of American liberalism. He rejected the laissez-faire inheritance of nineteenth-century liberalism— the arguments for free markets, property rights, and small government that defined Andrew Jackson's world—and embraced the idea of a strong government that could confront and combat the large industrial corporation. He understood that values such as individual freedom and equality now needed more ballast and thus stronger government capable of balancing out the growing centralization of national corporations.

Regulation and social legislation now needed to become a part of the liberal's vision more than freedom from state intervention. When Schlesinger defined "the great tradition of American liberalism" as combining a "fighting faith in the necessity of popular control of economic life" with "a fighting faith in the rights of the individual" or when he asserted that "big government, for all its dangers, remains democracy's only effective response to big business," he was clearly indebted to Croly and other thinkers during the Progressive Era. And he was also making connections to a popular American president, Teddy Roosevelt, who made use of Croly's ideas to justify building a regulatory state that helped confront issues of inequality and social justice. This only hammered home the idea that liberal ideas were not only coherent and defensible but capable of being put into practice by those with political power.[13]

It was not just for Schlesinger that the Progressive Era provided intellectual nourishment. Galbraith, for instance, was indebted to the noted curmudgeon Thorstein Veblen, an economic philosopher, who did much of his best thinking during this time. Reinhold Niebuhr noticed the transatlantic aspect of Progressive Era social thought by seeing how his own intellectual roots went back to Leonard Hobhouse, author of the classic work *Liberalism* (1911). Hobhouse was someone, Niebuhr explained, who "taught me almost all of the little I know." Hobhouse, like Croly, had expanded the liberal tradition, divorcing it from its prior obsession with small government and individual rights. Recognizing the realities of industrial society and the need to correct for growing social inequality, Hobhouse argued for an individual's obligation to a "common good" not just the private self and he did this in order to counteract the growing appeal of Marxist ideas to the British left.

So too did the great Progressive Era philosopher of America, John Dewey, a figure postwar liberals paid a debt to even though they criticized certain aspects of his thought. For example, Niebuhr disagreed with Dewey's faith in progress, the same way he disagreed with Rauschenbusch's, but he agreed with Dewey's overall hope of creating a society that balanced individualism and social obligation through experimental and incremental reform. Indeed, Niebuhr worked with Dewey in the League for Independent Action (LIPA), a group of radical liberals active during the Great Depression.[14]

It was of course during this time of depression that liberal thinking exploded in America. Faced with a collapse of capitalism, FDR sought

out ideas that could rescue the country from the Great Depression. But
he faced a plurality of ideas rather than any liberal consensus. Some
thinkers were studying the great British economist John Maynard
Keynes and believed government should stay on the sidelines of the
economy while trying to "revive purchasing power through government
spending." Other thinkers wanted more activist government intervention
to achieve "economic integration through structural reform."

This broad difference about the appropriate role of government grew
as FDR started to define the New Deal in its earliest stages, and others
came into play as the campaign of 1932 heated up. By this time,
Schlesinger explained that FDR as a "candidate found himself in the
center of a triangle of advice: at one corner, integration and social planning; at another, retrenchment, budget, balancing, and laissez faire; at
a third, trust busting and government regulation." FDR himself was a
pragmatist willing to try different approaches and see how they worked.
But he also had core beliefs, Schlesinger argued, such as the need for
"positive government as a means of redressing the balance of the
economic world," assistance to the poor, public works, conservation, and
some type of economic regulation.

Nonetheless, there was also a "vagueness" to FDR's vision because
the president, no matter what the intellectuals gathered in his "brains
trust" might have hoped for, wanted to avoid "rigid commitment." The
imperatives of politics forced political philosophy to temper its systematic
predilections. Liberalism, as Arthur Schlesinger saw it during the New
Deal and afterward, had core principles but also a loyalty to pragmatic
experimentation. Liberalism was an intellectual balancing act.[15]

By this account, liberalism during the New Deal, as it had been
throughout its history, was pluralistic. This inventory of Great Depression liberalism was a self-inventory for liberals in Schlesinger's own day
and age, a time when the memory of FDR still hung in the air but when
liberals were also aware they needed to move beyond the New Deal's
legacy. Pluralism and pragmatism would remain central to political thinking done by postwar liberals. Schlesinger and Niebuhr started with the
nationalism of original Federalists such as James Madison, appreciating
these thinkers' tough and dark views on human nature. They then
moved on to the transition of liberalism during the nineteenth century
and the Progressive Era and then the culmination of this political
philosophy during the New Deal. Both of these latter chapters in liberal

thought and political reform were unified by a faith in pragmatism and pluralism, ideas developed by William James and John Dewey during the Progressive Era and put into practice by FDR during the Great Depression. Liberals in the postwar period came to discover an enormous intellectual legacy in pragmatism and pluralism and tried to show just how they could provide Americans with a normative political theory that could guide them into the future.

PLURALISM: THE POLITICS OF AN IDEA

"Pluralism," according to Louis Menand, "is an attempt to make a good out of the circumstances that goods are often incommensurable. People come at life from different places, they understand the world in different ways, they strive for different ends." William James, for instance, counseled that the world was pluralistic and open-ended and that pragmatism, as he understood it, was simply about catching up to this reality. This was precisely the philosophical outlook for which postwar liberals were searching. Consider Niebuhr. His theory of the self led directly to an embrace of pluralism. The self for him was defined not only by its infatuation with itself but by its own limited perspective in relation to wider social relations and to the knowledge and power of God. The self's sense of "humility" was tied to seeing its own partiality in relation to other selves and to society at large. Pluralism, in Niebuhr's mind, was an ethical teaching as well as just a basic reality of existence, and it checked the "fanaticism of moralist idealists" who could not see the "corruption of self-interest in their professed ideals." Pluralism therefore served as an important corrective to liberalism's major intellectual enemies: fanaticism and totalitarianism in philosophy and politics.[16]

It is not surprising that in addition to James's pluralism, Niebuhr also recognized the importance of religious pluralism. During his life, Niebuhr was involved in many ecumenical practices, building relations among Jews, Catholics, and different sects of Protestants. Here again was an inheritance from the founding fathers with their belief in separation of church and state and appreciation of America's distinctly diverse set of religions. As Niebuhr saw it, faith was "an existential commitment. This commitment must not be restrictive so that it would prevent us from recognizing truth and grace in other lives with other commitments." A plurality of religious belief taught an ethic of tolerance that Niebuhr thought crucial to America's national identity. "The community," he pointed out, "taught the religions to moderate their pretensions." The existence of pluralism showed that religious belief was always marked by "finiteness and contingency," and therefore the need for being "humble and contrite" in one's own religious faith. This simply hammered home a philosophical idea about the partial nature of any belief that Niebuhr held to even before thinking about the reality of America's religious pluralism.[17]

It was easy to move from civil society (the realm of voluntary agencies such as churches) to politics while remaining a pluralist. As the sociologist David Riesman scanned America's political horizon during the early 1950s he noted business groups, farmers' associations, organized labor, and ethnic clubs. All vied for political influence, creating a "power dispersal among many marginally competing pressure groups." Schlesinger believed such an empirical observation provided an important lesson about political and philosophical values. In 1945, Schlesinger explained,

> American democracy has come to accept the struggle among competing groups for the control of the state as a positive virtue—indeed, as the only foundation of liberty. The business community has been ordinarily in the most powerful of those groups, and liberalism in America has been ordinarily the movement on the part of the other sections of society to restrain the power of the business community.

The state's role, as Schlesinger made clear, was not to step in, take over, and dictate the terms of the future. This would make government too powerful and potentially corrupt. Instead, the state should try to ensure that the voice of less powerful organizations be heard in the political discussion. This would nurture the source of American political health, its multiplicity and pluralism, while also making it more just and balanced. And so out of a philosophical belief in a pluralistic universe and a necessary reality of human existence came a political vision.[18]

To a large extent, Schlesinger and others here were making a claim that Alexis de Tocqueville made in his mid-nineteenth-century book *Democracy in America* and that political scientists seem to be coming back to today, the idea that a healthy and pluralistic civil society is central to American democracy. Voluntary associations that allow citizens to gain voice in political dialogue are now seen as crucial to a healthier politics. Theda Skocpol argues that in the wake of World War II labor unions helped shape public policy, as did the American Legion, a vast, national voluntary association made up of veterans that garnered support for the GI Bill, a legislative victory that opened up the world of higher education to those denied it before. Federated and voluntary organizations helped constitute participation and public voice in national political deliberation, as Skocpol and others argue. Voluntary associations help network power from the bottom up, at least during the period we're discussing here. In the case of the OPA, Galbraith recognized how state power relied upon the voluntary and local associations formed by housewives who monitored the prices set by local merchants. Again, liberalism was not just about regulatory power coming from government bureaucrats but also connected to local voluntary associations working their power upward.[19]

With this said, though, it's crucial to note that Schlesinger's arguments here were normative and value-laden, not just an exercise in political sociology or empirical assessment of American society. Pluralism was not just a description of the way American politics actually operated. A multiplicity of voices, especially those voices that traditionally lacked power, ensured a better political situation than when a single interest dominated. Indeed, liberals used pluralism as a political ideal to describe what went wrong with American politics during the 1950s. Schlesinger chastised Eisenhower's administration by elaborating on Niebuhr's ideas about pluralism. He warned,

> The urgent necessity today—as always in our history—remains that of remembering the limitations and possibilities of man. If our government and our society are to work, they must rest, not on the presumed superior wisdom and infallibility of a single-interest, but on the diverse and reciprocally conditioned judgments of a plurality of interests; for this alone can faithfully represent the brilliant and wonderful variety that is America.

Schlesinger struck a tone similar to James Madison who argued that the best solution to "factions" in early American history was a strong federal government capable of mediating conflict by filtering out complaints and finding realistic solutions. But in the context of the 1950s, Schlesinger was also arguing that pluralism needed to become a weapon of criticism, lest American politics reflect the vision of only one interest group—in this case, business—and thus violate a sense of fairness.[20]

Although Schlesinger was articulating a value-laden vision here, one that believed a common good could grow out of multiplicity, he knew his vision would not satisfy those who wanted to find passion in their politics. A residue of Federalist political thought could be found once again in Schlesinger's ideas during the Cold War. After all, America was a large nation, and its political system was not conducive to a politics of immediate engagement, the way Greek citizens had once entered the ancient polis or colonial New Englanders the town meeting house in order to register their voices in discussion and decision making.

Madison had warned against too much passion in politics and differentiated between a direct democracy and a constitutional republic. In the former, citizens could engage immediately in political deliberation, whereas in the latter they had to delegate power to representatives. Schlesinger knew full well that a pluralistic politics at the national level, with its inherent ethic of compromise and negotiation, could not garner high levels of passion (this was a theme JFK would articulate during the early 1960s as he took up the arguments about an "end of ideology"). Indeed, he noted a growing gap during the 1950s between the "politically apathetic majority" and the "politically conscious minority." This would pose difficulties for political mobilization, and Schlesinger worried about that, but he also recognized that a certain amount of political apathy and cynicism were inevitable. After all, even if citizens committed to a political cause (and Schlesinger still believed in causes), they could never expect immediate results, only the complicated and drawn-out process inherent in America's political system, a system of compromise, distillation, small victories, and many disappointments. Although recognizing the frustrations inherent in a representative form of government, these liberals never gave up their faith in it. As Reinhold Niebuhr explained to June Bingham in 1955, "I think a mixed economy and the balances of political democracy come closer to the truth than any alternative system, and I would want to say that even though I know that our nation may sink further and further into complacency."[21]

The danger, therefore, wasn't that liberal pluralism would create apathy. The real danger was when liberals confused their normative vision with the empirical realities of 1950s America. Here a major tension emerged within liberal political thought. Sometimes these thinkers forgot they were creating a normative vision and instead believed they were describing the world that presently existed around them. This became true for both Schlesinger and Galbraith. In developing conceptions of "countervailing power" and "cycles of history," both ideas that related back to their pluralist political philosophy, these thinkers moved out of political theory and into sociological description and forecasting. Recognizing this tension is central to understanding both the strengths and the weaknesses of liberal thought in the postwar era.

COUNTERVAILING POWER AND CYCLES OF HISTORY: THE TENSIONS OF IDEAS

The progressive tradition in America always feared that business would gain too much power in American society. One historian sums up Progressive era reform movements as being centered around "the discovery that business corrupts politics." And when FDR condemned "the unscrupulous money changers" in his first inaugural address, most citizens knew to whom he was referring. A populist fear of corruption and business power became apparent in the language of Progressive era and New Deal reformers. Following this, liberals, in the wake of World War II, naturally feared a trend that began during the war and persisted in its wake, a further centralization of corporate power. The U.S. government had worked closely with large corporations in order to fulfill production for war, and small businesses watched their numbers dwindle. If the large corporation grew in size and became cozier with the federal government, what exactly could check its influence? This was a primary question that liberals needed to answer once the emergency of war passed.[22]

John Kenneth Galbraith thought he had some answers to this question and provided them in his important book *American Capitalism* (1952), a central text in the postwar liberal canon. Galbraith began his book by taking note of the problems corporate centralization posed for liberals who wanted to ensure a pluralistic political sphere. He cited statistics about corporate centralization as evidence of a secular trend in the economy that seemed unstoppable. This meant the classical model of the free market now operated as a myth. "In the competitive mode," Galbraith explained, "the restraint on the power of any producer was provided by the competition of other producers—it came from the same side of the market." The logical conclusion from this seemed that big business would reign supreme in the new era. But Galbraith didn't think so. For alongside the power of large corporations had grown something called "countervailing power," the collective initiatives of farmers' organizations and labor unions that checked the wishes of businessmen. There were also "food chains, the variety chains, the mail order houses" that prevented businesses from setting prices any way they wished. This seemed an accurate assessment of the changes in the American economy, especially due to the victories of labor and farmer organizations won during the New Deal and sustained after the war.[23]

But Galbraith's assessment of countervailing power took a turn from empirical description to abstract theory in the pages of *American Capitalism*. It was not enough for him to see labor unions and farmer organizations collectively vying for power against big business, a standard story in any American history course or at least the sort that Schlesinger likely taught. He seemed to want a firmer grounding for his politics. And so, countervailing power became a mystical concept. From describing organizations and leaders, Galbraith moved to describing a metaphysical entity. Galbraith wrote, "Countervailing power is a self-generating force." This account robbed people of what today we call "agency." If countervailing force simply generated itself, then there would seem little need to engage people in organizing against the power of big business. And this is precisely the way Galbraith sounded when discussing labor organizing in the steel industry, an important episode in the history of labor organizing. "In the ultimate sense," he wrote, "it was the power of the steel industry, not the organizing abilities of John L. Lewis and Philip Murray, that brought the United Steel Workers into being." From this perspective, countervailing power seemed almost magical, operating behind the backs of people trying to change the course of history. Max Lerner, who was generally sympathetic to Galbraith's arguments, rightfully called his account of countervailing power a form of "Newtonianism" that depicted society as a "self-regulating mechanism."[24]

Galbraith knew his thesis would be controversial. Some believed he was suggesting that labor and farmer organizations were just as, if not more, powerful than big business. But the term *counter*vailing power clearly suggested that farmers and organized labor were pushing back against the original power of business. A year after *American Capitalism* came out, Galbraith pleaded with his British friend John Strachey to understand that he was not saying that unions were more powerful than big business. But it was really the Newtonianism of the concept that posed the biggest problems. It sounded too magical, turning empirical observations about certain conditions into an elaborate and abstract theory.

All of this is especially curious inasmuch as when Galbraith spoke at a Milan gathering of the CCF in 1955, he railed against intellectuals who constructed ideological abstractions and then treated them as realities. When defending his conception of countervailing power, Galbraith took strange turns. For instance, he explained during one of his many defenses of the concept of countervailing power: "I would not wish to argue that countervailing power emerges as an antidote to every position of economic power. (Many of my colleagues advanced this as a flaw in the theory while failing to observe that a similar bill of exceptions could always be advanced against competition.)" This was strange logic indeed, seeing as it failed to defend its original presuppositions and only asserted that his point was just as debatable as a previous viewpoint (there were plenty of those who would have asserted that classical models of free competition were indefensible).[25]

The problem here was that Galbraith tried to find a stronger grounding for his own political vision than it deserved. If countervailing power simply grew out of the natural operations of advanced capitalism, then why worry about pressing for political reform? It would simply come about of its own accord. Galbraith was at his best when he recognized that government needed to help support countervailing power (one thinks of the Wagner Act passed in 1935 that placed government more squarely on the side of organized labor). But by suggesting government should intervene, countervailing power could no longer be seen as "self-generating." Instead, it was *political*, reliant upon the hard work and initiatives of farmers and laborers who decided to take it upon themselves to organize in order to improve the quality of their lives. It relied also upon progressive political leaders who helped pass legislation that could promote, in the words of Schlesinger, "the countervailing pluralisms of society" and to counteract those with a different agenda for America. To think otherwise was to succumb to what the historian Nelson Lichtenstein rightfully calls the "wishful thinking" that marked certain elements of postwar liberal thought.[26]

Schlesinger also succumbed to wishful thinking when he spoke of "cycles of history," a concept that he inherited from his father and used consistently in his accounting of contemporary politics. Depressed by the conservative nature of the Eisenhower administration as well as the general apathy of the 1950s, Schlesinger, at times, argued that American politics had developed patterns, moving between conservative and liberal eras. So, for instance, the Progressive Era was a liberal period of time, dominated by the presidencies of Theodore Roosevelt and Woodrow Wilson, but was then followed by the conservative 1920s. The 1930s and New Deal symbolized a break from the era of Coolidge and Hoover as well as the emergence of a liberal heyday, but it too was followed by an era of national exhaustion during the conservative 1950s.

Thus, Schlesinger predicted, a new liberal era would dawn in the 1960s. This observation would turn out to be accurate (although the 1960s were not as truly a liberal decade as some perceive), but its general presupposition seemed to contradict Schlesinger's otherwise pragmatic and historical cast of mind. Schlesinger placed faith in "an inherent cyclical rhythm in our national affairs." Like Galbraith, Schlesinger turned an historical and empirical observation into a metaphysical one. Remarking on the idea that American history moved through "cycles," Schlesinger wrote, "Our reality has always been dialectic." There seemed a contradiction here with Schlesinger's pragmatism, his belief that political understanding came from empirical observation rather than theoretical and philosophical abstraction and that empirical reality was contingent upon the experimentation of people acting within it. Like "countervailing power," "cycles of history" appeared to be little more than abstraction and metaphysical reasoning coming from the mind of someone who otherwise abhorred such theorizing.[27]

This "wishful thinking" on the part of both Galbraith and Schlesinger led directly to a devaluation of their political opponents. They knew conservatives existed (they both debated William Buckley during the 1950s), but sometimes they pretended they didn't. This became all too easy when confronting the Eisenhower administration. Here was a president whose original political affiliation was nebulous at best (it was a long-lasting political embarrassment that the ADA actually tried to draft Eisenhower in order to oppose Harry Truman). Ike might have parroted Republican rhetoric about the "creeping socialism" of the New Deal welfare state, but, as president, he governed as a centrist. Essentially, as the historian John Patrick Diggins points out, "Eisenhower accepted the welfare state, agreeing to modest expansion of social security, minimum wage, unemployment insurance, and public housing." Galbraith reasoned from this side of the Eisenhower administration that some marginalized hard-right politicos might still believe in a "conservative utopia"—small government and free markets—but that big government and social welfare programs would have to be accepted by Eisenhower and other Republican Party politicians who wanted to win office.[28]

The problem with Galbraith's assessment here was not its empirical accuracy. He was right in noting Eisenhower's acceptance of social security. But he went a step further than this, as he had in his thinking about countervailing power. In 1955, he wrote, "Social welfare legislation is almost entirely noncontroversial." Schlesinger made the same mistake when he asserted that the welfare state did not have "many serious opponents left." He argued as early as 1949 that "we are all supporters of the welfare state." These assertions ignored Eisenhower's rhetoric about "creeping socialism" and the influence of a "radical right" that would start getting behind Barry Goldwater later in the decade.

As they observed certain conservatives making peace with the New Deal, many liberals started to believe the radical right was falling off the American political spectrum of the 1950s. James Wechsler, for instance, depicted arch-conservatives who believed in repealing the federal government's power as marginalized radicals: "There are moments when the modern conservative seems to be the spiritual descendant of the anarchist." So, too, Richard Hofstadter who argued that the arch-conservative "stands psychologically outside the frame of normal democratic politics." Lionel Trilling felt safe to say that the "conservative impulse" did not "express" itself in "ideas but only in . . . irritable mental gestures which seek to resemble ideas." This might have been applicable during the Eisenhower administration, when radical right ideas seemed marginalized by a more middle-of-the-road conservatism, but it ignored the ability of rightist ideas to continue to live on and speak to the American populace at large.[29]

This interpretation also contradicted another tendency in postwar liberal thinking that saw the world of the right riddled with contradictions but also capable of remaining a powerful voice in American politics. Thinkers like the Harvard political scientist Louis Hartz and the historian Richard Hofstadter took note that America lacked the feudal history of Western Europe. When colonists landed on America's shores, there was no feudal society of lords and serfs. And it was feudalism, with its veneration of social hierarchy, rigid class structure, and religious tradition, that provided the necessary background for classical conservative thinkers like Edmund Burke and Joseph Marie de Maistre. Because America never knew the world of barons or serfs, these liberals reasoned, American conservatives like Russell Kirk had "to unite the feudal traditions of British conservatism with the laissez-faire policies of American business." This made the right's political thought a "doctrinal . . . confusion," Schlesinger rightfully claimed. After all, tradition and organic hierarchy were inimical to the values of individualism and competition necessary for capitalism.[30]

But this confusion did not disempower the right. It simply forced it to stress the second of the two traditions Schlesinger noted, namely, laissez-faire policies or antiregulatory policies. This political philosophy was a truly American form of conservatism, what Reinhold Niebuhr called the "creed of the business community." As Schlesinger noted, this libertarian side of conservative political thought allowed Russell Kirk to downplay his praise for organic communities and religion and instead condemn school lunch programs as a form of totalitarianism, as an encroachment of the state on individual liberty. Kirk's thought could thus link up with the business community's desire to repeal the economic regulation of the New Deal. Worrying about the infatuation with self-interest, so rampant on the right, Reinhold Niebuhr had warned during the 1940s that "America, for all its vaunted democracy, still has a plutocracy which is unwilling to grant the most basic democratic rights to labor." The business community would try to not only hamper organized labor—a central component of Galbraith's countervailing power—but also push forth conservative legislation throughout the 1940s and 1950s, even as Eisenhower was making a certain amount of peace with the New Deal legacy.[31]

After condemning the OPA during World War II (as Galbraith could testify), the right pushed successfully to dismantle the program in the wake of the war and made it difficult to reinstate price controls during the Korean War. After this victory, the right decided to take on labor unions and pushed through the Taft–Hartley Act even against Truman's veto in 1947. The act was an enormous blow against the countervailing power of labor. As Jimmy Wechsler's paper documented it:

> The bill, the most far-reaching program for union curbs in U.S. history, bans the closed shop, requires a majority vote of all employees for a union shop, prohibits union-administered welfare funds, drastically alters the Wagner Act, deprives Communist-led unions of the protection of labor laws, permits the government to obtain 80-day injunctions against strikes imperiling the "national safety" and alters many other union-management procedures built up under the New Deal.

Schlesinger and others kept pressing to repeal this legislation, but to no avail. The National Association of Manufacturers and Chamber of Commerce were successful on this front, and the American Medical Association (AMA) successfully stymied Truman's attempt to expand national health coverage to include all Americans. Bernard DeVoto documented the success of the AMA's propaganda campaign that denounced "Old Doc Truman's Pink Pills" and "socialized medicine." And alongside these successful lobbying initiatives, there were conservative pundits arguing for even more radical right policies. Westbrook Pegler, for instance, called for the U.S. government to exit the United Nations and abolish the National Labor Review Board (the organization that upheld labor law since its creation during the New Deal). All of this symbolized the right's power in arguing against and actually repealing the "countervailing power" of labor and citizen organizations, in the name of an American conservatism based around a laissez-faire philosophy.[32]

In addition, it is important not to overestimate the centrist nature of the Eisenhower administration. The president was unfriendly toward the civil rights movement, even suggesting he thought the *Brown v. Board* Supreme Court decision was wrong and only responding to the crisis prompted by the civil rights movement when pro-segregation ideologues attacked school children in Little Rock, Arkansas. Eisenhower also did nothing to stop McCarthy's anticommunist crusade (although he did not support the senator). Most important, in terms of how liberal pluralism related to questions of economic power, the president wanted an administration more friendly toward business than his predecessor's. Eisenhower cut taxes for the wealthy and thus challenged FDR's earlier "soak the rich" approach. James Wechsler knew of Eisenhower's more conservative nature, reporting on a speech that Truman gave in 1953 denouncing Ike as having "wrecked public housing, slashed funds for enforcement of the minimum wage, . . . surrendered offshore oil to the power-oil interests, promised that the private-power lobby will finally be enabled to recapture its old privileges, and in general served notice that creeping Hooverism can walk right in." Schlesinger condemned Eisenhower's "give away" state, pointing out to Adlai Stevenson how the president had encouraged the turnover of public lands to private companies and the privatization of the federally controlled power program of dams and energy management created under the New Deal. Schlesinger believed that Eisenhower's pro-business leanings represented a desire to repeal pluralism and institute a single-interest government.[33]

Schlesinger's criticism of Eisenhower highlighted the normative side of pluralism. After all, Schlesinger was arguing that pluralism was a *good* thing and was being unfairly violated by Eisenhower's single-interest model of governance. Pluralism, in this account, was not some force that could simply generate itself magically and withstand the whims of conservative politicians. Galbraith's Newtonian conception of countervailing power could not account for the political choices being made by Eisenhower. And if Republicans were not defeated at the polling booths in 1958 and 1960, no counter "cycle of history" would have emerged. Pluralism, just as any other component of liberal political philosophy, constituted a "fighting faith" that faced enemies who were willing to do battle. There was the natural proclivity of human nature, Niebuhr reminded his fellow liberals, to valorize the self and therefore resist anything that threatened self-interest (and what did this more than having to listen to another group with counterinterests?). There was the power of the right in this country, its ability to harness wealth and make arguments that appealed to American ideals of individual freedom. And there were powerful businessmen who wanted to seek out a single-interest form of politics more to their liking.

When postwar liberals argued that they could rely upon the self-generating capacities of countervailing power or the "dialectic" of historical cycles, they ironically ignored the importance of their own activities. After all, pluralism relied upon the activism of labor leaders such as Walter Reuther who led the United Auto Workers and worked within the Democratic Party and who, as Jimmy Wechsler noted, combined the "humanism of European social democracy and the pragmatism of indigenous American progressives." It relied also upon the politicians whom people like Schlesinger and Galbraith did so much to support, such as Hubert Humphrey and Paul Douglas. It relied upon the voice of the ADA itself, pushing politicians to articulate a more progressive vision of American politics and then pressing them to make that vision a reality. It relied upon an often overlooked component of postwar liberalism: its support of citizen-operated cooperatives that organized against the power of business on a voluntary basis. All of these activities—the work of labor leaders, politicians, political organizations on the left, and cooperative organizers—served as the basis of liberalism's fighting faith in making American politics more pluralistic. And none of these things were self-generating; rather, they relied upon the hard work of committed citizens.[34]

But pluralism also relied upon something more: an overriding claim in a national interest. After all, groups such as labor unions and farmer associations looked after their own members' self-interest. Pluralism, if allowed to degenerate to its most base element, could become a war of group self-interest pitted against group self-interest. A lesson from World War II remained important for these pluralists here. Niebuhr knew that groups, including the labor unions he championed, had to sacrifice something in the name of winning the war. Working with farmers' organizations prior to joining the OPA, Galbraith cautioned that they would have to "subordinate group policy to national policy." Although the crisis of the war passed, there was still a need to maintain a national interest that could ultimately check group self-interest. As the Eisenhower administration came to a close, Schlesinger argued that a "pressure group" state was not enough, that there was a need for "an overriding public interest." Balancing pluralism against a public and national interest (something that would rely upon a set of values that transcended those of different interest groups) constituted what Schlesinger called, quite simply, "liberalism."[35]

CHAPTER FOUR

Loves
The Nation as Beloved Community

*What the new liberalism must do is make the point that our country
can grow only if we develop a positive philosophy of the public interest
to be asserted against the parochial interests of any special group.*
                                                Arthur Schlesinger[1]

A VICTORY NOW DANGEROUSLY FORGOTTEN

When Niebuhr and Schlesinger were busy sifting through the past,
they came across another not so surprising hero: Abraham Lincoln—
not so surprising because Lincoln had become a mythological character by the 1940s. His image was enshrined in a statue perched over the
National Mall in Washington, D.C., where Americans could gather as
apostles at his feet, reading his sacred words chipped into marble walls.
Boys and girls memorized Lincoln's famous Gettysburg Address in high
school, and numerous popular tales were told of his life, about the
young boy growing up in a log cabin who became a frontier lawyer
and then saved the country from ruin during the Civil War. While
Americans sank into the despair of the Great Depression, poet Carl
Sandburg and playwright Robert Sherwood made his words sing again,
and during World War II, he was remembered as a great national leader
who had taught Americans, in the words of Bernard DeVoto, that "the
nation is worth fighting for." So four years after the war, it is easy to
understand why Richard Hofstadter described the "Lincoln legend" as
America's highest form of "political mythology." Hofstadter quoted a
contemporary of Lincoln's who called him "the greatest character since
Christ."[2]

When the thinkers studied here expressed a love of Lincoln, they drew a more complex portrait than that of national sainthood. As America entered World War II, Niebuhr explained that he loved Lincoln precisely because he *wasn't* a God, because he "judged and condemned the system of slavery severely, and then declared 'but let us judge not that we not be judged.'" Niebuhr also cherished Lincoln's "frontier humor," his ironic, often droll wit in the face of adversity. The historian C. Vann Woodward added to this more complex portrait by pointing out that Lincoln did not think of himself as "the incarnation of the Archangel Michael" when he did things like write the Emancipation Proclamation. If anything, Schlesinger added, Lincoln was an ironic figure because he wound up abolishing slavery even while never becoming a passionate abolitionist. Lincoln was also a realist who had a good read on how far American public opinion could be pushed. He often put aside his conscience in order to win a political victory, but he never forgot it. "He knew," Woodward explained, "that there were limits beyond which popular conviction and conscience could not be pushed in time." Therefore, as far as liberal intellectuals were concerned, Lincoln was no saint but rather a human being who grappled with what could be accomplished within an imperfect world. At the same time, he was America's greatest nationalist who preserved the union in a time of crisis.[3]

There were pressing intellectual reasons to claim Lincoln a liberal hero. For during the late 1930s and through World War II and its aftermath, a "revisionist" school of historians arose to challenge the idea that the Civil War was necessary or just. Avery Craven and James Randall were two northern scholars who penned many books and articles during the late 1930s and 1940s, all arguing that the Civil War could have been averted. They depicted abolitionists and Radical Republicans as borderline lunatics itching for a fight and stoking up the North for unnecessary battle. Slavery, these scholars reasoned, would have fallen of its own accord, and thus the North was overreacting and embarking on what Craven called "the repressible conflict."

Schlesinger saw these ideas as dangerous, immoral when they came to slavery, and sentimental in the face of conflict and war. Schlesinger knew full well that Southerners had been arguing since the time of Jefferson that slavery would collapse eventually; the problem was that it hadn't even by 1860. When historians argued slavery would have fallen without the Civil War, evidence was lacking. More important, Civil War revisionists were refusing to pay any attention to moral questions. They were part of a larger "modern tendency to seek in optimistic sentimentalism an escape from the severe demands of moral decision." Drawing an analogy between the Civil War and World War II (just four years finished, at the time he wrote these words), Schlesinger pointed out that the "extension of slavery, like the extension of fascism, was an act of aggression which made a moral choice inescapable." Schlesinger didn't even need to add the obvious conclusion that Lincoln deserved praise for taking the right stance against slavery, even if he didn't do it for all the right moral reasons.[4]

Schlesinger was joined by another "tireless opponent" of the "neo-Confederate historians," namely, Bernard DeVoto, who served as Schlesinger's mentor at Harvard University (where DeVoto had taught English for numerous years). A journalist and historian, DeVoto joined in bashing the "Randall–Craven" thesis that slavery would simply have gone away if no one had pushed it and that Lincoln was malicious for not going cool on the issue. DeVoto followed Schlesinger by reminding readers of *Harper's* magazine, where he held court in a monthly column known as "The Easy Chair," that slavery "involved moral questions." But DeVoto had his own complaint about the revisionists: They ignored the power of American nationalism. "My strongest point," he explained to a friend, "apart from the revisionists' failure to understand the moral urgency of slavery, is the revisionists' failure to understand on the one hand the geographical and social necessity of continental unity and on the other hand the inherent impossibility of confederacy."

By the time that DeVoto was sparring with the Civil War revisionists, he had written two books about America's westward expansion during the eighteenth and nineteenth centuries, *The Year of Decision* and *Across the Wide Missouri*. There was an important message underneath the stories he told here and that he was about to tell in *The Course of Empire*, stories about Thomas Jefferson purchasing the Louisiana territory, Lewis and Clark first exploring all the way to the West Coast, mountain men settling the lands, and trappers pressing onto the plains. It was the story of nationalism spreading across the American continent, a lesson that the Civil War revisionists were too quick to forget. "All of my work" in his books about "Western history," DeVoto explained with remarkable honesty, had been a kind of psychological evasion of an inner feeling that I ought to write about the Civil War. The job of explaining the Civil War, which I regard as the key fact in American life, is so enormous that I was always afraid to embark on an inquiry that would have taken all my life, and so I have hoped that focusing on the Western frontier as a nation-making energy might serve as my assist to the men who ultimately write about the Civil War as I see it.

The problem was that Craven and Randall saw the war in exactly the wrong way, as unnecessary and immoral. And so they deserved what the slave-owning secessionists got in 1860, war, if only the intellectual type.[5]

DeVoto's nationalism was not foreign to America during the 1940s. World War II, after all, increased Americans' sense of belonging to a national community. There were baby steps taken toward making the community more inclusive. For instance, officer training programs in the army and higher positions in the navy were made open to African Americans (in addition, Executive Order 8802 created the Fair Employment Practices Committee (FEPC) that encouraged industries with defense contracts not to discriminate against blacks). Of course, Japanese Americans were treated horrendously and stuffed into relocation camps during the war, but this did not stop immigrants during and after the war from seeking national citizenship. Naturalization rates boomed during this time. A sense of national culture consolidated, or at least a "mass culture" growing out of movies and radio (and soon during the 1950s, television). Americans were watching the same images and singing the same songs more than before. And scholars were arguing that America had a national culture distinct from Europe's and deserving serious study. "American Studies" boomed in academia during the 1950s. Historians such as Henry Steele Commager and Henry Nash Smith and literary critics such as Daniel Aaron pioneered in this area, arguing, as Commager did in his book *The American Mind*, that "there is a distinctively American way of thought, character, and conduct." The idea of an American nation seemed a surer thing during the 1940s and 1950s, especially as the "American way of life" was increasingly defined against the threat of communism found in the Soviet Union.[6]

For liberals, the national community was crucial to questions of political theory. It served as a source of the public interest Arthur Schlesinger alluded to (see the ending of the last chapter) and that transcended pluralist interest groups. If Americans were to take seriously the claim that they lived in a national community, they had to make that community more of a reality. Rarely did Schlesinger or Niebuhr speak of "patriotism" when discussing their attitude toward America (that is not to say they didn't consider themselves patriots, just that they used the term sparingly). Patriotism is a sense of duty that can be invoked in times of emergency (war especially), but it does not necessarily infer true belongingness on the part of a nation's members.

Take the issue of race in America. When African Americans were asked to serve in World War I and World War II, they were asked to exhibit their patriotism, but they did not have a feeling of belonging to a national community, at least not in terms of having the rights that white citizens possessed. President Eisenhower, for instance, was a great patriot, but he did not believe in a national community's responsibility to grant full and equal rights to all citizens. This difference is crucial, especially in defining the meaning of liberalism in the wake of World War II. Race was placed squarely at the center of debates about America's national identity during World War II, what the Swedish sociologist Gunnar Myrdal labeled the "American creed" in his famous sprawling book about racial inequality, *The American Dilemma*. Race became that much more important as the Cold War heated up. The Soviet Union never ceased pointing out, especially to Asian and African countries, that the American faith in equality and democracy contradicted its treatment of black citizens. Liberals knew this and during the 1940s and 1950s made racial equality central to their political arguments for national reform.[7]

Nationalism was also related to another issue pressing in on the liberal conscience during the 1940s and 1950s: conservation. The desire to protect America's public lands from special interest groups who wanted to use them for cattle grazing and mining highlighted a weakness in the idea of pluralism and "countervailing power." John Kenneth Galbraith and Arthur Schlesinger made conservation a key part of their vision of "qualitative liberalism," and they relied a great deal on Bernard DeVoto on this matter. As DeVoto pointed out, those arguing for a public good that transcended the demands of special interest groups such as stockmen organizations faced an uphill battle. The stockmen's association, a quintessential interest and pressure group, was well funded, whereas there were, as Bernard and DeVoto pointed out, only a "few conservation organizations, whose membership is small, whose voice is feeble, and whose treasury is almost non-existent." Conservationists could not invoke any material interest the way a labor union or a farmers' organization could; instead, they aimed to articulate a common good (defending things such as watersheds that benefited all citizens, not just special interest groups). Unfortunately, they lacked force behind their countervailing power. And so, liberals needed to go beyond pluralism and embrace nationalism to seek power for their ideals. In the process, they tried to make the national community truly inclusive, open to voices historically ignored.[8]

Both issues of race and environment highlighted not just the problems of pluralism but the broader problem of regionalism in America. After all, racism plagued the northeastern region of America, where these liberals resided during the 1950s, but it was in the South where the most egregious violations of racial equality took place, in legal disfranchisement and segregation and extra-legal means such as lynching. The same was true for the regional nature of conservation. Easterners certainly faced conservation issues, but it was in the western regions of the United States where there were large swaths of public land owned by the federal government (the "public domain") and where cattle grazers and miners exerted pressure to open these up to private exploitation.

Regional differences of the South and West maintained themselves even as America became more of a nation during the 1940s and 1950s. Liberals desired a national community, to be sure, but recognized the country's internal differences. Of course, regions could serve as a source of national health, that is, a geographical mirroring of civil society's pluralism, a resistance against a bad sort of cultural homogeneity. But they also prompted warnings for any hope in a liberal consensus. After all, and here we can draw upon the vantage of historical hindsight, conservative political leaders would increasingly come out of the southern and western regions of the United States. As the historian Alan Brinkley notes, "Of the most successful national conservative leaders of the postwar era— Barry Goldwater, George Wallace, Richard Nixon, and Ronald Reagan— all but Wallace were westerners." Of course, Wallace was a Southerner, only accentuating the general point about the West and the South.[9]

There was more evidence of how regional differences played a role in the formation of a conservative politics prior to the rise of conservative leaders such as Barry Goldwater. For instance, the social critic W.J. Cash noted that labor unions might have tried but generally failed to organize the South during the 1930s. A concerted effort was made to do exactly this in the wake of World War II ("Operation Dixie"), but it failed due to racial divisions among the southern working class and the power of business leaders in the area who often used tactics of personal intimidation to block unionization efforts. At the same time, Southerners bemoaned the "lost cause" of the Civil War, asserting a "states' rights" doctrine to resist attempts to improve race relations, the way they had since John Calhoun wrote his treatises on "nullification" during the 1820s. Indeed, the sanctity of the state became Barry Goldwater's chief rationale to vote against the Civil Rights Act of 1957. Finally, in terms of the American West, there had been a long-standing opposition to federal land policy among ranchers and miners, dating all the way back to Teddy Roosevelt's early initiatives in conservation during the first decade of the twentieth century. A cursory examination of the first half of the twentieth century should have made liberals aware of the tough realities incurred by regionalism.[10]

Liberals were also aware of the power of regional "myths." For instance, it was nostalgia for the olden days of plantations and an agricultural society that conservative Southerners conjured up. This outlook found expression in 1939 in *Gone with the Wind*, with its romanticization of slavery and a culture of "honor" now dead. The West, too, was populated by myths, becoming a place that DeVoto claimed was enshrined in "a mist of enchantment," of "wonder" and "spectacle." He assumed that most Americans believed the West a "place where the Lone Ranger rides horses and John Wayne shoots outlaws." Westerners were especially enamored with what the western historian Frederick Jackson Turner once labeled the frontier ideal, an ideal that glorified in the gutsy activities of rugged individuals. The cowboy—that lone wanderer cast against an open landscape—was a staying symbol in the western collective mentality, even though actual cowboys were practically nonexistent in the West by the 1940s.

This "culture myth" of rugged individualism allowed Westerners to forget the collective aspects of frontier settlement, or what DeVoto described as the historical reality of nineteenth-century "cooperation enforced by the wilderness" that required "choices to be made in the common interest." During the postwar era, the frontier myth allowed Westerners to overlook the federal government's massive role in their social development (the cities that grew up around defense plants during World War II and the enormous assistance provided by federal dams generating power and providing water). The frontier ideal fueled a libertarian politics that rejected any idea of governmental action for a common good. Individuals were responsible only for themselves; for, in the wake of failure, a person could simply light out for open land.[11]

These myths and their conservative political implications made a regionalist voice within the larger liberal vision so crucial. And there were, no matter what at first appearances might seem an impossibility, regional liberals. Here our story takes a distinct turn and two characters step on stage for a brief interlude. After all, the cast so far has been from the Midwest (Niebuhr born to a German immigrant family that had moved to the Midwest before moving as an adult to New York City, and Schlesinger growing up in Ohio before going to Massachusetts), New York (Wechsler), and Canada (Galbraith).

Bernard DeVoto and C. Vann Woodward were true regionalists. DeVoto was born and raised in Utah, his father a failed land speculator and miner, personifying the boom-and-bust personality type central to the American West. Woodward grew up in Arkansas, in a family with a "slaveholding background." Both thinkers' backgrounds shaped their views and their line of work. DeVoto might have disliked being called a regionalist, once telling an editor that "so far as I have a field, it is nationalism, not regionalism." He lived most of his adult life on the East Coast, in either New York City or Cambridge, Massachusetts. Nonetheless, every chance he got, he traveled to see the West again and loved the area. The place seemed to stick in his blood (he called it a "good place to grow in" in a later article). So too with C. Vann Woodward who went to graduate school in North Carolina and taught at Johns Hopkins University during much of his adulthood (a university located in the "upper" south of Maryland). When he left for California to teach for a year in 1940 after graduate school, he wrote his mentor Howard Odum, who taught at the University of North Carolina, "I shall always call the South home and I shall want to come back to it before so very long." Both Woodward and DeVoto were regionalists, their identity wedded to a specific place in America's vast geography.[12]

To talk about them here might seem a detour to some readers. Rather, they are, in certain ways, at the center of this story due to both personal and broader intellectual connections. Schlesinger knew Woodward and DeVoto and tried to get them to meet. Writing to DeVoto, Schlesinger explained that Woodward is "an admirer of yours and eager to meet you, so give him a drink." Schlesinger always looked up to DeVoto, in a way similar to his relationship with Niebuhr. In a dedication he wrote for a DeVoto memorial in 1962, Schlesinger called DeVoto "a great American patriot who gave of himself without limit in the cause of decency, freedom, clear thinking, and common sense and whom I am proud to have had as a teacher and a very dear friend." Before DeVoto died in 1955, Schlesinger made sure to involve him in conversations with Adlai Stevenson about politics in the West and was always talking him up to colleagues. With Woodward, the relationship was more one of equals. Woodward admired Schlesinger's work, and the two corresponded throughout their lives, sharing a mutual friend in Richard Hofstadter. Woodward also admired Reinhold Niebuhr who had a large impact on his work, and once again Schlesinger tried to put them in contact (sending copies of Woodward's articles to Niebuhr). DeVoto and Woodward were loosely connected to but remained partially independent of the liberal circles traced here.[13]

Most important of all, Woodward and DeVoto traveled a similar trajectory in their intellectual biographies. They imbibed the radical political tradition known as populism that had once dominated the southern and western regions of the United States during the late nineteenth century (the way Niebuhr had embraced socialism). This tradition extended itself from the Jacksonian era's critique of "privilege" and championing of the "people," arguing for the interest of the small farmer against the railroads and banking interests (a tradition Schlesinger had traced in *The Age of Jackson*). Both DeVoto and Woodward moved from being the sort of populists who saw their regions exploited by a northeastern elite—"outside" capitalist interests, so to speak—to nationalists who saw their regions needing the support of the Northeast and the nation at large in remaking themselves along more just lines. That is, they went beyond seeing their regions as defenseless pawns, or "colonies" as they were often called, of the more powerful Northeast (a typical view among certain southwestern populists of the late nineteenth century) and started seeing that their own regions were indulging in self-destructive activities, be it regarding race or the environment. These problems needed national action to be solved. Both Woodward and DeVoto understood that, in the case of conservation of civil rights, liberals had to commit to action, not simply wait for the magical forces of "countervailing power." Describing DeVoto's and Woodward's intellectual transformation and their actions helps us understand a crucial element of postwar liberal thought.[14]

DeVoto: The Making of a Conservationist

Bernard DeVoto was many things besides a Westerner. And by the time of the 1940s, he was entering his fifties with a life of accomplishments. He had written numerous novels, some of them works of "pulp" fiction done under a pseudonym and only to make money. During the 1920s, he was associated with Mencken's tribe of writers at the *American Mercury*, writing a piece about his home state, Utah, that he would later regret as being too harsh and mean. During the Great Depression, DeVoto was considered one of the foremost experts on Mark Twain and a literary critic with a penchant for nationalist American literature. He was also a college professor, first at Northwestern University during the 1920s and then at Harvard where he was denied tenure in 1936. Afterward, he tried his hand at editing the *Saturday Review*, America's foremost middle-class literary publication. By the early 1940s, he started moving away from literary criticism and toward western history, becoming a free-lance writer with a regular column at *Harper's*. He also became an avid interventionist and used his skills as a writer to coax Americans to enter World War II. As the war came to a close, he took up the cause of civil liberties by defending Lillian Smith's novel *Strange Fruit* against censorship in Massachusetts and supported, although not in a high-profile manner, racial integration. But by 1946, he would become associated with one major cause until his death in 1955: the fight against America's abuse of its western public lands.

If DeVoto's life took many diverse turns, so did his politics. In certain ways, he traveled the map politically. Schlesinger saw that his life "oscillated" between "poles of activism and skepticism." He was also an independent populist who swung between supporting Democrats and Republicans (as late as 1946, he claimed to vote Republican). Sometimes he would support the New Deal; at other times, he offered a vague criticism of it. Nonetheless, the major trajectory in his life after 1946 was toward the party of Jackson and away from the party of Lincoln. His fight over public lands, by 1952, would place him squarely within the Democratic Party, as would his friendship with Adlai Stevenson and Harold Ickes, FDR's secretary of the interior (no man "has been on

the right side oftener than he has," DeVoto remarked in 1946). That
year, DeVoto would describe himself as "55 or 60 percent New Dealer"
and someone who had voted "for every Democratic Presidential candidate since 1928." As he saw western Republicans pressing to open public lands for grazing and mining and the Democrats making conservation
more central to their party's plank, his partisanship became more pro-
nounced. By the 1950s, DeVoto was fully in line with the circles of ADA
and "egghead" liberals. As he would put it himself, "The study of
history" held him to "the working principles of American liberalism."[15]

DeVoto's views on the West changed with his politics. In 1944 he
wrote a famous piece in which he described the West as a "plundered
province." His birthright region, he explained, had "mostly been
exploited for the benefit of other sections." The problem with the West
was a problem of "absentee ownership" and the power of eastern capitalist interests setting the terms of economic development. Here was
the anti-eastern, populist tinge to his views on the West. "The West is
systematically looted and has always been bankrupt" and "bound to the
industrial system of the East." DeVoto explored this populist theme in
his writings on western history. In *Across the Wide Missouri*, published
in 1947, for instance, he described the West as having "always been
exploited by absentee owners and managers under the sanction of
imported law." But there was a problem with this argument: much of the
western exploitation, as DeVoto himself explained, was actually done by
those settling in the West, by trappers and mountain men who planned
to stay awhile. They might ship their goods out East, but they themselves did the plundering on their own terms, keeping much of the profits themselves. The reality of this hit home for DeVoto during a defining
event in his life, the infamous "landgrab" of 1946–1947. It changed
the way he saw his home province for the rest of his life.[16]

It began on August 17, 1946, in Salt Lake City, Utah, when leaders
of the National Livestock and National Woolgrowers Associations met
to form what they called a "Committee of Ten." The meeting was
closed, but the call that emanated from it was made public: sell National
Forest Service (NFS) lands to local cattlemen and sheepherders who were
presently grazing them. The Committee of Ten did what all interest
groups do: they organized in order to influence their allies in national
government, in this case, Senator McCarran of Nevada (a conservative
Democrat) and Congressman Barrett of Wyoming (a Republican).

McCarran swung into high gear as part of the Committee on Public Lands and Surveys, crafting Bill S-32 that would have sold public lands to private stockmen for as low as sixty cents an acre. Barrett held a series of public hearings in western states and loaded them up with cattlemen, many of them his friends (Barrett, after all, was a large sheep and cattle rancher himself).

When reading the proceedings from these meetings, DeVoto highlighted evocative passages in which cattlemen compared the public lands system to Soviet totalitarianism, an argument that he was hearing more often as the Cold War heated up. This push of Barrett's and McCarran's failed, precisely because "public opinion" saw it as a private raid on the national trust and because Clinton Anderson, Truman's secretary of agriculture who oversaw NFS lands, opposed it. The cattlemen regrouped a year later in 1948 and called for turning NFS lands over to local states like Wyoming or Utah, believing rightfully, that state governments would be more pliable to ranchers and incapable of managing public lands, and thus willing to sell them eventually. After this failed, they tried in 1951 to turn NFS lands over to the Bureau of Land Management (BLM), a federal agency run by local committees full of ranchers. They failed on this count as well but continued to press for the D'Ewart Bill in 1953, another cattlemen-sponsored bit of legislation.[17]

DeVoto led an outcry against this long succession of "landgrabs." He was joined by politicians and private organizations such as the Izaak Walton League, a group of sportsmen (hunters and fishermen) concerned with the abuse of public lands. DeVoto explained that this landgrab consolidated "a kind of informal network of newspapermen, businessmen, sportsmen, and others interested in conservation." But it was DeVoto's articles in *Harper's* magazine that did the most to raise the ire of national public opinion against the cattlemen and that got cited by congressmen and senators opposed to Barrett and McCarran. DeVoto knew that the court of "public opinion" was the only place to beat the cattlemen, and he blasted them every chance he got. He made fun of how their arguments for strong tariffs against Australian beef (protectionism) contradicted their otherwise laissez-faire attitudes. He ridiculed their desire to "sacrifice" the West's environmental health (including the devastation of "watersheds") for short-term profit. He pointed out that Utah's water problems were due to "overgrazing the Wasatch watersheds," arguing this would become worse if cattlemen had their way

(DeVoto had a knack for describing environmental ideas such as watersheds to a lay audience). Perhaps most important, he reminded his readers that the national forests were *theirs*. They did not belong to the cattlemen but to the American people as a whole.[18]

Noting that McCarran and Barrett were western politicians and that many cattlemen were locals, DeVoto had a harder time seeing the West as a "plundered province." It seemed increasingly like a province plundering itself, one that needed to be saved from its own worst ambitions. This is, after all, why cattlemen wanted to turn public lands over to the states: because local government was more willing to satisfy local interests. DeVoto explained, "The plan is to get rid of public lands altogether, turning them over to the states, which can be coerced as the federal government cannot be, and eventually to private ownership." "Only the federal government," DeVoto wrote around the same time, "is able to withstand the pressure of special interest groups, is able to regulate and protect" the public lands "properly, or is willing to spend sums necessary for repair and maintenance." And only the nation could save the West from destroying itself, DeVoto admitted in 1952. "In my opinion it is, as in the past it has always turned out to be, up to the East. The West will destroy the public land system if it is permitted to." The nation therefore had to "prevent the West from committing suicide." By 1952, DeVoto was no longer a regional populist calling for an end to eastern exploitation of his beloved province but a national liberal calling for the federal government (including eastern politicians) to take up a course of conservation in the nation's best public interest.[19]

He didn't stop his crusading with the landgrab. There were other fights to be had, all giving shape to the modern environmentalist movement that many associate with the later 1960s. First, there were dams being built on rivers that didn't need to be. Key here was the Echo Park Dam proposed by the Bureau of Reclamation (a New Deal federal agency) and the Army Corps of Engineers as part of a general plan to provide energy and water to the southwestern United States, an arid desert region apart from its few major rivers. The dam would be built around the confluence of the Yampa and Green Rivers in Dinosaur National Monument in Utah. Some locals wanted the water for development; the Army Corps of Engineers was hot on testing their engineering acumen wherever possible. DeVoto didn't care much about motivation here, just the wreckage the dam would cause. Now, though, it would seem the tables had been turned, because the Federal government was pushing the dam, not a private interest group such as the cattlemen.

But DeVoto challenged this perception, arguing that "sectional and local interests" were behind the dam and would force the "general public" to pay for it and thus ruin "an area of great natural beauty" that belonged to the public. He also feared engineers would fixate on the technical issues and thus ignore aesthetic questions about the beauty of the land to be submerged under water. Most important of all, Echo Park Dam would be built in a national monument, and seeing as national monuments were part of America's national park system (most national monuments, declared by presidential decree, would go on to become national parks, backed up with a congressional vote), DeVoto saw the dam as a threat to the "national park system as we know it." How couldn't he oppose it?[20]

For DeVoto, the dam threatened the same national interest the cattlemen had. "What the West and the Bureau of Reclamation disregard," he explained, "is that the problems are not local but national, that the rest of the country is involved in them and will have a voice." But it was difficult to conjure up a voice against a dam in a little-visited area of Utah. The "national interest," as DeVoto called it, did not have "any effective representation against purely sectional interests as represented by the Bureau of Reclamation and the Western activities of the Army Engineers." The only thing to do was to garner public opinion against the initiative, the way he did against the landgrab. This he did by writing popular articles that drove some people to go see the beauty of the Echo Park region, prompting a tourist spurt in a region lacking developed roads. DeVoto was joined by David Brower of the Sierra Club, the Izaak Walton League, and his friend Alfred Knopf, a book publisher, who helped release *This Is Dinosaur*, a photographic collection about the beauty of the place in threat of being flooded. In the end, these initiatives worked in saving Echo Park, even though they couldn't prevent a dam in Glen Canyon or a continued push to build dams that would even come to threaten national parks such as the Grand Canyon. As with many liberal "victories," this one was partial, not final, and always open to challenge. Actually, building "countervailing power" was an uphill battle.[21]

As much as these battles against landgrabs and dams might build a portrait of DeVoto as a naysaying curmudgeon, he wasn't. He was a nationalist who loved his country. His conservation protests grew out of a trip he took west in 1946, scurrying about with his wife and kid in a packed sedan in order to see as many national parks as possible. He fell in love with them. "An American who does not know his national parks has missed a priceless part of his heritage," DeVoto beamed in an article published posthumously. He was proud of the national park system and not afraid to say so: "If it classifies me as a do-gooder to believe that the great scenic spectacles preserved in the national parks should continue to be preserved there so that posterity can enjoy them as much as we have done, then I am a do-gooder and will remain one."

Here, DeVoto took up a tradition begun in the early twentieth century that the historian Alfred Runte calls "scenic nationalism." The early national parks such as Yellowstone and Yosemite showed that "the United States had something of value in its own right to contribute to world culture." Why go to the Swiss Alps when you could see the mountains of Glacier National Park? some naturalists asked in 1910. DeVoto continued this line of argument when he persuaded Alfred Knopf, in 1948, to travel to see the national parks. DeVoto claimed that Knopf "returned enthusiastic and swearing he would never again go to Europe" for his vacations. The preservation of beautiful lands, DeVoto argued, could nurture national pride and prompt historical memory about America's distinct history. "We were a wilderness people," DeVoto wrote, "and there must be places where we and our great-grandchildren can revisit our roots."[22]

Precisely because they were such a source of national pride, DeVoto bemoaned how the parks were being treated during the 1950s. In confronting problems of the national park system, he diagnosed, before John Kenneth Galbraith, the perils of an increasingly "affluent society." For the postwar boom in consumerism (pent-up demand flooding the market) meant a boom in national tourism. People went to national parks in droves during the late 1940s and 1950s, with the numbers of visitors literally doubling. This "enormous postwar increase in tourist travel" meant that people were being turned away or facing traffic jams and increased vandalism in the parks. This was made worse by "financial anemia." Parks did not receive the public funds they needed to operate, especially considering this increased visitation. Quantity thus fouled quality. Even those who made it into the parks rarely stayed very long, whizzing into them via car and then whizzing out, thus missing the "more profound educational or emotional or aesthetic experience" the parks could offer. DeVoto was not just bemoaning what was happening in the national park system but a broader problem in American culture: the bleeding dry of the public sector of society (parks, schools, etc.) accompanied by an increasing supply of private goods such as automobiles. It would be this concern that fueled a change in liberal thinking during this time (see the next chapter).[23]

DeVoto was no elitist who hated the masses trampling his cherished national parks. He had rejected this sort of snobbery in his own writing when he threw off Mencken's influence during the 1920s. During the 1950s, he criticized those within the National Park System who chastised visitors for gathering at "evening dances" in Yosemite (held by a private concessionaire that ran numerous businesses in the park) and who demanded people "come on one knee and be crammed full of both information and inspiration." DeVoto was not concerned with tourists doing silly things in the parks but with how Americans failed to support public endeavors such as the park system and thus allowed a source of great national pride to fall into disarray. He believed that this problem could be redressed, and he tried his best to do so. Not only did he write about the matter in such provocatively entitled articles as "Let's Close the National Parks," he acted upon it, serving on the Advisory Committee on Conservation to the secretary of the interior from 1948 to 1949 and then, for the rest of his life, with the National Parks Advisory Board. He also provided advice to politicians active in this area, especially Senators Paul Douglas and Eugene McCarthy (both ADA members).[24]

When the Democratic presidential candidate asked for help, DeVoto was there too, writing speeches for Stevenson in 1952. And when Schlesinger was thinking of putting together a "Western conference" for Stevenson, he of course asked DeVoto to participate. The hope here was to articulate a Democratic Party vision for the West that could synthesize regional populism (i.e., better train rates for raw materials shipped from the West) with more sensible conservation programs regarding national forests and parks. DeVoto jumped at the opportunity. In 1954, he took Stevenson on a tour of the area surrounding Missoula, Montana, educating him about the difficulties of managing national forests. "I never had a better time in my life than those few days in Missoula," DeVoto wrote Stevenson. "I'd like to do it all over again. If you ever want a trout or a Douglas fir, yell and I'll come running." Of course, it wasn't just fun to hang out. DeVoto was pushing the Democratic Party to make conservation issues and support of the national parks a central plank in the 1956 party platform, and he was starting to see some success. He hoped "eggheads" in the party would be the major instigators in conservation policy. As Arthur Schlesinger pointed out, DeVoto had his "faith in politics" renewed by Stevenson, because he appreciated the candidate's keen sense of "national welfare."[25]

It should be obvious why DeVoto would focus his energy on plying national leaders. Public lands, conservation, and the national parks were all *national* issues that demanded intelligent leadership. When Americans decided to reserve western lands as part of a public domain, they committed themselves to a project with a great legacy: the demand to "protect posterity in our natural wealth." This was the challenge of taking seriously the idea of "public property" or what one historian calls the "principle of a national commons." It was a challenge to limit America's materialistic avaricious desire to expand endlessly. This was a lesson that the cattlemen wanting cheap lands for the taking and the politicians chintzy with federal dollars for national parks were too quick to ignore. Only national leaders could push back against these forces and prevent short-term aims to profit from the public's legacy.[26]

If this task could be accomplished, DeVoto believed that the nation could learn something from the West. Once the selfishness of cattlemen was cleared off the table, there were other elements of western culture that could inform a richer national identity. There was, of course, the beauty of the land that DeVoto wanted to defend. But there was also something about the humans living there. For instance, DeVoto loved the western sense of humor, which was "understated, oblique, ironical, and paradoxical." He embraced the region's plain language and lack of pretension, good qualities for any democratic nation to imbibe.

The primary lesson the West offered though was one that the Bureau of Reclamation and the Army Corps of Engineers seemed to forget: a lesson about "limits." "We know that limits are absolutely fixed by the topography and distances of the West, by its capacity to sustain population, by its soils and climate, by the amount of water, and by the facts of life." Humans could not magically transcend the geographical limits that the West had inherited. "The enduring drama of the West," DeVoto explained, "is provided by its aridity; lack of water sets an absolute limitation to its development." Western settlement had to be more careful and sensitive than the rugged frontier ideal suggested, confronting the reality of mountains, deserts, and the distances between water sources. If the nation could learn a lesson from the nature of the western landscape, it might be able to check its own hubris and sense that material progress could solve any and all problems standing in its way. It might be able to listen to the ironic voice of the western settler, that "self-derision of a man who has shot the moon and missed," as DeVoto put it. If the region could teach the nation, the nation might become more humble.[27]

WOODWARD: FROM SOUTHERN POPULISM TO NATIONAL LIBERALISM

It's probably clear by now that DeVoto rarely checked his opinions at the door. He was especially ruthless toward southern intellectuals: "Too many of them instantly become a section-conscious, caste-conscious, passion-dominated mob, throwing reason to the winds and reaching for a gun to defend their personal honor." He believed there was a dearth of southern intellectuals who could examine their own region critically and confront its legacy of racism. Too many were lost in a fog of myth and romanticism about the past. That belief on the part of DeVoto might have been why Arthur Schlesinger asked him to invite C. Vann Woodward up for a drink. Woodward was a southern intellectual who himself complained about the "mists of romanticism" in southern intellectual life as much as DeVoto did.[28]

Woodward had grown up in Arkansas and knew the realities of its social and race relations. His anger with the racism and depressed conditions of the South pushed him to the left, and in his young adult years he flirted with communism, helping to support Angelo Herndon, a black communist prosecuted by the state of Georgia (a state in which Woodward taught briefly). Woodward experienced the same sort of disillusionment with communists as James Wechsler, watching them infiltrate progressive organizations in order to take them over. Woodward even traveled to the Soviet Union (as had Wechsler), and this trip sobered him further to the realities of communism.

He then attended graduate school at the University of North Carolina during the 1930s, where he met the southern liberal and sociologist Howard Odum. There he wrote his dissertation on Tom Watson, a great southern populist who became a rabid racist after the failure of the farmers' movement of the 1890s, and then published it with a trade press during the late 1930s. This book expressed Woodward's growing faith in liberalism, seeing as he appreciated populism's desire to temper capitalism with state regulation and a mixed economy without eradicating private enterprise (Woodward would label the New Deal "neo-Populism" later in his life). After serving in the navy during World War II (and quickly writing a book about the experience), Woodward got a full-time teaching job at Johns Hopkins University, moving to a border state of the South.[29]

Although DeVoto never really inherited any western intellectual legacy (some would say there was none), Woodward knew that the South had its own intellectual tradition. First, there was the richness of southern literary expression. Woodward had read deep, impressed by writers like Thomas Wolfe, Katherine Anne Porter, and especially Robert Penn Warren and William Faulkner (the latter Woodward started "reading in college (1929) avidly without knowing what the hell he was saying but without ever a doubt that he was saying it to me"). There was also a long tradition of writers thinking hard about what made the South distinct and expressing themselves in nonfiction, a tradition that stemmed at least as far back as Thomas Jefferson (in his famous "Notes on the State of Virginia") and that, in Woodward's graduate school days, found clearest expression in a group of thinkers known as the southern "regionalists." Their essays collected in a book entitled *I'll Take My Stand*, these southern writers rebelled against the impersonal nature of modernity and the "apologists of industrialism" while celebrating an agricultural way of life (and even segregated race relations) found in the South. They hoped to renew the Old South's social practices in order to resist modernity's heartless individualism.[30]

Woodward knew that this regionalist tradition wound up supporting a politics he abhorred. But he also believed there was the possibility of a regionalism without racism or nostalgia. He had heard tones of this in the thinking of Howard Odum while at the University of North Carolina. Odum began as a racist in the 1910s but gradually came to a liberal faith in racial inclusion by the 1930s and 1940s. Odum also saw both the good and bad in regional identity (he insisted on using the term regionalism rather than sectionalism since he thought it didn't conjure up negative connotations of national division or civil war). Odum was never one to deny that the South had certain distasteful features, namely, a penchant for racism, mob rule, demagoguery, and anti-intellectualism. But he also believed, as did Lewis Mumford during the 1930s, that a region like the South could serve as a manageable unit capable of planning solutions for its own problems. And so he held out faith in southern regionalism as a means to create a more integrated and yet decentralized nationalism, local regions forming the basis of a more cooperative ethic. Odum not only wrote on these issues but served as part of cross-racial alliances, building up the basis of a white liberalism in the South before the civil rights movement took off during the 1950s. He helped in organizations such as the Southern Conference for Human Welfare and Commission on Interracial Cooperation. Drawing hope from Odum's life and thought, Woodward believed regionalism could throw off nostalgia, embrace realism, and become the basis of a future liberalism.[31]

Woodward himself would write history that recognized the distinct regional aspect of southern history. In 1951, he published *The Origins of a New South*, a book that depicted the region as a colony of the North. This was not a terribly difficult argument to make, seeing that up to the time of Reconstruction, the South had focused most of its energy on producing a single crop, cotton, that was finished in the textile mills of the North, cementing the typical mother country–colony relationship (albeit within a nation's borders). Although the South industrialized after the Civil War, it still did most of its work producing raw materials. Woodward pointed out that its newer forms of industrialism, found in a "textile industry," showed signs of a "general pattern of colonialism." "The chief products of the Southern cotton mills," he pointed out, "were yarn and coarse or unfinished cloth, much of which was shipped north for final processing before going to the consumer." Reliance upon "Northern capital" also betrayed the South's colonial status. By depicting the South as a colony of the North, Woodward told a regional story within a broadly national context, relating these stories from the South to wider processes occurring in the North as well. The South was distinct—even subservient—but still part of a nation.[32]

This relation between region and nation was echoed in another book, *Reunion and Reaction*, released the same year as *Origins of the New South* and one that connected him to the civil rights movement. Here Woodward argued that the national rush toward wealth during the Gilded Age, on the part of both North and South, had been the basis of a national betrayal of African-American rights initially ensured by the passage of the Fourteenth Amendment. This line of argument grabbed the attention of lawyers working at the National Association for the Advancement of Colored People (NAACP), including Thurgood Marshall who was just starting to press his now famous case *Brown v. Board of Education*. Marshall had been involved in a number of cases that tried to punch holes in the 1896 Supreme Court decision *Plessy v. Ferguson*, which argued that public schools could be racially segregated as long as they were given "equal" funds ("separate but equal" was the ideal, whereas underfunding of black schools was the reality). At first, the NAACP had tried to demand equal funding for racially segregated public schools in the South, not directly challenging segregation itself. But then came World War II and the Cold War, and, by the early 1950s, the organization had decided to challenge segregation full-on. Because Woodward told a story of national betrayal during Reconstruction, the NAACP's research team working on the *Brown* case was interested in learning more. It was at this point that Woodward, a white southern liberal intellectual, went from telling stories about his region in order to understand that region better to telling a story about the nation as a whole, for distinctly political reasons.[33]

John Davis, the head of the NAACP's research division and a political science professor at Lincoln University, wrote Woodward in June of 1953, asking him to write a paper about the "political and economic factors" behind Reconstruction and to become part of a wider group (including Woodward's friend John Hope Franklin) that would discuss the merits of the NAACP's case in New York City. Explaining himself a bit further in August the same year, Davis wrote that he hoped the paper would "indicate that the drive for complete immediate equality for the newly freed Negro was caught up in a complex economic, historical and political situation. The Constitutional mandate remains, and present complex world racial, economic, and political factors now demand its effectuation." Davis also made clear that his essay would be used only if it supported the NAACP's case. Legal demands would trump scholarly truth here. He made this point to ensure that Woodward knew what he was getting into.

In the end, Woodward wrote the paper by elaborating on his book about Reconstruction and wound up making an argument with which the NAACP was quite pleased. Woodward was more than willing to make historical inquiry relevant to what he thought might become one of the most important Supreme Court cases in America's national history. After the case was won, Robert Carter from the NAACP wrote Woodward to thank him, saying that he was one "of those who greatly aided in the successful preparation, development and presentation of the theory which won the vote of the Court." Woodward had successfully put his intellect to national service.[34]

Woodward's arguments in the paper "The Background of the Abandonment of Reconstruction" had something to say about American historiographical debates, as they are called today, but were also straightforward enough to be understood by a nonacademic audience. His scholarly argument was to call into question the importance of the Wormley House meeting of 1877, a meeting held after the presidential election of 1876 was too close to call. At this meeting, which came to symbolize a "great compromise," the Democrats granted the presidency to the Republicans in return for an agreement that they would pull the troops that had backed up Reconstruction out of the South, thus ensuring that support for civil rights would diminish. Woodward knew this event mattered but also believed that Reconstruction's demise could not be explained by one meeting. The history of Reconstruction, as all history is, was "more complex and elaborate." Woodward argued that economic pressures had threatened the idealistic edge of the Reconstruction from its beginnings, that is, right in the wake of the Civil War when Radical Republicans started to remake the South along lines of racial equality. The Republican Party was split as to how much effort it should make in order to ensure full civic equality for blacks. Business-minded Southerners had gained the hearing of the Republican Party, arguing they deserved railroads and economic infrastructure that could help them rebuild back their economy and thereby be able to increase trade with the North. This economic vision of reunion—a vision in place in the immediate aftermath of the Civil War—won out over the political and egalitarian vision of Reconstruction. The Wormley meeting was simply the crowning blow to racial equality. The meeting "preserved," Woodward explained, "the pragmatic and material ends of Reconstruction at the expense of the idealistic and humanitarian ends."[35]

Woodward's argument offered a nice historical rationale for the NAACP's arguments to abolish segregation. Any lawyer could read his paper and see a natural conclusion: the nation was now wealthy enough, in the 1950s, that it could finally deal with the racial problem more squarely; it could live up to the more idealistic promise of the Fourteenth Amendment. Even though his was a powerful argument, Woodward knew when he looked back on the case that "the Court was more impressed by sociological evidence than by historical arguments."

As many know, it was a famous set of "doll tests" that became the most evocative element of Thurgood Marshall's case against segregation. Drawing upon a growing respect for social-scientific research in the postwar years, the social psychologist Kenneth Clark had presented evidence that children living under segregated conditions suffered psychic damage, that segregation made black children feel inferior to white children no matter how much money was poured into their schools. Clark did this by presenting two sets of dolls to black children living under segregated conditions and then observing their reactions. One set of dolls was black, the other white, and invariably the black children said they would prefer to play with the white dolls. Clark inferred from this that black children suffered from self-loathing due to the social messages segregation gave them. Although the Supreme Court weighed many different elements when deciding *Brown*, the doll test was clearly one of the most persuasive bits of evidence the NAACP had mustered.[36]

Ironically, one of the strongest elements of the NAACP's case might have been one of its weakest. There had always been doubt about using social-scientific arguments in the *Brown* case. After all, social science could not move apace with the work of lawyers (as both social scientists and lawyers working on the case openly worried). If there was a hole found in the research presented, for instance, it was doubtful that a social scientist could arrange another study to provide counterevidence (social science relied upon arranging "control groups" and large enough samplings of people to carry statistical significance). In addition, there would always be questions raised about the objectivity of those submitting social-scientific research findings for a case that had a clearly set-out goal (racial equality). And in the case of the doll tests, there were more specific problems. When Kenneth Clark tested black children in the North—and more specifically, children not living under segregated conditions—he got the same negative reactions to black dolls. This posed a problem for a case stating that segregation was the most important cause of psychic damage among children.[37]

All of this is, of course, historical hindsight. The doll tests were persuasive in their own day and age, or at least they helped win over the Supreme Court. Nonetheless, if we consider Woodward's arguments, they teach us that an emphasis on psychological damage was not the only case made for the *Brown* decision, that the liberal worldview (as well as the Supreme Court) had other reasons to argue for an end to segregation. The first and most obvious is that race could not serve as a reason for denying citizenship to anyone. The "American creed," with its constitutional faith that all people were created equal, needed to become a reality that guided the country into the future; if necessary, the national interest needed to trump local practices, as Reinhold Niebuhr argued in the wake of the *Brown* decision.

Liberals placed their faith in reforming the law rather than in changing the attitudes that stood behind laws. If the law changed, so the reasoning went, racist attitudes would eventually and gradually change. A faith in a legal constitutional decision followed by a gradual change in social institutions over the years was *the* liberal vision for changing race relations in the South. This explains why liberals were not terribly interested in the original claims made for nonviolent direct action by Martin Luther King. During the 1950s, King was envisioning a long and protracted set of local struggles, the first being the Montgomery Bus Boycott of 1955. He argued that one aim of nonviolence was to "awaken a sense of moral shame in the opponent," that is, the southern racist standing in the way of reforming segregation. For a liberal, such an appeal to conscience and the hearts of local citizens would have seemed misguided. The real aim should be to change the federal laws and then gradually await attitudinal changes. This was what motivated Woodward to help Marshall and his staff to win the case.[38]

After the *Brown* decision was rendered, Woodward continued to utilize history as a means to analyze the present. During that following summer, Woodward gave a set of lectures at the University of Virginia and then quickly turned these lectures into a book entitled *The Strange Career of Jim Crow.* It became the "Bible of the Civil Rights movement." Focusing on the years from 1877 through the 1890s, the book's purpose was set out clearly from its beginning. Woodward saw his role as going against "the national discussion over the questions of how deeply rooted, how ineradicable, and how amenable to change the segregation practices are." Most thinking done so far, he argued, was based on "faulty or inadequate historical information." As an historian of the South, he could correct that. The book was a history of events following Reconstruction, but it was just as much a work that expressed a liberal sense of hope about changing race relations for the better. What Woodward showed was a sharp break in southern history, a cleaver coming down during the Civil War and continuing to cut its way through the South in the wake of Reconstruction.

Woodward set out to challenge the arguments of previous southern liberals such as W.J. Cash, who, in *The Mind of the South*, argued that "the South we encounter as we pass over into the 1900s is really one which has reached a sort of temporary equilibrium upon its ancient foundation." Unlike Cash, Woodward believed the South *had* changed in the past and thus could change in the future. Not surprisingly, Americans for Democratic Action designated the book one of its book club offers, arguing that it was important reading for all liberals.[39]

Getting down to historical detail, Woodward argued that the period of time from 1877, when Reconstruction ended, to the 1890s, when the first Jim Crow laws emerged (and when *Plessy v. Ferguson* was decided by the Supreme Court), was a time of incredible chaos in the South. In 1877, blacks were voting and running for office and traveling where they wished, and by the 1890s, they were disfranchised and segregated. Debates surrounded southern race relations from 1877 onward, and segregation, which, Woodward pointed out, had been practiced in northern urban communities for some time, was one among differing visions for the South's future.

Populists emerged during this period of time, arguing that racism kept poor blacks and poor whites fighting with one another instead of identifying their real enemy in landlords and bankers. "You are made to hate each other because upon that hatred is rested the keystone of the arch of financial despotism which enslaves you both," Woodward quoted Tom Watson, speaking to a gathering of black and white farmers. Southern "liberals" such as Lewis Harvie Blair were probably queasy about such radical egalitarianism but still argued for racial integration as the basis of building a new, more productive industrial South. There were also those who would have been quite happy simply exterminating blacks or imposing a more violent form of domination (i.e., lynching) than would necessarily be allowed by segregation. These visions collided with one another, with segregation winning out only when Populism was defeated during the 1890s and when liberals accepted segregation as a more "peaceful" form of race relations in the "new south."[40]

The shift to segregation and disfranchisement happened rapidly during the 1890s. Woodward simply laid out statistics: "The effectiveness of disfranchisement is suggested by a comparison of the number of registered Negro voters in Louisiana in 1896, when there were 130,334 and in 1904, when there were 1,342." Plus, there were anecdotal stories, such as the one about T. McCants Stewart, a black newspaperman who went from Boston to South Carolina in 1885. He had expected poor treatment riding on trains. Woodward relates the following, "He found a seat in a car which became so crowded that several white passengers had to sit on their baggage," and he was never asked to move. Stewart concluded, "I had found traveling more pleasant" in the South "than in some parts of New England." This sort of experience would be nonexistent by the late 1890s. By telling these types of stories, Woodward wrote an exciting narrative that began with a period when things were up for grabs and race relations in flux. Voices then clashed in this void and then finally segregation won out. His story had the right measure of suspense and intrigue to attract a wide audience. It also helped explain to Americans how the South became what it was.[41]

There was an irony to all of this that Woodward couldn't help but point out (Woodward was keen to apply Niebuhr's theory of irony to American history). Immediately after segregation arose, the sociologist William Graham Sumner conjured up a justification for it that would live on to Woodward's own day. Sumner argued that cultural prejudices such as racism were simply "folkways" that rested on a "primeval rock of human nature," ignoring the obvious fact that segregation had arisen rapidly due to political pressures and legal reforms. Sumner's reasoning was taken up by conservatives after his death in order to justify racial segregation.

Woodward noticed a more recent variation on the argument as he moved up the timeline into the 1950s. He could barely repress a chuckle when hearing segregationists using laissez-faire arguments against proposals that the federal government should step in to solve the race problem, seeing as segregation relied upon political and legal force, not laissez-faire freedom. Southerners liked to pretend segregation was natural when in fact it was political. "The policies of proscription, segregation, and disfranchisement that are often described as the immutable 'folkways' of the South, impervious alike to legislative reform and armed intervention, are of a more recent origin." Thus, Woodward's historical inquiry suggested, change the law and you could change the behavior somewhere down the road, the one following the other. He claimed this was a "realist" position.[42]

Critics and historians looking back on Woodward's work find it lacking. As part of a general attack on liberalism, historians have honed in on its relation to the civil rights movement. Historian Christopher Lasch, for instance, argued that Gunnar Myrdal's arguments for defending the "American creed" through the "courts" and "an enlightened federal bureaucracy" was little more than elitism. "It never occurred to" Myrdal or other liberals, Lasch went on, "that black people might take the leading role in their own liberation." The scholar David Chappell takes Lasch's point and paints even wider strokes, arguing that the civil rights movement "caught liberals off-guard in the 1950s" because these secularists couldn't understand the religious motivation of civil rights workers who hit the streets. Other historians have concurred, and recently, Carol Polsgrove has taken this doubt about liberal intellectual commitment to the civil rights movement and applied it directly to Woodward (and others). Stressing Woodward's ironic tone and desire for historical accuracy and detachment (something that people at the time said he lacked), Polsgrove argued that he believed in "gradualism" and "going slow," terms that she never clearly defines but generally sees as detrimental to the civil rights movement.[43]

These critics have their points, but their attack is scattershot and misses what liberal intellectuals *did* contribute to the cause. First and most obviously, Woodward had provided hope for the struggle against segregation and for full voting rights. But there's something else as well, something much broader that goes beyond Woodward's own initiatives. As we have seen, liberal intellectuals argued that anticommunism required Americans to reform their own institutions. Woodward himself cited how a 1952 brief filed with the Supreme Court "in connection with the cases involving segregation in the public schools," had made this connection very clearly. The brief quoted the secretary of state: "The segregation of school children on a racial basis is one of the practices in the United States which has been singled out for hostile foreign comment in the United Nations and elsewhere."

Whereas conservative anticommunists such as Governor Talmadge argued that civil rights workers were communist agitators, liberal anticommunists argued that the country needed to take them seriously because the eyes of the world were watching. Liberals also argued that the American nation had to become an integrated community, to live up to its "creed" by granting equal rights to all citizens. Or as Arthur Schlesinger had already put it in *The Vital Center*, "The sin of racial pride still represents the most basic challenge to the American conscience." When Woodward heard of senators signing a "Southern Manifesto" opposing the *Brown* decision and hinting at resistance, he warned, "It is a real Constitutional crisis that we are facing." Woodward knew history well enough to argue that America could not allow for anything that smacked of nullification or secession.[44]

The civil rights movement took up these ideas as it developed after the original local success of the Montgomery Bus Boycott. By the early 1960s, Martin Luther King and other civil rights leaders had changed strategy. No longer would they hunker down to win local victories in southern cities, the way King had in Montgomery, Alabama, in 1955 and the way student protestors had during sit-ins in Greensboro, North Carolina, in 1960. When King failed in pursuing local direct action in Albany, Georgia, from 1961–1962, he explained to his followers: "The key to everything is federal commitment." As Harvard Sitkoff points out, "The idea of changing hearts and minds gave way to confrontation politics that would induce federal intervention"; that is, the civil rights movement needed to get the nation on its side and get legislation that would ensure full political equality for blacks.

The movement accomplished this best with the March on Washington in 1963 where King gave his famous "I Have a Dream" speech, not so surprisingly, at the Lincoln Memorial. King used Lincoln's "Gettysburg Address" as his model and trumpeted the cause of the "American creed" and nationalism. Victory was around the corner at this moment, for in 1964 and 1965 the president and Congress passed sweeping legislation that ensured blacks equal voting rights as well as an end to segregation. Woodward called this time a "period of restitution, an effort to fulfill promises a century old, the redemption of a historic commitment." Of course, there were numerous factors behind this victory—JFK's assassination in 1963, LBJ's strong leadership on civil rights, pressures from the Cold War, the growth of an urban middle class, the growing strength of the federal government—but the anticommunist nationalism expounded by liberal intellectuals cannot be dismissed by historians so easily.[45]

Nor should we dismiss the fact that Woodward was not only a nationalist but a regionalist. This brings us back to the broader theme of this chapter. Much like DeVoto, Woodward believed the southern region had something to teach the nation. Of course, the South needed to shed racism, the way the West had to throw off its landgrabbing libertarianism. But if it did, it could teach the nation a very Niebuhrian lesson. Woodward explained how the South's history offered something of a morality tale, "An age-long experience with human bondage and its evils and later with emancipation and its shortcomings did not dispose the South very favorably toward such popular American ideas as the doctrine of human perfectibility, the belief that every evil has a cure, and the notion that every human problem has a solution." By Woodward's account, Niebuhr should have been a Southerner: "The experience of evil and the experience of tragedy are part of the Southern heritage."

It was especially southern blacks who could teach the nation this lesson. Woodward took up the black novelist Ralph Ellison's remark that blacks held a "tragic-comic attitude" due to years of mistreatment. Woodward expressed his own ironic outlook when he asked if the South could actually learn its own lesson. As he explained to David Riesman two years after arguing the South had lessons to teach the nation, his home region was still extremely reactionary. Nonetheless, he explained, "I was holding up the South's unique historical experience in America as something that it *might*, and I hope someday will profit from." The South's lesson for the nation, like everything else in history, was contingent.[46]

BACK TO LINCOLN

DeVoto and Woodward shared both friends and ideas. They articulated the importance of nationalism for the liberal worldview without losing sight of the regions that made them who they were or what they hoped their nation could become. They recognized that to build a national community required serious attention toward regional differences as sources of both strength and weakness. By doing this, both historians confronted some of the most difficult problems America would face in the 1950s and beyond: conservation of natural resources and race relations. In their own ways, they not only addressed these problems but also tried to solve them, as men of ideas first and activists second. They helped the liberal mind understand that it could be both regional and national at the same time.

This chapter is best ended by conjuring up, once again, a vision of Martin Luther King making his famous "I Have a Dream" speech in 1963. For here we come full circle to Lincoln. Standing only a short distance from Lincoln's statue in the memorial behind him, King spoke of this nationalist hero and his legacy for the country. King alluded to the "nation" throughout the speech, arguing that "we have come to our nation's Capitol to cash a check" on the promise made African Americans in the original Constitution. "I have a dream," King proclaimed, "that one day this nation will rise up and live out the true meaning of its creed: 'We hold these truths to be self-evident; that all men are created equal.'" Niebuhr, who had grown more conservative about the civil rights movement over time, believed the march an enormous success and the speech a work of genius: "King's address was one of the most eloquent in recent years. It won't influence the hard core of racists, but it will influence the nation." Niebuhr was right; King had made the liberal nationalist vision speak to the country and did so in the metaphorical and literal shadow of Lincoln. The event, as the historian Mary Dudziak points out, also became international, showing the best side of America to the world.[47]

Just as important, King had made the speech at the Lincoln Memorial, a park that was part of the national system DeVoto had adored and labeled a great "inheritance of the American citizen." Geography matters here. Films and photographs of King's speech usually show a crowd of black and white citizens responding joyously as they stand next to the Reflecting Pool that extends out from the Lincoln Memorial. The monument evokes a sense of public beauty and collective space that belongs to the nation as a whole; the bodies gathered there seem like a surrogate for the nation, or at least those members committed to racial equality. There can be no doubt that the collective memories of the March on Washington and King's speech tell us something about the power of American liberalism, of its dreams for racial equality and its faith in public space and the national parks as a reminder of the best promise of American life.[48]

CHAPTER FIVE

Hopes
Liberalism and the Quality of Public Life

The Russians want more because we have more. But we must ask ourselves why we want more.

John Kenneth Galbraith

Morality in foreign policy consists not in applying one's standards to other nations but in living up to them oneself.

Arthur Schlesinger[1]

THE POLITICS OF FRIENDSHIP AND HOPE

In 1955, Bernard DeVoto died, just one year before the final defeat of the Echo Park Dam. At the same time, Reinhold Niebuhr continued to suffer from a stroke and the residual depression it incurred and therefore found himself receding from political activism, explaining that he was still involved in ADA but "not as deeply committed to it as I once was." At least by now, liberal intellectuals could look back on a track record, a history of their own accomplishments. They had begun their collective travels when FDR led the country to war, helping the president build national unity through their work in organizations like the OPA and explaining "why we fight" in the literature released by the OWI. As the intellectual barricades of World War II were dismantled, the eggheads moved on to build a Non-Communist Left (NCL) in both Europe and the United States, opposing the fellow travelers and communist sympathizers in Henry Wallace's Progressive Party campaign for president in 1948. Liberals formed their own political organization in the ADA and articulated a political philosophy that provided a deeper justification for the welfare state and that faced up to the realities of human nature and

140

the sins of the self made apparent in the Holocaust and Stalin's gulags. By toughening and deepening the liberal vision traced here, these thinkers made it live beyond the towering persona of FDR.[2]

By the end of the 1940s, liberal intellectuals hoped they could let their guard down about communism but found others rushing in to keep the American mind fixated on it. The rise of McCarthyism meant liberals had to watch their backs, so to speak, defining their own brand of anticommunism against a new and more dangerous breed of conservatism, one that welded anticommunism to an antiregulatory politics. The challenge was best captured when Jimmy Wechsler stared into the eyes of Joe McCarthy and told him that he was not only wrong but that he was destroying democracy. Risks were taken, nothing was clean here, and sometimes liberals felt their backs pressed against a wall. Nonetheless, liberal anticommunism was able to define itself clearly against the new enemy of McCarthyism and the new right. Then came threats to national solidarity—the basis of liberal political philosophy— from the regions of the South and West. By 1955, after numerous pitched battles, Westerners learned there really was a national interest that trumped their special pleadings on behalf of ranchers' private profits and other pressure groups. Landgrabs were halted, plans for a dam scratched. The same year, the Supreme Court's *Brown* decision echoed the voice of a southern white liberal who argued that the country had a responsibility to live up to the "American creed" and grant all of its citizens full equality.

While things changed within America, things outside moved ahead as well. If Stalinism wasn't dead, Stalin was by 1953. In 1956, Khrushchev documented Stalin's crimes to the Communist Party leadership, and thus the threat of communism seemed to weaken or at least relax itself for a moment. The CCF held a conference in Milan in 1955, and the conversations revolved more around questions of mass culture and conformity in the United States than around communism in Europe (five years later communism barely came up at all at a CCF conference). There was a growing feeling during the mid-1950s that anticommunism had triumphed in Europe. Now that eyes were turning to the third world—Asia and Africa—anticommunism seemed almost passé or at least too Eurocentric to be taken seriously by the world's poor. No one was very hopeful about Khrushchev ditching the dictatorship of the proletariat for actual democracy (in 1956, he ruthlessly crushed an uprising in the Soviet satellite of Hungary); nonetheless, many felt the Cold War was changing.

In 1956, Schlesinger argued the United States could tone down the military aspects of its foreign policy, and, as James Wechsler pointed out four year later, liberals believed communists could be "met most effectively by imaginative programs of aid to the underprivileged countries and by the perfecting of our own free institutions." It wasn't that communism had died, just that liberals now felt some room to move around politically. Although they had previously defined positive visions of liberalism, now was a time that offered real possibilities for change. After all, McCarthy had fallen into disgrace by 1954 (and was preparing to drink himself to death) and conservative bulwarks such as James Burnham and Whittaker Chambers had exited the ACCF. It seemed as if things had changed, as if there really *was* more room to move around.[3]

The year 1955 was pivotal in shaping the liberal vision. Although there was hope about changes occurring within the communist system, the waning of the communist threat posed a problem for liberal identity and vision. After all, liberals had defined themselves against communism for a number of years. But this negative definition made it seem that liberals lacked direction, unsure of where to go as the political landscape shifted. Take the ADA for instance. The organization had felt the pinch of McCarthyism, often finding itself the subject of smears that required a great deal of energy to retaliate against (some politicians, Jimmy Wechsler pointed out, believed the ADA's endorsements a "liability"). In addition, the organization had never fully defined what it was supposed to be. Was it a group of intellectuals formulating policy and independent of any political party (like the Fabian Society of England)? Was it to be a pressure group within the Democratic Party or its own political organization? Or maybe all of these things at once? Although the organization could postpone this debate about definition from 1947 to 1948, when the threat of communism abroad and at home in the Henry Wallace campaign seemed so pressing, it came right back during the 1950s, with many members openly frustrated about a lack of direction within the organization. Wechsler, for one, worried that the ADA was becoming an "Alumni Association" of old New Deal liberals with no other place to go.[4]

While Wechsler worried, Schlesinger took action the way intellectuals often do: by sitting down at his typewriter. In 1955, he banged out a memo about the current and future status of liberal political philosophy and labeled his vision "qualitative liberalism," circulating his memo to many friends and politicians. Maybe, Schlesinger suggested, liberalism could take a qualitative turn in its thinking and thus get itself out of its current slump. The memo received good feedback. But Schlesinger also found opponents. Leon Keyserling, an old New Deal liberal if ever there was one, took issue with the idea of "qualitative liberalism" (following an earlier critique by Max Ascoli of *The Reporter* magazine). Keyserling debated Schlesinger publicly, pointing out that his ideas seemed allied with those of John Kenneth Galbraith, both of them guilty in Keyserling's mind of trying to change the terms of liberalism during the last few years of the 1950s. Keyserling was certainly right at least on this point, for Schlesinger and Galbraith *had* formed a friendship around political ideas and had indeed traveled down remarkably parallel paths in life and thought.[5]

The friendship began during World War II, both Galbraith and Schlesinger serving the cause in Washington, D.C., where they first met. They discovered a shared wit and commitment to the life of ironic passion demanded of the liberal intellectual, in addition to smaller things such as the same birthday (Galbraith was the elder) and eventually geographical proximity in Cambridge, Massachusetts. Both liked to move back and forth from activism (OPA and OWI during the war, for instance) to the reflective life of the mind in academia, joining the faculty of Harvard University just a year apart from each other. Their paths constantly crossed. They would see each other not just at Harvard and in their shared neighborhood but at ADA gatherings (although Schlesinger was more committed than Galbraith), CCF meetings, counseling sessions with Adlai Stevenson, and Democratic Party functions. Both watched with great joy as Democrats, some of them counseled directly by Galbraith and Schlesinger, won congressional seats in 1958, and both decided to throw in with a young one-time Harvard student, Jack Kennedy, for his presidential run in 1960. Essentially, Schlesinger and Galbraith articulated the idea of qualitative liberalism during the middle to late 1950s and then tried to put it into practice as they watched the 1950s fade away into the 1960s, when a new president asked them to serve the country the way they had during World War II. Understanding their travels from 1955 into the early 1960s is crucial to understanding the fighting faith of liberalism. The idea of "qualitative liberalism" is deeply wedded to Schlesinger's and Galbraith's friendship.[6]

THE POLITICS OF MASS CULTURE

Galbraith and Schlesinger knew that America had changed since coming out of World War II. Although fears lingered that America might slip back into the Great Depression that preceded the war, by the mid-1950s prosperity seemed assured. It could be perceived in many social indicators: higher wages and more home ownership (especially in America's growing suburbs). Intellectuals noticed it mostly in the growth of a consumer culture during the 1950s, taking note of some basic statistics. In 1948, only 3 percent of all electrically wired homes contained televisions; by 1956, the number was up to 81 percent. In 1948, 54 percent of American families owned automobiles, by 1956 73 percent did.

Credit cards took off during the 1950s, providing Americans with the means to purchase goods otherwise unaffordable. To ensure more spending on the part of the American public, corporations invested their earnings in advertising, becoming more sophisticated by doing things such as targeting different audiences who watched television throughout the week (i.e., kids on weekends, stay-at-home middle-class housewives during the day, husbands in the evening). They especially aimed their sights at adolescents who had more dispensable income and who were taking their cues from the mass media and peers more than from their families. Galbraith quipped that American culture seemed dominated by "high pressure salesmanship, singing commercials, and the concept of the captive audience." The new consumer culture even acquired a central monument of sorts in Disneyland, USA, founded in 1955 near Los Angeles. Its "Main Street, USA," one historian argued, served as "a community of consumption where you" could "buy everything you want." This was the new ethic that took America by storm during the 1950s.[7]

Intellectuals struggled to understand this new culture of prosperity and consumption and, in so doing, passed down to us today some of our key perceptions of what the 1950s were all about. Think 1950s America, and many conjure up images of grey flannel suit conformity, people buying refrigerators and cars in droves, suburban houses that all look the same. We also think of concepts that intellectuals developed at the time: the loss of individuality and "autonomy" as Americans became more "other-directed" in their behavior, "alienation" of the white-collar classes from working in large bureaucratic corporations, "standardization" of cultural products by a "culture industry" that pumped out streamlined commodities aimed at the lowest common denominator (movies replacing books, comic books replacing literature), and advertisements manipulating the tastes of isolated individuals who could no longer make up their own minds. Best-selling paperbacks expounded on these themes: *The Lonely Crowd, White Collar, The Organization Man, The Immediate Experience,* and *Growing up Absurd.* All of these books shared a concern with "mass culture," a term that haunted the American mind-set during the 1950s. Prosperity and consumption had brought with them a new culture with pernicious effects, that is, if we take seriously American intellectual life.[8]

This critique of mass culture helped provide the intellectual scaffolding of "qualitative liberalism." Liberal intellectuals had already expressed concern about "mass culture" in thinking about the threat of totalitarianism during the 1940s. This new political system isolated individuals from each other, turning them into a "mass," and then directly manipulating this mass through propaganda. Although neither Galbraith nor Schlesinger thought America was becoming totalitarian (that idea was stronger on the right end of the spectrum during the 1950s and wouldn't infiltrate left-wing thought until the late 1960s in the work of thinkers such as Herbert Marcuse), their concerns with totalitarianism made them especially sensitive to certain features of American mass culture.

By 1951, Arthur Schlesinger bemoaned a "uniform audience" growing in America. He championed his colleague David Riesman's conception of the "other-directed" individual and the problems of the "lonely crowd": conformity and loss of autonomy. He castigated a "conspiracy of blandness" that had hit America during the 1950s, and he considered starting a magazine with the social critic Mary McCarthy (and others) that would focus attention on problems of mass culture (it would have had the simple title *Critic*). Schlesinger linked this concern with mass culture to liberalism directly: "The central concern of American liberalism has been the status and growth of the free individual in the mass society. This concern has been moral and cultural as well as political and economic." Schlesinger and Galbraith worried about mass culture, like other intellectuals of their time. Galbraith's own book *The Affluent Society* (1958) stands as an exemplary work of mass culture critique, with its stinging satire about advertising and manufactured desire. Both Schlesinger and Galbraith were swimming in the mainstream of American intellectual life when they worried about a "uniform audience" and the manipulation of advertising in connecting these themes to the political thought of liberalism.[9]

This helps explain why these thinkers' liberal vision is forgotten today. Contemporary cultural theorists and historians have lambasted the mass culture critique of the 1950s as passé, elitist, and utterly irrelevant to contemporary political thought. A theory that grew out of concern with totalitarianism is now seen as an overreaction to those dark days. When intellectuals criticized movies or comic books in the past, we are told that this was little more than fear of ordinary people having fun. The historian Paul Gorman, in a book documenting "left intellectuals and popular culture" during the twentieth century, reduces critical ideas about the culture industry to snobbery. The critique of mass culture by New York City intellectuals, we are told, "grew out of a sophisticated philosophical rationale they created to support their tastes." The cultural studies theorist Andrew Ross depicts the story of intellectuals' relation to popular culture as little more than "paternalism, containment, and even allergic reaction." Intellectuals, for Ross, were simply jealous that they had lost cultural guardianship over their fellow citizens, as Americans took satisfaction in comic books and movies and not the ponderous writings of eggheads. Intellectuals couldn't understand that people might actually like the things they were buying or watching on television. The political theorist Stephen Holmes can't even imagine a critique of popular culture being anything but elitist and thus inherently "antiliberal."[10]

There's truth to some of these claims but, as with any critique with such sweep, a lot is left out. Sure, a critic like Galbraith recoiled at what he saw in the American cultural landscape of the 1950s. He obviously didn't like advertising and thought it manipulative. "Is a new breakfast cereal or detergent so much wanted if so much must be spent to compel in the consumer the sense of want?" he asked. You can imagine Galbraith rolling his eyes and switching off the radio when a singing commercial came on. Nor did he care much for the highways on which he drove. He found them "hideous," because the "billboard artists and the motel builders and the sellers of countless things and the neon signs" try to "turn the road into an efficient instrument of commerce." Take these words alone and out of context and you can build up an image of

Galbraith as a curmudgeon—an intellectual holding his nose as he drove down the highway, kicking his radio as commercial jingles blared, and cutting himself off from a world he couldn't understand or relax enough to enjoy. Here was a man, contemporary critics would seem right to argue, whose tastes transformed themselves into prejudices against the daily pleasures of the masses.[11]

Such a flippant characterization would be unfair though. A lot more than taste worried Galbraith when it came to America's consumer culture of the 1950s. What especially mattered was the *politics* behind the growth of a mass culture: how the new consumer culture had direct political ramifications in terms of limiting public choices and thinning out the content of democracy. So, for instance, take one of the key events that symbolized how consumer culture had invaded the political realm: the famous "Kitchen Debate" between Khrushchev and then Vice President Richard Nixon in 1959. Taking place at the American Exhibition in Moscow, Nixon took Khrushchev through a model home built especially for the occasion and pointed to a model kitchen's accoutrements, touting them as symbols of the American way of life. The dishwashers and refrigerators found here embodied "what freedom means to us," Nixon told a grouchy Khrushchev. Never before was there such a bold equation of freedom and consumerism made for the world to see, and it worried liberal intellectuals.

Reinhold Niebuhr noticed an irony in Nixon whittling down the meaning of democracy and freedom to dishwashers and refrigerators. "The whole debate was on the material and technical success of our culture. This is," Niebuhr explained "ironic" because, as most Americans understood the cultural imperative of the Cold War, "we were the original idealists and the Communists were the materialists." Galbraith agreed, pointing out that "those who argue that" freedom "is identified with the greatest possible range of choice of consumers' goods are only confessing their exceedingly simple-minded and mechanical view of man and his liberties." This had little to do with personal taste but rather with how consumer culture nurtured a thin view of democracy and the American creed, both at home and abroad. "It seems to many Europeans," Niebuhr explained, "that a nation as fortunate as ours could not possibly be either virtuous or 'cultured.'" This view could never be countered if Americans such as Nixon continued to equate democracy with consumer abundance.[12]

The central problem of a consumer culture for liberals was that it gave priority to private satisfaction while denigrating public life. This was its structural impact—what Galbraith called its social imbalance—seen by the priorities it set. Galbraith drove home this point by describing for his readers a trip their families might have recently taken. In one of the most memorable passages written by a liberal intellectual during the 1950s, Galbraith expounded:

> The family which takes its mauve and cerise, air-conditioned, power-steered, and power-braked automobile out for a tour passes through cities that are badly paved, made hideous by litter, blighted buildings, billboards, and posts for wires that should long since have been put underground. They pass on into a countryside that has been rendered largely invisible by commercial art. (The goods that the latter advertise have an absolute priority in our value system. Such aesthetic considerations as a view of the countryside accordingly come second. On such matters we are consistent.) They picnic on exquisitely packaged food from a portable icebox by a polluted stream and go on to spend the night at a park which is a menace to public health and morals. Just before dozing off on an air mattress, beneath a nylon tent, amid the stench of decaying refuse, they may reflect vaguely on the curious unevenness of their blessings. Is this, indeed, the American genius?

It was the "unevenness" between "private opulence and public squalor" that worried Galbraith (and Schlesinger), not just the ugliness of the highways. This is what contemporary cultural historians forget when they portray cultural critique in the 1950s as mere snobbery or fear. They also forget that critics like Galbraith and Schlesinger saw this as deeply political. Even before Nixon bragged about dishwashers to Khrushchev, Eisenhower (a president known for devouring western pulp fiction and playing golf) was busy touting the importance of business in his administration (Stevenson once quipped that Ike allowed the "car dealers" to take over for the "New Dealers") and denying the importance of public expenditure. Criticizing the cultural ethos of Eisenhower's presidency, Schlesinger argued that Americans needed to "end this belief that every dollar spent for private indulgence is good and every dollar spent for public service is bad—that, to put it simply, tail-fins are better than schools." Such beliefs had both cultural and political ramifications.[13]

Galbraith read the ramifications in his social landscape. When he complained about architecture, probably sounding like a snob to Andrew Ross or Paul Gorman, he was not simply complaining about ugliness but about a lack of investment in and care given to public space. "In our last twenty years our public construction has become much more utilitarian—much more determinedly practical." He saw this in the "square, functional and antiseptic" buildings that municipal, state, and federal governments erected (he especially hated the new State Department building in Washington, D.C.). This was a sign of cheapness as much as ugliness. "In public housekeeping," Galbraith explained, "the aim is not elegance but to get by."

He also saw this in the new highway system that Eisenhower had championed (the biggest public works project that America witnessed during the 1950s). Highways were an imperative for people who were rapidly purchasing automobiles so that they could move to the suburbs (encouraged by federal subsidies of home mortgages) and shop at the mall. Should it be a surprise to find these highways, these oddly public creations that facilitated private consumption, inadequately supported? Not so for Galbraith who once complained to Schlesinger about "highways that are crowded with traffic, disfigured by billboards, and laced with trash and garbage." He had probably seen littered roads by simply driving outside of Boston to Cape Cod, where Harvard's professoriate often vacationed. Such trashy appearances gave off an important political and cultural message to Galbraith: the only thing that seemed to matter was private consumption or how the air conditioner functioned inside a person's car, not public expenditure or care for public goods, certainly not the appearance of public areas.[14]

What was especially egregious was how highways were supported by federal tax dollars and yet facilitated the growth of shopping malls, motels, drive-in restaurants, and other private industries. The interstates channeled people, led them to certain places and not to others. They created a social environment in which public dollars helped buck up private industries and profit. Of course, Galbraith and Schlesinger weren't socialists. They believed in private industry but didn't like how private industry took advantage of public expenditures (the way stockgrowers out West wanted to).

Take television as a classic example. One of the biggest scandals in American culture during the late 1950s drove home this point. In 1958, it was discovered that the quiz show *Twenty-One* had been rigged. The show was part of a larger mania that had taken the country by storm ("movie theaters stopped their shows" and "bar patrons riveted their attention en masse" to tune in quiz shows). Charles Van Doren, a quintessential egghead himself, had pretended to be quizzed, sweating in an isolated booth and looking as if he were thinking hard about trivia questions, when in fact he had been fed the answers. Typically the discovery that *Twenty-One* was rigged is depicted as an event of great cultural disillusionment in America (as it was, for instance, by Robert Redford in the film *Quiz Show*).

But for Schlesinger the problem was *political*. He pointed out that the Communications Act of 1934 empowered the Federal Communications Commission (FCC) to grant licenses to networks that were to utilize the public airwaves in order to "serve the 'public convenience, interest, or necessity.'" That is, the public airwaves belonged to the people. When faced with something like the quiz show scandal, Schlesinger saw no reason government shouldn't step in to improve the quality of the public's fare. "Why," Schlesinger asked, "should the national government stand helplessly by while private individuals, making vast sums of money out of public licenses, employ public facilities to debase the public taste?" In fact, NBC, the hosting channel of *Twenty-One*, offered "free time for a series of presidential debates the following year," but it's likely that Schlesinger saw this as chump change when considering the sort of profits NBC had been making. The quiz show scandal illustrated that the public needed to seize back what was being lost to a society that prioritized entertainment, television, and consumerism.[15]

Some might have thought that shows like *Twenty-One* were simply sources of entertainment for the masses. Perhaps, but this point overlooks a more important one. The "private opulence and public squalor" that Galbraith and Schlesinger worried about hurt people on the lower end of the economic spectrum most of all. The wealthy might be able to purchase necessary services ignored by America's private prosperity (private schools stand out as an example), but the poor could not. When in 1951 Galbraith argued to attack the problem of the "poverty belt in American agriculture" (one that could be found in the deep South and Appalachia), he championed "better schools" and "local health services." He would continue to make this point up through his time in the Kennedy administration, arguing that "parks and swimming pools" supported by public dollars mattered to the poor more than the rich. "Public services have," he explained, "a strong redistributional effect." The problem with a consumer culture was that it encouraged middle- and upper-middle-class citizens (especially) to mistake their own private opulence for social well-being. Again, the problem wasn't one of liking or not liking tailfins or commercial jingles on the radio but rather of worrying that these things allowed citizens to ignore the problems incurred by "public squalor" and social imbalance. This was no critique based on elitism but one that concerned itself with the status of those at the bottom of America's economic hierarchy. And it is this concern that stands as the basis of qualitative liberalism.[16]

The Challenge of Qualitative Liberalism

In 1948, Bernard DeVoto and Arthur Schlesinger helped form a History Book Club. The idea was to have qualified historians (not necessarily academics) choose books they believed deserved a wide audience, some-times books that might not appear immediately entertaining to readers. Was this about championing a certain taste? Certainly, but it was also about a desire to create a voluntary association that stood between the lone consumer and the profit-driven book company (giving cultural weight to their theory of civic pluralism). Similarly, in 1953 Galbraith worked on an "Educational Television" initiative in Iowa that tried to provide high-quality programs to as large an audience as possible, an initiative that Reinhold Niebuhr applauded more in the abstract. What these voluntary efforts on the part of Schlesinger and Galbraith show is that liberal intellectuals were not alienated from mass culture. Instead, Schlesinger and Galbraith tried to provide an alternative to mass culture, finding voluntary mechanisms that could offer consumers more choices than what were presently being offered and therefore keep alive cultural products that might be ignored by vendors concerned with the bottom line. In the words of Reinhold Niebuhr, liberal intellectuals hoped to uphold "the breadth and depths of the arts" (be those literary works of history or shows about arts on television) "against the vulgarities of mass communications." They believed the intellectual might be able to change things for the better by helping to form intermediary institu-tions that stood between the corporate entities merchandising cultural products and consumers.[17]

Schlesinger and DeVoto pulled out of the book club because of disputes with other members, and it's not clear how sustained a relationship Galbraith maintained with educational television in Iowa. But both incidents are important to note for what they tell us about these intellectuals' relation to mass culture. Contrast their engagement with the reaction of their predecessor intellectuals who, after World War I, faced disillusionment with not only the war but the business culture that dominated the 1920s. Many key thinkers, including Ernest Hemingway, Harold Stearns, Malcolm Cowley, and Matthew Josephson, left for Europe during the 1920s in order to escape what they perceived as the inherently anti-intellectual and materialistic nature of American public life. In contrast, Schlesinger and Galbraith committed themselves to improving the status of American public culture. Their voluntary work failing, they started to reason that they could look to government in order to embrace a public interest and improve the quality of American civilization. In 1960, Schlesinger was outlining what he called a "national cultural policy" to do precisely this. This served as a central element in the informal platform of qualitative liberalism. It showed that the liberal mind was starting to think about the ways public purposes could be defended and nurtured by government.

Looking ahead to the 1956 presidential campaign, Schlesinger defined the idea of "qualitative liberalism" in some published articles and a memo entitled "Liberalism, The 'Middle-of-the-Road' and the Democratic Campaign." The central idea was straightforward. Schlesinger defined qualitative liberalism against "quantitative liberalism," which was "oriented against the unemployment, poverty and economic insecurity" and addressed these problems through "quantitative terms—in terms of raising mass living standards, of minimum wages, of farm price supports, of salvation through appropriation." Quantitative liberalism could be found in "the New Deal" and "to a large extent" Truman's "Fair Deal." In contrast, "qualitative liberalism" became more appropriate for a society that had achieved a certain level of economic prosperity through growth. Schlesinger made clear that qualitative liberalism was not opposed to quantitative liberalism but rather that it "absorbed the triumphs of the New and Fair Deal" and "moved beyond them" to aim at "improving the *quality* of the lives people live." Qualitative liberalism grew directly out of the mass culture critique found in America in the 1950s. It addressed, Schlesinger pointed out, the "spiritual uncertainty and anxiety" and "spiritual malaise" that accompanied prosperity and comfort. "It is this situation which provides 'qualitative liberalism' its challenge and its opportunity," Schlesinger explained.[18]

Qualitative liberalism was therefore the concrete political reform resulting from Galbraith's and Schlesinger's observations that the "affluent society" increased both "private opulence" and "public squalor." Schlesinger argued in his 1955 memo,

> The great point to be made is that this country is richer than ever before, and is getting even richer every moment—but it is devoting a *decreasing* share of its wealth to the common welfare. Our national wealth increases—but our schools become more crowded and dilapidated, our teachers more weary and underpaid, our playgrounds more crowded, our cities dirtier, our roads more teeming and filthy. . . .

The political conclusion was obvious: buff up the public sector and thereby enrich the community. Concretely, this meant improving the way Americans planned their cities and especially their sprawling suburban environment (Schlesinger was writing just as the number of Americans living in suburbs was topping that of city dwellers), increasing public investment in public schools, reforming the American health care system, and creating a national arts and cultural policy to counteract the pernicious tendencies of mass culture. Qualitative liberalism was also a natural extension of DeVoto's and Woodward's struggles. Thus, Schlesinger believed qualitative liberalism had to tackle the problem of the "unkempt" status of "our national parks" as well as to acquire "equal rights for minorities." Galbraith added to this growing list of qualitative liberalism's goals "urban redevelopment, housing and transportation." To create public opulence would put the public sector on new ground. Instead of public works addressing the immediate needs of the unemployed, the way they did during the New Deal by putting people back to work, they would now symbolize the importance of the public sector for its own sake, for the pride it symbolized and for its message of shared sacrifice and belief in a commonweal.[19]

In so doing, qualitative liberalism would rejuvenate a sense of national purpose. The consumer culture that was fast growing up around him, Schlesinger argued, could not "achieve for our own citizens what Herbert Croly used to call the promise of American life, for that is a moral and spiritual promise." By showing that community and public life mattered (and what showed this better than investing in it and correcting for its present slovenliness?), Americans could identify not just as consumers but as citizens who were part of a larger national community, as members of something that went beyond individuals. Schlesinger was not seeking the belonging incurred by a tight-knit homogeneous community (the nation was simply too diverse for that anyway) or the sort of absolute sacrifice incurred by war (he had faith in liberty and the right to privacy about which his friend Isaiah Berlin was writing). But he thought that unchecked private desires without any reminder of public obligation was a dangerous path for any country to take. And so Schlesinger called for "a shift from the private motives of the last decade to a new dedication of public purposes." Without a sense of national purpose, there could be no victory for African Americans struggling for full equality, no chance of improving national parks, and no chance of improving the collective lives of all Americans. A sense of national belonging and civic membership were crucial prerequisites for qualitative liberalism.[20]

In pledging himself to this vision of national purpose and qualitative liberalism, Schlesinger drew inspiration from the New Deal. After all, FDR had helped develop, in Schlesinger's own words, "new energies in a people who had lost faith." Qualitative liberalism needed to do the same thing, and, although it faced different circumstances, it could never break completely from the past. Schlesinger cautioned his fellow eggheads not to "sneer at quantitative liberalism" because they "owed too much to this tradition and the generation which executed it." The real challenge for qualitative liberalism was a competing version of liberalism that arose after the New Deal, one that prioritized economic growth as the only way to ensure full employment. This vision saw government's role as limited to stimulating the economy through fiscal means rather than engaging in direct regulation of economic activity. As Galbraith pointed out, "almost everyone in the United States is a Keynesian" (in fact, *Time* magazine ran a cover headline to that effect six years after Galbraith made his declaration). Nonetheless, there were liberal and conservative Keynesians and big differences between them.

Conservative Keynesians stressed things such as tax cuts as a means to grow the economy by putting more money into circulation and thus bulking up buying power and "demand." It was this sort of conservative Keynesianism that Schlesinger and Galbraith disparaged, precisely because it divested the public sector of necessary funds and thus threatened the programs of qualitative liberalism. Conservative Keynesianism also fetishized growth as an end in itself, with no larger purpose than upping the gross national product. If more Americans owned televisions things would be better, or so Galbraith thought conservative Keynesians believed. But just because there was more productivity and more money circulating in the economy, Galbraith argued, didn't mean American public life would improve. Nor could conservative Keynesians do anything about the new problem of inflation (although here we concentrate on the political and cultural aspects of Galbraith's arguments rather than the question of inflation).[21]

Galbraith was not arguing against growth here. Obviously an expanding economy ensured there would be jobs and fiscal resources. He knew the growing American middle class of the 1950s was important for national health. But in general, Galbraith's arguments were taken as critical of "post-Keynesian liberals," as Loren Okroi points out, because these economists "concentrated on maximizing aggregate output rather than pushing for social and economic change." One prominent Keynesian read Galbraith this way. Leon Keyserling, who had served under Truman on the Council of Economic Advisors, thought Galbraith had gone off the deep end and said so openly in the pages of *The New Republic*, prompting Galbraith to reply. Growth was essential to any liberal public policy, Keyserling argued, and to say otherwise struck him as sacrilege. Only continuous growth ensured Americans could solve the "two prime political problems of our times, . . . the vast impoverishment of millions of our citizens . . . and the vast impoverishment of our public services." Keyserling believed liberals needed to grow the economy, acquire public funds, and then put them to good use. But first grow the economy, Keyserling argued.

To a large extent, the heated debate that followed with Galbraith seemed really a matter of emphasis. For Galbraith believed in growth, but he thought liberals should stop putting this aim at the top of their agenda. He admitted in his response to Keyserling that this old New Dealer "does not minimize the importance of getting resources into public use, but he does continue to attach first importance to the rate of increase in total output." Growth, Galbraith pointed out, could simply generate more private wealth and consumerism and thus do nothing about addressing public squalor. Growth, without any direct corrective, does "not improve proportionately our public position, at least in the absence of a powerful determination to the contrary." Now was the time to deemphasize economic abundance and nurture public goods that could help enhance the quality of Americans' social experiences.[22]

Keyserling's approach to economic growth had a bit more tradition on its side. After all, Galbraith was breaking from Keynes's emphasis on upping economic demand for goods, and he had no track record for his political philosophy. It was not clear upon what foundation qualitative liberalism stood. Much of it seemed subjective. Take one of Galbraith's pet peeves: public architecture. As contemporary cultural theorists would be quick to point out, Galbraith's complaints about the public square were based on his own set of opinions about aesthetics. Galbraith admitted as much, "Those who are unwilling to pay for beauty and some elegance, and those who profit from commercial squalor, will be quick to say that [my] standards are too subjective and Americans cannot be concerned with them." Galbraith had little to say in reply to those critics; there *was* something subjective and aesthetic about qualitative liberalism. Seemingly it would be America's middle class, those already floating on a sea of prosperity, who would articulate the sort of demands Galbraith wanted pressed.

Schlesinger in fact placed a great deal of hope in middle-class reformers and intellectuals of his own day and age, those who were in politics not for their "livelihood" but because "they care deeply about issues and politics." At the same time, Schlesinger and Galbraith complained that the middle class of the 1950s had acquiesced to the comforts of prosperity. Galbraith argued that the Eisenhower administration suited "the comfortable and the contented and the unconcerned." But weren't these often members of the same middle class to whom qualitative liberalism needed to appeal? Finally, if the New Deal relied upon, as Schlesinger argued, a convergence of "discontent" represented by farmers, labor unions, social workers, and educated liberals, what power lay behind qualitative liberalism? Galbraith's earlier conception of countervailing power relied upon the material interests of labor union members and chain store operators looking to undercut the power of corporate producers. Qualitative liberalism, on the other hand, seemed to grow out of idealism, not always the best grounding for political commitment.[23]

This is what makes one of Schlesinger's earlier caveats so important: qualitative liberalism could never displace quantitative liberalism. The latter was still important, especially among the working classes and the poverty belt of the inner city and rural America. And qualitative liberalism needed to ensure its base by making certain the middle class remained stable. In addition, qualitative liberalism needed to build upon the strength of quantitative liberalism, suggesting perhaps a coalition between the poor and the middle class. The middle class might be motivated by aesthetic and moral concerns (anger at, say, the ugliness of highways, billboards, and sprawl) whereas the poor would be motivated by the material desire for making it into the middle class (which could only happen, so Galbraith reasoned, if they had access to public services such as education and housing). Under the right conditions (and unfortunately Galbraith and Schlesinger never elaborated on these things clearly enough) qualitative liberalism could work hand in hand with quantitative liberalism.

Although some might have questioned what exactly energized qualitative liberalism, Galbraith and Schlesinger believed they knew the answer: political leaders. They even had a person in mind, Adlai Stevenson. Stevenson was important because he differed from Truman, a politician who was part of the New Deal generation of Democrats and the Democratic Party machine. Because Stevenson didn't take his cues from those doling out political favors (or at least not as much as prior politicians), he could articulate a more idealistic and qualitative vision of politics. Schlesinger told Stevenson of a conversation that he had with Galbraith in 1955: "We feel that a key issue to be developed in the next twelve months is the anomaly of America's becoming simultaneously richer in wealth and poorer in public services and decencies under the Eisenhower administration." Indeed, the Finletter Group (which Galbraith organized with Schlesinger) advised Stevenson to make the 1956 campaign a combination of qualitative and quantitative liberalism, arguing that he should support the repeal of the Taft–Hartley Act (in order to support unions), attack Ike's unwillingness to raise taxes on the wealthy, follow DeVoto's advice against the public lands giveaway out West, support civil rights for blacks in the South, and increase public spending. Galbraith and Schlesinger certainly pressed their vision of national greatness upon Stevenson, and they had reason for hope inasmuch as their presidential candidate saw campaigning as a tool of popular education. Unfortunately, Stevenson seemed more comfortable focusing on questions of foreign policy rather than domestic policy. Besides, if the

1956 election could be considered a test case for Stevenson, there was little reason for optimism. He lost in a landslide.[24]

QUALITATIVE LIBERALISM AND JFK

Stevenson's loss in 1956 prompted some liberals to search for a new presidential candidate to run in 1960. Stevenson, after all, had lost two times in a row. Although Schlesinger and Galbraith respected Stevenson immensely, they thought he might have passed his prime and thus also started looking elsewhere. Galbraith had taught Joe Kennedy, the elder brother of Jack, at Harvard, and was thus introduced to one of America's most spectacular political families. Joe died during World War II, but his younger brother Jack went on to serve as a senator from Massachusetts, consulting with both Galbraith and Schlesinger (even briefly with DeVoto). Galbraith and Schlesinger both liked Kennedy for his energy, youth, and intellect (Jack had originally thought of becoming a writer). Essentially, JFK seemed like one of them. Schlesinger described him as a "man of action who could pass easily over to the realm of ideas and confront intellectuals with perfect confidence in his capacity to hold his own." He was also "an ironist" who did not allow "irony" to "sever the nerve of action." As Galbraith and Schlesinger grew attracted to JFK, they wondered how to break the news to Stevenson. The news was not well received. Nonetheless, they thought it best for the cause of qualitative liberalism.[25]

Galbraith and Schlesinger consoled themselves with the hectic nature of a political campaign. They immediately started to counsel JFK and crafted a vision through the speeches written for him. To make JFK a candidate who spoke to America was not necessarily an easy task, for many perceived few differences between him and the other candidate, Richard Nixon. As Schlesinger pointed out, both candidates appeared as "cool cats" and "junior executives on the make." But he argued that Nixon personified David Riesman's "other-directed" personality type, someone who had few internalized principles and took his cues in life from others. Nixon seemed obsessed with image (although, it will always be remembered, not enough to shave before participating in a nationally televised debate with JFK).

Beyond these personal attributes, the most important thing was that Kennedy wanted to reassert "national purposes" and fulfill the "real promise of American life." Galbraith added some substance to this stylistic view by arguing that Nixon criticized public spending on the basis of thrift. What mattered in the election, Galbraith explained, was the very different "attitudes towards public service" between Democrats and Republicans. Looking back on the 1960 campaign, the historian Steven Gillon confirms what Schlesinger and Galbraith believed at the time: "The platform that Kennedy supported was the most liberal in the party's history and echoed much of the ADA's program." It's no wonder JFK got egghead support. They were not just voting for one of their own but for someone they believed had championed the cause of liberalism and national greatness.[26]

Their mutual support of Kennedy helped cement Galbraith's and Schlesinger's friendship. (Niebuhr, like some other liberals, disliked Kennedy because he didn't do enough to oppose Joe McCarthy while in the Senate, and Wechsler saw the president as little more than a "charm boy.") They worked together on the campaign, traveling the country to stump for the candidate and writing numerous speeches. Galbraith would write up questions and answers about economics for Kennedy to prep for press conferences, and Schlesinger dashed off memos with political advice often grounded in history. Both agreed Nixon would target Kennedy's lack of experience. But they argued that the vice president was not as well experienced as some thought. In one memo, Galbraith alluded to Nixon's debate with Khrushchev, quipping that "one does not learn how to deal with Khrushchev by talking with him for a few minutes in a kitchen."

Schlesinger was especially concerned that liberals seemed to be peeling off from Kennedy's campaign and kept pressing how important they were to him (their idealism, he argued, was a key source of his political support). Not surprisingly, both thinkers pressed the theme of public squalor and private opulence on the candidate, and Galbraith took the time to show how more public spending was different from "creeping socialism" (a key term used by Eisenhower and Nixon). Galbraith pressed a tougher stance on civil rights, as did Schlesinger. These policies could be articulated under the wider rubric of national greatness, they argued. Schlesinger, in one memo to the president, explained that Americans needed to be reminded of their "historic mission. This becomes the campaign theme. America is not finished, nor is it rich, fat, and lazy." Qualitative liberalism and national greatness thus should serve as the campaign message, as far as Galbraith and Schlesinger were concerned.[27]

Among liberal intellectuals, Galbraith and Schlesinger stood out. Not only were they smart and helpful, but they differed from liberals who criticized JFK (some who backed Hubert Humphrey or Stevenson). Joe Rauh of the ADA wrote Jimmy Wechsler, describing Kennedy as "friendly but not adequately liberal." Wechsler concurred, having supported Hubert Humphrey in 1960. He believed rightfully that Kennedy, as a senator, had been silent on McCarthy and was too hawkish on military matters. The ADA itself would remain critical of JFK in terms of his weak stance on civil rights during the earliest part of his administration. And generally, many in the ADA saw JFK less as a committed liberal and more as a technocrat. It is no surprise then that in trying to figure out who to ask to work for him, JFK rewarded those who had been loyal and helpful. Schlesinger became Special Assistant to the President, and Galbraith was sent to India as an ambassador.[28]

The Perils of Power

More than ten years before accepting his position as Special Assistant to the President, Schlesinger wrote, "Our democratic tradition has been at its best an activist tradition. It has found its fulfillment, not in complaint or in escapism, but in responsibility and decision." In these words can be read Schlesinger's rationale for the decision he made to enter the halls of power. He had always been a realist who accepted the responsibilities that came with power (what the German sociologist Max Weber once called the "ethic of responsibility"). Now sitting within the seat of power he could see what this actually entailed. Under JFK, he later wrote, the "intellectual was no longer merely consultant or adviser but responsible official." This new job obviously had major challenges. It's easy to imagine Schlesinger first entering the Oval Office and hearing a whisper in the back of his mind, one that came from Niebuhr and warned about the self becoming infatuated with the pride of power. Galbraith too worried about what he was about to do when crossing from a life of the mind to a life of power and politics. "To rationalize and explain and cover up as Washington requires will come very hard," Galbraith wrote in his journal. This would serve as a key challenge as these two thinkers embarked on the project they held dear to their hearts: the merging of intellect and politics.[29]

Not surprisingly, the liberal ironist found the world of politics full of its own ironies. Schlesinger recalled his first day in the Oval Office, shaking JFK's hand and then saying, "I'm not sure what I'm supposed to be doing here." "Neither am I," Kennedy responded. This was a good beginning, for Schlesinger's position remained ill-defined. Tevi Troy argues that Schlesinger's role in the Kennedy administration was minimal. He worked on creating a presidential library, provided general advice (sometimes historical, sometimes political in nature), and served as a bridge to the intellectual community. He was also a "liberal lightning rod, giving cover to the rest of the staff." Lawrence Freedman agrees, saying that Schlesinger "spent much of his time keeping lines open to liberals and soothing their bruised egos." Although Schlesinger certainly did these things, he also remained an activist who tried to take up some key elements of qualitative liberalism and put them into practice. Most important was the national arts policy he had envisioned before taking the job.[30]

Schlesinger did a great deal to get intellectuals and artists invited to the White House, in order to show that the Kennedy administration, unlike its predecessor, cared about culture and intellect. The poet Robert Frost spoke at Kennedy's inauguration of the "next Augustan age," and part of Schlesinger's role was to try to make the poet's grandiose words a reality. In addition to helping arrange musical performances, Schlesinger invited the great sage Walter Lippmann for dialogues with the president and got the literary critic Alfred Kazin to visit and write a story about JFK for the *American Scholar*. The story was a mixed bag, seeing as it argued that Kennedy was certainly "highbrow" but not as promising as some thought. The president ribbed Schlesinger about the article. But this didn't stop Schlesinger from continuing to push JFK to improve the image of the White House in cultural and intellectual terms. When the great cellist Pablo Casals played at the White House, Schlesinger praised JFK, saying that such an event helped "transform the world's impression of the United States as a nation of money-grubbing materialists." Schlesinger saw Kennedy as continuing the fight in the cultural Cold War begun when the CCF originally emerged ten years earlier.[31]

But this was the superficial aspect of Schlesinger's work. A cello performance does not a national cultural policy make. So Schlesinger set to work creating a policy that could have longer-lasting ramifications. He knew that this would require political care, so he called upon someone who had identified himself as an Eisenhower Republican,

August Heckscher. Schlesinger and Galbraith both knew Heckscher as the director of the Twentieth Century Fund (TCF), a nonprofit policy organization whose board Galbraith and Schlesinger had joined by 1960. Heckscher had been influenced by the liberal intellectual Adolf Berle, who played a leading role at TCF, and his thinking started to become remarkably similar to the qualitative liberalism of Schlesinger and Galbraith. He had issued a paper from TCF that asked the question "Production for What?" Heckscher answered this question in ways similar to Galbraith's *The Affluent Society*. When Schlesinger asked Heckscher for help in creating a national arts policy, the director of TCF had just published *The Public Happiness* (1962). In this breezy and loosely organized book, Heckscher complained about a world of "advertising, commercialism, and public relations" that corrupted Americans' conception of happiness, in ways akin to Schlesinger's and Galbraith's arguments. Heckscher hoped to build a higher quality of "civilization," a term he used throughout the book, by improving the status of public architecture and art and cutting down on urban sprawl. He offered few concrete suggestions how to do any of this. So when Schlesinger asked him to help construct a national arts policy, it's not surprising that Heckscher jumped at the chance to put some meat on the bone.[32]

Schlesinger created the position that Heckscher moved into in March 1962 and made the transition for him as easy as he could. Heckscher remained director of TCF and planned to resign his position in the White House after only a year's service (which he did in May 1963). He had done some work under the Eisenhower administration on a national cultural policy (during which time a national cultural center, what would become the Kennedy Center for the Performing Arts, was conceptualized). But he believed that JFK brought new energy to this sort of initiative and was excited to be working with Schlesinger. Therefore, he might have been disappointed by his first meeting with the president in August 1962, where Kennedy took a "go-slow" approach, chafing at any direct federal subsidies to artists and suggesting that Heckscher survey only what presently existed in terms of federal and nonfederal support for the arts.

Although Heckscher, Schlesinger, and JFK agreed that the federal role in the arts would be kept to a minimum, that consensus did not prevent a flurry of open discussion about different ideas between August 1962 and May 1963. Along with conducting the survey that the president requested, Heckscher and Schlesinger debated different policy possibilities, such as changing federal tax law to make contributions to cultural institutions less burdensome, helping arts education programs in local communities, directly subsidizing state arts agencies, and creating an awards system for artists that would be run from the White House. These discussions reflected the seminar-style of government that JFK loved, including its productive and too often open-ended and indecisive nature.[33]

Discussions did solicit several concrete outcomes. First, the national cultural center proposed under the Eisenhower administration got closer to completion (it would be erected after Kennedy's death). Kennedy strongly backed this initiative, and Schlesinger plugged away at many of its details. Second, JFK's Executive Order 1112 of June 12, 1963, created an Advisory Council on the Arts. Schlesinger had argued for presidential action on this matter, knowing that Congressman Frank Thompson of New Jersey had been pushing similar legislation (as had Hubert Humphrey). The language used to justify the executive order had Schlesinger's ideas written all over it, declaring the purpose of the council to "promote and stimulate public understanding and recognition of the importance of the arts and cultural institutions to our national welfare and our international interests." Up until the time of JFK's assassination there was quibbling about the membership of the Advisory Council, Schlesinger constantly answering letters from this congressperson or that senator suggesting a friend or expert who seemed suitable. And this was part of the problem with the initiative: starting quite late in the course of the Kennedy administration, it always seemed a bit behind schedule, just getting started when the administration faced its awful fate in 1963.[34]

The third outcome from Schlesinger's and Heckscher's work was the one most expected: words on paper. On May 28, 1963, in preparation for the executive order, the White House released August Heckscher's report on "The Arts and National Government." The document reported on Heckscher's survey of what had been done to date. He spoke, in tones Galbraith must have warmed to, of the importance of the national mall and the beauty of the public architecture found there. He argued for the importance of the public environment in general, continuing themes developed in *The Public Happiness*. DeVoto would have been happy to see Heckscher write, "To shape an environment which meets the needs of men and women for a civilized existence is a long-range Federal interest going beyond mere preservation. The National

Parks should be seen in this light: they are important for recreation, but also, more broadly, as a means to fulfilling the characteristic American conception of the good life."

Heckscher also made clear that support for the arts had found a new justification that differed from FDR's earlier attempts to support the arts during the New Deal. Although the New Deal supported artists desperately searching employment during the Great Depression, the present interest in the arts had a deeper appreciation of the arts on their own grounds. "There has been a growing awareness," Heckscher wrote in words akin to Schlesinger's, "that the United States will be judged—and its place in history ultimately assessed—not alone by its military or economic power, but by the quality of its civilization." And so Heckscher gave expression to the dreams of qualitative liberalism in explaining why the federal government should take up the long-term project of supporting the arts as a means of improving the quality of public life.[35]

While Schlesinger tried to turn his idea of a national cultural policy into a reality, Galbraith served as a diplomat to India. His appointment as ambassador might at first seem odd. Why didn't JFK appoint him as an economic advisor? Galbraith's economic views would probably have been too controversial for the Kennedy administration, even too radical for JFK's own predilections. There were also some bitter memories of Galbraith's work at the OPA that would have angered the business community. Besides, Galbraith had always been deeply interested in questions of international aid and India itself, a country that played a central role in Cold War international politics. Its leader Jawaharlal Nehru pledged himself to neutralism, urging a third way between the Soviet Union and America. Galbraith and other liberals believed America faced a special challenge in making a direct appeal to Nehru, to show that America could provide aid and help and thereby win over a country not through military intervention but by living up to its own democratic ideals.

In many ways, India served as a test case for putting Galbraith's and Schlesinger's "qualitative liberalism" into global practice. When he went on *Meet the Press* in 1961, just on the heels of being appointed ambassador, Galbraith was asked what it was like shifting gears from being an American social critic to being an ambassador for the United States. His response was what would be expected: he believed he could be both critic and ambassador at once. "Much of the American charm," he explained, "lies in the fact that we [Americans] talk so much about ourselves. . . . If we only praised ourselves, we would be a very dull society and we wouldn't be loved anywhere." Galbraith's statement captured the challenge of making qualitative liberalism less of an idea and more of a reality.[36]

The ambassadorship proved just as murky a challenge as Schlesinger's ill-defined position within the White House. Nehru was a difficult man to negotiate with, especially when pushed by his pro-Soviet Defense Minister Krishna Menon. The legacy of Dulles's arch-anticommunism only added to Galbraith's difficulties. During his brief ambassadorship (it lasted just two years), Galbraith had to deal with Nehru's threat to buy Soviet missiles when the United States had to cut aid briefly. He succeeded in part by pointing to the creation of the Peace Corps and a general rise in American economic aid to India. Galbraith argued that America needed to give more than just money to India; it needed to give technical aid (what the Peace Corps promised) and support for education (Galbraith visited India's schools on a regular basis).

Economic aid, as it had under the Marshall Plan, had a lesson to teach Americans as well. The United States needed to accept the fact that economic assistance would go toward projects that were antithetical to free market ideology. Ironically, though, Galbraith's biggest success came not in the form of economic or technical aid but in his pledge of military support to India in order to fight off a Chinese invasion during the Sino–India War of 1962. This diplomatic wedge allowed Galbraith to improve relations between India and America more than anything else. It also gave him a brief opportunity to articulate the importance of keeping India on America's side, something that Galbraith continued to argue required economic, educational, and technical assistance—only this could ensure America could hold the attention of this third world country that refused alliance to American ideology based on words alone.[37]

Insider Critics

Both Schlesinger and Galbraith knew that something changed once they accepted positions within the Kennedy administration. They could no longer think of themselves as freewheeling intellectuals speaking truth to power. Acquiring power had changed that, for it provided not just the chance to see ideas being turned into practice but also the need to defend decisions before a wider public, that is, the ethic of responsibility. It is too easy to see these thinkers' decisions to join up with Kennedy as a sellout of principle. Intellect certainly changed as it entered the corridors of power, but it did not relinquish its claim to truth. Looking back in 1966 on his time in the Kennedy administration, Schlesinger argued, "It is entirely possible to deal with practical realities without yielding inner convictions; it is entirely possible to compromise in program and action without compromising in ideas and values." Critics from the left, such as Christopher Lasch, doubted this. For Lasch, Schlesinger's "pragmatism" illustrated a desire to "demonstrate . . . toughness and practicality" and thus a surrender of the real demand intellectuals should take to heart: to "imagine other alternatives" to existing political realities and the demands of power. Schlesinger, from this perspective, had surrendered the one thing that made an intellectual truly an intellectual: the ability to go beyond existing power structures and engage in social and political criticism.[38]

Certainly there were perils in Schlesinger's and Galbraith's decisions to serve in the Kennedy administration. The ethics demanded by their liberal worldview—passion infused with irony—already made this clear. But more important, neither thinker gave up on criticism even when working for the president. They knew that the ethic of responsibility demanded they be critics if necessary. This was clear from the beginning. For as much as Kennedy hoped to define his administration via the high-minded ideals of the "New Frontier," one of his first high-profile moves as president was the Bay of Pigs fiasco, when he approved the CIA's support of a band of anticommunist rebels and their botched attempt to overthrow Castro. When Schlesinger and Galbraith caught wind of the plan, they both protested. In late March, Schlesinger frantically wrote JFK two memos saying that he had met with American journalists who had heard of the plan simply by hanging out with Cuban exiles in Miami. If these journalists could learn so easily about it, wouldn't Castro know and be able to stop the invasion? Schlesinger argued to JFK.

At the same time that Schlesinger warned the president about the practical difficulties of such a high-profile risk, Galbraith spoke to broader concerns. Learning of the invasion, he wrote Kennedy in order to praise him for his "conservative, thoughtful, non-belligerent stance" in foreign affairs. Although he didn't mention the Bay of Pigs, his intention was clear. Neither his nor Schlesinger's plea worked, of course, but they made clear that Schlesinger and Galbraith were willing to speak truth to power even as part of the power structure itself. But there were limits here, seeing as Schlesinger and Galbraith could not speak *out* to the wider public as much as they could speak *in* toward the rest of the administration.[39]

The same thing occurred during one of Kennedy's major domestic initiatives, his decision to cut taxes, an idea that originated early on in the administration's life but only became reality after Kennedy's assassination. For Galbraith, JFK's decision here represented the conservative Keynesianism he had always despised. Nothing stopped him from continuing this protest even as ambassador. After all, qualitative liberalism could not survive if the president drained the public coffers, as any tax cut would necessarily do. In 1961, Galbraith wrote the president that "I am against a tax cut." In 1963, just as Kennedy had made the tax cut "must" legislation, Galbraith wrote the president again that he was "still not reconciled to tax reduction," being "alarmed at the applause" the proposal gained "from the wrong people" (in this case, corporate leaders and the wealthy). Galbraith rightfully believed the tax cut would prevent the president from doing something bigger, such as supporting an "assistance program for families of unemployed" and providing "loans for public facilities in towns with serious unemployment" or even a "Youth Conservation Corps" that could assist "unemployed teenagers." In 1963, still protesting the tax cut, he would bundle these sorts of initiatives under the rubric of a "Civil Equality Drive," linking it to his wider support for the civil rights movement. The protest, once again, failed, but it made clear that Galbraith was still a critic even when taking orders from the president.[40]

Galbraith did not stop with just these specific policy protests. He noted a general problem pervading the administration. After having just stepped into office, Kennedy received a memo from Galbraith. "If my experience of the last two or three weeks is fair," Galbraith complained, "I think the problem of the new Administration is going to be neither liberalism nor conservatism but caution. I am a little appalled at the eloquence of the explanations as to why things, neither radical nor reactionary but only wise, cannot be done." He continued to worry that the administration was "too professional—too aware of criticism." He noted an absence of "political buccaneers with a fine enthusiasm for action" among Kennedy's cabinet, arguing that the "New Frontier" lacked the passion of the New Deal. Here, Galbraith picked up on a central feature of the Kennedy administration that later critics (some in the New Left) honed in on: the president's "technocratic" side. It was the same concern that had worried Schlesinger during JFK's original campaign against Nixon. Although Kennedy was right to worry about *too much* passion entering politics—the warning provided by liberal irony—he too often forgot that liberalism still required idealism, energy, and commitment.[41]

If this criticism sounded an awful lot like the New Left's later critique of liberalism, the obvious cannot be forgotten: Galbraith served his president well, even when being a critic. So too did Schlesinger. Both tried to balance criticism with engagement. They did this by emphasizing those elements of Kennedy's administration they admired while also offering criticism where they thought it was deserved. Theirs was an "in-house" critique both literally and figuratively. Although they would offer a critique of the Bay of Pigs invasion (arguing that it put too much emphasis on military engagement and too little on other methods of diplomacy), they would tout the president's commitment to programs such as the Peace Corps and Alliance for Progress as well as his more adept handling of the Cuban missile crisis (during which time Kennedy rejected military solutions) and his work for a nuclear test ban. For Schlesinger, the missile crisis showed Kennedy's balance of "toughness and restraint" missing from the Bay of Pigs fiasco, whereas the test ban pushed the United States beyond the "illusion or language of total conflict" that the Cold War sometimes prompted, including JFK's own "brinksmanlike adventuring" that Galbraith saw in the Bay of Pigs imbroglio. Both Schlesinger and Galbraith praised the Peace Corps as an important outlet for youthful idealism and a well-rounded type of international aid.[42]

This same critical support is evident in domestic policy. Galbraith could criticize the president for his tax cut and a generally technocratic tone in the administration, and Schlesinger hoped for more action on a national cultural policy. Nonetheless, they both praised the president for his belated support for the civil rights movement in 1963. Kennedy began his presidency as someone who disliked what he referred to as "this goddamned civil rights mess," concerned only with the bad reputation the American South was gaining among third world countries in the midst of the Cold War. But by 1963, facing the pressure of the March on Washington, Kennedy would argue that America needed to confront the demand for civil rights as "primarily" a "moral issue." Schlesinger himself believed that this moral vision was always present within the Kennedy administration, captured in his sense of national greatness. "Civil rights is clearly the overriding domestic issue of our day," Schlesinger explained in January 1961, "and it is the moral crux which this presents to Americans that is going to be an organic part of the release of national energy which will be required if we are to have a full realization of the idea of the public interests and of the national welfare in the years to come." He would continue to press this point from 1961 onward, even when Kennedy didn't want to hear it. But Schlesinger also knew something that the civil rights movement leaders sometimes forgot: that as much as the civil rights movement relied upon morality to stake its claims, it also needed executive leadership to become a reality. Morality was not enough.[43]

This balanced approach—being at the same time both critic and partisan—sustained itself throughout Schlesinger's and Galbraith's tenure within the Kennedy administration. But at times it could falter. While in the White House, Schlesinger signed most of his letters to Jackie Kennedy "Love," reflecting the closeness of a family member rather than a public servant. Sometimes he sounded much less like an engaged intellectual than an effusive romantic when describing Kennedy during the early years. For instance, in his memoir *A Thousand Days*, he wrote that "the future everywhere, indeed, seemed bright with hope" and that "the capital city, somnolent in the Eisenhower years" now seemed "suddenly alive" and that the air had been once "stale and oppressive" but there now seemed "fresh winds blowing." And yet while he sounded effusive here, Schlesinger continued to hold, within his ideas, a tension that had marked qualitative liberalism all along. In the same article in which he praised Kennedy's moral commitment to civil rights, for instance, he also spoke of how JFK's presidency was due to "the existence of an inherent cyclical rhythm in our national affairs." There appeared a schizophrenic tone when Schlesinger discussed JFK's presidency: was it based on a moral vision, one that could serve as the basis of judgment in time of failure, or was it an historical inevitability based on mystical forces?[44]

Schlesinger's biggest problem emerged around his own pet cause of enhancing JFK's cultural leadership. Sometimes Schlesinger mistook intellectual style for concrete policy accomplishments. Kennedy, often prompted by his wife, was known for inviting writers, artists, and musicians to the White House. The Kennedys projected a style of so-phistication that writers at the time and historians since have noted. Schlesinger did this as well when he wrote in 1962 that the "government has already" shown "that American society, as symbolized by the Presidency, welcomes and honors artistic creation. In an Executive Mansion where Fred Waring once flourished, one now finds Isaac Stern, Pablo Casals, and the Stratford Players—and all this represents a revolution in the status of the serious arts." But perhaps it wasn't a revolution, just a change in taste. After all, Kennedy's national cultural policy was still fairly skimpy at the time that Schlesinger wrote those words. More important, Schlesinger seemed to be too prone to mistaking Kennedy's "wit" and commitment to "ideas" for real policy accomplishments. His friend Jimmy Wechsler, remaining distant from the administration as a journalist, never fell prey to this and pointed out, in 1963, that Kennedy had not accomplished a great deal. Even when the country was caught in the despair of Kennedy's assassination, Wechsler would remind his readers that Kennedy's "legislative program was stalled in the Congressional morass; the Alliance for Progress was floundering; his ability to rally the country was being disputed; there was an ominous lull in the battle for equal rights." Wechsler's points highlight that at times Schlesinger could do what many have done since: prioritize style over substance, image over policy.[45]

But too much can be made of this point. Kennedy's real problems had little to do with prioritizing style but rather the inherent limits of American politics. No matter how much Schlesinger might have hoped that Kennedy could represent the dreams of qualitative liberalism to the world, he could not make the world over. Much of his presidency became a process of reacting to different crises: to what took place in Cuba, to developments in other parts of the world, to the demands of civil rights workers. None of these were circumstances that Kennedy created, and many were problems inherited from the previous administration.

Similarly, Schlesinger's and Galbraith's ideas were not the only ones that vied for the president's attention. The administration had a much more conservative wing as well, seen in Dean Acheson and Dean Rusk in foreign policy and more conservative Keynesians in domestic policy. When Galbraith voiced his critique of Kennedy's tax policy, for instance, he knew others had won the debate. In the letter he wrote to Kennedy protesting the tax cut, Galbraith joked, "In accordance with Lenin's principles of democratic centralism, the decision having been taken I am lapsing into silence." Galbraith's ironic frustration here was that of an intellectual facing the fact that other voices, often with much more power and influence, had the ear of the president. In other words, Galbraith faced the "inordinately complex environment" of national politics that he had discussed as an abstraction before. The frustration of the intellectual in the Kennedy administration mirrored the larger frustration of liberal reform in an imperfect world, or, what Schlesinger, writing about Kennedy in 1965, would call "the paradox of power— that the exercise of power is necessary to fulfill purpose, yet the world of power dooms many purposes to frustration."[46]

With all of this in mind, we should not diminish the importance of these thinkers' vision. Certainly they could never accomplish all for which they hoped. But they already knew that by the time they entered the halls of power. Realism was inherent in their vision; it tempered their passion. Nonetheless, Galbraith and Schlesinger really did believe that Kennedy captured the better side of the American promise. They really did believe that a president could project an image of national greatness to the world and then try to live up to that image and coax citizens to as well. They thought the world a better place with a president who cared about the arts and who wanted to combat public squalor. Their vision was not realized during Kennedy's reign, but this failure should not be used to damn the vision itself. As with any vision, it could live beyond the time in which it was articulated. Precisely because it spoke of an American promise—a promise that transcended any specific president or political leader—it lives on today. Or so it might if we think harder about its possibilities in a changing world.

CHAPTER SIX

Tragedies and Conclusions

*The contemporary situation in Vietnam should certainly instruct us on
the limits of military power in the long cold war.*

Reinhold Niebuhr, 1955

*American liberalism certainly made its contribution to the mood that
led us into Vietnam. But liberal self-hatred can go too far.*

Arthur Schlesinger, 1969[1]

NOVEMBER 22, 1963 STANDS as a day etched permanently in America's
collective memory. Kennedy was shot to death that day, and so
ended, many people believe, a certain sense of national innocence and
hope. The murder weighed even more heavily on the figures studied
here, for obvious reasons. They had invested so much in Kennedy's
administration, not just their careers but their dreams. The tragedy was
felt politically, intellectually, and personally. Galbraith and Schlesinger
were together in New York City having drinks with Katherine Graham
of the *Washington Post* and *Newsweek* when they first received news of
Kennedy's fall to an assassin's bullet. Neither one of them could believe
it at first. They scrambled back in a daze to Washington in order to
attend the funeral. The daze didn't leave them anytime soon.

A month and a half after the assassination, Schlesinger wrote a friend,
"It has been a hard time—the worst I have ever known—and things do
not seem to get better, though I suppose I will snap out of it in due
course." As he wrote these words, he was tendering his resignation from
the White House, and Kennedy's successor, LBJ, who had asked him to
stay on, accepted it. Schlesinger left to write his book about the Kennedy
administration, *A Thousand Days,* and the sadness in which the book
was started never entirely left him. He became more gloomy and morose,

especially after witnessing the assassinations of Robert Kennedy (whose Senate run he had helped out with) and Martin Luther King in the tumultuous year of 1968. He started to note a form of violence inherent in the American character, one that he had rarely written about before. Galbraith, who had already resigned as ambassador when Kennedy was assassinated (turning his position over to Chester Bowles), simply described the "wretchedness of the time" that followed the murder. That expression was enough to describe the feel of those days for two people who had once been so hopeful.[2]

To add to the tragic nature of the event, the assassination took place in Dallas, Texas, a rising capital of America's burgeoning sunbelt. Just a few days before Kennedy appeared in Dallas, General Edwin Walker, a key spokesman for the "new right," had harangued that city's citizens, denouncing U.S. membership in the United Nations. Adlai Stevenson had recently visited Dallas only to face taunts and jeers. In *A Thousand Days*, Schlesinger pointed out that "Dallas school children applauded the news" of the assassination and that an anti-Kennedy sentiment had pervaded the city before and would live long after. The fact that Barry Goldwater, a senator from the state of Arizona, another sunbelt state, would run on a blatantly antiliberal message only a year after the assassination and the sick celebrations in Dallas should make clear that Schlesinger's and Galbraith's vision for America had not triumphed, at least not in the region that Bernard DeVoto had once called home. A liberal consensus never took hold in the Southwest, if anywhere in the United States.[3]

Death, of course, changes everything. We can only speculate what would have happened if Kennedy had lived. Historians generally avoid counterfactual speculation. Schlesinger, however, had had a boost of hope right before Kennedy's death, as he watched the president move to the left, captured in his willingness to embrace deficit spending and his consideration of more public sector expenditures, the sort that would have made Galbraith happy. By 1963, Kennedy had championed civil rights legislation and understood its moral significance. He had pushed through a weapons test ban that aimed to lessen the Cold War's arms race. But there is another area that historians continue to debate as they have for years: would JFK, as LBJ did in fact, have increased U.S. intervention in Vietnam? The question cannot be answered here, but its significance is crucial to consider at this moment because the Vietnam

War came to drown out everything else as the 1960s proceeded, even LBJ's "Great Society" program that these liberals embraced. If Kennedy's assassination was the first tragedy for liberalism during the 1960s, Vietnam was the obvious second one. It goes without saying that this war, in an area of the world Americans had known very little about before the mid-1960s, helped kill the liberal dream.[4]

Right before his death, Kennedy was certainly increasing America's intervention in southeastern Asia. Although he never gave direct approval to overthrow Ngo Dinh Diem, the dictator of South Vietnam that America had supported up until November of 1963, he had certainly come to believe that Diem was no longer worthy of U.S. support. He was also dispatching increasing numbers of military "advisors," hoping to prop up South Vietnam against the Vietcong and their communist brethren in the north. As Lawrence Freedman points out, the coup that took place against Diem in the same month Kennedy was assassinated presented a logic that seemed to "draw the United States even more deeply into responsibility for the government of the country and the prosecution of the war. It was by and large on this side of the argument [for the coup] that could be found some recognition that the events being set in motion could end with U.S. troops in combat." On the other hand, as the historian Fredrik Logevall documents in one of the most thorough histories of America's escalating intervention in Vietnam, Kennedy "in all likelihood" had "not decided" on the "day of his death" what "to do with his Vietnam problem. Like many politicians, he liked to put off difficult decisions for as long as possible." So JFK's plans were murky at best, pointing in different directions. What is certain is that LBJ pushed for further U.S. involvement in Vietnam. He made Vietnam an American war.[5]

So was the Vietnam War a logical extension of liberal anticommunism? Certainly the war was waged to prevent communism from spreading from North to South Vietnam, and thus some might argue the war was in line with Kennan's theory of containment. Certainly some liberal anticommunists supported the war (many of JFK's "best and brightest" continued under LBJ and lent support to the war). Certainly Kennedy seemed, in part, to drift toward commitment in 1963.

However, one needs to take note of the president's caution in this area. It cannot answer the question whether Kennedy would have dragged America into Vietnam the way Johnson did but his caution can help us ask a more important question in the context of this book: should liberal anticommunism, as a set of ideas, be seen as leading toward support of the war? After all, considering the extent of the Vietnam tragedy, with its death toll, destruction, and drain of the public coffers, it seems crucial to answer this question before drawing to a close. The question can be answered in the following ways. The first is to consider the world-view set out in this book, to get inside it, so to speak, and ask if it would seem to justify U.S. entry into the Vietnam War. The second is to extend the timeframe of this book a bit, if only very briefly, and ask what happened to the cast of characters considered here as they faced up to the increasing realities of the Vietnam War.

It seems obvious that Niebuhr's critique of national hubris would militate against U.S. entry into the war. Indeed, in 1955, he warned of the "limits of military power" in the "long Cold War," just as the United States was first starting to take up the slack of French colonial withdrawal from Vietnam. This caution was in line with the rest of his philosophy regarding American power abroad. It was a short step from warning about national hubris to arguing that if the United States intervened in Vietnam there would be a high price to pay. This was especially true considering that these liberals had seen Europe as the major stage for Cold War battles. A bond existed between Europe and the United States, a bond of shared history and "Western" democracy. Niebuhr didn't believe such a bond existed between the West and Asia (and the legacy of colonialism would temper whatever bond did exist), and he doubted, in language that some today would be uncomfortable with, that there was any "spiritual and cultural basis" for democracy in Asia.

There's no need to defend Niebuhr's cultural presuppositions here, just to remember that he never believed the Cold War could be easily extended into Asia, certainly not to a country like Vietnam. Considering this, it is no surprise to hear C. Vann Woodward, in 1972, recalling his critique of national hubris made back in 1959, and saying that he knew "there'd be wars like" Vietnam. The liberal critique of hubris and reliance on military power at the expense of other diplomatic initiatives seemed to dictate that. By all accounts, Cold War liberalism could easily turn into a critique of the Vietnam War.[6]

Indeed, John Kenneth Galbraith was one of the earliest liberal opponents of the war. As seen in the previous chapter, Galbraith was just as much a critic as a partisan of the Kennedy administration.

Seeing Kennedy supporting Diem in mid-1962, he zipped off a letter to the president, this one especially prescient: "I can't think Diem has made any significant effort to improve his government either politically or administratively or will. We are increasingly replacing the French as the colonial military force and we will increasingly arouse the resentments associated therewith." Galbraith sometimes hoped for a military coup, like the one Diem eventually faced, because at least that would rid the world of an awful dictator out of touch with the people. Still, Galbraith thought America might need to send in more "military police" and "security units," but he also wanted to move away from a purely military involvement in Vietnam (again in line with the general liberal outlook traced out here). "What about a combined corps of young Americans and young Viet Namese to rebuild villages and start schools?" Galbraith asked. What about more economic and diplomatic aid, he seemed to be hinting. Still, even while striking this optimistic note, he was deeply pessimistic about the situation: "Anyone who claims to have a formula for success and victory is fooling himself." And so this passionate ironist found himself opposed to Diem and further support but, at the same time, not clear what the next step should be.[7]

Johnson offered one answer to Galbraith's perplexed state, namely, to escalate the war. At that point, Galbraith quickly moved into opposition. He had given advice to Johnson and even written some speeches for him, like other "hangers-on" from the Kennedy administration. His position was therefore tricky, trying not to alienate the president but also standing firm. By the winter of 1965, Galbraith was arguing that "South Viet Nam is of no significant economic or strategic interest to the United States." He believed the "National Liberation Front" had "legitimate grievances" and that the United States should negotiate with its leaders. "The United States cannot," he warned "be a universal police power preventing revolts so motivated wherever they occur." Although he wouldn't go so far as to call for immediate withdrawal of troops, he did argue to "reduce air attacks on North Viet Nam" and open up negotiations. Whatever way possible, Galbraith argued, the United States should "limit" the "magnitude of our military commitment." Johnson, of course, ignored this point. And so by 1967, Galbraith was not only reenergizing ADA as an organization that would oppose the war but was ready to back Eugene McCarthy over Hubert Humphrey, the latter being too complicit with Johnson's policy in Vietnam.[8]

Schlesinger was slower in moving the way Galbraith did. After all, he had always been tougher when it came to fighting communism overseas, and so he stayed the course with LBJ a bit longer than Galbraith. Indeed, he even used the word "honor" in his defense of U.S. commitment to Vietnam in 1964, the sort of term that LBJ would later use to justify further escalation. But by 1965, he had his doubts. He wrote a letter to Sam Beer in May of that year that reflected his confusion about the situation: "I agree with you that ground forces are a risk; but I am sure that Johnson does not want to turn Vietnam into another Korea and that therefore the commitment will be limited. I fear that continued airstrikes will hurt us in the eyes of the world and make negotiation impossible."

Of course, Johnson did everything he could to turn Vietnam into something *more* than Korea, upping U.S. engagement and not simply containing the North but suppressing the National Liberation Front's fight within the South. By 1966, Schlesinger was saying what Galbraith had said a year earlier: stop the bombing, recognize the local nature of the Vietcong's struggle, and open up negotiations. By 1967, Schlesinger was more fully in Galbraith's camp, looking for anyone to oppose Hubert Humphrey, be it Robert Kennedy or Galbraith's own choice, Eugene McCarthy. And so Schlesinger and Galbraith's political friendship of the 1940s and 1950s carried through the tumultuous 1960s.[9]

What made Schlesinger slow to come to his Vietnam War opposition was likely a closeness to power. This can also be seen in the style of Galbraith's original protest. Never once did he lose his sense of civility. Because he and others "have been associated in the past with the government, and a few with this problem" of Vietnam, he pointed out, he "did not underestimate the difficulties involved." He knew "at first hand of the intelligence and dedication of those who have been seeking solutions," so he would not "engage in attacks and recriminations" that "have characterized so much of the debate on this subject." Galbraith's caution is understandable. It also contrasts with Niebuhr's early opposition to the war. After all, by 1955, Niebuhr expressed doubts about U.S intervention in Vietnam, and he remained independent of political power and therefore more critical of U.S. foreign policy, making his vision clearer by 1965 when he called the war "a scandal to the world." The same was true for Jimmy Wechsler, who, along with Niebuhr, had strong doubts about Kennedy. By 1965, he too called for an end to the bombings and for opening up negotiations. That made it unanimous: although Schlesinger would come a bit late, by 1965, all of the intellectuals studied here were critics of the course that America was taking in the Vietnam War. To call Vietnam the "liberals' war," as some have, is simply unfair.[10]

Nothing makes this clearer than when, in 1967, Galbraith, Schlesinger, and Wechsler met with Hubert Humphrey in a desperate attempt to convince the vice president that the Vietnam War was wrong. The meeting was awkward and made no better by the alcohol consumed. At one point, Schlesinger uncharacteristically lost his temper and screamed at his old political ally (although they always had their differences, Humphrey and Schlesinger knew one another from their work in the ADA during the 1940s). All three intellectuals now stood completely independent of political power in a way that Humphrey could never imagine. They argued that the bombing must cease, making a moral argument, but Humphrey insisted that the Joint Chiefs of Staff would never allow for such a thing. Sadly enough, Humphrey kept using the term "morass" to describe and justify why America was staying in Vietnam, frustrating the situation even more. This seemed an anemic justification for a policy so bloody and unending. Humphrey confessed his own guilt, making the meeting not only rancorous but sad. It made clearer more than ever that liberals were not unified, that Vietnam had created deep chasms, shattering consensus. The liberal worldview was no longer a cluster of ideas working together in synch but divided. All the while, as liberals screamed at one another, bodies kept piling up in Vietnam.[11]

The meeting between Humphrey and three of our main characters brings us full circle to the beginnings of this story, that is, the first years of the Cold War, those years when Humphrey and Schlesinger worked together as allies for the first time. At that time, liberals decided to resist alliances with fellow-traveling leftists. Responsibility dictated the need for a "fighting faith" of liberalism that took on enemies of the left as much as enemies of the right. Now, just twenty years later, liberals faced those who at first appeared to share values such as anticommunism but who were actually a new type of enemy. Evil, it was discovered, could be done in the name of liberalism—be it the "dough faced" progressivism of Wallace supporters that Schlesinger worried about in *The Vital Center* or the complicity that Humphrey admitted to with the "morass" of Vietnam. By the middle to late 1960s, there were new enemies on the left that helped remind liberals of their founding principles. Perhaps the most important one here was a critique of national hubris. As Schlesinger would write in 1969, "Little is more dangerous than a sense of world mission pushed too far or perceived too absolutely." Added to this was the lesson that liberalism could never rest easy. It would always have to mount protest in the face of power's abuse.[12]

* * *

If we disassociate the worldview traced here from the bloodbath of Vietnam, we are left with the question of what these liberal thinkers and activists accomplished. If there is an answer, it can be given by sketching the broadest outlines of the ideas and arguments these intellectuals left behind. First, and perhaps most fundamentally, the characters in this book showed how a passionate commitment to virtues and ideals could be balanced against complexity, nuance, and irony. In opposing totalitarianism, for instance, these thinkers and activists argued that their own brand of liberal anticommunism could not become fanatical. Nor should it transmute into a simplistic celebration of the American way of life. Rather, the variant of liberalism I have delineated here demanded Americans improve the quality of their own civilization, the shared resources that chastened the self-love dangerously engrained in human nature. This tradition prompted collective self-examination and thus prevented chauvinism and hubris, especially important as Americans turned their attention to the wider world and applied the demands of anticommunism to foreign policy. Liberalism called on Americans to embrace greatness, in the deeper and more complex sense of that term.

That's why these thinkers believed their ideals grew out of the mainstream of America's own history. They pointed to a tradition that stemmed from the Founding Fathers, Abraham Lincoln, and Franklin Delano Roosevelt. Sometimes these thinkers mistakenly took their own time as one of liberal consensus. Clearly, this was not the case as their own era and the history since the 1960s make brutally evident. These thinkers' vision lost—think Adlai Stevenson during the 1950s—just as much as it squeaked by to win—think JFK's 1960 election. There was always a hearty opposition from the right, one that continued to grow past the era on which this book focuses. The ideas delineated here might have grown out of a central tradition in American political thought and activism, but that did not mean they were ensured victory or acceptance across the country. Liberalism has always been a "fighting faith" that faced opponents. Indeed, the ideas explored here went down to defeat: first as New Left protestors made liberalism their enemy during the late 1960s and when the new right gained momentum and popularity from 1980 onward. Even so, the belief in the nation as a beloved community, an ideal at the center of the political thought traced in this book, will always linger if not always dominate American political debate. That the idea of a nation as beloved community can push us to conceptualize our public purposes better should be clear by now.

With this in mind, it would be hubris of a different kind to think that this tradition can solve the political challenges of the present. It would be especially wrong considering that these thinkers, as all do, made mistakes and could not always translate their ideas into concrete political realities. I have discussed mistakes as well as strengths in this book. If it seems that I focus more on the strengths, that is because I think we are more in danger of forgetting them today. Needless to say, times have changed since these thinkers wrote. We cannot apply the ideas found in books written fifty years ago or the advice given to politicians now dead to our present-day world. But it would be wrong to believe that the thinking and activism outlined here have no contemporary relevance. We can remember this history creatively today and think of American greatness in a subtle, ironic, and complex manner. This is not the place to do this; after all, this is a work of history, not contemporary public policy or political theory. Nonetheless, it has been my premise that if we started to think more creatively about national greatness and the liberal tradition from this time period, we could not just improve our understanding of the past but think more clearly about the present as well.

Notes

Notes to the Introduction

1 Reagan quoted in Gerald Pomper, "The Presidential Nominations," in *The Election of 1988: Reports and Interpretations*, ed. Gerald Pomper et al. (Chatham, NY: Chatham House, 1989), p. 65.

2 Buckley quoted in George Nash, *The Conservative Intellectual Movement in America* (Wilmington, DE: ISS, 1998), p. 136. See also John Judis, *William F. Buckley, Jr., Patron Saint of the Conservatives* (New York: Simon and Schuster, 1988) and Sidney Blumenthal, *The Rise of the Counter-establishment* (New York: Harper and Row, 1988).

3 Richard Flacks quoted in James Miller, *"Democracy Is in the Streets": From Port Huron to the Siege of Chicago* (New York: Simon and Schuster, 1987), p. 174; *Studies on the Left* editor quoted in Kevin Mattson, "Between Despair and Hope: Revisiting *Studies on the Left*," in *The New Left Revisited*, ed. John McMillian and Paul Buhle (Philadelphia: Temple University Press, 2003), p. 34. For more on the New Left attack on liberalism, see Ronald Berman, *America in the Sixties: An Intellectual History* (New York: Harper and Row, 1970), Chapter 5, and Todd Gitlin, *The Sixties* (New York: Bantam, 1987), p. 130. I should make clear that this attack on liberalism was only one strain within the New Left, one that became stronger as the 1960s proceeded, and that liberalism and the New Left shared a great deal more in common: see my *Intellectuals in Action: The Origins of the New Left and Radical Liberalism* (University Park: Pennsylvania State University Press, 2002).

4 Michel Foucault, *Discipline and Punish* (New York: Pantheon, 1977); on Foucault, see Thomas Haskell's excellent dissection in his *Objectivity Is Not Neutrality* (Baltimore: Johns Hopkins University Press, 1998).

5 Michele Mitchell, *A New Kind of Party Animal: How the Young Are Tearing Up the American Political Landscape* (New York: Simon and Schuster, 1980), p. 34. For more on Mitchell and young pundits who are critical of liberalism, see Kevin Mattson, *Engaging Youth: Combating the Apathy of Young Americans towards Politics* (New York: Century Foundation Press, 2003), Chapter Four. On neoconservatives, see Peter Steinfels, *The Neoconservatives* (New York: Simon and Schuster, 1979). The best communitarian critique of liberalism is the work of Michael Sandel in his *Liberalism and the Limits of Justice* (Cambridge, UK: Cambridge University

Press, 1982). See also Alan Brinkley, *Liberalism and Its Discontents* (Cambridge, MA: Harvard University Press, 1998), p. x.

6   Ann Coulter, *Treason: Liberal Treachery from the Cold War to the War on Terrorism* (New York: Crown, 2003).

7   Arthur Schlesinger, *The Vital Center: The Politics of Freedom* (1949; New York: DaCapo, 1988), p. 245; Archibald MacLeish at a dinner conference of Americans for Democratic Action (ADA), reprinted in *ADA World*, February (1951): 7. For the problem of entering the world of punditry and popular debate, see my "The Perils of Michael Moore," *Dissent*, Spring (2003): 75–81.

8   Alexander Bloom, *Prodigal Sons: The New York Intellectuals and Their World* (New York: Oxford University Press, 1986), pp. 201, 310; "deradicalization" comes from Howard Brick, *Daniel Bell and the Decline of Intellectual Radicalism* (Madison: University of Wisconsin Press, 1986); T.J. Jackson Lears, "A Matter of Taste," in *Recasting America*, ed. Lary May (Chicago: University of Chicago Press, 1989), pp. 38–39; for the point on the growing comfort of intellectuals during the Cold War, see Richard Pells, *The Liberal Mind in a Conservative Age* (Middletown, CT: Wesleyan, 1989), Chapter Three, and Stephen Longstaff, "The New York Family," *Queen's Quarterly* 83 (1976): 567. A more "classic" statement of this interpretation is found in Christopher Lasch, *The Agony of the American Left* (New York: Knopf, 1969).

9   There are numerous sources of the sort of historical research I allude to here. For a critique of liberal intellectuals in terms of the civil rights movement, see David Chappell, "Niebuhrisms and Myrdaleries: The Intellectual Roots of the Civil Rights Movement Reconsidered," in *The Role of Ideas in the Civil Rights South*, ed. Ted Ownby (Jackson: University of Mississippi Press, 2002), p. 4, and Tony Badger, "Fatalism, Not Gradualism: Race and the Crisis of Southern Liberalism, 1945–1965" and Walter Jackson, "White Liberal Intellectuals, Civil Rights, and Gradualism, 1954–1960," both in *The Making of Martin Luther King and the Civil Rights Movement*, ed. Brian Ward and Tony Badger (New York: New York University Press, 1996) as well as Carol Polsgrove, *Divided Minds: Intellectuals and the Civil Rights Movement* (New York: Norton, 2001), pp. 32, 37. For a view of liberal intellectuals as complicit with the CIA, see Frances Stonor Saunders, *The Cultural Cold War* (New York: Free Press, 2000) and Christopher Lasch, *The Agony of the American Left* (New York: Norton, 1969). For a more sweeping historical work that depicts liberal intellectuals as elitists, see Christopher Lasch, *The True and Only Heaven: Progress and Its Critics* (New York: Norton, 1991).

10 Reinhold Niebuhr, "Ten Years That Shook My World," *Christian Century*, April 26 (1939): 546.

11 On how, for instance, Arthur Schlesinger sought out Jimmy Wechsler due to their shared anticommunism in the 1940s, I rely upon Schlesinger's

remarks during Wechsler's funeral, found in the James Wechsler Papers, State Historical Society, Madison Wisconsin, Box 1 of Third Accessions.

12 Numerous sources exist on the New York Intellectuals, more than can be mentioned here. See for a helpful and concise treatment, Neil Jumonville, *Critical Crossings: The New York Intellectuals in Postwar America* (Berkeley: University of California Press, 1991) and the documentary movie, *Arguing the World*.

13 Edwin Yoder, *Joe Alsop's Cold War: A Study of Journalistic Influence and Intrigue* (Chapel Hill: University of North Carolina Press, 1995), p. 19; Bernard DeVoto to Ray Dovell, February 28, 1946, found in Bernard De-Voto Archives, Stanford University, Box Three. See also, Joyce Hoffman, *Theodore White and Journalism as Illusion* (Columbia: University of Missouri Press, 1995), p. 110; on the paperback revolution, J. Ronald Oakley, *God's Country: America in the Fifties* (New York: Red Dembner, 1990), p. 16; on Schlesinger's seriously considering journalism, I rely upon his correspondence with Barry Bingham, especially a letter he wrote on February 3, 1946, Arthur Schlesinger Papers, JFK Library, Boston, MA, Series One. For interesting comments on being a generalist, man of letters, and an editorialist, see Max Lerner, *The Unfinished Country* (New York: Simon and Schuster, 1959), pp. xvi–xvii. See also Neil Jumonville, *Henry Steele Commager: Midcentury Liberalism and the History of the Present* (Chapel Hill: University of North Carolina Press, 1999).

14 Eric Goldman, *Rendezvous with Destiny: A History of Modern American Reform* (New York: Knopf, 1952), p. 434; John Kenneth Galbraith, *Economics and Public Controversy* (New Brunswick, NJ: Rutgers University Press, 1955), p. 81; John Kenneth Galbraith, "Reflection on the Asian Scene," *Journal of Asian Studies* 23 (1963–64), p. 504; Daniel Bell, in *The Radical Right*, ed. Daniel Bell (Garden City, NY: Doubleday, 1964), p. 3. On Eisenhower's support for the New Deal, see R. Michael Oakley, *God's Country*, p. 157. On postwar exhaustion, see John Morton Blum, *V Was for Victory: Politics and American Culture during World War II* (New York: Harcourt Brace Jovanovich, 1976), p. 332.

15 For the general business push against the New Deal legacy, see Fred Siegel, *Troubled Journey: From Pearl Harbor to Ronald Reagan* (New York: Hill & Wang, 1984), p. 9, and Elizabeth Fones-Wolf, *Selling Free Enterprise: The Business Assault on Labor and Liberalism, 1945–1960* (Urbana: University of Illinois Press, 1994). There is general recognition throughout the ADA Papers of NAM's power and influence. For opposition to the Marshall Plan, see the *New York Post*, January 26, 1948, p. 2. For more on these conservative journalists, see Neil Gabler, *Winchell: Gossip, Power, and the Culture of Celebrity* (New York: Knopf, 1994); Oliver Pilat, *Pegler, Angry Man of the Press* (Boston: Beacon, 1963); and Booton Herndon, *Praised and Damned: The Story of Fulton Lewis, Jr.* (New York: Duell, Sloan and Pearce, 1954). More and more scholars have challenged

the "liberal consensus" model of postwar history: See Rick Perlstein, *Before the Storm* (New York: Hill and Wang, 2001) and Maurice Isserman and Michael Kazin, *America Divided* (New York: Oxford 2000), pp. 47–48.

16   Bernard DeVoto, "The Civilian Outpost," *Harper's*, March (1942): 446; Richard Lingeman, *Don't You Know There's a War On?* (New York: Putnam, 1970); Richard Polenberg, *One Nation Divisible: Class, Race, and Ethnicity in the United States* (New York: Penguin, 1980), pp. 48–49.

17   On rising hopes of African Americans during the war, see James Wechsler, "Pigeonhole for Negro Equality," *The Nation*, January 23 (1943): 122; Bernard DeVoto, *The Letters of Bernard DeVoto*, ed. Wallace Stegner (Garden City, NY: Doubleday, 1975), p. 176; Blum, *V Was for Victory*, p. 249; and John Patrick Diggins, *The Proud Decades* (New York: Norton, 1988), p. 21. Eleanor Roosevelt seemed most committed to fusing the humanitarian ethic of the New Deal to the war effort: see Lois Scharf, *Eleanor Roosevelt: First Lady of American Liberalism* (New York: Twayne, 1987). For more on issues of nationalism, see Benedict Anderson, *Imagined Communities* (London: Verso, 1983); on the difficulty of creating "obligation" within the American nation, see Robert Westbrook, "Fighting for the American Family," in *The Power of Culture*, ed. Richard Fox and Jackson Lears (Chicago: University of Chicago Press, 1993); on nationalism and American intellectual life, see Jonathan Hansen, *The Lost Promise of American Patriotism* (Chicago: University of Chicago Press, 2003); James Kloppenberg, "Aspirational Nationalism in America," *Intellectual History Newsletter* 24 (2002): 60–71; Yael Tamir, *Liberal Nationalism* (Princeton, NJ: Princeton University Press, 1993).

18   Archibald MacLeish, *A Time to Speak* (Boston: Houghton Mifflin, 1941), p. 109; Scott Donaldson, *Archibald MacLeish: An American Life* (Boston: Houghton Mifflin, 1992), pp. 333–334 and Richard Pells, *Radical Visions and American Dreams* (New York: Harper and Row, 1973), p. 314; Lewis Mumford, *Values for Survival* (New York: Harcourt, Brace, 1946), p. 37; Donald Miller, *Lewis Mumford* (New York: Weidenfeld and Nicholson, 1989), p. 419; Arthur Schlesinger on Lewis Mumford: Schlesinger, "Preacher Manque," *The Nation*, April 20 (1946): 473–474.

19   Reinhold Niebuhr, "The Crisis," *Christianity and Crisis*, February 10 (1941): 1; "Is the Bombing Necessary," *Christianity and Crisis*, April 3 (1944): 1; "Just or Holy?," *Christianity and Crisis*, November 3 (1941): 1; *Discerning the Signs of the Times* (New York: Scribner's, 1949), p. 139. For a treatment that sees more similarities between Mumford and Niebuhr than I do here, see Richard Fox, "Tragedy, Responsibility, and the American Intellectual, 1925–1950," in *Lewis Mumford: Public Intellectual*, ed. Thomas Hughes and Agatha Hughes (New York: Oxford, 1990). It should be noted that Niebuhr had been a critic of pacifism prior to World War II, which is not to say that World War II did not make an impact on his

political philosophy. It obviously did. On this point, see June Bingham, *Courage to Change* (New York: Scribner, 1961), pp. 109–110.

20 Reinhold Niebuhr to John Bennett, May 31 ("about 1940" written across top of letter), Reinhold Niebuhr Papers, Library of Congress, Box 42; "Limits of Liberty," *The Nation*, January 24 (1942): 87; "Civil Liberties in War Time," *Christianity and Crisis*, February 23 (1942): 1; "Ethics of Loyalty," *Confluence*, December (1954): 481. On Niebuhr's condemnation of America's treatment of Japanese Americans, see his "The Japanese Atrocities," *Christianity and Crisis*, February 21 (1944): 1.

21 Reinhold Niebuhr to David Dubinsky, October 7, 1941, Niebuhr Papers, Box 12; Arthur Schlesinger, "Arms and the Young Man," article written for the *Harvard Defense* in 1940, found in Box W-33, Arthur Schlesinger Papers; Bernard DeVoto to Elmer Davis, November 26, 1943, Bernard DeVoto Archives (Stanford University), Box 2; Galbraith to Professor Drummond, February 24, 1941, John Kenneth Galbraith Archives (JFK Library), Box 2. On *Christianity and Crisis*'s origins, see "Our Fifteenth Birthday," *Christianity and Crisis*, February 7 (1955): 1–3. On Niebuhr's service with OFF and OWI, see Richard Fox, *Reinhold Niebuhr: A Biography* (New York: Pantheon, 1985), pp. 207–208, 217. On Wechsler's induction, see Paul Milkman, *PM: A New Deal in Journalism, 1940–1948* (New Brunswick, NJ: Rutgers University Press, 1997), p. 193; Arthur Schlesinger, *A Life in the Twentieth Century* (Boston: Houghton Mifflin, 2000), p. 263; John Kenneth Galbraith, *A Life in Our Times* (Boston: Houghton Mifflin, 1981), Chapters 10–12; June Bingham, *Courage to Change*, p. 284.

22 Richard Lingeman, *Don't You Know There's a War On?*, p. 235; John Kenneth Galbraith, *The Great Crash* (Boston: Houghton Mifflin, 1955), p. 31; David Kennedy, *Freedom from Fear* (New York: Oxford University Press, 1999), p. 620; Meg Jacobs, "'How about Some Meat?': The Office of Price Administration, Consumption Politics, and State Building from the Bottom Up, 1941–1946," *Journal of American History* 84 (1997): 910–941. For Galbraith's difficulty in conveying the reasons behind price regulation to the American public, see materials found throughout the Galbraith Papers, Box 2.

23 Lizabeth Cohen, *A Consumer's Republic* (New York: Knopf, 2003), pp. 66–67, on the role of women, see p. 75; Jacobs, "'How about Some Meat?'" pp. 933, 912. For the impact of World War II on Galbraith, see his *A Life in Our Times*, p. 179. For how World War II consolidated America's economy, see Richard Adelstein, "The Nation as an Economic Unit: Keynes, Roosevelt, and the Managerial Ideal," *Journal of American History* 78 (1991): 160–187.

24 James Wechsler, "Landlords' Field Day," *The Nation*, February 15 (1947): 175–176; see *PM*, May 3, 1943, p. 5, for instance; James Wechsler, *Labor Baron: A Portrait of John L. Lewis* (New York: Morrow, 1944), pp. 234–244.

25   James Wechsler and Harold Lavine, *War Propaganda and the United States*
      (New Haven, CT: Yale University Press, 1940), p. 89; my account of the
      OFF and MacLeish draws from John Morton Blum, *V Was for Victory*,
      pp. 21–31. On the CPI, see Stephen Vaughn, *Holding Fast the Inner Lines*
      (Chapel Hill: University of North Carolina Press, 1980); on MacLeish's
      fear of re-creating the CPI's worst tendencies, see Brett Gary, *The Ner-
      vous Liberals: Propaganda Anxieties from World War I to the Cold War*
      (New York: Columbia University Press, 1999), pp. 152–153. For more
      on the transition from the OFF to the OWI, see William O'Neill, *A
      Democracy at War* (New York: Free Press, 1993), p. 140.

26   The memo on Japanese stereotypes comes from Gregory Black and Clayton
      Koppes, "OWI Goes to the Movies," *Prologues* 6 (1974): 54. On the lib-
      eral staff at OWI, see Koppes and Black, "What to Show," p. 88. On the
      movies' special problems for OWI, see Black and Koppes, "OWI," p. 51.

27   Arthur Schlesinger to Bernard DeVoto, April 1943, Bernard DeVoto
      Archives, Box 19. For more on this rift between advertisers and writers at
      OWI, see Malcolm Cowley, "The Sorrows of Elmer Davis," *The New
      Republic*, May 3 (1943): 591–592; Alan Winkler, *The Politics of Propa-
      ganda: The Office of War Information, 1942–1945* (New Haven, CT: Yale
      University Press, 1978), pp. 63–65; Sydney Weinberg, "What to Tell
      America?: The Writers' Quarrel in the Office of War Information," *Journal
      of American History* 55 (1968): 82; John Morton Blum, *V Was for Victory*,
      pp. 37–38; John Patrick Diggins, *The Proud Decades*, p. 157. On the War
      Advertising Council, see O'Neill, *A Democracy at War*, p. 253.

28   See on the distinction between the OWI and OSS, Clayton Laurie, *The
      Propaganda Warriors: America's Crusade against Nazi Germany*
      (Lawrence: University Press of Kansas, 1996), p. 3.

29   Jeffrey Isaac, *Arendt, Camus, and Modern Rebellion* (New Haven, CT: Yale
      University Press, 1992), pp. 21–22; William Graebner, *The Age of Doubt:
      American Thought & Culture in the 1940s* (Prospect Heights, IL: Waveland,
      1991), p. 18.

30   Bernard DeVoto, Commencement Address at Goddard College, 1954,
      found in Bernard DeVoto Papers, Box 49. Erika Doss, "The Art of Cul-
      tural Politics," in *Recasting America*, ed. May; George Cotkin, *Existential
      America* (Baltimore: Johns Hopkins University Press, 2003).

31   Arthur Schlesinger, "Two Years Later—The Roosevelt Family," *Life*, April
      7 (1947): 113; Eric Goldman, *Rendezvous with Destiny*, p. 405; Arthur
      Schlesinger, *The Vital Center*, p. xvii. For how FDR's death influenced the
      most important organization of liberals in the 1940s, ADA, see Clifton
      Brock, *Americans for Democratic Action* (Washington, D.C.: Public Affairs
      Press, 1962), p. 39.

32   Arthur Schlesinger, *The Vital Center*, p. 38; Arthur Schlesinger, "Liberal
      Faith Needs Guts," *Labor and Nation*, November–December (1948): 13;
      Arthur Schlesinger, "The Future of Socialism," p. 235; Bloom, *Prodigal*

Sons, p. 179. For Trilling's distinction, I rely upon a crucial and undated letter he wrote to Madame Deuette Mavez, found in Box 12, Folder 199 of the Lionel Trilling Papers, Columbia University Rare Book and Manuscript Division. See also Marian Morton, *The Terrors of Ideological Politics: Liberal Historians in a Conservative Mood* (Cleveland, OH: Case Western Reserve University, 1972).

Notes to Chapter One

1 William James, *Pragmatism and the Meaning of Truth* (Cambridge, MA: Harvard University Press, 1978), p. 11.
2 John Kenneth Galbraith, *A Life in Our Times* (Boston: Houghton Mifflin, 1981), Chapters 9–12. For a brief overview of Galbraith's life, see James Ronald Stanfield, *John Kenneth Galbraith* (New York: St. Martin's, 1996).
3 This information relies upon *A Life in Our Times* and materials found throughout the Galbraith Papers.
4 On Galbraith's ambassadorship, see David Mayers, "JFK's Ambassadors and the Cold War," *Diplomacy and Statecraft* 11 (2000): 196–198; John Kenneth Galbraith, *Ambassador's Journal* (Boston: Houghton Mifflin, 1969), p. 376.
5 *Ambassador's Journal*, p. 72; Schlesinger to Galbraith, May 17, 1965, Schlesinger Archives, Box P-33; Galbraith, *American Capitalism* (1952; reprint, Boston: Houghton Mifflin, 1962), p. x; *Life in Our Times*, p. 495.
6 Arthur Schlesinger, Jr., "Ideas and Responsibility: The Intellectual and Society" (An Inaugural Lecture, October 25, 1966, given at CUNY), p. 23, found in Schlesinger Archives, Box W-33; *The Vital Center: The Politics of Freedom* (1949; NY: Da Capo, 1988), p. 9; James Wechsler, *Age of Suspicion*, (1953; reprint, New York: Donald I. Fine, 1985), p. 213; James Wechsler to Page Wilson of ADA, April 13, 1962, James Wechsler Papers, Box One, of First Addition.
7 Schlesinger, *The Politics of Hope* (Boston: Houghton Mifflin, 1963), p. 235 (the essays in this book were published from 1949 to 1962); Schlesinger, "The Administration and the Left," *New Statesman*, February 8 (1963): 8.
8 "Author James A. Wechsler, Editor of the *New York Post*," *The Publisher's Auxiliary*, May 21 (1960): 4; Arthur Schlesinger, Jr., *A Life in the 20th Century* (Boston: Houghton Mifflin, 2000), p. 411 (these comments were also given at Wechsler's funeral); "Wechsler Proves Liberal Daily Need Not Be Dull," *News Workshop* (a publication of New York University), May (1957): 5. See also comments made at *You and the Press* (on CBS), Friday January 20, 1950, found in Wechsler Papers, Box 14. On Wechsler's failure to get Galbraith to write for the *Post*, I rely upon Galbraith's response to Wechsler's request for a weekly column: Galbraith to Wechsler, September 22, 1958, Galbraith Papers, Box 64.

9   James Wechsler, *Age of Suspicion* (1953; reprint, New York: Donald I.
     Fine, 1985), p. 157; "24th Columnist," *Newsweek*, September 25 (1961):
     64; Wechsler, "The Techniques of Showmanship," *Saturday Review of
     Literature*, June 24 (1950): 8; Bernard Lefkowitz, "Good Bye to Dolly's
     New York Post," *Present Tense* 4 (1977): 54; "Is Sex Necessary?" *Time*,
     July 3 (1950): 35; "The Things We Believe," *New York Post*, May 27,
     1949, p. 35. Schlesinger wrote James Wechsler on January 23, 1950, that
     he thought "the sex and human interest formula is sometimes overdone
     in the POST." Wechsler Archives, Box 8, First Accessions.
10 Pete Hamill, *A Drinking Life* (Boston: Little, Brown, 1994), p. 225;
     Reinhold Niebuhr to James Wechsler, November 9, 1953, Wechsler
     Papers, Additions Box: 1953–1958.
11 Reinhold Niebuhr, *Discerning the Signs of the Times* (New York: Scribner,
     1946), pp. 122, 126; Henry Beckett, "Niebuhr—The Grim Crusader,"
     New York Post, April 20, 1943, p. 39. On Niebuhr's sense of humor, see
     June Bingham, *Courage to Chang* (New York: Scribner, 1961), p. 311.
12 Niebuhr to Schlesinger, April 15, 1954, Reinhold Niebuhr Archives, Box
     27; Niebuhr, "Address to Alumni, 1960," found in Niebuhr Archives, Box
     41. See Charles Kegley, ed., *Reinhold Niebuhr: Handbook of Religious,
     Social, & Political Thought* (New York: Macmillan, 1956).
13 Robert Fitch pointed out Niebuhr's interest in "attitude" and disposition
     when it came to religious thought: see his "Reinhold Niebuhr as Prophet
     and as Philosopher of History," *Journal of Religion* 32 (1952): 39–40. On
     the "egghead" in American culture, see John Patrick Diggins, *The Proud
     Decades*, p. 127 and George Cotkin, "The Tragic Predicament: Post War
     American Intellectuals, Acceptance and Mass Culture," in *Intellectuals and
     Politics: From the Dreyfus Affair to Salman Rushdie*, ed. Jeremy Jennings
     and Anthony Kemp-Welch (New York: Routledge, 1997), pp. 261–264.
14 Trilling to Eleanor Roosevelt, February 26, 1954, Lionel Trilling Papers,
     Columbia University, Box 5. Niebuhr and Trilling's relation can be gleaned
     from correspondence found in the Lionel Trilling Papers, Box 4. Trilling's
     praise of Schlesinger can be seen in a letter he wrote Schlesinger: Trilling
     to Schlesinger, June 30, 1963, Lionel Trilling Papers, Box 5.
15 Diana Trilling, *The Beginning of the Journey* (New York: Harcourt Brace,
     1993), p. 373; John Rodden, "The Opposing Selves of Lionel Trilling,"
     Modern Age 38 (1996): 173. On "the moral responsibility to be intelli-
     gent," see the collection of writings that Leon Wieseltier has compiled,
     The Moral Obligation to Be Intelligent (New York: Farrar, Straus, and
     Giroux, 2000); on complexity see Mark Krupnick, *Lionel Trilling and the
     Fate of Cultural Criticism* (Evanston, IL: Northwestern University Press,
     1986), p. 58.
16 Lionel Trilling, "The Progressive Psyche," *The Nation*, September 12
     (1942): 216; Lionel Trilling, *A Gathering of Fugitives* (Boston: Beacon,
     1956), p. 57; Lionel Trilling, *The Liberal Imagination* (1950; reprint,

New York: Anchor, 1953), p. 7; Lionel Trilling, "From the Notebooks of Lionel Trilling," *Partisan Review* 51–52 (1984–1985): 509 (this article is made up of excerpts from the 1930s to the 1950s or so). For more on Freud's impact on Trilling, see William Chace, *Lionel Trilling* (Stanford, CA: Stanford University Press, 1980), p. 88. In many ways, *Billy Budd* served as a model for Lionel Trilling's own *Middle of the Journey.*

17   *Middle of the Journey* (1947; reprint, New York: Avon, 1966), p. 34. Trilling recognized the importance of growing up and tossing aside any nostalgic beliefs in his own literary criticism: See Trilling, *The Liberal Imagination*, pp. 143–144.

18   *Middle of the Journey*, pp. 166, 111–112, 229, 279; Trilling to Madame Deuette Mavez, undated, Trilling Archives, Box 12.

19   Arthur Schlesinger to Lionel Trilling, August 26, 1947, Trilling Archives, Box 5; Whittaker Chambers, *Witness* (New York: Random House, 1952), p. 12. For more on Chambers, see Sam Tanenhaus, *Whittaker Chambers* (New York: Random House, 1997).

20   Schlesinger's Review of *Witness* (originally 1952), in *Politics of Hope*, p. 195; Niebuhr to Schlesinger, May 29, 1952, Schlesinger Papers, Box P-20; Niebuhr, "Liberals and the Marxist Heresy," *The New Republic*, October 12 (1953): 14. For Will Herberg, see John Patrick Diggins, *Up from Communism* (New York: Harper and Row, 1975), p. 282; and on Elizabeth Bentley, see Kathryn Olmsted, *Red Spy Queen: A Biography of Elizabeth Bentley* (Chapel Hill: University of North Carolina Press, 2002), esp. p. 147 on Bentley's conversion to Catholicism.

21   Reinhold Niebuhr, *Pious and Secular America* (New York: Scribner, 1958), p. 21, and "Differing Views on Billy Graham," *Life*, July 1 (1957): 92; Richard Hofstadter, "The Pseudo-Conservative Revolt" (1955), in *The Radical Right*, ed. Daniel Bell (New York: Doubleday, 1963); on the "authoritarian personality," see Martin Jay, *The Dialectical Imagination: A History of the Frankfurt School and the Institute of Social Research, 1923–1950* (Boston: Little, Brown, 1973), Chapter 7. For an example of the invective against John Foster Dulles, one that is replete throughout all of these thinkers' arguments, consider Niebuhr's dislike of how "Dulles has confused the picture by his simple moral preachments." Niebuhr to Ernest Lefever, June 19, 1956, Niebuhr Archives, Box 8. On Billy Graham's popularity, see Stephen Whitfield, *The Culture of the Cold War* (Baltimore: Johns Hopkins University Press, 1996), pp. 79–81.

22   Richard Hofstadter, "Democracy and Anti-Intellectualism in America," *Michigan Alumnus Quarterly Review*, Summer (1953): 282, 286; David Riesman and Nathan Glazer, "Intellectuals and the Discontented Classes," in *The Radical Right*, ed. Daniel Bell, p. 133; Mark Krupnick, *Lionel Trilling*, p. 69.

23   H.L. Mencken, "The Educational Process," in *A Mencken Chrestomathy* (New York: Vintage, 1949), p. 301. On Mencken, I rely upon Fred Hobson's

fine biography, *Mencken: A Life* (New York; Random House, 1999). For more on the intellectual culture of the 1920s, see Christopher Lasch, *The True and Only Heaven* (New York: Norton, 1991), Chapter 10.

24   Schlesinger, *Crisis of the Old Order* (Garden City, NY: Doubleday, 1975), pp. 148, 150; Bernard DeVoto, *Letters of Bernard DeVoto* (Boston: Houghton Mifflin, 1957), p. 24; Bernard DeVoto, "The Easy Chair," *Harper's*, March (1943): 440. For more on Schlesinger's indebtedness to Mencken, see his comments in *Pastmasters*, ed. Marcus Cunliffe and Robin Winks (New York: Harper and Row, 1969), pp. 295, 460. Schlesinger also realized that he slipped into Mencken's mode of invective when writing about General MacArthur. See his opening remarks in the reissue of his book on MacArthur (originally published in 1952): Arthur Schlesinger, Jr. and Richard Rovere, *General MacArthur and President Truman* (New Brunswick, NJ: Transaction, 1992). The liberal historian Eric Goldman also recognized the importance of Mencken's influence while criticizing it. He pointed out that Harold Stearns's *Liberalism in America* redefined liberal thought along Mencken's line of invective, resulting in a liberalism of "despair." Eric Goldman, *Rendezvous with Destiny: A Modern History of American Reform* (New York: Knopf, 1952), p. 319.

25   Reinhold Niebuhr, *Nature and Destiny of Man*, Volume II (New York: Scribner, 1943), p. 332; *Nature and Destiny of Man*, Volume I (New York: Scribner, 1941), p. 301; John Kenneth Galbraith, "John Strachey," *Encounter*, September (1963): 53; Niebuhr to June Bingham, Niebuhr Archives, Box 26; Schlesinger, "Benjamin Franklin," *New York Post*, January 15, 1956, p. M5.

26   Lionel Trilling, "From the Notebooks," p. 508; Reinhold Niebuhr, *Irony of American History* (New York: Scribner, 1952), pp. vii, viii, 2, 158; David Riesman, *Individualism Reconsidered* (Glencoe, NY: Free Press, 1954), p. 55; Reinhold Niebuhr, *Self and Dramas of History* (New York: Scribner, 1955), p. 233. Schlesinger, who was friends with Riesman (as was Galbraith), praised his idea of autonomy: See Schlesinger, "Entertainment versus the People," *The Reporter*, February 6 (1951): 39.

27   Arthur Schlesinger, *Politics of Hope*, p. 67; Arthur Schlesinger, *The Vital Center*, p. 159; Arthur Schlesinger, *The American as Reformer* (Cambridge, MA: Harvard University Press, 1950), p. 49, see also p. 6. Schlesinger's interest in nineteenth-century reform movements can be seen in his honors thesis, *Orestes Brownson, A Pilgrim's Progress* (Boston: Houghton Mifflin, 1939), especially p. 20. For Hofstadter's critique of the reform tradition and concomitant celebration of the New Deal, see his *Age of Reform* (New York: Knopf, 1955), p. 303; for his ridiculing of "do-gooder" intention behind reform, see his *The American Political Tradition* (New York: Knopf, 1948), p. 177.

28   John Kenneth Galbraith, "What Makes the Good People Good," *The Reporter*, December 8 (1953): 44; James Wechsler, "The Liberal's Vote

and 48," *Commentary*, September (1947): 224; Michael Ignatieff, *Isaiah Berlin* (New York: Metropolitan, 1998), p. 227.

29   Arthur Schlesinger, "Political Culture in the U.S.," *The Nation*, March 13 (1948): 306; Schlesinger, "Ideas and Responsibility," p. 23.

30   James Wechsler to Arthur Schlesinger, August 18, 1954, Wechsler Archives, Box 8; Reinhold Niebuhr to William Scarlett, December 13, no year, Niebuhr Archives, Box 33; Steven Gillon, *Politics and Vision: The ADA and American Liberalism, 1947–1985* (New York: Oxford University Press, 1987).

31   Schlesinger, *Crisis of the Old Order*, p. 410; *Coming of the New Deal*, p. 553.

32   James Wechsler, "What Makes Wallace Run?" *The Progressive*, February (1948): 20; James Loeb to Reinhold Niebuhr, September 17, 1948, ADA Papers, Series 1: Folder/Frame 1, Microfilm Documents; *New York Post*, August 31, 1948, p. 5; *New York Post*, September 5, 1948, p. 21. For more on Wallace's political positions, see Norman Markowitz, *The Rise and Fall of the People's Century: Henry Wallace and American Liberalism, 1941–1948* (New York: Free Press, 1973), p. 166.

33   Arthur Schlesinger, "Ideas to Watch in 1949," *Vogue*, January (1949): 174; Stevenson quoted in Jean Baker, *The Stevensons: A Biography of an American Family* (New York: Norton, 1996), p. 370; Wechsler in *Reminiscences of James Arthur Wechsler, Oral History on Stevenson*, p. 19, in the Columbia University Oral History Research Office Collection; Niebuhr, "The Political Situation in America," *Christianity and Society*, Winter (1956): 5.

34   For Wechsler's disappointment in Stevenson, I rely on letters he wrote to Naomi Sachs on March 26, 1956, and to Stevenson himself on November 25, 1955, both in Wechsler Archives, Box 8 (with the latter there is some angry correspondence that comes from Schlesinger to Stevenson as well); the complaint about Stevenson made publicly is in the *New York Post*, February 9, 1956, p. 29; Schlesinger's statistics come from a letter he wrote to Averell Harriman, July 9, 1952, Schlesinger Archives, Box P-16. On Stevenson's political record, see Jean Baker, *The Stevensons*, p. 342, and Steven Gillon, *Politics and Vision*, p. 83.

35   Galbraith to "Dear Governor," September 23, 1953, Galbraith Archives, Box 22; DeVoto on the Western Conference: DeVoto to Arthur Schlesinger, January 18, 1955, DeVoto Archives, Box 6. On the list of Finletter Group suggestions, see a Memo for Discussion, dated September 7, 1955, in Schlesinger Archives, Box P-13.

36   Galbraith remarks to *New York Herald Tribune* meeting, February 25, 1959, Box 46 of Galbraith Archives; Galbraith, "The Age of the Wordfact," *Atlantic Monthly*, September (1960): 87, 88; Galbraith to JFK, January 9, 1961, Galbraith Archives, Box 76; Wechsler to Stevenson, October 1, 1954, Wechsler Archives, Box 20; John Kenneth Galbraith to JFK, January 9, 1961, Galbraith Papers, Box 76.

37   Henry Luce, *The American Century* (New York: Farrar and Rinehart, 1941),
     p. 37; Reinhold Niebuhr, *Christian Realism and Political Problems* (New
     York: Scribner, 1953), p. 30; *The Irony of American History*, p. 74; Rein-
     hold Niebuhr, "Why They Dislike America," *New Leader*, April 12 (1954):
     3.

Notes to Chapter Two

1   *Stenographic Transcript of Hearings before the Senate Permanent Subcom-
     mittee on Investigations*, U.S. Senate, May 5, 1953, Volume 83, p. 6441.
     Document found in the James Wechsler Papers, State Historical Society of
     Wisconsin, Madison, WI.
2   I rely here upon David Oshinsky, *A Conspiracy So Immense: The World of Joe
     McCarthy* (New York: Free Press, 1983); David Caute, *The Great Fear*
     (New York: Simon and Schuster, 1979); and Richard Fried, *Nightmare in
     Red: The McCarthy Era in Perspective* (New York: Oxford, 1990). Arthur
     Schlesinger wrote to Adlai Stevenson about Eisenhower's relation to McCarthy
     that he was "putting his finger in his ears and wishing to hell that McCarthy
     would go away." Schlesinger to Adlai Stevenson, April 1, 1953, Schlesinger
     Papers, Box P-23. See also on this point, J. Ronald Oakley, *God's Country:
     America in the Fifties* (New York: Red Dembner, 1990), pp. 176–177.
3   *New York Post*, June 6, 1954, p. 9M; on the Cohn and Schine trip, see
     Oshinsky, *A Conspiracy So Immense*, p. 279; for "overreaching," see Fried,
     Nightmare in Red, p. 136.
4   Arthur Schlesinger, "Dangerous Nonsense," *The Progressive*, September
     (1953): 8; Richard Nixon to James Wechsler, January 30, 1950, Wechsler
     Papers, Box 7; for Wechsler's fight with *PM* and then the Newspaper
     Guild, see his *Age of Suspicion* (1953); reprint, New York: Donald I. Fine,
     1985), pp. 163, 167. See also Paul Milkman, *PM: A New Deal in Jour-
     nalism, 1940–1948* (New Brunswick, NJ: Rutgers University Press, 1997),
     p. 123. On Heywood Broun's fight against communists in the Newspa-
     per Guild, which he founded, see Richard O'Connor, *Heywood Broun: A
     Biography* (New York: Putnam, 1975), pp. 186, 197, and John Adam
     Moreau, "The Often Enraged Heywood Broun: His Career and Thought
     Revisited," *Journalism Quarterly* 44 (1967): 506.
5   The Winchell pieces can be found in the *New York Post*, January 18, 1952,
     p. 5; January 20, 1952, p. 5; January 24, 1952, p. 5 (the last citation in-
     cludes Wechsler's depiction of Winchell's love of Joe McCarthy);
     Winchell's labels for the *Post* come from Neal Gabler, *Winchell: Gossip,
     Power, & the Culture of Celebrity* (New York: Knopf, 1994), p. 441; on
     Winchell's accusation about Wechsler still being a communist, I rely upon
     Wechsler's letter to Philip Graham of the *Washington Post*, September 15,
     1952, Wechsler Papers, Box 4; for Winchell's apology, "Winchell 'Regrets'
     anti-Wechsler Dope," *America*, March 26 (1955): 664.

6 *New York Post*, September 4, 1951, pp. 3, 32; September 22, 1951, p. 4. McCarthy might also have been hopeful that Wechsler would be vulnerable, as seen in the fact that a sponsor of a show he had been on (*Starring the Editors*) had pulled the plug once the sponsor found out about Wechsler's communist background. See "Half Happy Ending," *Newsweek*, September 8 (1952): 121.

7 Max Lerner, *The Unfinished Country* (New York: Simon and Schuster, 1959), p. 184.

8 "Excerpts from Testimony of Wechsler before McCarthy Inquiry," *New York Times*, May 8, 1953, p. C14; *Stenographic Transcript of Hearings*, pp. 6145–6146; "Excerpts from Testimony," C14. For more on Rushmore's presence, see "Behind Closed Doors," *Time*, May 11 (1953): 53.

9 *Age of Suspicion*, p. 270; *Stenographic Transcripts of Hearings*, p. 6443; *By Elmer Davis*, ed. Robert Lloyd Davis (Indianapolis, IN: Bobbs-Merrill, 1964), p. 69.

10 *Age of Suspicion*, p. 304; *New York Post*, p. 40; "Excerpts from Testimony of Wechsler," C14; Leslie Fiedler, *An End to Innocence* (Boston: Beacon, 1955), p. 72; see also Arthur Schlesinger's argument against the Fifth Amendment: "Academic Freedom," *Journal of Higher Education* 27 (1956): 350.

11 Undated memo to Joe McCarthy from James Wechsler, Wechsler Papers, Additions Box: 1953–1958.

12 Note found in Folder on ASNE investigation: Box 13 of Wechsler Papers; *Stenographic Transcript*, p. 6392. For more on ASNE, see "Freedom and McCarthy," *Newsweek*, August 17 (1953): 52, 54. Bernard DeVoto, *Easy Chair* (Boston: Houghton Mifflin, 1955), p. 218; Joe Alsop to Arthur Schlesinger, May 29, 1953, showing that Schlesinger was trying to persuade him to take a tougher stand on Wechsler's case and the ASNE: Schlesinger Papers, Box P-8. Schlesinger was hopeful that Wechsler's case would help destroy McCarthy: See Schlesinger's letter to Paul Douglas, April 29, 1953, James Wechsler Papers, Box 8.

13 Lillian Hellman, *Scoundrel Time* (Boston: Little Brown, 1976), pp. 62–64 (it is interesting to note that Hellman says she chucks liberalism for "decency" during this time period: p. 113); Victor Navasky, *Naming Names* (New York: Viking, 1980), p. 46; Richard Pells, *The Liberal Mind in a Conservative Age* (Middletown, CT: Wesleyan, 1989), p. 321.

14 Stephen Whitfield, *The Culture of the Cold War* (Baltimore: Johns Hopkins University Press, 1996), pp. 104–106; Pells, *The Liberal Mind in a Conservative Age*, p. 325. On the rise of Americans for Intellectual Freedom, see Job Dittberner, *The End of Ideology and American Social Thought, 1930–1960* (Ann Arbor, MI: UMI Research Press, 1977), p. 106.

15 Lawrence Freedman, *Kennedy's Wars* (New York: Oxford, 2000), p. x; for the dehumanization thesis, see Ellen Schrecker, *Many Are the Crimes: McCarthyism in America* (Boston: Little Brown, 1998), pp. xii–xiii; Andrew Ross, *No Respect: Intellectuals and Popular Culture* (New York:

Routledge, 1989), p. 35; for a good corrective to these views, see Richard Gid Powers, *Not without Honor: The History of American Anti-Communism* (New York: Free Press, 1995). Arthur Schlesinger argued that Miller's play unfairly characterized anticommunism in a letter to John Fairbank, February 2, 1953, and pointed out that Jimmy Wechsler had editorialized against the play: Letter found in Schlesinger Papers, Box P-13.

16 Christopher Lasch, *The Agony of the American Left* (New York: Knopf, 1969), p. 94; Frances Stonor Saunders, *The Cultural Cold War: The CIA and the World of Arts and Letters* (New York: Free Press, 2000). For criticisms of these points, see Jeffrey Isaac, "Rethinking the Cultural Cold War," *Dissent*, Summer (2002): 29–38; Hugh Wilford, "Playing the CIA's Tune?: The New Leader and the Cultural Cold War," *Diplomatic History* 27 (2003): 15–34. The neoconservative critic Hilton Kramer points out an irony in that the CCF has been condemned by those on the left for "demonology" when it was actually quite a liberal organization. See his *The Twilight of the Intellectuals: Culture and Politics in the Era of the Cold War* (Chicago: I.R. Dee, 1999), p. 312.

17 Arthur Schlesinger, *The Vital Center*, pp. 64, 132; "The U.S. Communist Party," *Life*, July 29 (1946): 87.

18 Eugene Kamenka, ed., *The Portable Karl Marx* (New York: Viking, 1983), p. 203.

19 Arthur Schlesinger, *The Vital Center*, p. 47; James Wechsler, "The Liberal's Vote and 48," *Commentary*, September (1947): 225; Schlesinger, *The Vital Center: The Politics of Freedom* (1949; New York: Da Capo, 1988), p. 171; *The Federalist Papers*, ed. Isaac Kramnick (New York: Penguin, 1987), p. 124; Arthur Schlesinger, *The Age of Jackson* (Boston: Little Brown, 1945), p. 90. William Graebner argues that Schlesinger gave up talking about class after 1945. This misinterpretation is due to the fact that Graebner sees Marxism as the only real way to talk about class: see his *The Age of Doubt: American Thought and Culture in the 1940s* (Prospect Heights, IL: Waveland, 1991), p. 49.

20 For the critique of Marx's predictions, see Arthur Schlesinger, "The World We Want and How to Get It," Speech at State College, Indiana, PA (March 12, 1964), in Schlesinger Papers, Box P-6. See also here, Reinhold Niebuhr, *Christian Realism and Political Problems* (New York: Scribner, 1953), p. 39, and Daniel Bell, *The End of Ideology* (Glencoe, NY: Free Press, 1960), p. 394.

21 Arthur Schlesinger, *The Vital Center*, pp. 152, 153; Reinhold Niebuhr, "Halfway to What?" *The Nation*, January 14, 1950, p. 27. See, too, John Kenneth Galbraith, *The Affluent Society* (1958; Boston: Houghton Mifflin, 1976), pp. 57–58, 61.

22 Reinhold Niebuhr, "Will Civilization Survive?" *Commentary*, December (1945): 5; Reinhold Niebuhr, *The Children of Light and the Children of Darkness* (New York: Scribner, 1944), p. 59.

23 Reinhold Niebuhr, *Christian Realism and Political Problems*, pp. 34, 36; Schlesinger, *The Vital Center*, p. 71; Reinhold Niebuhr, "New Allies, Old Issues," *The Nation*, July 19 (1941): 51. For an excellent dissection of Marx's weak understanding of rights, see Steven Lukes, *Marxism and Morality* (Oxford: Clarendon, 1985), pp. 61–70.

24 Reinhold Niebuhr, *Christian Realism and Political Problems*, p. 38; Hannah Arendt, *The Origins of Totalitarianism* (Cleveland: Meridian, 1951), p. 317. See also Silone's contribution to *The God That Failed*, ed. Richard Crossman (New York: Harper, 1949), p. 99.

25 Reinhold Niebuhr, *Irony of American History* (New York: Scribner, 1952), p. 170; *The Children of Light and the Children of Darkness*, p. 41; see here John Lewis Gaddis, *The Origins of the Cold War* (New York: Columbia University Press, 1972); on the Cominforn, Giles Scott-Smith, *The Politics of Apolitical Culture: The Congress for Cultural Freedom, the CIA, and Post-War American Hegemony* (New York: Routledge, 2002), p. 86; and on the French Communist Party, see Walter LaFeber, *America, Russia, and the Cold War* (New York: Wiley, 1967), p. 42.

26 James Wechsler, "Politics on Campus," *The Nation*, December 30 (1949): 733; Arthur Schlesinger, *The Vital Center*, p. 128. Schlesinger documents the communist infiltration of labor unions in his "The U.S. Communist Party," *Life*, July 29 (1946): 90.

27 Congress for Cultural Freedom Papers, University of Chicago, Box 7, Folder 10: These are comments Schlesinger made during the Milan Conference of 1955; "How to Rid the Government of Communists," *Harper's*, November (1947): 440; Reinhold Niebuhr, "Introduction," to Benjamin Ginzberg, *Rededication to Freedom* (New York: Simon and Schuster, 1959), pp. vii–viii; Arthur Schlesinger, "What Is Loyalty?: A Difficult Question," *New York Times Magazine*, November 2 (1947): 50; Arthur Schlesinger, "The Right to Loathsome Ideas," *Saturday Review of Literature*, May 14 (1949): 17; Arthur Schlesinger, *The Vital Center*, p. 210. Sidney Hook's writing on the "ethics of controversy" can be found in *Sidney Hook on Pragmatism, Democracy, and Freedom: The Essential Essays*, ed. Robert Talisse and Robert Tempio (Amherst, MA: Prometheus, 2002).

28 Steve Gillon, *Politics and Vision*, p. 72; see also *ADA World*, May (1950): 2; James Wechsler, "How to Rid the Government," p. 442; *New York Post*, October 7, 1947, p. 2; *New York Post*, March 3, 1949, p. 2; James Wechsler, "The Brass and Samuel Wahrhaftig," *The New Republic*, May 23 (1949): 17. A key complaint about Truman's loyalty act was that it failed to distinguish between employees who posed a high internal security risk and other federal employees. See Alonzo Hamby, *Man of the People: A Life of Harry S. Truman* (New York: Oxford University Press, 1995), p. 487.

29 Arthur Schlesinger, "What Is Loyalty?" p. 50; "The Right to Loathsome Ideas," p. 18. On the University of Washington case, I rely upon Ellen Schrecker,

No Ivory Tower: McCarthyism and the Universities (New York: Oxford University Press, 1986), pp. 100–104. For the fear of wiretapping, see the *New York Post*, January 13, 1950, p. 37, and Schlesinger's comments in *ADA World*, January (1954): 3.

30   Richard Fried, *Nightmare in Red*, p. 47; James Wechsler, "The Christian Front and Martin Dies," *The Nation*, January 27 (1940): 89; Arthur Schlesinger, "Dangerous Nonsense," p. 7; James Wechsler, "Small Fry," *The Nation*, October 3 (1942): 326–328; James Wechsler, *Age of Suspicion*, p. 181. For more on the Federal Writers Project and Dies, see Jerre Mangione, *The Dream and the Deal* (Boston: Little, Brown, 1972), Chapter 8.

31   Galbraith to Austin Robinson, April 11, 1955, Galbraith Papers, Box 34; Galbraith in undated note to ACCF in ACCF Archives, Tamiment Labor Archives, Box 12; Galbraith, *The Great Crash* (Boston: Houghton Mifflin, 1955), p. xiii; James Wechsler, "How to Rid the Government," p. 440. For the attack on ADA, see Stephen Whitfield, *The Culture of the Cold War*, p. 20.

32   *New York Post*: p. 30; Arthur Schlesinger, "Dangerous Nonsense," *The Progressive*, September (1953): 10; J. Ronald Oakley, *God's Country*, p. 68; Schlesinger's opposition to the Communist Control Act can be seen in his letter to Hubert Humphrey, September 14, 1954, Schlesinger Papers, Box P-16; Wechsler's opposition to McCarran Bill: See the *New York Post*, September 7, 1950, p. 33.

33   Wechsler to Judith Crist at *New York Herald Tribune*, February 19, 1952; Schlesinger, "The Right to Loathsome Ideas," p. 17; "Dangerous Nonsense," p. 8. Because of this stance, Schlesinger refused to sign statements of the ACCF that favored the firing of communist teachers: see Arthur Schlesinger to Irving Kristol, February 22, 1953, ACCF Records, Box 8. Throughout this box, there is a great deal on ACCF statements regarding communism and teaching.

34   Schlesinger to Sol Stein, February 15, 1954, ACCF Records, Box 4; on *The Best Years of Our Lives*, see Schlesinger, "What Is Loyalty?" p. 7, and the *New York Post*, May 26, 1947, p. 4. For more on HUAC's search for communists in Hollywood, see Caute, *The Great Fear*, p. 488.

35   Sidney Hook, *Out of Step: An Unquiet Life in the 20th Century* (New York: Harper and Row, 1987), p. 421.

36   Hook, *Out of Step*, pp. 421–423; James Wechsler to James Farrell (then head of ACCF), February 23, 1955, Wechsler Archives, Box 2; Pearl Kluger to Nicolas Nabokov about the split, letter dated April 14, 1952, CCF Archives, Box 30; Rovere's attack on the Kristol article ("'Civil Liberties,' 1952—A Study in Confusion," *Commentary*, March (1952): esp. p. 229) is seen in Rovere's comments in "Communists in a Free Society" (Typed MS in ACCF files): Box 9. For Burnham's smear against Schlesinger, see his "The Case against Adlai Stevenson," *American*

Mercury, October (1952): 18–19; Richard Rovere to Arthur Schlesinger, December 11, 1952, Schlesinger Archives, Box P-22; on McCarthyites leaving ACCF, see Sol Stein to David Riesman, September 22, 1954, ACCF Archives, Box 4. On the Schlesinger–Burnham feud, see John Patrick Diggins, *Up from Communism*, pp. 327–331.

37 David Riesman to Norman Thomas, February 7, 1955, explaining his resignation: ACCF Records, Box 4 (see also the earlier letter that Riesman writes to Sol Stein on May 6, 1954, about meetings); David Riesman to Sol Stein, February 24, 1954, ACCF Records, Box 4. On the "hardening" of Burnham's anticommunism, see Daniel Kelly, *James Burnham and the Struggle for the World* (Wilmington, DE: ISI, 2002).

38 See Page Douherty to Reinhold Niebuhr, April 5, 1957 (attached to this letter is Schlesinger's plea for ACCF members to join the ADA): found in Niebuhr Archives, Box 1 (Americans for Democratic Action folder).

39 Irving Kristol to Arthur Schlesinger, January 8, 1952, ACCF Records, Box 4; Kelly, *James Burnham*, p. 125; the term "ideological crusade" comes from ADA, *Toward Total Peace* (Washington, DC: ADA Publications, 1947), p. 26 (therefore it is not clearly Schlesinger's but as I show, it reflects his vision quite nicely).

40 Reinhold Niebuhr, "America and Enslaved Nations," *Christianity and Crisis*, October 6 (1941): 1; Schlesinger, "Foreign Policy and National Morality," *Foreign Service Journal*, October (1961): 22; Reinhold Niebuhr, "American Conservatism and the World Crisis: A Study in Vacillation," *Yale Review* 40 (1951): 388.

41 Reinhold Niebuhr, *World Crisis and American Responsibility* (New York: Association Press, 1958), pp. 89, 109 (the essays in this book were written at an earlier time than the book's publication; Niebuhr, "The Myth of World Government," *The Nation*, March 16 (1946): 313; Niebuhr, *Christian Realism and Political Problems* (New York: Scribner, 1953), p. 23.

42 Reinhold Niebuhr, "Frustrations of American Power," *New Leader*, November 29 (1954): 8; "The Plight of China," *Christianity and Society*, Winter (1949): 6.

43 Arthur Schlesinger, "Need Seen for Path between Moralism and Retreatism," *Foreign Policy Bulletin*, February 23 (1951): 1; Schlesinger to Alsop, June 1, 1954, Schlesinger Papers, Box P-8; Galbraith to Alsop, October 10, 1960, found in Schlesinger Archives, Box P-30; Reinhold Niebuhr, "For Peace We Must Risk War," *Life*, September 20 (1948): 38.

44 Arthur Schlesinger and Richard Rovere, *General MacArthur and President Truman* (1951; reprint, New Brunswick, NJ: Transaction, 1992), p. 227; see also Arthur Schlesinger and Richard Rovere, "The Story of Douglas MacArthur," *Harper's*, July (1951): 35.

45 Walter LaFeber, *America, Russia, and the Cold War*, p. 131; Morgenthau and Niebuhr met in 1944, and Morgenthau always appreciated Niebuhr's political views. See Christoph Frei, *Hans J. Morgenthau: An Intellectual*

Biography (Baton Rouge: Louisiana University Press, 2001), pp. 110–111, 186–188, 213. For Morgenthau's debt to Niebuhr, I rely upon a letter he wrote to Niebuhr on November 13, 1970, in the Niebuhr Archives, Box 61; Lippmann's views can be gleaned from John Patrick Diggins, *The Proud Decades* (New York: Norton, 1988), p. 82, and Ronald Steel, *Walter Lippmann and the American Century* (New York: Vintage, 1984), p. 437. On Wallace's realist views, I rely upon John Lewis Gaddis, *Origins of the Cold War*, pp. 338–340. To a large extent, Lippmann and Morgenthau's views squared with the views of FDR before he died: see Daniel Yergin, *Shattered Peace* (Boston: Houghton Mifflin, 1977), p. 55.

46 Reinhold Niebuhr, "Geography, Christianity, and Politics," *Christianity and Crisis*, June 16 (1941): 6; George Kennan, *American Diplomacy, 1900–1950* (New York: Mentor, 1951), p. 93; Reinhold Niebuhr, "Europe, Russia, and American," *The Nation*, September 14 (1946): 288; James Wechsler, *Age of Suspicion*, p. 119; Reinhold Niebuhr, *Essays in Applied Christianity* (New York: Meridien, 1959), p. 97; Niebuhr, *The Irony of American History*, p. 148; Niebuhr, *World Crisis and American Responsibility*, p. 33. On Kennan's view of foreign policy, see Daniel Yergin, *Shattered Peace*, p. 169, and John Lewis Gaddis, *Origins of the Cold War*, pp. 302–303. In 1966, Kennan wrote Niebuhr, "I don't think I ever learned from anyone things more important to the understanding of our predicament, as individuals and as a society, than those that I have learned, so to speak, at your feet." Letter of April 12, 1966, found in Niebuhr Archives, Box 49.

47 Reinhold Niebuhr, *World Crisis and American Responsibility*, p. 35; Reinhold Niebuhr, "Germany and Western Civilization," in *Germany and the Future of Europe*, ed. Hans Morgenthau (Chicago: University of Chicago Press, 1951), p. 7.

48 On Niebuhr's marriage to his British wife, Ursula, see June Bingham, *The Courage to Change* (New York: Scribner, 1961), p. 277, and Elisabeth Sifton, *The Serenity Prayer: Faith and Politics in Times of Peace and War* (New York: Norton, 2003), p. 35; on Schlesinger's friendship with Berlin I rely upon correspondence between the two of them in the Schlesinger Archives, Box P-9, and Michael Ignatieff, *Isaiah Berlin*, pp. 101–103. See also David Cesarani, *Arthur Koestler: The Homeless Mind* (New York: Free Press, 1999). For more on cosmopolitanism and American intellectuals, see Terry Cooney, *The Rise of the New York Intellectuals* (Madison: University of Wisconsin Press, 1986).

49 Clifton Brock, *Americans for Democratic Action* (Washington, DC: Public Affairs Press, 1962), p. 64; Schlesinger, *Vital Center*, pp. 223–224.

50 Reinhold Niebuhr, "American Liberals and British Labor," *The Nation*, June 8 (1946): 684; Reinhold Niebuhr, "America's Precarious Eminence," *Virginia Quarterly Review* 23 (1947): 487; for Niebuhr's criticism of dismantling of the OPA in terms of its international implications, see his

"Europe, Russia, and America," *The Nation*, September 14 (1946): 288–289; see also his "The Sickness of American Culture," *The Nation*, March 6, 1948, p. 270. See also John Kenneth Galbraith, "Challenges of a Changing World," *Foreign Policy Bulletin*, December 15 (1958): 51 and "Europe's Great Last Chance," *Harper's*, January (1949): 48.

51 Michael Josselson to Daniel Bell, April 27, 1956, CCF Records, Box 6; Nabokov to Schlesinger, July 19, 1951, Schlesinger Archives, Box P-20; on Josselson's background, see Saunders, *The Cultural Cold War*, pp. 11–12, and on the conflict with Russell and the ACCF, pp. 231–232.

52 Reinhold Niebuhr to William Benton, Assistant Secretary of State, April 28, 1947, Niebuhr Archives, Box 2; Statement on "American Culture: Menace or Promise," in ACCF Records, Box 9. On Coca-Cola's infiltration into France, see Richard Kuisel, *Seducing the French: The Dilemma of Americanization* (Berkeley: University of California Press, 1993), p. 52; on 1920s anti-American literature's impact on Europe, see Richard Pells, *Not Like Us: How Europeans Have Loved, Hated, and Transformed American Culture since World War II* (New York: Basic, 1997), p. 20.

53 Report No. 1 to the American Committee, from the CCF, May 22, 1951, found in CCF Records, Box Three; Lionel Trilling to Mr. Laughlin, July 12, 1952, Trilling Archives, Box 12.

54 Trilling to Faulkner, undated letter (but from 1956), Trilling Archives, Box 2; Trilling to Kristol, no date (but certainly 1953, since Kristol left ACCF to edit *Encounter* in England that year), Trilling Archives, Box 12.

55 Mary McCarthy, "America the Beautiful," *Perspectives*, Winter (1953): 11–22; Reinhold Niebuhr, "The French Do Not Like Us," *Christianity and Society*, Winter (1954): 10. Niebuhr's vision was also captured in Richard Hofstadter's praise for the Salzburg Seminar in his "The Salzburg Seminar, Fourth Year," *The Nation*, October 28 (1950): 392. This was a privately funded cultural exchange program for intellectuals that arose prior to the CCF.

56 Reinhold Niebuhr, "American Conservatism and World Crisis," *Yale Review* 40 (1951), p. 385; John Kenneth Galbraith, "Democratic Foreign Policy and the Voter," paper found in Galbraith Papers, Box 98, dated January 20, 1958, p. 8; Niebuhr makes the argument in "American Pride and Power," *American Scholar* 17 (1948): 393 and "America's Precarious Eminence," p. 481. Henry Luce disagreed with Reinhold Niebuhr's call for America to be more ambivalent about its power in the world in a letter he wrote to him, dated January 8, 1949, Niebuhr Papers, Box 8.

57 Reinhold Niebuhr in "Our Country, Our Culture," *Partisan Review* 19 (1952): 302. For the standard view of "Our Country, Our Culture," see, for instance, Jackson Lears, "A Matter of Taste," in Larry May, ed., *Recasting America* (Chicago: University of Chicago Press, 1989), pp. 39–40. George Kennan was quite uncertain if America had the internal moral

resources to fight the Cold War: See Waler Hixson, *George F. Kennan: Cold War Iconoclast* (New York: Columbia University Press, 1989), p. 240.

58 Reinhold Niebuhr, *Faith and Politics*, p. 159; Arthur Schlesinger, "Where Does the Liberal Go from Here?" *New York Times Magazine*, August 4 (1957): 36. Two recent historical treatments of the Cold War point to the importance of civil rights: See Thomas Bostelmann, *The Cold War and the Color Line: American Race Relations in the Global Arena* (Cambridge, MA: Harvard University Press, 2000) and Mary Dudziak, *Cold War Civil Rights* (Princeton, NJ: Princeton University Press, 2000).

NOTES TO CHAPTER THREE

1 Reinhold Niebuhr, *The Children of Light and the Children of Darkness* (New York: Scribner, 1944), p. 118.

2 Reinhold Niebuhr to Irving Barshop, May 24, 1940, Reinhold Niebuhr Papers, Box 11; Clifton Brock, *Americans for Democratic Action* (Washington, D.C.: Public Affairs Press, 1962), p. 49; Niebuhr's comments are made in "Dogmas and Principles of Politics," included with a letter to James Loeb, dated April 12, 1943, found in UDA File of ADA Papers, Series 1: No. 222. For Niebuhr's 1930s voting record and his run for Congress in 1930, see June Bingham, *Courage to Change* (New York: Scribner, 1961), p. 163. On how Niebuhr's break with the Socialist Party symbolized the first step toward accepting the New Deal, see Charles Brown, *Niebuhr and His Age* (Harrisburg, PA: Trinity Press, 2002), p. 119, and Richard Fox, *Reinhold Niebuhr: A Biography* (New York: Pantheon, 1985), Chapter 9.

3 W.A. Swanberg, *Norman Thomas, The Last Idealist* (New York: Scribner, 1976), p. 260 (for the quote on "critical support" and the other details about Thomas, see pp. 340–380); Michael Wreszin, *A Rebel in Defense of Tradition: The Life and Politics of Dwight Macdonald* (New York: Basic, 1994), p. 239; Gerald Sorin, *Irving Howe: A Life of Passionate Dissent* (New York: New York University Press, 2002), p. 121.

4 Arthur Schlesinger to June Bingham, January 7, 1954, in Niebuhr Archives, Box 27; see also Perry Miller, "The Influence of Reinhold Niebuhr," *The Reporter*, May 1 (1958): 39–40; James Wechsler believed that the importance of Niebuhr was that he helped "deepen our awareness of human frailty without destroying our belief in the capacity to combat social justice." Wechsler to Robert Good, February 17, 1954, Wechsler Papers, Box 7.

5 Gary Gerstle, "The Protean Character of American Liberalism," *American Historical Review*, 99 (1994): 1045; see also Dorothy Ross, "Socialism and American Liberalism: Academic Social Thought in the 1880s," *Perspectives in American History* 11 (1977–1978): 7–79. I rely also upon James Weinstein, *The Decline of Socialism in America, 1912–1925* (New York:

Vintage, 1967). For the soft socialism of William Morris and its impact
on American social thought, see Casey Blake, *Beloved Community* (Chapel
Hill: University of North Carolina Press, 1990), p. 137.

6 Reinhold Niebuhr, *The Children of Light and Children of Darkness*, pp. 4,
   9, 78; *Europe's Catastrophe and the Christian Faith* (London: Nisbet,
   1940), p. 17. For Niebuhr's debt to Augustine, see Niebuhr, "Intellectual
   Autobiography," in *Reinhold Niebuhr: His Religious, Social, and Political
   Thought*, ed. Charles Kegley (New York: MacMillan, 1956), p. 9; for his
   belief in Augustine being a more fruitful thinker on original sin than
   the Old Testament, see his "Human Creativity and Self-Concern in Religious Thought," in *Freud and the 20th Century*, ed. Benjamin Nelson
   (New York: Meridian, 1957), p. 272, and "Morality," in *The Search for
   America*, ed. Huston Smith (Englewood Cliffs, NJ: Prentice Hall, 1959),
   p. 150.

7 Walter Rauschenbusch, *A Theology for the Social Gospel* (New York:
   MacMillan, 1917), pp. 48 and 223–225.

8 Reinhold Niebuhr, *The Nature and Destiny of Man*, Volume II (London:
   Nisbet, 1943), p. 39; Arthur Schlesinger, *The Vital Center*, p. 169.

9 Niebuhr, *Nature and Destiny of Man*, Volume I (London: Nisbet, 1941),
   p. 240; "Ideology in the Social Struggle" (1946) in *Love and Justice*
   (Philadelphia: Westminster, 1957), p. 117; "The Spirit of Justice," (1950),
   in *Love and Justice*, p. 26.

10 Arthur Schlesinger, *The Age of Jackson* (Boston: Little, Brown, 1945), p. ix.

11 Niebuhr, *Irony of American History*, p. 96; *World Crisis and American
   Responsibility*, p. 31; Arthur Schlesinger, "Reinhold Niebuhr's Role in
   American Political Thought and Life," in *Reinhold Niebuhr*, ed. Kegley,
   p. 126.

12 Arthur Schlesinger, *The Age of Jackson*, pp. 273, 279; Schlesinger, "The
   Legacy of Andrew Jackson," *American Mercury*, February (1947): 171;
   Age of Jackson, p. x. On debates about Schlesinger's work in American
   historiography, see Schlesinger's own admission that he got the Whig Party
   wrong in *The Age of Jackson*: Schlesinger, *A Life in the Twentieth Century*
   (Boston: Houghton Mifflin, 2000), pp. 366–367. The language that
   Schlesinger sees in Jackson is further supported in Michael Kazin, *The
   Populist Persuasion* (New York: Basic, 1995), Chapter 1.

13 Arthur Schlesinger, *Crisis of the Old Order*, pp. 20–21; Schlesinger, "Third
   Force," *ADA World*, February 19 (1948): 2; *The Vital Center*, p. 182.

14 Reinhold Niebuhr to John Bennett, August 1 (early 1930s written in on
   this letter), Niebuhr Archives, Box 42; Stefan Collini, *Liberalism and
   Sociology: L.T. Hobhouse and Political Argument in England, 1880–1914*
   (New York: Cambridge University Press, 1979), p. 125. See also C.T.
   Hobhase, *Liberalism* (1911; reprint, New York: Oxford, 1964), On
   Niebuhr's work with Dewey in LIPA, see June Bingham, *The Courage to
   Change*, p. 162.

15 Arthur Schlesinger, *The Crisis of the Old Order*, pp. 202, 420, 455.

16 Louis Menand, *The Metaphysical Club* (New York: Farrar, Straus and Giroux, 2001), p. 377; Reinhold Niebuhr, "The Commitment of the Self and the Freedom of the Mind," in *Religion and Freedom of Thought*, ed. Henry P. Van Dusen (Garden City, NY: Doubleday, 1954), p. 57; Niebuhr, *Children of Light and Children of Darkness*, p. 151.

17 Niebuhr, "Reply," in *Reinhold Niebuhr*, ed. Kegley, p. 450; *Children of Light and Children of Darkness*, p. 134; for Niebuhr's ecumenical work, see Elisabeth Sifton, *The Serenity Prayer: Faith and Politics in Time of Peace and War* (New York: Norton, 2003).

18 David Riesman, et al., *The Lonely Crowd* (1950; reprint, New Haven, CT: Yale University Press, 1969), pp. 163, 213; Arthur Schlesinger, *The Age of Jackson*, p. 505; Schlesinger, *The Vital Center: The Politics of Freedom*, (1949; reprint, New York: Da Capo, 1988), p. 182.

19 Theda Skocpol, *Diminished Democracy: From Membership to Management in American Civic Life* (Norman: University of Oklahoma Press, 2003), esp. pp. 69–73. See also Alexis de Tocqueville, *Democracy in America* (1848; reprint, New York: Doubleday, 1969), pp. 513–517.

20 Arthur Schlesinger, "Eisenhower Won't Succeed," *The New Republic*, April 5 (1954): 12.

21 Arthur Schlesinger to David Riesman, September 17, 1954, Schlesinger Archives, Box P-22; Reinhold Niebuhr to June Bingham, April 6, 1955, Reinhold Niebuhr Papers, Box 26.

22 Richard McCormick, "The Discovery That Business Corrupts Politics: A Reappraisal of the Origins of Progressivism," *American Historical Review* 86 (1981): 247–274; FDR, "First Inaugural Address," in *Great Issues in American History: From Reconstruction to the Present Day*, ed. Richard Hofstadter (New York: Vintage, 1969), p. 353.

23 John Kenneth Galbraith, *American Capitalism* (Boston: Houghton Mifflin, 1952), pp. 58, 199.

24 *American Capitalism*, pp. 113, 115; Max Lerner, *America as Civilization* (New York: Simon and Schuster, 1957), p. 350.

25 "Economic Power in the American Setting," speech given in May 1958 while in Poland, found in the Galbraith Archives, Box 50; John Kenneth Galbraith to John Strachey, May 25, 1953, in Galbraith Archives, Box 60 (see also in Box 97 an interesting and undated speech on "Countervailing Power: The Concept and the Criticism"); "Economics, Ideology, and the Intellectual," found in CCF Records, Series 2, Box 7, Folder 7.

26 Arthur Schlesinger, "'Liberalism' in the 'Isms in 1957," *Saturday Review*, June 8 (1957): 37; *American Capitalism*, p. 126; on "wishful thinking," see Nelson Lichtenstein, *State of the Union* (Princeton, NJ: Princeton University Press, 2002), p. 152.

27 Arthur Schlesinger, "Coming Shape of American Politics," *Progressive*, September (1959): 23; Arthur Schlesinger, *Politics of Hope*, p. x.

28 John Kenneth Galbraith, "Eisenhower and the Conservative Revolution," *Commentary*, August (1953): 101; John Patrick Diggins, *The Proud Decades* (New York: Norton, 1988), p. 131.

29 John Kenneth Galbraith, *Economics and the Art of Controversy* (New York: Vintage, 1955), p. 81; Arthur Schlesinger, "The Welfare State," *The Reporter*, October 11 (1949): 29; James Wechsler, "State of Mind and Heart," *The American Editor* 3 (1959): 20; Hofstadter in Daniel Bell, ed., *The Radical Right*, (Garden City, NY: Doubleday, 1964), p. 101. Galbraith also believed the Eisenhower administration had pledged itself to deficit spending, a key Keynesian policy. See his "Economics for 1955," *The Reporter*, February 24 (1955): 19.

30 Arthur Schlesinger, *Politics of Hope* (Boston: Houghton Mifflin, 1963), p. 78; Schlesinger, "The Threat of the Radical Right," *New York Times Magazine*, June 17 (1962): 55.

31 Reinhold Niebuhr, "American Conservatism and the World Crisis," *Yale Review* 40 (1951): 390; Reinhold Niebuhr, "The Threat of Reaction," *Christianity and Society*, Summer (1940): 8–9; Schlesinger's point about Kirk is made in *Politics of Hope*, p. 78.

32 *New York Post*, June 6, 1947, p. 5; Reinhold Niebuhr, "The Character of Ideology," *Christianity and Society*, Summer (1947): 4; Bernard DeVoto, "Letter to a Family Doctor," *Harper's*, January (1951): 520 (see also *New York Post*, June 3, 1947, p. 4); Oliver Pilat, *Pegler, Angry Man of the Press* (Boston: Beacon, 1963), p. 261. On Galbraith's difficulty implementing the OPA, I rely upon an unpublished manuscript in his Archives entitled "No Little Heat" (June 23, 1944), found in the Galbraith Archives, Box 95.

33 *New York Post*, September 9, 1953, p. 31; "Give away" state remark; Schlesinger to Stevenson, May 11, 1953, Schlesinger Archives, Box P-23; Schlesinger, "Eisenhower Won't Succeed," p. 12.

34 James Wechsler, "Labor's Bright Young Man," *Harper's*, March (1948): 265; the faith in cooperatives is seen in Arthur Schlesinger, *The Vital Center*, p. 186 (and throughout the ADA's many constitutional statements on economics). For more on the cooperative movement, see Lizabeth Cohen, *A Consumers' Republic*, Chapter 1.

35 Reinhold Niebuhr, "The End of the Beginning," *Christianity and Crisis*, November 30 (1942): 1–2; Arthur Schlesinger, "Coming Shape of American Politics," p. 25; Reinhold Niebuhr, "Ethics of Loyalty," *Confluence* 3 (1956): 484–485.

NOTES TO CHAPTER FOUR

1 Arthur Schlesinger, "The Future of Liberalism: The Challenge of Abundance," *The Reporter*, May 3 (1956): 10.

2 Bernard DeVoto, "The Easy Chair," *Harper's*, December (1943): 39; Richard Hofstadter, *The American Political Tradition* (New York: Knopf,

1948), p. 93. For more on nationalism and its connection to the civil war, see Cecilia Elizabeth O'Leary, *To Die For: The Paradox of American Patriotism* (Princeton, NJ: Princeton University Press, 1999). On the legacy of Lincoln in American culture, see Barry Schwartz, *Abraham Lincoln and the Forge of National Memory* (Chicago: University of Chicago Press, 2000).

3 Reinhold Niebuhr, "Just or Holy," *Christianity and Crisis*, November 3 (1941): 2; Niebuhr quoted in June Bingham, *Courage to Change* (New York: Scribner, 1961), p. 311; C. Vann Woodward, *The Burden of Southern History* (Baton Rouge: Louisiana University Press, 1960), p. 87; Arthur Schlesinger, *The American as Reformer* (Cambridge, MA: Harvard University Press, 1950), pp. 38–39. See also Reinhold Niebuhr, *The Children of Light, The Children of Darkness* (New York Scribner, 1944), p. 181.

4 Arthur Schlesinger, "The Causes of the Civil War: A Note on Historical Sentimentalism," *Partisan Review* 16 (1949): 976, 978; for the revisionists, see Betty Fladeland, "Revisionists and Abolitionists: The Historiographical Cold War of the 1930s and 1940s," *Journal of the Early Republic* 6 (1986): 1–21; James Harvey Young, "Randall's Lincoln: An Academic Scholar's Biography," *Journal of the Abraham Lincoln Association* 19 (1998): 1–13; Peter Novick, *That Noble Dream* (Cambridge, UK: Cambridge University Press, 1988), p. 355.

5 Bernard DeVoto to Dr. Bernstein, February 13, 1948, found in the Bernard DeVoto Archives, Box 4; Bernard DeVoto, *The Easy Chair* (Boston: Houghton Mifflin, 1955), p. 157; DeVoto to Ronald Kayser, February 27, 1946, DeVoto Archives, Box 3; DeVoto to Mr. Bunn, April 4, 1949, Box 5. DeVoto was just about to write *The Course of Empire*. Here he made an interesting leap in historical chronology, from Jefferson's Louisiana Purchase to Lincoln's argument against Southern secession: *The Course of Empire* (Boston: Houghton Mifflin, 1952), pp. 401–402.

6 Henry Steele Commager, *The American Mind* (New Haven, CT: Yale University Press, 1950), p. vii. On racial integration of the armed forces, see Harvard Sitkoff, *The Struggle for Black Equality* (New York: Hill and Wang, 1981), p. 12; on the FEPC, see John Morton Blum, *V Was for Victory*, pp. 185–186; on naturalization rates, see Richard Polenberg, *One Nation Divisible: Class, Race, and Ethnicity in the United States since 1938* (New York: Viking, 1980), p. 57; on a national mass culture, see William Graebner, *The Age of Doubt: American Thought and Culture in the 1940s* (Prospect Heights, IL: Waveland, 1991), pp. 78–79; on Commager and American Studies, see Neil Jumonville, *Henry Steele Commager: Midcentury Liberalism and the History of the Present* (Chapel Hill: University of North Carolina Press, 1999), pp. 209–210.

7 Two recent books have highlighted the relationship between the Cold War and the struggle for civil rights for African Americans: see Thomas Borstelmann, *The Cold War and the Color Line: American Race Relations*

in the Global Arena (Cambridge, MA: Harvard University Press, 2001) and Mary Dudziak, *Cold War Civil Rights: Race of the Image of American Democracy* (Princeton, NJ: Princeton University Press, 2000). See also Alan Brinkley, *Liberalism and Its Discontents* (Cambridge, MA: Harvard University Press, 1998), p. 101. On Myrdal, I rely upon Walter Jackson, *Gunnar Myrdal and America's Conscience: Social Engineering and Racial Liberalism* (Chapel Hill: University of North Carolina Press, 1990), especially pp. 204–205; see also Gunnar Myrdal, *The American Dilemma* (New York: Harper and Brothers, 1942), pp. 8–12 on the "American creed" and p. 1015 on the international implications of racial inequality in America. Lillian Smith argued after the *Brown v. Board* decision that "communist demagogues" were exploiting the race issue for political advantage: *Now Is the Time* (New York: Dell, 1955), pp. 62–64; see also L.D. Reddick's comments about Little Rock in *The Southerner as American* (Chapel Hill: University of North Carolina Press, 1960), p. 145. C. Vann Woodward also understood the power of international arguments against racial segregation.

8   Bernard DeVoto to General Sturgis, September 14, 1950, DeVoto Archives, Box 5.

9   Alan Brinkley, *Liberalism and Its Discontents*, p. 285; see also Rick Perlstein, *Before the Storm: Barry Goldwater and the Unmaking of the American Consensus* (New York: Hill and Wang, 2001).

10 W. J. Cash, *The Mind of the South* (New York: Norton, 1941), pp. 246–247; Barbara Griffith, *The Crisis of American Labor: Operation Dixie and the Defeat of the CIO* (Philadelphia: Temple University Press, 1988); on western opposition to federal land policy, see Samuel Hays, *Conservation and the Gospel of Efficiency: The Progressive Conservation Movement* (1959; reprint, New York: Atheneum, 1980), pp. 256–258. For two examples of liberal awareness regarding regional differences, see remarks about a "Southern-Republican" coalition against the OPA and for the Taft–Hartley Act in *The Southerner as American*, ed. Sellers, p. 174, and Arthur Schlesinger's remarks about an increasing awareness of the conservative politics of the Southwest and Sunbelt in his *A Thousand Days: John F. Kennedy in the White House* (Boston: Houghton Mifflin, 1965), p. 1012.

11 Bernard DeVoto, "The Wild West," *Holiday*, July (1954): 35; DeVoto lecture on "Safeguarding Our National Wealth," typed on notecards with no date given, found in Box 53 of DeVoto Archives; DeVoto, "The Easy Chair," *Harper's*, November (1948): 60; DeVoto, *The Year of Decision: 1846* (Boston: Houghton Mifflin, 1942), p. 343. For the South's nostalgia about a "lost cause" after the Civil War, see David Blight, *Race and Reunion: The Civil War in American Memory* (Cambridge, MA: Harvard University Press, 2001).

12 C. Vann Woodward, *Thinking Back: The Perils of Writing History* (Baton Rouge: Louisiana State University Press, 1986), p. 85; Bernard DeVoto to

Mr. Peattie, April 9, 1944, DeVoto Archives, Box 17; Woodward to Odum, May 30, 1940, Woodward Archives, Box 14; "good place to grow in" comes from "Good Place to Grow In," *Lincoln Mercury Times*, March–April, 1956, pp. 1–3. On DeVoto's father, see Wallace Stegner, *The Uneasy Chair: A Biography of Bernard DeVoto* (New York: Doubleday, 1974), pp. 5–6. DeVoto claimed that he always liked returning east after his trips out west, believing he could never move back to his homeland: DeVoto to Madeline, January 18, 1947, DeVoto Archives, Box 15.

13 Arthur Schlesinger to Bernard DeVoto, December 30, 1945, DeVoto Archives, Box 19; Arthur Schlesinger to Robert Sykes, September 7, 1962, Schlesinger Archives, Box P-32; for Woodward's appreciation of DeVoto's work, see Woodward, "Report on Current Research," *Saturday Review*, April 4 (1953): 16; for Woodward's appreciation of Schlesinger's work, see his review of *The Crisis of the Old Order*, *Saturday Review*, March 2 (1957): 11–12.

14 Woodward, like Schlesinger, resisted the tendency in postwar intellectual thought to see populism as essentially some sort of irrational, anti-Semitic revolt of the mob. In *The South in Search of a Philosophy* (Phi Beta Kappa Lecture, 1938), he called populism a "tough-minded realism that was modern" (p. 10). In his book *Tom Watson* (New York: MacMillan, 1938), he described populism's reasonable anger at the way poor farmers were exploited and kept apart by racial divisions in the South. He also stressed the voices of intellectuals such as Henry Demarest Lloyd in the populist movement in this book. Woodward continued to stress this rational, self-interested model of populism in *The Burden of Southern History*, p. 153, calling it an "interest politics, more specifically 'agricultural interest politics.'" This belief of Woodward's prompted many a debate with his friend Richard Hofstadter who saw populism as being an irrational revolt against the "status anxiety" created by industrialization.

15 Arthur Schlesinger, *The Politics of Hope* (Boston: Houghton Mifflin, 1963), p. 156; the remark on Ickes comes from Bernard DeVoto to Mr. Gurkee, January 19, 1946, DeVoto Archives, Box 3; Bernard DeVoto, "Personal and Otherwise," *Harper's*, April (1952): 14; "The Easy Chair," p. 9. For DeVoto's critique of the New Deal, see, for instance, his "Luke II, I," *Harper's*, December (1939): 110; for his Republican vote in 1946, see his "Easy Chair," *Harper's*, December (1946): 537; on DeVoto's respect for Ickes, see T.H. Watkins, *Righteous Pilgrim: The Life and Times of Harold Ickes* (New York: Holt, 1990), p. 846; for his critique of western Republicans, see his "An Old Steal Refurbished," *Harper's*, October (1952): 66.

16 Bernard DeVoto, "Easy Chair," February 1944, p. 243; *Across the Wide Missouri* (Boston: Houghton Mifflin, 1947), p. 301.

17 Senator McCarran's Bill is described in an editorial found in the DeVoto Archives: "Ike Walton Jr.," *Daily News*, September 30, 1947, found in the DeVoto Archives, Box 69; the communist comment made by a cattleman

is found in "Hearings before the Subcommittee on Public Lands Committee on Public Lands, House of Representatives," H. Res. 93: August 27, 1947 (Glasgow, Montana), p. 171 (found in DeVoto Archives, Box 76a: DeVoto has underlined the comment). The best source on the land grab is Arthur Carhart, "Don't Fence Us In," *The Pacific Spectator* 1 (1947): 251–264. For more on the cattle industry in the postwar period, see Gerald Nash, *The American West Transformed: The Impact of the Second World War* (Bloomington: Indiana University Press, 1985), p. 199.

18 Bernard DeVoto to Mr. Butler, December 1, 1952, DeVoto Archives, Box 6; DeVoto, "The Easy Chair," *Harper's*, June (1947): 543, 545; DeVoto, "The Easy Chair," *Harper's*, January (1947): 46; on his articles' use by politicians, I rely upon DeVoto's letter to Fred Allen, March 31, 1947, DeVoto Archives, Box 3. For more on the Izaak Walton League, see its pamphlet, *Our Public Lands: Their Administration and Use* (Chicago: Izaak Walton League, 1947) and William Voigt, *Born with Fists Doubled: Defending Outdoor America* (Iowa City, IA: Izaak Walton League of America Endowment, 1992).

19 Bernard DeVoto to Mr. Buchanan (undated correspondence), DeVoto Archives, Box 6; DeVoto to Mr. Butler, December 1, 1952, DeVoto Archives, Box 6; "An Old Steal Refurbished," p. 66. It should be noted that the western states boomed after World War II due to massive federal investments during that war. Thus, it became harder at this time to understand the West as a plundered province: see Richard White, *"It's Your Misfortune and None of My Own": A History of the American West* (Norman: University of Oklahoma Press, 1991), p. 497, and Robert Hine and John Faragher, *The American West: A New Interpretive History* (New Haven, CT: Yale University Press, 2000), p. 518.

20 Bernard DeVoto, "Shall We Let Them Ruin Our National Parks?" *Saturday Evening Post*, July 22 (1950): 19 (DeVoto intentionally wrote this article for a widely read publication, and wound up getting it reprinted in *Reader's Digest*); DeVoto, "Intramural Giveaway," *Harper's*, March (1954): 10; on criticism of technical mentality, see DeVoto, "Our Hundred Year Plan," *Harper's*, August (1950): 64. For more on the Echo Park Dam battle, see Russell Martin, *A Story That Stands like a Dam: Glen Canyon and the Struggle for the Soul of the West* (New York: Holt, 1989), Chapter Three; Marc Reisner, *Cadillac Desert: the American West and Its Disappearing Water* (New York: Penguin, 1986), pp. 294–295; and Craig Allin, *The Politics of Wilderness Preservation* (Westport, CT: Greenwood, 1982), pp. 89–94.

21 Bernard DeVoto, "And Fractions Drive Me Mad," *Harper's*, September (1954): 16; "Shall We Let Them Ruin Our National Parks?" p. 48; on Knopf's book, see Russell Martin, *A Story That Stands like a Dam*, pp. 64–65. For the Izaak Walton League's work against dams, see Voigt, *Born with Fists*, pp. 100–102. See also Wallace Stegner, *This Is Dinosaur: Echo Park and Its Magic Rivers* (New York: Knopf, 1955).

22 Bernard DeVoto, "Uncle Sam's Campgrounds," *Ford Times*, June (1956): 4; DeVoto to Mr. Smiley, January 4, 1955, DeVoto Archives, Box 6; Alfred Runte, *National Parks: The American Experience* (Lincoln: University of Nebraska Press, 1979), pp. 22, 71, 93–94; DeVoto to James Phinney Baxter, January 28, 1949, DeVoto Archives, Box 5; "Safeguarding Our National Wealth" Lecture Notes, DeVoto Archives, Box 53, and similar language in "The National Parks," *Fortune*, June (1947): 120.

23 For the numbers of park visitations, see J. Ronald Oakley, *God's Country, America in the Fifties* (New York: Red Dembner, 1990), p. 259. DeVoto, "Parks and Pictures," *Harper's*, February (1954): 12; DeVoto, "Let's Close the National Parks," *Harper's*, October (1953): 49; "The National Parks," p. 120.

24 DeVoto to Alfred Knopf, February 3, 1949, DeVoto Archives, Box 5.

25 DeVoto to Stevenson, August 24, 1954, DeVoto Archives, Box 6; the "Western conference" is outlined in Schlesinger's correspondence with DeVoto found in the Schlesinger Archives, Box P-12; DeVoto, "One-Way Partnership Derailed," *Harper's*, January (1955): 14, 16; Schlesinger, *Politics of Hope*, p. 181.

26 DeVoto to Mrs. Grant, May 30, 1953, DeVoto Archives, Box 6; DeVoto, *The Easy Chair*, p. 307; John Thomas, *A Country in Mind: Wallace Stegner, Bernard DeVoto, History, and the American Land* (New York: Routledge, 2000), p. 125.

27 DeVoto, "Two Points of a Joke," *Harper's*, October (1951): 75; DeVoto, "The Western Paradox," in *The Western Paradox: A Conservation Reader*, ed. Douglas Brinkley and Patricia Limerick (New Haven, CT: Yale University Press, 2001), pp. 22–23 (this is an unfinished manuscript left at DeVoto's death); DeVoto, "Our Hundred Year Plan," *Harper's*, August (1950): 62; DeVoto, "And Fractions Drive Me Mad," p. 18.

28 DeVoto, "The Easy Chair," *Harper's*, November (1944): 556; C. Vann Woodward, "Hillbilly Realism," *Southern Review* 4 (1939): 677.

29 Woodward, *The Burden of Southern History*, p. 142. For the details here on Woodward's biography, the best source is John Roper, *C. Vann Woodward: Southerner* (Athens: University of Georgia Press, 1987); see also James Green, "Past and Present in Southern History: An Interview with C. Vann Woodward," *Radical History Review* 36 (1986): 80–100, and C. Vann Woodward's own *Thinking Back*. Roper does an excellent job at relating biographical and historical developments to Woodward's ideas. For a nice treatment that shows Woodward's relation to liberal political philosophy after World War II, see Robert Westbrook, "C. Vann Woodward: The Southerner as Liberal Realist," *South Atlantic Quarterly* 77 (1978): 54–71.

30 Woodward to Robert Penn Warren, April 8, 1966, Woodward Archives, Box 21; Twelve Southerners, *I'll Take My Stand* (1930; reprint, New York: Harper Torchbook, 1962), p. xxiii (and Robert Penn Warren's essay

collected here that justifies segregation); on the literary tradition, see also C. Vann Woodward, "The Historical Dimension," *Virginia Quarterly Review* 32 (1956): 259. For the Southern "regionalists," I rely upon Twelve Southerners, *I'll Take My Stand*; Richard Pells, *Radical Visions and American Dreams* (New York: Harper and Row, 1973), pp. 102–103; and for a sympathetic account, Mark Malvasi, *The Unregenerate South: The Agrarian Thought of John Crowe Ransom, Allen Tate, and Donald Davidson* (Baton Rouge: Louisiana State University Press, 1997).

31 Howard Odum, *The Way of the South* (New York: MacMillan, 1947), pp. 44, 141–142, 301. Woodward makes his point about regionalism in *The South in Search of a Philosophy*, p. 17. On Odum changing from racist to an inclusive liberal, see *Folk, Region, and Society: Selected Papers of Howard Odum*, ed. Katharine Jocher et al. (Chapel Hill: University of North Carolina Press, 1964), p. 4; on Odum's relation to regionalism, I rely upon George Tindall, "The Significance of Howard Odum to Southern History," *Journal of Southern History* 24 (1958): 294; John Egerton, *Speak Now against the Day: The Generation Before the Civil Rights Movement* (New York: Knopf, 1994), and Morton Sosna, *In Search of the Silent South: Southern Liberals and the Race Issue* (New York: Columbia University Press, 1977), pp. 21, 51, 90.

32 C. Vann Woodward, *Origins of the New South*, p. 308.

33 For the story behind the *Brown v. Board of Education* decision, I rely upon the magisterial work of Richard Kluger, *Simple Justice* (New York: Knopf, 1975) and Howard Ball, *A Defiant Life: Thurgood Marshall and the Persistence of Racism in America* (New York: Crown, 1998), Chapter 6; and the opening remarks of Laura Kalman, *The Strange Career of Legal Liberalism* (New Haven, CT: Yale University Press, 1996), esp. p. 2.

34 John Davis to Woodward, July 8, 1953, Woodward Archives, Box 13; Davis to Woodward, August 7, 1953, found in Subject File on NAACP School Segregation Case in Woodward Archives; Carter to Woodward, June 21, 1954, found in Box 13.

35 C. Vann Woodward, "The Background of the Abandonment of Reconstruction," paper found in Woodward Archives, pp. 3, 27; see also *Reunion and Reaction*, pp. 13, 35, and throughout.

36 C. Vann Woodward, *Thinking Back*, p. 89; Richard Kluger, *Simple Justice*, 492–493; see especially here John Jackson, *Social Scientists for Social Justice: Making the Case against Segregation* (New York: New York University Press, 2001).

37 I rely here upon the rich history told by John Jackson, *Social Scientists for Social Justice*.

38 Reinhold Niebuhr, *Love and Justice*, ed. D.B. Robertson (Philadelphia: Westminster Press, 1957), p. 149. Another figure not dealt with here is Lillian Smith, an important Southern writer who also stressed the psychic impact of racism especially on children. She was an anticommunist and

worked with Americans for Democratic Action. But she also stressed that racism was part of an "ancient psychological mechanism" and thus not so easily changed. Lillian Smith, "Addressed to White Liberals," *The New Republic*, September 18 (1944): 331. Additionally, she defined the issue as "spiritual" in this article, thus requiring the change of belief on the part of Southerners, something she bravely committed herself to doing. See her remarks in *The Winner Names the Age: A Collection of Writings*, ed. Michelle Cliff (New York: Norton, 1978), pp. 30, 43. Smith's emphasis on psychology made her differ from Woodward's stress on law and historical reform. Schlesinger himself counseled ADA to overlook Smith for Woodward when dealing with the South: see Schlesinger to Joe Rauh and James Loeb, January 25, 1950, ADA Papers, 5:264, Reel 103. For more on Smith, see Randall Patton, "Lillian Smith and the Transformation of American Liberalism," *Georgia Historical Quarterly* 76 (1992): 373–392.

39 Woodward, 1955 Introduction in *The Strange Career of Jim Crow* (New York: Oxford University Press, 1974), pp. xvi–xvii; W.J. Cash, *The Mind of the South*, p. 195; *ADA World*, February (1956): 4M. See also here Michael O'Brien, "C. Vann Woodward and the Burden of Southern Liberalism," *American Historical Review* 78 (1973): 596; on Cash, see Woodward's critical review, "The Mind of the South," *Journal of Southern History* 7 (1941): 401. See also Bruce Clayton, *W.J. Cash, A Life* (Baton Rouge: Louisiana State University Press, 1991): pp. 195–199, and Richard King, *A Southern Renaissance: The Cultural Awakening of the American South, 1930–1955* (New York: Oxford University Press, 1980), pp. 168–170.

40 *Strange Career of Jim Crow*, p. 63.

41 *Strange Career*, pp. 39, 85.

42 *Strange Career*, p. 103; Woodward, "Young Jim Crow," *The Nation*, July 7 (1956): 9; *Strange Career*, p. 65. For Woodward's statement on gradualism, see his "The 'New Reconstruction' in the South," *Commentary*, June (1956): 508. Here he wrote, "Undesirable or not, gradualism is an unescapable fact and a basic characteristic of the New Reconstruction." He equated gradualism with realism.

43 Christopher Lasch, *The True and Only Heaven: Progress and Its Critics* (New York: Norton, 1991), p. 441; David Chappell, "Niebuhrisms and Myrdaleries: The Intellectual Roots of the Civil Rights Movement Reconsidered," in *The Role of Ideas in the Civil Rights South*, ed. Ted Ownby (Jackson: University of Mississippi Press, 2002), p. 4 and Tony Badger, "Fatalism, Not Gradualism: Race and the Crisis of Southern Liberalism, 1945–1965," and Walter Jackson, "White Liberal Intellectuals, Civil Rights, and Gradualism, 1954–1960," both in *The Making of Martin Luther King and the Civil Rights Movement*, ed. Brian Ward and Tony Badger (New York: New York University Press, 1996); Carol Polsgrove, *Divided Minds: Intellectuals and the Civil Rights Movement* (New York: Norton, 2001), pp. 32, 37.

44 Woodward, *Strange Career*, p. 132; Woodward quoted in Walter Jackson, "White Liberal Intellectuals," p. 178; Arthur Schlesinger, *The Vital Center*, p. 190. On conservative versus liberal anticommunism as related to civil rights, see Thomas Bostelmann, *The Cold War and the Color Line*, p. 108; on the "Southern Manifesto," see Brent Aucoin, "The Southern Manifesto and Southern Opposition to Desegregation," *Arkansas Historical Quarterly* 55 (1996): 173–193. Woodward also believed the North was largely responsible for segregation, not only because it was complicit with the original decision to end Reconstruction but also because the jingoistic imperialism of the late 1890s found in America's expansion into the Philippines and other imperial excursions was tied to the consolidation of racism in the South: *The Strange Career*, pp. 72–73.

45 King quoted in David Garrow, *Bearing the Cross: Martin Luther King, Jr. and the Southern Christian Leadership Conference* (New York: Vintage, 1986), p. 228; Harvard Sitkoff, *The Struggle for Black Equality*, p. 97; Woodward, *The Burden of Southern History*, p. 176. On King's "I Have a Dream" speech, I rely upon Drew Hansen, *The Dream* (New York: Harper Collins, 2003). For the civil rights movement, Garrow's book is an excellent source as is Taylor Branch, *Parting the Waters: America in the King Years, 1954–1963* (New York: 1988). Both tell the story of a growing nationalism within the movement. Nationalism was also why Woodward would come to be a staunch critic, like Arthur Schlesinger and James Wechsler, of black separatism. See his "After Watts—Where Is the Negro Revolution Headed?" *New York Times Magazine*, August 29 (1965): 24–25, 81–84.

46 Woodward, *The Burden of Southern History*, pp. 21, 183; Woodward to David Riesman, March 21, 1962, Woodward Archives, Box 11.

47 Martin Luther King, "I Have a Dream," in *Great Issues in American History*, ed. Richard Hofstadter, pp. 485, 487; Reinhold Niebuhr to William Scarlett, September 4 (obviously 1963, though not dated): Niebuhr Archives, Box 33. For more on the speech, see Hansen, *The Dream*. Mary Dudziak, *Cold War Civil Rights*, p. 192.

48 DeVoto, "The National Parks," p. 121.

NOTES TO CHAPTER FIVE

1 John Kenneth Galbraith, *The Liberal Hour* (Boston: Houghton Mifflin, 1960), p. 11; Arthur Schlesinger, "Foreign Policy and National Morality," *Foreign Service Journal*, October (1961): 22.

2 Reinhold Niebuhr to June Bingham, March 1, 1957, Niebuhr Archives, Box 26.

3 James Wechsler to Philip Schuyler, April 4, 1960, Wechsler Papers, Box 8; on the CCF's declining attention toward communism (and its own

declining relevance from the mid-1950s onward), see Giles Scott-Smith, *The Politics of Apolitical Culture: The Congress for Cultural Freedom, the CIA, and Post-War American Hegemony* (New York: Routledge, 2002), pp. 156–157; Schlesinger remarks in *ADA World*, February (1956): 2; see also Reinhold Niebuhr, "The Long Ordeal of Co-Existence," *The New Republic*, March 30 (1959): 10–12.

4   James Wechsler to Elmer Davis, March 11, 1955, found in Wechsler Papers, Box 2; James Wechsler, *Reflections of an Angry Middle Aged Editor* (New York: Random House, 1960), p. 57. See Joe Rauh's comments on how ADA needed to be a Fabian Society, political organization, and pressure group all at once: *ADA World*, April (1958): 3M; on ADA frustration with drift, see Clifton Brock, *Americans for Democratic Action* (Washington, D.C.: Public Affairs Press, 1964), p. 165.

5   Leon Keyserling, "Eggheads and Politics," *The New Republic*, October 27 (1958): 14.

6   On Schlesinger and Galbraith's friendship, see Arthur Schlesinger, *A Life in the 20th Century* (Boston: Houghton Mifflin, 2000), pp. 282–283; see also the remarks by John Kenneth Galbraith, *A View from the Stands* (Boston: Houghton Mifflin, 1986), p. 322. About geographical proximity in Cambridge, see Peggy Lamson, *Speaking of Galbraith: A Personal Portrait* (New York: Ticknor and Fields, 1991), p. 104.

7   John Kenneth Galbraith, *American Capitalism* (Boston: Houghton Mifflin, 1952), p. 95; Warren Susman, "Did Success Spoil the United States," in *Recasting America*, ed. Larry May (Chicago: University of Chicago Press, 1989), p. 31; the statistics come from John Patrick Diggins, *The Proud Decades: America in War and in Peace, 1941–1960* (New York: Norton, 1988), p. 186; on early methods of targeting different types of consumers, see Lizabeth Cohen, *A Consumers' Republic: The Politics of Mass Consumption in Postwar America* (New York: Knopf, 2003), p. 302; on credit, see J. Ronald Oakley, *God's Country: America in the Fifties* (New York: Red Dembner, 1990), p. 231.

8   See, for instance, Richard Pells, *The Liberal Mind in a Conservative Age* (Middletown, CT: Wesleyan, 1989), Chapter Four (entitled "Conformity and Alienation").

9   Arthur Schlesinger, "Entertainment versus the People," *The Reporter*, February 6 (1951): 36; Schlesinger, "The Challenge to Liberalism," in *An Outline of Man's Knowledge of the Modern World*, ed. Lyman Bryson (Garden City, NY: Doubleday, 1960), p. 472; on the attempt to form *Critic Magazine*, there are many letters found in the Schlesinger Archives, but a reader can also consult Carol Brightman, *Writing Dangerously: Mary McCarthy and Her World* (New York: Potter, 1992), pp. 359–360. For the mass culture thesis and its tie to totalitarianism, see Martin Jay, *The Dialectical Imagination: A History of the Frankfurt School of the Institute of Social Research, 1923–1950* (Boston: Little Brown, 1973), Chapter 6.

10 Paul Gorman, *Left Intellectuals and Popular Culture in Twentieth Century America* (Chapel Hill: University of North Carolina Press, 1996), p. 138; Andrew Ross, *No Respect: Intellectuals of Popular Culture* (New York: Routledge, 1989), p. 227; Stephen Holmes, *The Anatomy of Antiliberalism* (Cambridge, MA: Harvard University Press, 1993), p. 260. Patrick Brantlinger argues that mass culture theories draw too much from classical and ancient views to be of much use to modern thinkers: see his *Bread and Circuses: Theories of Mass Culture as Social Decay* (Ithaca, NY: Cornell University Press, 1983). For a critique of these types of criticisms of the original mass culture critique, see Thomas Frank, *One Market Under God* (New York: Doubleday, 2000), Chapter Eight, and Chris Lehmann, *Revolt of the Masscult* (Chicago: Prickly Paradigm, 2003). See also my "Mass Culture Revisited," *Radical Society* 30 (2003): 87–93.

11 John Kenneth Galbraith, *The Affluent Society* (Boston: Houghton Mifflin, 1958), p. 131; "Some Thoughts on Public Architecture and Public Works," p. 10: Article found in Galbraith Archives, Box 106.

12 Nixon quoted in Lizabeth Cohen, *A Consumers' Republic*, p. 126 (see also Stephen Whitfield, *The Culture of the Cold War* [Baltimore: Johns Hopkins University Press, 1996], pp. 73–74 on this event); Henry Brandon, "A Christian View of the Future: A Conversation with Reinhold Niebuhr," *Harper's*, December (1960): 74; John Kenneth Galbraith, "How Much Should a Country Consume?" in *Perspectives on Conservation*, ed. Henry Jarrett (Baltimore: Johns Hopkins University Press, 1958), p. 96; Reinhold Niebuhr, "Why They Dislike America," *New Leader*, April 12 (1954): 3.

13 John Kenneth Galbraith, *The Affluent Society* (Boston: Houghton Mifflin, 1958), p. 253; Schlesinger's remarks to the New Jersey ADA (December 8, 1957), found in ADA Papers, Reel 5: 264; see also Schlesinger, *The Politics of Hope* (Boston: Houghton Mifflin, 1963), p. 89.

14 John Kenneth Galbraith, "For Public and Potent Buildings," *New York Times Magazine*, October 9 (1960): 64; John Kenneth Galbraith to editor of *New York Times Magazine*, September 16, 1960, about his forthcoming article on public architecture: This is where he names the State Department building and it is found in Galbraith Archives, Box 58; Galbraith makes the comment about highways in a short piece he sent Schlesinger: "Some Reflections on Resource Allocation" (1958 was scribbled on the top of the piece): see Schlesinger Archives, Box P-14. There can be little doubt that Schlesinger and Galbraith saw ugliness in their immediate local landscape, especially the sprawl around Boston and Cape Cod (where they often spent summers). Bernard DeVoto described Cape Cod as "the modern vacation suburb, a seaside zone of amusement parks." DeVoto, "Outdoor Metropolis," *Harper's*, October (1955): 18. Also see Kenneth Jackson, *Crabgrass Frontier: The Suburbanization of the United States* (New York: Oxford University Press, 1985), Chapter 14.

15   Kent Anderson, *Television Fraud: The History and Implications of the Quiz Show Scandals* (Westport, CT: Greenwood, 1978), p. ix; *The Politics of Hope*, pp. 245–254; Stephen Whitfield, *The Culture of the Cold War*, p. 176.

16   Galbraith, "An Effective and Liberal Farm Policy" (1951 written in on top), p. 2: found in Galbraith Archives, Box 99; "Let Us Begin: An Invitation to Action on Poverty," *Harper's*, March (1964): 23.

17   Reinhold Niebuhr, "Higher Education in America," *Confluence* 6 (1957): 14; on the History Book Club, I rely upon correspondence found in the Bernard DeVoto Archives, especially a letter DeVoto wrote to Alfred Knopf on June 30, 1947, Box 3; for Galbraith's work on education television, I rely upon a letter he wrote to Carl Spaeth of the Ford Foundation, March 3, 1953, found in the Galbraith Archives, Box 28; on Niebuhr's support of educational television, see Reinhold Niebuhr, "Introduction," to *Responsibility in Mass Communication*, ed. Wilbur Schram (New York: Harper and Brothers, 1957), p. xviii, and Charles Brown, *Niebuhr and His Age*, p. 195. For more on book clubs, see Joan Shelley Rubin, *The Making of Middlebrow Culture* (Chapel Hill: University of North Carolina Press, 1992), p. 109; Lionel Trilling was also involved in various book club ventures during the 1950s: see Mark Krupnick, *Lionel Trilling and the Fate of Cultural Criticism* (Evanston, IL: Northwestern University Press, 1986), p. 105.

18   Arthur Schlesinger, "Liberalism, the 'Middle-of-the-Road' and the Democratic Campaign," October 11, 1955, pp. 1, 2 (emphasis in original): I originally found this document in the Wechsler Papers but it can also be found in Box W-34 of the Schlesinger Papers.

19   Schlesinger, "Liberalism, the 'Middle-of-the-Road' and the Democratic Campaign," p. 2; "The Coming Shape of American Politics," *The Progressive*, September (1959): 27; "The Future of Liberalism: The Challenge of Abundance," *The Reporter*, May 3 (1956): 11; John Kenneth Galbraith, "Some Unfinished Business for Liberals," *The New Republic*, February 9 (1957): 7.

20   Schlesinger, *The Politics of Hope*, p. 83; "America's Domestic Future: Its Perils and Prospects," *Spelman Messenger*, February (1961): 15.

21   Schlesinger, *The Coming of the New Deal* (Boston: Houghton Mifflin, 1958), p. 22; "Liberalism, the Middle-of-the-Road and the Democratic Campaign," p. 3; John Kenneth Galbraith, "Keynesians in Washington," *The Financial Times*, March 19, 1958, p. 3; for the *Time* Magazine cover about Keynesianism, see Alan Matusow, *The Unraveling of America: A History of Liberalism in the 1960s* (New York: Harper & Row, 1984), p. 57; on "growth" liberalism, see Alan Brinkley, *The End of Reform* (New York: Alfred Knopf, 1995) and Robert Collins, *More: The Politics of Economic Growth in Postwar America* (New York: Oxford University Press, 2000). It should be pointed out that both Galbraith and Schlesinger were

Keynesians, just more on the left end of the spectrum of this philosophy. Schlesinger had a Keynesian explanation of the Great Depression: see *The Crisis of the Old Order* (Boston: Houghton Mifflin, 1957), p. 68.

22   Loren Okroi, *Galbraith, Harrington, Heilbroner: Economics and Dissent in an Age of Optimism* (Princeton, NJ: Princeton University Press, 1988), p. 51; Leon Keyserling, "Eggheads and Politics," *The New Republic*, October 27 (1958): 15; "Galbraith and Schlesinger Reply to Leon Keyserling," *The New Republic*, November 10 (1958): 14; on Keyserling, see W. Robert Brazelton, "Retrospectives: The Economics of Leon Hirsch Keyserling," *Journal of Economic Perspectives* 11 (1997): 189–197, and Alonzo Hamby, *Man of the People: A Life of Harry S. Truman* (New York: Oxford, 1995), p. 500.

23   Galbraith, "Some Reflections on Public Buildings and Public Works" (undated), Galbraith Archives, Box 102; Schlesinger in a memo to JFK, August 26, 1960, found in the Galbraith Archives, Box 74; "Address by John Kenneth Galbraith, Chairman, Economic Policy Commission," p. 3 (found in Galbraith Archives, Speech Files); Arthur Schlesinger, *Crisis of the Old Order*, p. 125.

24   Arthur Schlesinger to Adlai Stevenson, September 22, 1955, Schlesinger Archives, Box P-23; Arthur Schlesinger, "Liberalism, Middle-of-the-Road . . . ," p. 3; the Finletter memo (dated September 7, 1955) is found in Box P-13 of the Schlesinger Archives; on Stevenson's view of campaigning, see Jean Baker, *The Stevensons: A Biography of an American Family* (New York: Norton, 1996), p. 335; Stevenson's focus on foreign policy can be seen in his lack of comment on domestic policy anywhere in his *Call to Greatness* (New York: Harper and Brothers, 1954).

25   Schlesinger, *A Thousand Days: John F. Kennedy in the White House* (Boston: Houghton Mifflin, 1965), pp. 104, 111; the discomfort can be seen in some of the correspondence between Galbraith and Stevenson, especially a letter from Galbraith to Stevenson on August 12, 1960, found in Box 59 of the Galbraith Archives.

26   Schlesinger, *Kennedy or Nixon: Does It Make Any Difference?* (New York: Macmillan, 1960), pp. 4, 15, 51; Galbraith, "Mr. Nixon's Remedy for Inflation," *Harper's*, February (1960): 29–34; Galbraith, "The Democrats: Profile of the Popular Party," November 27, 1959, p. 12, found in Galbraith Archives, Box 98; Steven Gillon, *Politics and Vision: The ADA of American Liberalism, 1947–1985* (New York: Oxford, 1987), p. 133.

27   James Wechsler, *Reflections of a Angry Middle Aged Editor*, p. 38; all of Galbraith's and Schlesinger's remarks come from various memoranda and notes in the Galbraith Archives, Box 74: Galbraith to JFK, Memo of July 29, 1960; Budget Speech notes; Schlesinger follow-up memo to Galbraith's "Campaign Strategy, 1960" memo.

28   Joe Rauh to James Wechsler, May 4, 1961, Wechsler Archives, Box 5; Wechsler to Schlesinger, July 9, 1959, Wechsler Archives, Box 8; on the

continued ADA critique, see Maurice Isserman and Michael Kazin, *America Divided: The Civil War of the 1960s* (New York: Oxford, 2000), p. 64.

29   Arthur Schlesinger, *The Vital Center: The Politics of Freedom* (1949; New York: DaCapo, 1988), p. 159; Schlesinger, *A Thousand Days*, p. 728; Galbraith, *Ambassador's Journal* (Boston: Houghton Mifflin, 1969), p. 72. Schlesinger also knew that not everyone accepted the role of the intellectual as advisor: see his "The Administration and the Left," *The New Statesman*, February 8 (1963): 185–186.

30   The story of Schlesinger and JFK comes from *The Liberal Persuasion: Arthur Schlesinger, Jr. and the Challenge of the American Past*, ed. John Patrick Diggins and Michael Lind (Princeton, NJ: Princeton University Press, 1997), p. 3; Tevi Troy, *Intellectuals and the American Presidency: Philosophers, Jesters, or Technicians?* (Lanham, MD: Rowman and Littlefield, 2002), p. 29; Lawrence Freedman, *Kennedy's Wars: Berlin, Cuba, Laos, and Vietnam* (New York: Oxford University Press, 2000), p. 36. The other program that Schlesinger worked on was the Alliance for Progress (AFP), an attempt to revise America's relations with Latin America. To a large extent, this work was similar to Schlesinger's earlier search for a Non-Communist Left (NCL) in Europe during the 1940s. He looked for reformers in Latin America with whom America could make alliances. Schlesinger himself believed AFP in 1963 was a "mingling of disappointment and progress." The first word was more important than the second ("The Alliance for Progress: Prospects, Perils, and Potentialities," talk given in Venezuela, May 11, 1963, found in Schlesinger Archives, Box WH-2). The historian Lawrence Freedman argues the program was stymied by "bureaucratic inertia and poor understanding of the societies to be rescued" and by "local power structures" that resisted U.S. interference: *Kennedy's Wars*, p. 229. For our sake here, I focus more on the national arts policy because this is more in line with Schlesinger's earlier vision of national greatness and qualitative liberalism. But this does not discount the energy he threw toward the AFP.

31   Reference to Robert Frost's speech is found in a memo that Max Isenberg of the State Department wrote about "A National Cultural Policy" (September 15, 1961), found in the Schlesinger Archives, Box WH-16; Ronald Steel, *Walter Lippmann and the American Century* (New York: Vintage Books, 1981), pp. 524–525; Alfred Kazin, "The President and Other Intellectuals," *American Scholar* 30 (1961): 507; Schlesinger to JFK, November 22, 1961, Schlesinger Archives, Box WH 16.

32   "Production for What?" found in Twentieth Century Fund's Records (New York City), with letter from Heckscher to Berle, dated March 24, 1958; August Heckscher, *The Public Happiness* (New York: Atheneum, 1962), p. 161. For Schlesinger and Galbraith serving at the Twentieth Century Fund, I rely upon the Century Foundation's records in New York

City (the TCF newsletter of fall 1959 announces Schlesinger's arrival, the fall 1960 issue announces Galbraith's) and upon Adolf Berle, *Leaning against the Dawn* (New York: Twentieth Century Fund, 1969). Schlesinger labeled Heckscher a conservative (albeit a centrist) in "The New Conservatism in America," *Confluence* 2 (1953): 62.

33 August Heckscher thanked Schlesinger for making his transition into his new position easy in a letter dated March 19, 1962, found in the Heckscher Papers, Box 5; Heckscher resigns in a letter to John F. Kennedy, May 28, 1963, found in the Schlesinger Papers, Box WH-1; Memo from August Heckscher to "The Files," dated August 7, 1962, about meeting with JFK, found in Heckscher Papers, Box 40; on the discussions with Schlesinger and Heckscher's own thoughts on what could be done, see two memos he wrote to the president, August 7, 1962, and November 27, 1962, both found in the Heckscher Papers, Box 40.

34 The copy of the Executive Order was found in the Schlesinger Papers, Box WH-1. On the history of the Performing Arts Center, see Ralph Becker, *Miracle on the Potomac: The Kennedy Center from the Beginning* (Silver Spring, MD: Bartleby Press, 1990).

35 "The Arts and National Government," pp. 5, 27 (found in Schlesinger Papers, Box WH-1).

36 Transcript of *Meet the Press* (November 12, 1961), found in Galbraith Archives, Box 43; for Galbraith's early interest in foreign aid, see his "The Poor Countries," *Encounter*, October (1953): 68–72, and "Making 'Point Four' Work," *Commentary*, September (1950): 229–233.

37 This paragraph relies upon David Mayers, "JFK's Ambassadors and the Cold War," *Diplomacy and Statecraft* 11 (2000): 183–211; Galbraith, *Ambassador's Journal* and "The Poverty of Nations," *Atlantic Monthly*, October (1962): 47–53.

38 Arthur Schlesinger, "Ideas and Responsibility: The Intellectual and Society" (Inaugural Lecture, October 25, 1966), reprinted pamphlet found in Schlesinger Archives, Box W-36, p. 23; Christopher Lasch, "Arthur Schlesinger and 'Pragmatic Liberalism,'" *Iowa Defender*, May 6, 1963, p. 1, and *Iowa Defender*, May 13, 1963, p. 1. See also my own "The Historian as a Social Critic: Christopher Lasch and the Uses of History," *The History Teacher* 36 (2003): 375–396.

39 John Kenneth Galbraith, letter to the White House, April 3, 1961, reprinted in *Letters to Kennedy*, ed. James Goodman (Cambridge, MA: Harvard University Press, 1998), p. 64; Arthur Schlesinger to the president, March 31, 1961, telling of meetings with Haward Handleman from *US News and World Report* and Joseph Newman of the *Herald Tribune*: Schlesinger Archives, Box WH-5. See also Lawrence Freedman, *Kennedy's Wars*, pp. 68, 132.

40 Galbraith to Kennedy, March 25, 1961, reprinted in *Letters to Kennedy*, p. 39; Galbraith to Kennedy, January 29, 1963, Galbraith Archives, Box 76;

Letters to Kennedy, p. 42; Galbraith in memo to Attorney General Kennedy, June 11, 1963, found in Schlesinger Archives, Box WH-11. For the setting of Kennedy's tax cut, see Allen Matusow, *The Unraveling of America*, Chapter 2.

41 Galbraith to Kennedy, February 2, 1961, Galbraith Archives, Box 77; *Ambassador's Journal*, p. 23.

42 Schlesinger, *A Thousand Days*, p. 841; Galbraith, "Foreign Policy: The Stuck Whistle," *Atlantic Monthly*, February (1965): 67; Galbraith, *Ambassador's Journal*, pp. 53, 95.

43 Kennedy quoted in Richard Reeves, *President Kennedy* (New York: Simon and Schuster, 1993), pp. 53, 522; Arthur Schlesinger, "America's Domestic Future," p. 16; for Schlesinger's pressing of the civil rights issue, see for example the memo he wrote to the president on June 8, 1963, found in the Schlesinger Archives, WH-66.

44 Schlesinger, *A Thousand Days*, p. 206; Schlesinger, "America's Domestic Future," p. 10.

45 Schlesinger, "Government and the Arts," *Show*, October (1962): 101; Wechsler editorial in *New York Post*, November 26, 1963, found in Schlesinger Archives with cover letter, Box P-30.

46 Galbraith to Kennedy, January 29, 1963, Galbraith Archives, Box 76; Galbraith, "What Makes the Good People Good," *The Reporter*, December 8 (1953): 44; Schlesinger, *A Thousand Days*, pp. 116–117.

NOTES TO CHAPTER SIX

1 Reinhold Niebuhr, *Love and Justice* (Philadelphia: Westminster, 1957), p. 192; Arthur Schlesinger, *The Crisis of Confidence* (New York: Bantam, 1969), p. 125.

2 Schlesinger to Mrs. Benjamin Johnson, January 7, 1964, Schlesinger Archives, Box P-30; Galbraith, *A Life in Our Times*, p. 445.

3 Schlesinger, *A Thousand Days: John F. Kennedy in the White House* (Boston: Houghton Mifflin, 1965), p. 1027.

4 For Schlesinger's optimism about deficit spending and more public spending, see Schlesinger, *A Thousand Days*, pp. 1002-1004.

5 Lawrence Freedman, *Kennedy's Wars* (New York: Oxford University Press, 2000), p. 396; Fredrik Logevall, *Choosing War: The Lost Chance for Peace and the Escalation of War in Vietnam* (Berkeley: University of California Press, 1999), p. 73.

6 Niebuhr, *The Irony of American History* (New York: Scribner, 1952), p. 126; Woodward's statement here is taken from a story clipped by him and placed in his personal papers (the uncatalogued portion). It was entitled "Vann Woodward Warned There'd Be Wars Like This," and was published in the *Baltimore Sun* (with the year 1972 written on top but with no other date on it).

7 Galbraith, *Letters to Kennedy* (Cambridge, MA: Harvard University Press, 1998), p. 98; Galbraith, "Program in Vietnam" (undated memo, marked Confidential) and found in Arthur Schlesinger Papers, Box WH-11.

8 Galbraith, "A Private White Paper on Vietnam," presented in the winter of 1965 and found in Box 146 of the Galbraith Papers.

9 On Schlesinger's use of "honor," see Steven Gillon, *Politics and Vision: The ADA and American Liberalism, 1947–1985* (New York: Oxford, 1987), pp. 181, ff.; Schlesinger to Sam Beer, May 21, 1965, Schlesinger Papers, Box P-30; Schlesinger, "A Middle Way out of Vietnam," *New York Times Magazine*, September 18, 1966, 47–49, 111–115, 117–120.

10 Galbraith, "A Private White Paper on Vietnam"; Niebuhr to William Scarlett, December 23, 1965, Niebuhr Archives, Box 33; *New York Post*, November 19, 1965, M4; on the "myth" of the "liberals' war" thesis, see Fredrik Logevall, *Choosing War*, p. 57.

11 This meeting is documented in a memo that Wechsler wrote to himself, dated, April 26, 1967 (a copy was sent to Dorothy Schiff), Wechsler Papers, Box 4.

12 Schlesinger, *Crisis of Confidence*, p. 120.

Index

A

Aaron, Daniel, 113
Advisory Council on the Arts, 163
Alliance for Progress, 168
Alsop, Joe, 76
American Capitalism, 101
American Congress for Cultural
    Freedom (ACCF), 71, 72,
    see also Congress for Cultural
    Freedom (CCF)
  Disintegration of organization, 74
  Troublesome relation with
    Congress for Cultural Freedom
    (CCF), 81
American Heritage Foundation, 13
American Medical Association (AMA),
    107
American Society for Newspaper
    Editors (ASNE), 58
American South, 115
  Intellectual tradition of, 128
American Student Union, 67
American Studies, 113
American West, 116, 120, 126–127
Americans for Democratic Action
    (ADA), 9, 10, 32, 34, 45–46, 68,
    74, 86, 104, 120, 134, 140, 142,
    160, 176, see also Union for
    Democratic Action (UDA)
  Attacked as communist, 70
  Shift in emphasis during the 1950s,
    142
Americans for Intellectual Freedom
    (AIF), 59

Anderson, Clinton, 121
Anticommunism, 60–66, 141
  Difference between liberal and
    right-wing variant, 72–73
  Distinction between ideas and
    action, 67
  Relation to Civil Rights Movement,
    137
Anti-intellectualism, 40–41
Arendt, Hannah, 11, 65
  Theory of totalitarianism, 65
Army Corps of Engineers, 122, 126
Ascoli, Max, 143
Augustine, 89

B

Barrett, Frank (Congressman), 120–121
Bay of Pigs, 166, 168
Bell, Daniel, 10, 13
Bentley, Elizabeth, 67
Benton, Thomas Hart, 24
Berle, Adolf, 162
Berlin, Isaiah, 44, 79
Best Years of Our Lives, The, 72
Blair, Lewis Harvie, 134
Blum, John Morton, 21
Brinkley, Alan, 115
Broun, Heywood, 53
Brower, David, 123
Brown v. Board of Education, 107
  Doll Tests as evidence, 132
  Importance of Constitutional and
    historical arguments in favor of,
    133

Brownson, Orestes, 63
Buckley, William, 1, 3, 4, 6, 13, 104
Budenz, Louis, 54
Bureau of Land Management (BLM), 121
Bureau of Reclamation, 122–123, 126
Burke, Edmund, 105
Burnham, James, 40, 73, 74, 76, 142
   Support for "offensive policy" towards USSR, 75

C
Calhoun, John, 116
Capehart, Senator Homer, 70
Carter, Robert, 131
Casals, Pablo, 161, 170
Cash, W.J., 115–116, 134
Central Intelligence Agency (CIA), 6, 61
Chamber of Commerce, 13, 80, 91, 107
Chambers, Whittaker, 38, 54, 67, 73, 142
Chaplin, Charlie, 72
Chappell, David, 136
Christianity and Crisis, 18
Civil liberties, 71
Civil Rights Movement, 130–137
Clark, Kenneth, 132
Coca Cola, 81
Cohen, Lizabeth, 20
Cohn, Roy, 53
Cold War, 66, 67, 91
   Impact on culture, 5–6
   Impact on civil rights movement, 137
Commager, Henry Steele, 113
Commission on Interracial Cooperation, 129
Committee on Public Information (CPI), 21
Committee on Public Lands and Surveys, 121
Communist Control Act, 70

Communitarianism, 3
Congress for Cultural Freedom (CCF), 6, 9, 10, 59, 81, 87, 141, See also American Congress for Cultural Freedom (ACCF)
   Desire to improve relations between Europe and America during Cold War, 81–82
   Ties to the Central Intelligence Agency, 61
Conservatism
   Difficulty in establishing itself in American political culture, 105
   Importance of southern and western United States for constituency, 115
   Relation to liberalism, 1–2
Containment, 75
Cosmopolitanism, 79
Coulter, Ann, 4, 6
Countervailing Power, 102
Cowley, Malcolm, 152
Craven, Avery, 111–113
Croly, Herbert, 94, 153
Cuban Missile Crisis, 168

D
Dallas, Texas, 173
Davis, Elmer, 19, 22, 57, 58
Davis, Helen Gahagan, 47
Davis, John, 130
Democratic Advisory Council, 27
Democratic Party, 93, 119, 125
DeVoto, Bernard, 9, 11, 12, 18, 19, 56, 58, 119–127, 173
   Activism on behalf of National Parks, 125
   As populist, 118
   Battle against Echo Park Dam, 122–123
   Battle against landgrab, 121–122
   Belief in limits, 126–127
   Biographical information, 112, 117, 119

Changing political outlook,
119–120
Changing views on the American
west, 120
Criticism of National Park
management, 124–125
Death, 140
Debate with Civil War revisionist
historians, 112
Embrace of American West, 126
Formation of History Book Club
with Arthur Schlesinger, 151
Friendship with Adlai Stevenson, 119
Friendship with Alfred Knopf, 124
Hope that public opinion could
support conservation initiatives,
123
Love of National Parks, 124
On Abraham Lincoln, 110
On health care reform and
American Medical Association
(AMA), 107
On importance of public lands
being governed by federal
government, 122
On postwar conservation
movement, 114–115
Opinion about southern
intellectuals, 127
Pushing Democratic Party to take
tougher stand on conservation,
125–126
Regionalism, 117
Relation to H.L. Mencken, 41,
119, 125
Writing speeches for Adlai
Stevenson, 49, 125
Dewey, John, 95
Dies Committee (Martin Dies), 69
Diem, Ngo Dinh, 174, 176
Diggins, John Patrick, 104
Dissent, 87
Doll Tests, 132, see also *Brown v.
Board of Education*

Doren, Charles Van, 150
Douglas, Paul, 10, 46, 108, 125
Dulles, John Foster, 75, 76

E
Eastman, Max, 73
Echo Park Dam, 122, 140
Economic Cooperation Association
(ECA), 29
Egghead, Conception of, 33–34
Eisenhower, Dwight (President), 12,
40, 99, 103, 104, 107, 109, 114,
148, 156
Elitism, 40
Ellison, Ralph, 11, 138
Emancipation Proclamation, 111

F
Fair Deal, 91
Fair Employment Practices
Committee (FEPC), 113
Fallibility, 43
Fascism, 15
Faulkner, William, 83, 128
Federal Communications Commission
(FCC), 150
Federalist Papers, 6, 93
Fiedler, Leslie, 57
Finletter, Tom, 27
Ford Foundation, 83
Foucault, Michel, 3
Fourteenth Amendment, 130, 132
Franken, Al, 4
Franklin, John Hope, 130
Freedman, Lawrence, 161, 174
Freud, Sigmund, 35
Frontier myth, 116–117
Frost, Robert, 161

G
Galbraith, John Kenneth, 9, 13, 79,
124
Affluent Society, The, 145
Ambassador to India, 164

Analysis of Eisenhower
Administration, 105
Attacked by Senator Homer
Capehart, 70
Belief in Civil Equality Drive, 167
Belief in humility in foreign policy,
84
Belief that the poor are most in
need of public services, 150–151
Biographical information, 26–28
Concept of countervailing power,
102–103
Conception of political speeches, 50
Concern about accepting a position
within the White House, 160
Concern with Kitchen Debate, 147
Criticism of conservative
Keynesianism, 155–156
Criticism of contemporary public
architecture, 149
Criticism of growth economics, 155
Criticism of highway system in
America, 149
Criticism of JFK's political timidity,
167
Criticism of JFK's tax cut, 167
Criticism of mass culture, 146
Debate with Leon Keyserling, 155
Diplomat to India, 27–28, 160,
164–165
Examination of post-war capitalism,
101–102
Formation of Finletter Group to
advise politicians, 49, 157
Friendship with Arthur Schlesinger,
143–144
Indebtedness to Thorstein Veblen, 95
Ironic disposition, 28
Opposition to Vietnam War,
175–176
Protest against Bay of Pigs invasion,
166
Recognition that JFK followed
others' advice, 170–171

Relation to Adlai Stevenson, 27
Relation to Lyndon Baines
Johnson, 176
Relation to Keynesian economics,
154
Sorrow in light of JFK assassination,
173
Support for JFK, 158
Support for public television, 151
Support for qualitative liberalism,
153
Theory of social imbalance, 148
Work at Office of Price
Administration (OPA), 19–20,
26–27, 99
Work on JFK Presidential Campaign
(1960), 158–159
Galbraith, Kitty, 11
Gillon, Steven, 46, 159
Glacier National Park, 124
Glen Canyon, 123
Goldman, Eric, 13
Goldwater, Barry, 1, 2, 115,
116, 173
Gorman, Paul, 146, 149
Graham, Billy, 39
Graham, Katherine, 172

H
Hartz, Louis, 105
Harvard University, 143
Heckscher, August, 162–164
Report on arts and national
government, 163
Hegel, G.W.F., 63
Heller, Walter, 27
Hellman, Lillian, 59
Hemingway, Ernest, 17, 152
Herndon, Angelo, 127
Highway system, 149
Hiss, Alger, 36, 52, 67
History, 92
History Book Club, 151
Hobhouse, Leonard, 95

Hofstadter, Richard, 10, 40, 105
  Conception of "anti-
    intellectualism," 40
  On Abraham Lincoln, 110
Holmes, Oliver Wendell, 68
Holmes, Stephen, 146
Hook, Sidney, 10, 67, 71, 73
  Role in American Congress for
    Cultural Freedom (ACCF), 73
House Committee on Un-American
  Activities (HUAC), 69, 71
Howe, Irving, 84, 87
Humphrey, Hubert, 10, 45, 46, 47,
  70, 108, 160, 163, 176, 178–179

I
Ickes, Harold, 119
I'll Take My Stand, 128
Irony, 43–44, 138
Isaac, Jeffrey, 24
Isolationism, 79
Izaak Walton League, 121, 123

J
Jackson, Andrew, 94
Jacobs, Meg, 20
James, William, 26, 97
Jefferson, Thomas, 93, 128
Johnson, Lyndon Baines, 172, 176
Josephson, Matthew, 152
Josselson, Michael, 81

K
Kazin, Alfred, 161
Kennan, George, 77–78
Kennedy, John F. (JFK), 10, 143,
  158–171
  Assassination, 172–173
Kennedy, Joseph, 158
Kennedy Center for the Performing
  Arts, 162
Keynes, John Maynard, 96
Keynesianism, 154–156
Keyserling, Leon, 143, 155

Debate with John Kenneth
  Galbraith and Arthur Schlesinger,
  155–156
Khrushchev, Nikita, 141, 159
King, Martin Luther, 11, 133
  "I Have a Dream Speech," 137,
  139
Kirk, Russell, 106
Kitchen Debate (Nixon versus
  Khrushchev), 147
Knopf, Alfred, 123, 124
Koestler, Arthur, 79
Korean War, 52, 77
Kristol, Irving, 73, 74, 83

L
Labor unions, 102
LaFeber, Walter, 77
Landgrab, 120–121
Lasch, Christopher, 61, 83,
  136, 166
League for Independent Political
  Action (LIPA), 95
League of Nations, 16
Lears, Jackson, 5
Lenin, V.I., 64–65
Lerner, Max, 55
  Criticism of John Kenneth
    Galbraith, 102
  Description of confrontation
    between Joseph McCarthy and
    James Wechsler, 55
Lewis, Fulton, 14, 27
Lewis, John L., 20
Lewis, Sinclair, 82
Liberal Consensus, 13
Liberalism
  Attacks against, 1–5
  Belief in voluntary associations,
    98–99
  Belief in reform, 44
  Concept of balancing pluralism and
    nationalism, 109
  Conception of virtue, 42

Concern with cultural impact of
    capitalism, 88
Criticism of Marxism, 62
Definition, 6–8
Faith in individualism, 43–44
Faith in law, 133
Race Relations, 11
Relation to civil society, 7–8
Relation to conservatism, 105
Relation to irony, 43
Relation to political
    representatives, 46
Relation to socialism, 88
Reliance on the concept of
    pluralism, 97–101
Roots in American Revolution and
    Constitution, 92–93
Support for granting civil rights to
    African Americans, 136
Lichtenstein, Nelson, 103
Lincoln, Abraham, 6, 92, 93, 110,
    139, 179
Lippmann, Walter, 77, 161
Little Rock, Arkansas, 107
Logevall, Fredrik, 174
Loyalty Act (President Truman), 68
Luce, Henry, 50, 84

M

MacArthur, General Douglas, 76, 77
Macdonald, Dwight, 87
MacLeish, Archibald, 5, 16–17, 21
Madison, James, 63, 93, 99, 100
Mailer, Norman, 84
Maistre, Joseph Marie de, 105
Marshall Plan, 13, 80, 81, 165
Marshall, Thurgood, 130
Marx, Karl, 62, 88
Marxism, 62–66
    Relation to Soviet totalitarianism,
        63–64
    Tendency to predict the future, 63
    Theory of class division, 62
    Theory of government, 64

Mass Culture, 144–145
    Criticisms of by intellectuals,
        144–145
McCarran, Patrick (Senator), 70, 120
McCarthy, Eugene, 125, 176
McCarthy, Joseph (Senator), 2, 4, 52,
    69, 73
    Accusation that James Wechsler was
        a communist, 56
    Calls James Wechsler to testify,
        53, 55
    Rise to power, 52–53
McCarthy, Mary, 11, 83, 145
Melville, Herman, 82
Menand, Louis, 97
Mencken, H.L., 40, 82
Menon, Krishna, 165
Middle of the Journey, The, 36–37
Miller, Arthur, 59, 60, 66
Mills, C. Wright, 84
Mitchell, Michelle, 3–4
Montgomery Bus Boycott, 133
Moore, Michael, 4
Morgenthau, Hans, 77
Morris, William, 88
Mumford, Lewis, 17, 129
Myrdal, Gunnar, 114, 136

N

Nabokov, Nicholas, 81, 82
National Association for the
    Advancement of Colored People
    (NAACP), 130–131
National Association of Manufacturers
    (NAM), 13, 80, 91, 107
National Forest Service, 120, 121
National greatness, 159
National Livestock and National
    Woolgrowers Associations, 120
National Maritime Union, 66
National Park System, 124–125
National Parks Advisory Board, 125
National Review, 1, 13–14
Nationalism, 113–114

Race relations and concept of nation, 114
Relation to scenic beauty (scenic nationalism), 124
Navasky, Victor, 59
Nehru, Jawaharlal, 164
New Deal, 91, 164
New Left, 2
New York Intellectuals, 10, 71, 72
New York Post, 14, 68, 70
Niebuhr, Reinhold, 9, 11, 70, 118
  Appeal to secularists, 87
  Appreciation of James Madison and Constitutional thought, 93
  Argument in favor of World War II, 17–18
  Attitude toward labor unions, 109
  Belief in "limits" regarding foreign policy, 76
  Belief in pluralism, 97–98
  Biographical information, 32, 86
  Change in political philosophy from socialism to liberalism, 86–87
  Conception of humility, 33
  Concern over "Coca-colonialism," 83
  Criticism of belligerence in foreign policy, 84
  Criticism of Billy Graham, 39
  Criticism of capitalism, 89
  Criticism of hubris, 50, 84
  Criticism of Marxism, 64–65
  Criticism of mass culture, 151
  Criticism of progress, 90
  Criticism of Richard Nixon during Kitchen Debate, 147
  Criticism of Whittaker Chambers, 38–39
  Defense of the welfare state, 90–91
  Definition of sinfulness and relation to individualism, 89
  Disagreement with Hannah Arendt about totalitarianism, 65
  Disagreement with idea of predestination, 89
  Disagreement with Walter Rauschenbusch, 90
  Health problems, 140
  Importance of America's relation with Europe, 80–81
  Indebtedness to Leonard Hobhouse, 95
  Marriage, 79
  On Abraham Lincoln, 111
  On political apathy, 100
  On Vietnam, 175
  Opinion about "I Have a Dream Speech," 139
  Opinion about the United Nations (UN), 75–76
  Relation to John Dewey, 95
  Relation to Social Gospel tradition, 89
  Understanding of conservatism, 106
  Understanding of the Soviet Union's foreign policy, 78
Niebuhr, Ursula, 11
Nixon, Richard, 54, 147
Non-Communist Left (NCL), 80, 140
Nuclear Test Ban, 168

O

Oakley, J. Ronald, 70
Odum, Howard, 127, 128–129
Office of Facts and Figures (OFF), 21
Office of Price Administration (OPA), 19–20, 80, 91, 99, 106, 109, 140
Office of Strategic Services (OSS), 19, 23, 29
Office of War Information (OWI), 19, 22–23, 29, 140
Okroi, Loren, 155
"Our Country, Our Culture" symposium, 84

P

Partisan Review, 84
Peace Corps, 165, 168

Pegler, Westbrook, 14, 107
Pells, Richard, 59
Perspectives, 82–83
Pilat, Oliver, 54
Plessy v. Ferguson, 130
Pluralism, 97–101
    As basis of political criticism, 99
PM (newspaper), 20, 53
Pollock, Jackson, 24
Polsgrove, Carol, 136
Populism, 118, 134
Porter, Katherine Anne, 128
Post-structuralism, 3
Preuves, 82
Preventive war, 77
Progressive Era, 96, 101
Progressive Party, 47, 55, 140

Q
Qualitative liberalism, 143–171
    Connection to national greatness,
        159
    Relation to quantitative liberalism,
        154, 157
    Weaknesses in philosophy, 156
Quiz Show Scandal, 149–150

R
Race Relations, 114, 115
    Interaction with the Cold War, 114
Randall, James, 111–113
Randolph, A. Philip, 15
Rauh, Joseph, 160
Rauschenbusch, Walter, 89–90
Reagan, Ronald, 1, 3
Realism, 45, 50, 75–79, 171
    Distinction between "old school"
        and liberal form of concept, 77
    Relation to concept of "limits" on
        power, 76
Red Scare (1919), 69
Redford, Robert, 150
Regionalism, 115–116, 138–139
Republican Party, 1

Reuther, Walter, 108
Riesman, David, 40, 43, 74, 98, 138,
    145, 158
Roosevelt, Franklin Delano (FDR), 6,
    15, 21, 25, 46, 92, 96, 101, 141,
    154, 164, 179
Roosevelt, Theodore, 6, 92, 94, 95,
    104, 116
Rosenbergs, 60, 67
Ross, Andrew, 60, 146, 149
Rovere, Richard, 73
Runte, Alfred, 124
Rushmore, Howard, 55
Russell, Bertrand, 81

S
Sandburg, Carl, 110
Saunders, Frances Stonor, 61, 73, 83
Schiff, Dorothy, 11, 30
Schine, David, 53
Schlesinger, Arthur, Jr., 4, 9, 12, 17,
    18, 22, 44
    Argument against hunting
        communists in Hollywood, 72
    Argument for public uses of
        television networks, 150
    Attitude toward American middle
        class, 156
    Belief in political compromise, 45
    Belief in public purposes, 154
    Belief that communists had
        infiltrated the federal
        government, 67
    Biographical information, 29
    Changing attitude towards Vietnam
        War, 177–178
    Conception of "cycles of history,"
        103–104
    Conception of intellectual purpose,
        29
    Conception of government's
        relation to liberalism, 95
    Conception of political pluralism,
        98–99

Concern over ridding college campuses of communists, 69
Concern with political apathy, 100
Criticism of concept of "preventive war," 77
Criticism of conservatism, 106
Criticism of Dies Committee, 69
Criticism of Joseph McCarthy, 53
Criticism of Marxism's predictions about capitalism, 62
Criticism of mass culture, 85, 145–146
Criticism of Whittaker Chambers, 38
Debate with Civil War revisionist historians, 111–112
Definition of qualitative liberalism, 143, 152–153
Desire to be connected to political power, 46
Experience in Congress for Cultural Freedom (CCF), 81
Faith in political compromise, 100
Formation of History Book Club with Bernard DeVoto, 151
Friendship with John Kenneth Galbraith, 143–144
Infatuation with Kennedy family, 169
Interpretation of Andrew Jackson, 93
Interpretation of New Deal, 96
On Abraham Lincoln, 111
On Franklin Delano Roosevelt's relation to liberalism, 25, 46–47
On Reinhold Niebuhr's appeal to secularists, 87
Opinion about prosecuting communist teachers, 71
Opinion of Eisenhower Administration, 107
Opinion of *The Middle of the Journey*, 37
Outline of "national cultural policy," 152

Poor assessment of Kennedy administration, 169–170
Protest against Bay of Pigs invasion, 166
Rationale for "containment" in foreign policy, 75
Relationship with Bernard DeVoto and C. Vann Woodward, 117–118
Role as Special Assistant to the President, 161
Sadness at JFK Assassination, 172–173
Speech writing for Adlai Stevenson, 49
Support for Adlai Stevenson, 157
Support for Americans for Democratic Action (ADA), 74
Support for civil rights movement, 137, 168–169
Support for Kennedy, 158
View that intellectuals could assist political power, 166
Work at Office of War Information (OWI), 23
Work with August Heckscher on national arts policy, 162–164
Work on JFK Presidential Campaign (1960), 158–159
Work on national arts policy at the White House, 161–164
Shannon, William, 54
Sherwood, Robert, 110
Sierra Club, 123
Sino-Indian War, 165
Skocpol, Theda, 99
Smith, Henry Nash, 113
Smith, Lillian, 119, 209–210 (endnote Number 38)
Social Gospel, 89
Socialist Party, 86, 88
Southern Conference for Human Welfare, 129
Soviet expansionism, 66

Stalinism, 62, 141
State Department, 68
Stearns, Harold, 152
Stern, Isaac, 170
Stevenson, Adlai, 9, 10, 12, 27, 32,
　　48, 70, 107, 118, 119, 125, 143,
　　148, 157, 160, 173
　　Loss of presidential campaign in
　　　1956 and ramifications, 158
Strachey, John, 102
Stratford Players, 170 Students for a
　　Democratic Society (SDS), 2
Sumner, William Graham, 135

T
Taft-Hartley Act, 13, 106
Technocracy, 168
This is Dinosaur, 123
Thomas, Norman, 87
Thompson, Frank (Congressman),
　　163
Tocqueville, Alexis de, 98
Totalitarianism, 65
Trilling, Lionel, 10, 25, 71, 82–83,
　　105
　　Conception of tragic element of life,
　　　35
　　Relation to liberalism, 34–36
Troy, Tevi, 161
Truman, Harry, 47, 80, 107
Truman Doctrine, 80
Twain, Mark, 82, 119
Twentieth Century Fund, 162

U
Union for Democratic Action (UDA),
　　18, 32, 86, see also Americans for
　　Democratic Action (ADA)
United Auto Workers (UAW), 108
United Electrical, Radio, and Machine
　　Workers of America, 66
United Mine Workers (UMW), 20
United Nations (UN), 75
University of Washington, 69

V
Veblen, Thorstein, 95
Vietnam War, 2, 9, 173–179
　　Destruction of liberalism, 178
　　JFK's involvement, 174
　　Relation to liberal anticommunism,
　　　174–179
Voice of America, 53
Voluntary Associations, 98

W
Wagner Act, 103
Waldorf Conference, 59
Wallace, Henry, 47, 55, 66, 70,
　　78, 140
Walker, Edwin (General), 173
Warren, Robert Penn, 128
Watson, Tom, 127, 134
Weber, Max, 160
Wechsler, James, 9, 127, 142, 160
　　Admiration of Walter Reuther, 108
　　Argument that American Congress
　　　for Cultural Freedom (ACCF)
　　　should confront Joseph
　　　McCarthy, 73
　　Argument that Communism
　　　differed from Fascism, 78
　　Assessment of right wing in
　　　American politics, 105
　　Bad experiences with communists,
　　　67
　　Battle against Joseph McCarthy,
　　　58–59
　　Belief that the federal government
　　　had been infiltrated by
　　　communists, 67
　　Biographical information, 30–31
　　Conception of Americans for
　　　Democratic Action and its work,
　　　46
　　Criticism of Adlai Stevenson on civil
　　　rights, 48–49
　　Criticism of Americans for
　　　Democratic Action (ADA), 142

Criticism of Henry Wallace, 47
Criticism of JFK, 170
Criticism of President Truman's
  Loyalty Program, 68
Criticism of Marxism's belief in
  predicting the future, 63
Criticism of Marxism's theory of
  capitalism, 62
Decision to name Communists,
  57–58
Dislike of JFK, 159
Distinction between ideas and
  action when attacking
  communists, 67
Experience during World War II,
  20–21
Exposure of Joseph McCarthy's
  anticommunist hunt, 54
Membership in Young Communist
  League, 54
On Taft-Hartley Act, 106
Opinion of Eisenhower
  Administration, 107
Opposition to Vietnam War, 178
Testimony to Senator Joseph
  McCarthy, 53, 55
Wechsler, Nancy, 11
Whig Party, 93
White, Morton, 87
Whitman, Walt, 82
Wilson, Woodrow (President),
  16, 104
Winchell, Walter, 14, 54
  Influence on Joseph McCarthy, 54
Wiretapping, 69
Wolfe, Thomas, 128
Woodward, C. Vann, 9, 11, 127–138
  Admiration for Reinhold Niebuhr,
    118, 135
  As a regionalist, 129

Belief in irony, 138
Belief in populism, 118–119, 128
Biographical information, 117,
  127–128
Criticism of secession and
  nullification, 137
Criticism of segregation, 135–136
Criticism of W.J. Cash, 134
Disillusionment with communism,
  127
Influenced by Howard Odum, 128
Interpretation of post-
  Reconstruction period, 134–135
Interpretation of Reconstruction,
  130–132
Interpretation of rise of segregation
  and disfranchisement, 135
Knowledge of southern intellectual
  tradition, 128
On Abraham Lincoln, 111
On Vietnam, 175
Opinion that South was a colony of
  the North, 129
Regionalism, 117
Support for *Brown v. Board of
  Education*, 131
Support of Angelo Herndon, 127
Work for the National Association
  for the Advancement of Colored
  People (NAACP), 130–131
Writing of *Strange Career of Jim
  Crow*, 133–134
World War I, 16
Propaganda initiatives during, 21
World War II
Relation to liberalism, 14–25

Y
Yellowstone National Park, 124
Yosemite National Park, 124